Child Brides and Intruders

Child Brides and Intruders

Carol Wershoven

Bowling Green State University Popular Press
Bowling Green, OH 43403

Women's Studies Series
Jane Bakerman, General Editor

Copyright © 1993 by Bowling Green State University Popular Press

Library of Congress Catalogue Card No.: 93-72344

ISBN: 0-87972-627-X Clothbound
     0-87972-628-8 Paperback

Cover design and type by Laura Darnell-Dumm/Dumm Art.

For John Sheridan Biays, Jr.

Contents

"In the English novel (by which of course I mean the American novel as well), more than in any other, there is a traditional difference between that which people know and that which they agree to admit they know, that which they see and that which they speak of, that which they feel to be a part of life and that which they allow to enter into literature....The essence of moral energy is to survey the whole field...."

Henry James, "The Art of Fiction" (405-06)

Introduction

"Are there any women in it?" This was the question my female friends and I asked when we were teenagers, choosing which movie to see. We enjoyed movies about male adventure and sympathized, even identified, with male conflicts, but we generally found a film more interesting if it included some mirror—or model—for ourselves. We were not necessarily seeking a "woman's picture," but one with a significant female character, a developed one, in a significant conflict. We did not demand that this character fill the screen with her virtues and triumphs, but that she be a central presence, a character to observe and react to, to criticize, judge, even analyze. It is possible that my friends and I were looking for heroines.

We looked for heroines in books as well. Heroines were fairly easy to find in the movies, given the variety of choices and our ignorance of critical standards for judging film. The same indiscriminate kind of reading introduced us to a number of memorable women characters: we read about everyone from Nancy Drew to Jane Eyre, from Anna Karenina to Scarlett O'Hara. It was not until later that the heroines, significant women in significant conflict, began to disappear from the books we read.

They disappeared for me because I became a student of American literature and learned about the classics. I became familiar with those "melodramas of beset manhood," as Nina Baym calls them (*Melodramas* 130), novels about males in the forest, on the battleground, at sea—fighting, hunting, sailing, whaling, shooting. I read about white men and their conflicts with blacks or Indians or fish or other white men. I studied the canon of American literature, and I did not study many significant female characters. Learning to discriminate, to recognize literature, I was taught another lesson: the best American literature does not have interesting women in it. They are in British or European works or in inferior American ones.

Judith Fetterley says, "To read the canon of what is currently considered American literature is perforce to identify as male" (xii).

1

2 Child Brides and Intruders

Even when we read *The Scarlet Letter*, we are advised to study its hero, Dimmesdale, not its heroine. After all, her story is fundamentally over when the novel begins, isn't it?[1] And as for the rest of the "greats," women have no logical place in them. Why would a woman be on a raft with a runaway slave, or killing her first bear and wearing the badge of its blood?

As a student of American literature, I learned not to ask, "Are there any women in it?" I stopped looking for novels about relationships other than those defined by war, or crime-and-punishment, or hunting, or sport. I stopped looking for any setting other than nature or some other kind of open space; I gave up on finding novels set in a house, or a workplace, or a factory, or a school, or a church. I accepted the stories of men relating to men, in men's worlds: the literary equivalent of a steady diet of John Wayne and Sylvester Stallone movies, only better written, better produced.

The classic American novels, I was told, explore the great conflicts, the allegorical, metaphysical struggles of man against nature, or man at war, or man alone in lofty strife. These novels are not about male-female relationships. Women are irrelevant to these worlds, and so they disappear. Richard Chase acknowledges that a world without women characters is missing something, and that the writer who cannot imagine "a fully developed woman of sexual age" is imagining an incomplete, deficient culture. Yet he insists that no such woman appears in American literature "until the age of James and Edith Wharton" (63-64).

Chase hints that there *are* heroines somewhere in American literature, but says they appear long after the classic writers have set other standards. Chase is right: there are "fully developed women of sexual age" after the standard romances. But he is wrong, too. There are heroines, in varied stages of development yet nevertheless significant, within the classics as well. The secret of finding the heroines, in both places, is in the way we look. We must widen our vision, to examine the socio-political nature of American literature, and then sharpen our sight. We must look further into the fiction itself to find the hidden heroines.

Baym discusses the construction of the American canon as a deliberate limitation of vision. Within the canon are those works of "a sort of non-realistic narrative, a romance, a story free to catch an essential, idealized American character, to intensify his essence and convey his experience in a way that ignores the details of an actual social milieu." The construction of the canon, she notes, begins "with the hypothesis that American literature is to be judged less by its form than its content" (*Melodramas* 131). American literary theory and criticism, then, began as "a nationalistic enterprise" (125), and "has retained a nationalist orientation to this day" (126). Much feminist criticism, like Baym's, explores the connection of the literary and the political. For an understanding of American heroines and their roles begins on socio-political ground.

That turf first appears as the new Eden, generally discussed in terms of new Adams rather than as a place for Eves. The new place of endless possibility and promise was to be the site of re-birth. Here, man was to re-create himself, free of the constraints of church and king, of class and convention. Shedding his past, man was to design a future based solely on his desires.

The design invariably omitted woman from the blueprint. The new dream-culture created new constraints and barriers that kept woman irrelevant and near-invisible. A world void of tradition soon hungered for a new order, and within that new order, woman seemed to disappear. As Eric Sundquist notes, "Against the spirit of repudiation that upholds any revolutionary performance there must weigh an anxiety over the loss of those forms of practical and ceremonial behavior in which are dramatized the sacraments of a new culture." Thus, according to Sundquist, the new land experiences "a longing to return to those sacraments or to place in their stead others that are yet more potent and binding" (*Home* xi). Repudiating the sacraments of king, church, and class, America designed a new order, more powerful than any of the past, concentrating that power on one value.

America found one father/priest in money. The sacrament of the new culture was the exchange of cash. Possession, production and consumption replaced the practical and ceremonial behavior of the aristocracy or of established religion. Progress, expansion, industrial development became the new virtues. Endless possibility came to mean the chance for endless exploitation, an exploitation, Jan Dietrichson comments, encouraged by "the absence of inhibiting feudal institutions and the fluidity of class lines" (3).

But a very basic class division quickly appeared. The country was divided into those who could produce and acquire and those who could not. And the chief members of that second class were women. Lacking the means or the training to produce, denied entry into the economic arena, women watched their roles diminish. As Nancy Reeves says, "in a cash nexus society, to be outside the economic structure is also to be outside the mainstream of purposeful activity—to be irrelevant" (35). And so women seemed to disappear.

In Europe, of course, industrial capitalism flourished as well, and women were driven from the marketplace and relegated to the home and the church. Unlike her American counterpart, however, the European woman retained a significant function and identity. Vestiges of traditional values such as respect for home, family life, social hierarchy and religion allocated her remnants of power and prestige. But in America, with its blithe disregard for tradition, only one value mattered. Man defined himself by what he could produce and assessed his progress by what he could acquire. And all that existed outside of man—land, natural resources, human beings—became valued only insofar as they could enhance male identity.

In America, the new system pushed the new Eves into the corners of the culture.[1] Alexis de Tocqueville, writing in 1835, noted that in America, "more than anywhere else in the world, care has been taken constantly to trace clearly distinct spheres of action for the two sexes, and both are required to keep in step, but along paths that are never the same" (601). For what did women's limited world of family, home, and church matter, when real life was not by the fireplace but in the marketplace? One American novel identifies American values most succinctly. Edith Wharton's *The Custom of the Country* asks, "Where does the real life of most Americans lie? In some woman's drawing room or their men's offices?"

The answer's obvious, isn't it? The emotional center of gravity's not the same in the two hemispheres. In the effete societies it's love, in our own new one it's business. In America the real "crime passionel" is a "big steal"—there's more excitement in wrecking railways than homes. (207)

Excluded from the marketplace, the American woman became the child-prisoner of the domestic sphere. Incapable of acquiring cash, she became dependent on one who could get it. The male who supported her, whether father, brother, or husband, emerged as Big Daddy, a powerful patriarch bored in his domain. Family life, to him, wasn't really life at all, for the real action was elsewhere. "How people are used depends on what needs to be done," explains Reeves, and women just weren't very useful in the new economy. Granted, a woman could reproduce and thus perpetuate the male line, but, as Reeves notes, "The lifestream of industrial societies...is money not blood, and production, not reproduction, has transcendent value" (77). Like the land itself, like the slave, woman was a resource to be used up and discarded.[2]

The new Eden of endless possibility came to mean a place of endless desire, not for love or family, but for getting and spending. And man could never be sure he had enough. Again it is Wharton who notes the obsessive nature of American materialism by comparing America to France, where money-making "is a far more modest ambition and consists simply in the effort to earn one's living and put by enough for sickness, old age, and a good start in life for the children." Such a modest ambition, she feels, "has the immense superiority of leaving time for living, time for men and women both" (*French Ways* 108). But "living" in America was equated with acquisition, essentially a male function. The limited roles permitted women were merely outgrowths of the new, dominant activity, the deal. Woman herself became an acquisition, or as Veblen noted, a living embodiment of her man's financial power, a vicarious consumer. In either role, she became a kind of wholly-owned subsidiary, never a full participant in the art of the deal.

This picture of an America consecrated to cash is hardly pretty, and it is not surprising that men of sensitivity deplored it. And from the beginning of this new order, men condemned it. James Fenimore Cooper warned,

A people that deems the possession of riches its highest sense of distinction, admits one of the most degrading of influences to preside over its opinions. At no time, should money ever be ranked as more than a means, and he who lives as if the acquisition of property were the sole end of his existence, betrays the dominion of the most sordid, base and groveling motive, that life offers. (qtd. in Dietrichson 5)

Such "sordid, base and groveling" goals are hard for even the insensitive to acknowledge. They are a terrible departure from the initial American dreams. The disparity between the ideal and the new order was extremely unpleasant to face. And so many chose not to face it.

Robert Richardson, Jr., in *Myth and Literature in the American Renaissance*, differentiates between a definition of myth as a kind of imaginative, intuitive, universal truth, and "a sociological view of myth, an intellectual tool for discerning a society" (48). This second definition views American mythology as "a limited, culture-based reflection of the values and aspirations of a group of people" (71), and this is the kind of myth I am referring to when I say that American myth is an evasion of economic reality. Elizabeth Janeway says that "economic considerations have a terrible aptitude for getting tangled up with myth" (184), and the values of a money-obsessed culture created a need for such myth. Myth could conceal the implications of such values and even deny the existence of the values themselves. It could conceal the sovereignty of acquisition under a veneer of individualism. Rapaciousness and opportunism could be presented as a genius for seizing the right chance.

Myth could justify the ways of cash to man. A set of national verities, based on the old dreams of Eden, could maintain the status quo and function as sacred form of social contract. "What myths tell us about the world," says Janeway, "is not a description of the way things are...but instructions for action, imperatives to be followed on pain of 'destroying the order of the universe' "(295).

"Closed minds accept myth most easily," Janeway adds, "but a frightened society seeks it actively" (191). To question such myth is painful and dangerous. To recognize the underside of a national dream as nightmare might lead a person to action, perhaps even to rebellion. And when there is still a chance that a fresh place of endless promise might be available for oneself, if not for others, it is easier to evade than to question. Such evasion was possible if a person did not look too closely at American women.

American women subverted the myth. Their very presence provoked unease and challenged a nation's security. To feel safe, man had to avoid those corners, the kitchens, bedrooms, drawing rooms, where American women lived. Like the black people accidentally included in the street scenes of early American films, American women needed to be edited out of the picture. To acknowledge their presence and their problems was to face a reality too disturbing to know.

And yet the reality was always there, one of those elements Henry James calls "the things we cannot possibly not know, sooner or later, in one way or another" ("Preface" 9).Thus there is an ongoing conflict, in American life and in American literature, between myth and reality. And in that struggle, women, forever intruding into myth, are the catalysts.

One way to handle such conflict is to look at other things. It is to write fiction that takes place where women do not go, to write of a hero on a ship or a raft or battlefield, to allow him to discover himself in a prizefight or bullfight or on a fantastic journey. Such heroes may explore metaphysical questions, like the nature of man's relation to evil or to the physical universe, outside of that society where women, the subversives, live. By changing the focus of literature from society to "space,"[3] the writer can avoid the nightmare side of the American dream.

Classic American writers have, to a certain extent, done just that. Whether out of conscious revulsion for a narrow, materialistic society, or out of a fear of its power to disfigure the self, many American writers have chosen to locate their fictions where society—and women—are not. Many critics of American literature recognize that a great deal of American fiction is set in one of two places: a large, wide, outer world of great ideas, or the small and private inner world of the self. Marius Bewley, for example, says that the greatest American novels contain "a deep and emotional concern with abstractions" (15); F.O. Matthiessen says that Hawthorne and Melville were "more concerned with human destiny than with every man in his humor" (270). Richard Chase notes the concern with both the big and little worlds, citing American novelists' "talent for depicting the largest public abstractions and the smallest and most elusive turn of the inner mind" (41). Richard Poirer defines the world of the classic American writer as "a world elsewhere" (7), bearing little relation to the real world, emanating only from the self. And whether this world is the large one of abstractions or the small one of the inner self, it is indeed elsewhere than where women are.

To study the classics, then, is to read many novels that avert their gaze from women. To study those who study the novels is to discover more writers who prefer to look elsewhere. This preference is manifest even when a novel in the canon has a significant woman character in a central role. Thus, many critics who discuss *The Scarlet Letter* find Dimmesdale more interesting than Hester, and others dismiss Zenobia of *The Blithedale Romance* with a few words while endlessly analyzing

Coverdale. More significantly, some who have established the criteria for a great American novel appear to have decided that, if the book is set within a recognizable society, it does not merit much examination at all.

There are many American writers whose novels are filled with heroines: James, Wharton, Dreiser, Fitzgerald, Howells, Cather, Glasgow, for instance. But, aside from mixed opinions on James and Fitzgerald, American literary critics largely rate these writers as of the second rank. They are variously denigrated as realists or naturalists or novelists of manners or social critics or social historians. What each shares with the others, aside from labels of disparagement, is a tendency to set his or her novels within society and to populate that place with heroines. The concerns of such novels are not always abstract or uniquely personal; instead, the books often deal with specific characters in a specific time and place, living within a specific culture described in detail. And those characters and their time and place may in fact correspond to a historical time and place. Such works, then, may encourage the reader to connect fiction and historical fact.

If such works are to be slighted as realistic, we might consider one definition of the term. Geoffrey Wagner explains that "realistic" once meant "subversive"; it meant the supposed pornographic quality of early novels, considered unfit for women. Later, it was a label used to sell movies with sexual content, to circumvent the restrictions of the Hays Code (192). In either case, realism was a presentation of the taboo.

For whatever reasons, literary study continues to focus elsewhere than where the heroines are. First, critics defined the greats in such a way that novels with heroines went largely ignored. Even when one of the books of the romantic canon contained a heroine, critics found ways to avoid her. The realists and naturalists were damned with faint praise, so that scholars could skip past them to the more acceptable moderns. Modernism, as Julia Bader says, "challenges the ontological and epistemological premises of realism: it casts doubt on the very existence of any reality independent of human perception, and it questions whether individual perception can yield an understanding of the world that has more than subjective validity" (177). The critical preference for modernism over realism is one valid response to an important movement, but it is also another move *away* from a study of people in an objective historical context. It is another return to the small world of the social isolate: a person's history, in this world, is merely personal history,[4] and each version of that history is challenged by metaphysical, unanswerable questions. Thus, the move away from realism is a double return to romanticism: to the small world of the inner life, and to the big, boundless abstractions.

There are, of course, those who move toward the heroine, whatever kind of world includes her. Recent feminist scholarship has explored women characters and women writers, recovering and rediscovering American works and writers. Nevertheless, there is still a sense that such study is a sideline, that the truly important work is taking place elsewhere. Carolyn Heilbrun says that, in both the artistic and academic worlds, "the point of view that women commit themselves to with complete conviction is likely to be labeled by the dominant men as 'trivial,' or insubstantial. It is placed, by assumption, outside the mainstream" (*Reinventing Womanhood* 164). And recent mainstream literary study appears to prefer a shift of focus—again, away from the heroine and her recognizable, historically connected territory, to something larger or smaller.

The study of how a text works often dismisses connection between work and world. At its worst, such study becomes a kind of criticism-as-high-technology, a new kind of computer game. To move inside in this way suggests a withdrawal into manageable boundaries, a deliberate limiting of activity to puzzles, formulas and codes.

Then there is the parallel movement to the larger world. To approach a work as an artifact whose meaning can change with the frame of reference of each reader appears, initially, a hopeful stance. It seems to identify literature as the source of a multiplicity of meanings, of ever-renewable exploration and discovery. But the potential for an infinitude of meanings can lead to the possibility of meaninglessness. In either case, whether the vision is narrowed or widened, the activity becomes increasingly self-referential.

The missing element—in the novels, in those who study them—is the social context, the place where the heroines are, and where what happens to them says something about American life and how it was, and is, actually lived. To find the hidden heroines, we need to look for that social context, whether it be concealed within the classics or exposed within the "second tier" of novels. We will find the subversive heroines not in the wide metaphysical or narrow psychological spaces, not in endless expansions of meaning or neat contrivances of a code, but in depictions of the society that traps these women.

American heroines are subversives *because* they are trapped. Unlike heroes, these characters cannot head for the territory, go to war, retreat to the forest. Because these figures represent the half of America denied an escape from society, they must either conform to it or confront it. In either case, they function as a challenge to society's myths.

Those forced to remain within society must deal with it as best they can. The story of the American heroine is different from that of the American hero because the woman cannot flee to a wide world in which to develop herself. Fiction about heroines, therefore, repeatedly explores confinement and its consequences and is highly critical of society. The catalysts for such criticism are usually the heroines. Warner Berthoff comments on American works of the late nineteenth century, many of them by women writers, all involving heroines. Such works, he says, offer "a powerful and comprehensive indictment of the official creed of equal opportunity and generally diffused happiness in the land of the free. The plight of women speaks pathetically for the plight of all" (27). His comment is equally applicable to a wider range of American fiction, from the American Renaissance to the present, which depicts the conflicts of American women. And, as Berthoff notes, the conflicts of women mirror the struggles of all those who live with women or who flee from such connection. To examine American heroines, then, is to look at all of American life from a new perspective.

Such an examination demands a recognition that American heroines themselves see differently than American heroes do. In *The Reign of Wonder*, Tony Tanner explores the recurring use of the naive vision in American literature. As he describes the point of view of the "innocent eye," he identifies its components: a preference for wonder over analysis, a passive receptivity to all that experience can show, a childlike stance that is vulnerable and hopeful. American heroines, too, see in characteristic ways, in two divergent ways which classify the heroines themselves. There are American heroines who see too little and those who see too much.

The first group of heroines may well be called "innocent," but in a sense of the word very different from Tanner's use of it. These women are the survivors in society, and they have survived by limiting their vision. The typical heroine in this group has learned to fulfill her role as desired object, and to do so, she must not be touched by experience; she must be nearly blind. Far from even wondering at what life reveals, she must not even see it. To see, to question, to grow would be to diminish her marketability. Like Tanner's naive eye, the innocent heroine sees in a passive way, but it is far more passive than the hero's way, for the heroine never questions and is only slightly changed by what little she sees. This heroine remains forever a child, a blank slate on which the male buyer can make his mark. Her innocence is not merely sexual; it is emotional and intellectual. This woman has learned the lessons of conformity, and she knows that her value is her newness, her vacuous innocence. She must remain a child, and she must find a father drawn to her helplessness, willing to indulge her uselessness. This nearly blind heroine is a doll, a pet—a child bride.

From the beginning of American fiction, this heroine is described as not only innocent but dangerous.[5] By playing the role assigned to her and by playing it well, this heroine becomes a destructive force. The better she is at becoming an image of arrested development, the more she spreads paralysis and dehumanization. As man's most cherished possession, she is an expensive purchase, for she inevitably *costs too much*. Deprived of a chance to grow, the child bride offers her buyer a dehumanized connection. To wed her is to marry emptiness. No lover can lift her veil and give her vision, for she has been trained never to see.

Such a heroine appears in the earliest American literature. In Hawthorne's *The Blithedale Romance*, the blind child who brings disease and death to all she touches is Priscilla, the little medium, transmitter of others' desires and dreams. Priscilla, who can see only through others, mirrors their defeat and despair.

Characterized initially by helplessness and vulnerability, the child bride evolves from the mesmerist's darling to become other heroines who will not see: Hawthorne's Hilda and Phoebe Pycheon, James's Verena Tarrant and Pansy Osmond, Howells's Margaret Vance. As she evolves, her sexual purity may become stained, as in the case of Jennie Gerhardt (in Dreiser's novel) or Ada Forrester (Cather's *Lost Lady*). In later versions, the heroine becomes more dangerous until her passivity becomes a powerful weapon and her receptivity to social norms becomes an insatiable hunger for society's prizes. And so the heroine becomes Dreiser's Carrie Meeber, the consummate receptor, "yours truly," all appetite and longing.

12 Child Brides and Intruders

When the child bride adopts the male belief that enough is never enough, and when she learns to trade herself more effectively, she becomes a dynamo of destruction. She is Undine Spragg, learning and exploiting *The Custom of the Country*. Undine is the eldest sister in a large family of such child-entrepreneurs; she is kin to Wharton's Lita Wyant, Glasgow's Stanley Kingsmill and Jenny Blair Archbold, Fitzgerald's Daisy Buchanan. In these characters, the endless desires of the perpetual child become an active force for evil.

In the world of child brides, the standard romantic relationship is, as Leslie Fiedler notes, incest (397). In James's *The Golden Bowl*, we see the emblematic marriage of father and child, and we see hints of marriages to come. As the heroine continues to evolve, the incest pattern assumes a new form, becoming the marriage of two children. The man who seeks a child bride regresses into innocence himself; he falls from his position as father-lover to become his bride's twin. Howells's *A Modern Instance* and Fitzgerald's *Tender Is the Night* chart the transformation of the husband from father to child; child couples populate Wharton's *The Age of Innocence*, Fitzgerald's *The Beautiful and Damned*, Dreiser's *An American Tragedy*. In these marriages, there is no father, only a demand for instant gratification, a pathetic hunger for society's toys. The unions, reducing the partners to the status of lost children, reveal the hollow core of the society that shapes them.

Even as the child brides and the men who chose them respect society's values, they subvert those very standards. In the novels containing child brides, the consequences of living by the American code are exposed, repeatedly, as a diminished identity and a corresponding diminution of adult and loving connection. Because such characters see so little and question even less, we are prompted to see further and to analyze what we see.

Child brides don't see. The second group of heroines both see and question.[6] They are the women caught in society, but not of it. Forever trapped in a culture that offers them no adult role, they are forever intruders. The intruders feel little allegiance to a world in which they are kept apart from the mainstream. As outsiders, they often see more—and see more clearly—than those safe and comfortable inside. As they see, we share their vision. As they rebel, we note their frequent failures and occasional successes. Many break their spirits in a struggle against things as they are; a few, true to an alternative vision, begin to realize that vision, creating themselves and constructing a new world. All, defeated or triumphant, struggle to become adults. For them, to see is to grow.[7]

The line of intruders, like the line of child brides, starts with Hawthorne. Hester Prynne, having broken her culture's rules, is nonetheless caught within its judgments. Devalued by a hostile society, she must learn to see beyond it while she lives inside it. Hester is followed by a series of damaged and destroyed women, all characterized by a threatening capacity to see and to question. These are heroines who either will not or cannot conform, who will not or cannot limit their vision to the picture society prepares for their edification. In their struggle to look beyond, to create a new self, such heroines are often outcast, their lives characterized by violence and loss. Wharton's Lily Bart dies estranged from the man she loves, Cather's Lucy Gayheart and Chopin's Edna Pontellier drown, and James's Charlotte Stant is tamed and chained.

Others, who seek refuge from loneliness, compromise their values. Glasgow's Ada Fincastle becomes a mother to her husband; Howells's Dr. Grace Breen becomes a wife and worker, but her husband is her employer. Whatever the struggle or its outcome, the intruder fights a world that would diminish her and that works relentlessly to break her rebellion. Formed in that world, this heroine must resist the temptation she has been trained for: the surrender to dependence, the lure of the father. Denied the luxury of self-discovery in endless space, this heroine fights not only her inner weakness but a whole culture dedicated to freezing her in eternal childhood.

A few strong women survive the double danger. Some—Wharton's Ellen Olenska, Adams's Mrs. Henry Lightfoot Lee, Glasgow's Millie Burden—survive alone. Others learn to connect to men who are not fathers or brothers. They love out of choice, not desperation. Lewis's Carol Kennicott and Ann Vickers, Cather's Antonia Shimerda, Alexandra Bergson and Thea Kronborg all move through a powerful initiation to a new kind of union. These marriages are imperfect and incomplete, for the partners have no models to guide them, no established roles to play. Their stories have no happy endings, for they are merely beginnings—visions of a new design for adult marriages.

All the intruders attempt to build a new world within the old one. By proposing an alternative society, a grown-up world of self-discipline

14 Child Brides and Intruders

and courage, they expose the existing one, showing the specious qualities of its declared ideals. They reveal American myth to be desire, not fulfillment. These heroines grow by fidelity to their own vision, and they do not flinch from what they see around them.

American heroes grow and define themselves in space. Their Eden is the endless frontier, and that space is their sanctuary, free of the taint of society. American heroines grow, too. But they must define themselves against a world forever impinging on the alien, adult self they strive to create. They live on the eternal borderline, born and formed within the limits of convention, growing beyond those limits. The place where these adult women confront a hostile world is a kind of frontier territory. And perhaps, in surviving, even growing on that frontier, the heroines enact their own version of the American dream.

Part One:

Child Brides

Chapter One:
Society's Darlings

he felt himself oppressed by this creation of factitious purity, so cunningly manufactured by a conspiracy of mothers and aunts and grandmothers and long-dead ancestresses, because it was supposed to be what he wanted, what he had a right to, in order that he might exercise his lordly pleasure in smashing it like an image made of snow.

Edith Wharton, The Age of Innocence (46)

there was no single and unchangeable set of features, beneath the veil, but...whosoever should be bold enough to lift it, would behold the features of that person, in all the world, who was destined to be his fate; perhaps he would be greeted by the tender smile of the woman whom he loved; or, quite as probably, the deadly scowl of his bitterest enemy would throw a blight over his life.

Nathaniel Hawthorne, The Blithedale Romance (102)

All weakness tends to corrupt, and impotence corrupts absolutely.

Edgar Friedenberg, Coming of Age in America (47-48)

Section One:
The Veiled Ladies

The Blithedale Romance

The innocent heroine is introduced to American literature with a stage entrance, for she is a performer of some renown. Her sensational appearance is heralded by her manager/impressario, who tantalizes the audience with a description of what it will see and what that spectacle means. As he describes his protegée, he links her powers, her visionary gift, to a larger vision that will please the crowd.

17

18   Child Brides and Intruders

He spoke of a new era that was dawning upon the world; an era that would link soul to soul, and the present life to what we call futurity, with a closeness that should finally convert both worlds into one great, mutually conscious brotherhood. (185)

He is describing the dream of a "white" country village (180), the dream of so many American villages and cities. He offers the audience a fantasy of a world without a past, where, through the rapidity of progress, the present *is* the future. In the new era, not only will all time blend into an explosion of possibility and potentiality, but all those individuals in the white villages will become one, in a blending of lost souls into one great being, united in thought and purpose.

The token of this dream, its sign, is the heroine about to appear on stage. From her lips her manager/mesmerist will elicit the dream, for she is a psychic who can transmit the ideal. Priscilla, the center of attention in this scene, and in many ways the center of Hawthorne's *The Blithedale Romance*, is an instrument. To this rural crowd she appears as one who selflessly dedicates her gift, her very being, to the realization of this ideal. She is a pure vessel containing all that is best in America. As such, she is loved and even revered. She finally appears on stage, above her audience, on a platform, dressed in shimmering, silvery white. In her gauzy veil, she is everyone's dream of a bride.

She is universally loved—the darling of nearly everyone, not just in this audience, but in the novel itself. Zenobia is moved to nurture her, Hollingsworth will marry her, Moodie/Fauntleroy prefers her to his other daughter and ultimately bestows the riches of the world upon her. Coverdale secretly loves her. Even crusty Silas Foster, the Yankee farmer, indulges Priscilla.

She is the silver, shining princess, an emblem of America's hopes, a realization of America's longings. For she is pure and sweet and full of the promise of a being that is all potential, all possibility. Her potential for something less than pure goodness becomes apparent only when we return to Priscilla in theatrical tableau and re-examine the scene.

As we look again, we see a crowd that is less in awe of the princess than pruriently curious about her. They are trying to peer through her gauzy draperies to discover the shape of the body beneath. The exhibition of Priscilla is a kind of pornography, and her manager, the mesmerist Westvelt, is a sly huckster. With his shifty appearance, his disguises, his leers, he is a trickster. He is hardly human—more a compendium of all the disguises that money can buy and that social skills can teach. His gold-banded false teeth signify the spuriousness of all his body parts. Is he human at all?

His power over Priscilla is at once thrilling and threatening. Because it seems based on science, his power is a symbol of both the opportunities and dangers of material progress. As A.N. Kaul says, "In its remote control it suggests the exploitative power which technology was putting into the hands of men: the power to bring individuals into total bondage while leaving them free and untouched" (304). Westervelt's power allows him to exploit his audience as well as Priscilla; he can mesmerize them into mass unconsciousness by selling them a dream. To sell that dream, he must sell the girl who can make it come true—the medium of the world's desires. Thus Priscilla is truly, as D.H. Lawrence notes, "the little psychic prostitute" (107).

She is the first of a long line of innocents, the darlings of the new world. She has been created for the men of that world, men terrified of losing their own place and identity in a country of too many challenges. This new milieu where man must create himself and form his own values is a threatening one, and in it, man becomes frightened of those who offer more challenge to his fragile selfhood. For the weak, a world of endless choices, endless responsibility and guilt is not Eden. Such men perceive paradise as terrifying. To them, the promises of potentiality become taunts of their own inadequacy. Laing's description of the plight of the schizoid individual is an apt description of the besieged individual of the new world:

His whole effort is...to preserve his self. This...is precariously established; he is subject to the dread of his own dissolution into non-being.... His autonomy is threatened with engulfment. He has to guard himself against losing his subjectivity and sense of being alive. In so far as he feels empty, the full, substantive, living reality of others is an impingement which is always liable to get out of hand and become implosive, threatening to overwhelm and obliterate his self completely.... The schizoid individual fears a real live dialectical relationship with real live people. He can relate himself only to depersonalized persons, to phantoms of his own phantasies...perhaps to things. (80)

Like Laing's schizoid individuals, the men of the emerging nation perceive the humanness of others as a threat to self. And, in America, the threat is exacerbated by the absence of traditional ways to define self and by the presence of a new challenge to re-make one's self. Each man is pressured to grow, to meet the demands of a future that impinges on the present, to link his own strength in brotherhood with other men, without sacrificing self. When Westervelt sells his audience a world of "futurity" and brotherhood, he may be offering the promise of unity but also hinting at the terror of failure and of dissolution. The woman who embodies the dream, therefore, must not threaten the men who will invest in it, but must soften its hard edges, conceal its frightening implications. Like any good trader, this woman must promise the buyer what he wants. The buyer wants a bride-as-thing, a fantasy set apart from the challenges and inevitable failures of his real life.

Priscilla is that fantasy: the innocent heroine. She appears utterly dissociated from the workings of everyday life. She is blind to externals: on stage, she is oblivious to the crowd that observes her. Messages, even sunlight, run through her but leave no mark. All experience is refracted by the veil. It protects her and keeps her away from the imperfections of life as it is actually lived, for she embodies a dream of life as it should be. Priscilla is completely untouched, the perfect consumer item. She is brand new, perfect yet perfectible. Utterly malleable, subservient, she offers to become anything the buyer desires. She is ready to adore her beloved and to give him everything, without ever questioning or challenging him.

Like every product designed to enhance the buyer's status, she is a luxury item, created for pleasure, not utility. She offers man the luxury of superiority. He can protect her fragility, soothe her trembling, encase her in a lover's world away from the world itself.

She is cleverly marketed: her shimmering veil is a subtle packaging that indicates the mystery surrounding her.[1] She is wrapped in the unknown, hinting at secret delights, offering a delicious reward for the man who invests in her. Only one owner will ever know what is behind the veil, and then only after the purchase has been completed. Priscilla is at once enticing and inaccessible, utterly pure yet susceptible to the buyer's violation.

Thus she is the dream of a bride, promising devotion and trust, swearing perpetual innocence. She will live, untouched and blind, in her lover's sanctuary. She has been designed for one man, and she knows it. For the man who chooses her, she will lift her veil of mystery. And her lover will be forever trapped in its netting. He will soon learn that the dream is also nightmare. Even the most vulnerable and victimized of innocents destroys.

Each attraction of the fantasy bride leads to her man's undoing. Priscilla's blindness is a refusal to see; her veil cannot be removed. She is forever sheltered from experience, an emblem of stasis, an eternal child. Her lover will never make his mark upon her because she is empty. Her lover can decorate her shell, but he cannot make the thing he desired into a human being. Janeway describes the marriage customs of the nomad Marri tribe in an analogy to modern Western marriage, and questions the consequences of marriage to a child-bride: "How can one love a creature whom one owns? She has lost the power to say no, and so her yes has no value and can bestow no virtue.... She has nothing to give because everything has been taken from her" (207-08).

Loving woman-as-thing, man has embraced an emptiness. Ironically, in seeking a fantasy apart from the world, he has chosen a being truly *of* the world. For the child bride is the quintessential product of society, a thing to be purchased and consumed, not a person to be known and understood. The relationship of man to child bride replicates the getting-and-spending at the center of all American activity, and, as such, it degrades the most intimate of connections. Buying the innocent heroine, he, too, becomes an emptiness. Enticed by his own ego into a foolish purchase, he diminishes his very self. Zenobia, Priscilla's sister, recognizes this transaction and its consequences when she identifies Priscilla as "the type of womanhood, such as man has spent centuries in making it. He is never content, unless he can degrade himself by stooping towards what he loves. In denying us our rights, he betrays even more blindness to his own interests, than profligate disregard of ours!" (113).

Priscilla, on stage, is the true symbol of the innocent. Blithely and blindly, she is the medium for man's most secret values. On her pedestal above the crowd, draped in white, she is the virgin in a new cathedral—the American market. As such, she is, of course, also a whore.[2]

In her first appearance in American literature, then, the child-bride is a figure of ambivalence. She is man's beloved, but she has the power to become his secret adversary. Her weakness is the strength of the leech; her purity is an erotic temptation but it is also a terrible void. As the innocent heroine evolves in the course of American literature, the feared side of her nature emerges and dominates. The character becomes more distorted and grotesque. But even in the helpless Priscilla we see glimpses of a dark side.

Hawthorne fills both the portrait of Priscilla and the pattern of her actions with ambiguity. Her dual nature is established even before she appears on the scene, when the veil she wears is described as shimmering like "the sunny side of a cloud" (6). In this juxtaposition of light and dark, and in the image of a layer of light concealing darkness, there is an immediate warning of ambiguities to come. The sunny side promises what cannot be; it deceives us into believing there will be no storm. And yet we see the cloud. In a novel full of veils, masks, disguises, pretense, and self-deception, Priscilla takes center stage by introducing this theme.[3]

The ambiguities multiply. Priscilla is weak, but she is also a gentle parasite whose love for her sister grows like a grape vine twisting itself out of rock and onto a strong young tree (71). Because Priscilla can't do anything—cook, or milk cows, or care for children—she isn't required to do anything. Everyone at Blithedale perceives her weakness as "pleasant" (69) and looks out for her. Like a baby, Priscilla can get what she wants precisely by remaining unable to get it herself.

Repeatedly, the novel stresses Priscilla's vulnerability. She calls herself a helpless leaf, blown about; Coverdale sees her as a leaf caught up in strong currents that threaten her. For the greater part of the novel, Coverdale worries about Priscilla; to him, she is always about to be victimized by the other characters. Coverdale torments himself endlessly with visions of Hollingsworth breaking Priscilla's heart, Zenobia casting her aside, Westervelt returning her to some unspeakable activity, and he himself allowing it all to happen. Yet, of all the characters in the novel, only Priscilla wins all of the novel's games and gets what she wants. How can this happen to a girl everyone perceives as a born victim?

Other ambiguities seem to hint at an answer. Coverdale himself ultimately recognizes that the seemingly vulnerable child is, in fact, untouchable. The leaf may flutter in every breeze, but it survives each storm. By the end of the novel, noting Priscilla's serenity in the midst of disaster, Coverdale notes that "while we see that such a being responds to every breeze, with tremulous vibration, and imagine that she must be shattered by the first rude blast, we find her retaining her equilibrium amid shocks that might have overthrown many a sturdier frame" (222). Throughout the novel, each hint of Priscilla's susceptibility to others' ill will or to the blows of fate is countered by comments on her ability to remain untouched by life and by others. Neighbors call her the ghost-child, implying that she is a being apart from the processes of human life; Priscilla herself avoids any environment where there is risk or change or chance. When she first comes to Blithedale, she shuns open spaces; in fact, she only learns to enjoy them when they have been domesticated into scenes of May festivities and girlish play. Like the sunbeam, experience seems to pass through Priscilla and to leave no trace behind. Priscilla seems to feel those emotions traditionally most expected of a young woman—devotion, love, adoration, loyalty—but her capacity to feel is limited. Like her notorious silk purses, Priscilla's heart cannot hold much; she "has room for only a single predominant affection" (222). Chase notes that Priscilla's psychic powers, which might be an indicator of a great receptivity to others' needs and desires, in reality "bypass or merely symbolize an emotional life" (84).

Priscilla cannot learn or feel much because her identity is predicated on a denial of growth. Only a child can fulfill the requirements of the role she has been created for, and Priscilla is Blithedale's little girl, frozen in an infantile pose. She alone, of all the major characters at the community, wishes for stasis. Impervious to the hidden conflicts in the Happy Valley, she perceives Blithedale as her personal playground and those who suffer within it as her loving protectors. Even as Coverdale prepares to leave the place in disillusionment and Hollingsworth and Zenobia struggle for mastery of their own situations, Priscilla remains serene, wishing only that "there might never be any change, but one summer follow another, and all just like this!" (133). Unpleasantness must be kept from children, and the other characters and Priscilla's own nature shield her from harsh experience: "with all her delicacy of nerves, there was a singular self-possession in Priscilla, and her sensibilities seemed to be sheltered from ordinary commotion, like the water in a deep well" (132). To be impervious to experience, incapable of change is, of course, a kind of living death, so Priscilla is indeed the ghost-child. And in a novel filled with ominous water imagery, the implications of Priscilla as a deep well extend far beyond the sense of her as a guarded being. The well is a dark and hidden enclosure, a trap for the unwary.

Multiplied ambiguities meet in one central scene. The scene is, like the mesmerist's show, a fantastic entertainment. Hawthorne sets his tableau in the very middle of the novel, and its meanings radiate throughout the book. Zenobia, the teller of the fantasy, derives her inspiration from Priscilla's eyes, and Priscilla herself stands above the Blithedale audience as the focus of the story. She is the main character, the Veiled Lady, in what Zenobia calls "not exactly a ghost story…but something so nearly like it that you shall hardly tell the difference" (99). It is the story of one nearly devoid of human life, and of others who ally themselves to her.

From the first description of the Veiled Lady, we are warned that we may see and hear more than we expect. The life of the Lady is presented as fantasy. But it is also a mirror, a distorted dark one, since the Veiled Lady's lack of substance is like "the candlelight image of one's self, which peeps at us outside of a dark window-pane" (100). Her life reflects men's fears and desires, but also women's doom.

What is behind the Lady's veil? Rumors say it may be great beauty, or a hideous face, or the head of a corpse or a skeleton, or even a Medusa. Other rumors say that what is behind the veil may vary, according to who lifts that veil: the man who lifts the veil will find the face of that one person destined to be his fate. Theodore, a young man obsessed with discovering the identity behind the veil, wagers that he will solve the mystery that very night.

When he confronts the Veiled Lady, she is at once pathetic and sinister. She is, she says, a sad and lonely prisoner of her gauze disguise, and she pleads for a pledge of love and trust. If Theodore will kiss her and make that pledge before he lifts the veil, he will be rewarded with eternal happiness. But if he violates her selfhood in idle curiosity, without faith, the woman beneath the veil will forever be his "evil fate" (105), and he will be forever doomed. The young man, influenced by the rumors he has heard, is unwilling to pledge himself to "so questionable a creature" (106). When he lifts the veil without commitment or understanding, treating its wearer as an alien, he sees what is forever to be denied to him—great beauty. Then the lady disappears from his life. Theodore and the Lady remain apart, each trapped in loneliness.

Thus far the story is an allegory of American marriage. The Veiled Lady is the American bride, an object sequestered from the world and formed to be an impossible and mysterious ideal. Behind her shining cover, she waits for the touch of one man to give her some connection to life. Yet her veil transforms her into a stranger, and man fears what has in fact been created for his delectation. Baym explains, "The ideal is diabolic, for it thoroughly corrupts the natural growth of a strong human personality. It promises a fulfillment that is in fact an incompleteness" (*Shape* 197). Unable or unwilling to provide the Lady with the self she lacks, perceiving her as a thing, not a person, man is doomed to ally himself with a stranger, or, worse, to an emptiness. The ideal vanishes and is replaced by a longing that will never be met. Man unwraps the package he has purchased and finds himself cheated. Seeking an object, instead of a person, to relieve his loneliness, he has denied himself any human bond. And so husband and wife remain locked in mutual solitude, the isolation created when all relationships are transactions, and every buyer is wary and faithless.

This is only the first half of the tale. Its second half applies more directly to the impact of the Veiled Lady on her audience. In this part of Zenobia's story, the Lady finds refuge in a group of visionary people, where one woman in particular becomes her protector. Again, the innocent Lady becomes a sinister figure, this time when the Magician warns her protector that "this stranger is your deadliest enemy. In love, in worldly fortune, in all your pursuit of happiness, she is doomed to fling a blight over your prospects" (107). To save herself from this evil, the protector must re-capture the Lady and net the captive in the Veil. And this, of course, is what Zenobia, ending her story, does to Priscilla.

Superficially, this part of Zenobia's tale is only Zenobia's subtle recounting of her meeting with Westervelt and her recognition of Priscilla's past life and present rivalry. But on another level, this tale summarizes Priscilla's impact on Blithedale and its inhabitants: her power to disrupt the community, to diminish Hollingsworth, and to destroy her sister.

Zenobia's entertaining little tale encapsulates the conflicts of the entire novel, for the intrusion of Priscilla transforms the lives of those around her. From her first moments at Blithedale, Priscilla begins to poison the community, and the images of her entry make her function clear. The setting for that entrance is a warm hearth, a sanctuary filled with good fellowship and the glow of Zenobia's smile. Coverdale repeatedly describes the hearth, stressing the blaze, the extravagance of the kitchen fire and the cheerfulness of the supper gathering. Outside, a terrible snowstorm rages, and when Priscilla comes inside, she is the snow-maiden—slim, insubstantial, sickly, trembling all over. In her helplessness, she makes an appealing figure. Blithedale takes her in, the group takes her to their hearts, and they thus doom themselves.

To let Priscilla into their midst is to invite the world to Blithedale.[4] Priscilla chills the heart and, eventually, extinguishes the fire of every character's dreams. Frederick Crews remarks on the pattern of regression to childhood that develops in the novel (205), and Priscilla is the seamstress who stitches that pattern. Devoid of ideas or goals, she is the city girl,[5] alien in this rural Utopia, and capable of subverting it, for she functions as a constant temptation to return to the ways of the old world. When men choose her, they choose the socially approved item and the socially approved roles they have been trying to escape. When one woman emulates her, that woman destroys her identity.

Priscilla's effect on Blithedale is most dramatically shown in her effect on Blithedale's most vital member, Zenobia. Hawthorne begins the novel using the sisters as contrasting figures: Zenobia all activity, physical grace, and sexual energy; Priscilla all lassitude, awkwardness, and virginal purity. Zenobia is the queen of Blithedale, an independent, strong woman presiding over the fireside when the novel begins. Initially, she is the focus of desire for both Hollingsworth and Coverdale; she fascinates and challenges them. She is the woman who embodies the ideals of Blithedale, for she is unconventional, generous, and free. But like the others, she soon succumbs to the influence of the snow maiden when she and Priscilla battle for the love of the same man.

Zenobia destroys herself by trying to become Priscilla. She, like the men at Blithedale, becomes caught in the net of social roles, and she reverts to the very role she claims to despise, that of the vapid and submissive child-woman. She does so because the presence of Priscilla brings out that poisonous, hidden part of Zenobia's nature.

Like Priscilla, Zenobia is wearing a veil, but her veil is the veil of feminism. Like the others at Blithedale who are trying to escape social constrictions, Zenobia has assumed a radical identity, but it is only tentative. When Zenobia perceives that another guise is more pleasing to her lover, she tries to assume it. Out of love for Hollingsworth, she discards her radical self, denying her intelligence, her energy, and, ultimately, her very being.

Zenobia's story is told through symbolism of tricks and masks. Zenobia is the flower she wears every day, fresh, luxuriant, and exotic. Shortly after Priscilla arrives on the scene and is adopted by Hollingsworth, something happens to that flower. In what appears to be a lighthearted exchange, Coverdale accuses Zenobia of being an enchantress and mockingly tells Hollingsworth, who is listening to the banter, "That flower in her hair is a talisman. If you were to snatch it away, she would vanish, or be transformed into something else!" (42). But Hollingsworth needs to exert no physical force to transform Zenobia. She takes the flower from her hair, and thus, in the early pages of the novel, initiates the surrender that becomes her doom.

That flower keeps reappearing, and changing, and changing hands, as Zenobia falls further and further towards her degradation. Desperate to win the love of the dominant, conventionally masculine Hollingsworth, Zenobia becomes what he demands,[6] a helpless creature, subservient to his will. Coverdale at least partly perceives the transformation. When he observes Hollingsworth look tenderly upon Priscilla, he comments that "Zenobia...would have given her eyes...for such a look" (67). To bask in his approving gaze, Zenobia does indeed relinquish her own power to see and act. Soon the exotic flower is replaced by an artificial, jeweled flower; like the new Zenobia, it is a false material object, an ornament appropriate for social gatherings.

Having become Priscilla, Zenobia becomes *not* herself. But she is denied Hollingsworth, the reward she expected for her transformation. The shock of disappointment forces Zenobia to face her disgrace, and she recognizes her error. Finally "awake, disenchanted, disenthralled" (201), she perceives that she has chosen "a woman's doom," and that she has "deserved it like a woman" (206). She has traded a free self for a false and disfiguring feminine role, and she has done so because Priscilla's presence tempted Zenobia to assume that role; Priscilla's enactment of it demonstrated its power and made it attractive.

Now, in despair, Zenobia addresses her sister/rival with "a sort of contempt," calling her "my evil fate," but adding, "there never was a babe with less strength or will to do an injury" (203). Priscilla enjoys the triumph of the weak. Zenobia, acknowledging her mistake, can only cast off the false self. She gives the jeweled flower to Priscilla. It is both the product Zenobia tried so hard to be and the item Priscilla has always been, so it rightly belongs to the girl, not the woman. But without the decorative self, there is nothing left of Zenobia. Confronted with her own emptiness, she dies in the pose characteristic of her sister: on her knees. Ironically, remnants of the earlier Zenobia remain, for when her corpse is found, Zenobia's fists are clenched in defiance. The attitude defines her life, the conflict of the adult woman tempted to assume the child's role.

Zenobia's life does not end like her story of the Veiled Lady. Instead of imprisoning her female enemy, Zenobia assumes the veil herself, and it becomes her shroud. Her sister is left the victor in the romantic struggle and, in relating to her lover, again enjoys the power of the weak.

The marriage of the helpless bride to the dominant male is the typical American union, and Hollingsworth fits his role as well as Priscilla does hers. Even though he is a philanthropist, he is in many ways the quintessential American businessman, a work-obsessed monomaniac. Like other businessmen, he perceives marriage as a trade, an exchange of female adoration in return for his protection. In a neat reversal, however, Hawthorne enables Priscilla, funded by her father's inheritance, to buy Hollingsworth, thus corrupting him further than the more traditional exchange. In deciding to marry Priscilla for her new-found riches, Hollingsworth betrays the last of his principles; like Theodore in the tale of the Veiled Lady, he takes his bride not out of love but out of lust—in this case, lust for money.

Hollingsworth's dark secret is his greed for power, and to attain that power he takes Priscilla and cruelly casts her sister off. Like Theodore, he realizes too late that he has chosen his own damnation, for he has wed his own dark secret, a living mirror of his sin. In Priscilla's eyes he will forever see his own evil; in Priscilla's being he will see an image of what Zenobia became. As Coverdale notes, "in all the world, there was nothing so difficult to be endured, by those who had any dark secret to conceal, as the glance of Priscilla's terrible and melancholy eyes" (172). Priscilla will be inescapable; she is the living twin of her wronged dead sister. And, paradoxically, her blind adoration is the worst kind of judgment, for it offers no understanding and thus no possibility of forgiveness.

Marriage reduces Hollingsworth to a pitiful and broken figure. Soon after the union, Hollingsworth relinquishes all his dreams of reforming prisoners and himself becomes a prisoner of despair, characterized by a childish tendency to press close to his wife. Her "unquestioning reverence" and veiled happiness" (223) reflect her total inability to share his pain. Priscilla refuses to see any evil in her beloved; she remains safe and happy behind her veil of innocence. Blithedale has fallen apart, Zenobia has killed herself, Priscilla, as Lawrence says, has drained her "blacksmith of his blackness and his smith-strength," (107) and she alone has attained her dream. That it is only a dream, that her beloved neither cares for nor supports her, is, of course, not significant to Priscilla. For she has been created *as* a dream, to live in one.

Priscilla is not directly responsible for the misery of Blithedale. She did nothing. Alone among the main characters, she did not change. She did not plan, think, or act to any purpose. She was simply what she was formed to be—a beautiful, empty thing. She was—and remains—the lovely ideal of the child-bride, a vessel each man can fill with his own fantasies. If she appeared to be what she was not, and if she promised what she could not give, it was others, and not she, who clothed her in a veil of promises. Daniel Hoffman says the theme of *The Blithedale Romance* is that "the price of pure idealism is the extinction of reality" (212). Priscilla represents that pure ideal, and her price is very high.

The House of the Seven Gables

There are versions of Priscilla elsewhere in Hawthorne's novels. Although Phoebe Pyncheon of *The House of the Seven Gables* is a sunshine girl rather than a snow maiden, she represents the same ideal as Priscilla. Granted, she is capable where Priscilla is useless, bustling and bright where Priscilla is fearful and shrinking, but in her allegiance to the ways of the world and her ability to live by the world's standards, Phoebe is another Priscilla.

Like Priscilla, she is characterized by her innocence. Clark Griffith recognizes that innocence is Phoebe's defect and defines it as her lack of insight, her inability to recognize both the evils of the Pyncheon-Maule past and the present dangers within the family (387). Like Priscilla, Phoebe is blind. On one level, her blindness may be considered an asset, for it enables her to move blithely through the miseries of the family and to spread a layer of cheer wherever she goes. But unending cheerfulness and light keep Phoebe from becoming fully human. She is, Hawthorne says, an angel, but even angels of sunshine and sweetness are not human, and in her lack of conflict and passion, Phoebe is a kind of ghost, just like the rest of the Pyncheons. As an angel, she is an angel of conformity, bringing tidings of conventional joys within the Pyncheon house.

She remains the conventional child bride. Clifford perceives her as an earthly rosebud (142), never a wild-flower, "for wildness was no trait of hers" (143). "The path, which would have best suited her, was the well-worn track of ordinary life; the companions, in whom she would most have been delighted, were such as one encounters at every turn" (142-43). Far from being a wild-flower, Phoebe is not really a flower at all; she is the perpetual bud of a flower. She will never blossom into adult life. Instead, she remains forever the adorable child in a domestic hideaway; in Phoebe's garden, little birds are nesting as Phoebe casts her spell over Holgrave.

Like Priscilla, Phoebe is most at home in a conventional setting, and since conventional values are determined by economic needs, it is not surprising that Phoebe understands the rules of trading. She can manage the one-cent shop well. And, like, Priscilla, Phoebe is rewarded, at the end of the novel, with riches.[7] Although she appears vulnerable and powerless, Phoebe attains material and emotional dominance simply by remaining a child.

Phoebe enjoys the same kind of triumph-through-submission as Priscilla. At Maule's Well, Holgrave senses his mesmerist's power over the pure ray of sunshine, but he refrains from exercising it. His influence over Phoebe is actually minimal; a mesmerist might transmit his values *through* Phoebe, but experience does not remain within her simple being. Phoebe is essentially unchanging and unchangeable. For all her appearance of adaptability, Phoebe is incapable of one adaptation—she cannot grow up. She will forever see through the eyes of a happy child. Her life, then, is a kind of death-in-life, and it is fitting that, as Gloria Erlich notes, Holgrave decides to marry Phoebe in the presence of a corpse (142).

By marrying Holgrave to Phoebe, Hawthorne provides the typical "happy ending" of every romance. A young, energetic, intelligent man of talent and promise unites with a pure and loving girl dedicated to creating a home for him. This is the wedding that should happen, according to all conventional standards. Yet the ending is bitter because the union signals a defeat and a regression. The young man will never fulfill his promise; he will relinquish his radicalism, deny his ability to question and challenge. He will be blinded by the domestic ray of

sunshine, trapped in the nest she is so carefully building. At the end of
the novel, Holgrave is being tamed and taught his conventional role.
Hawthorne, again, challenges us with his ambivalence, for he gives us
the marriage we expect, and leaves us unsatisfied.

The Marble Faun
Phoebe reappears as Hilda in Hawthorne's last completed novel,
The Marble Faun. Once again we meet an American girl of sunshine,
surrounded by those ever-present birds, this time doves. Once again,
Hawthorne's maiden is loved by all, cheerful and meek, an image of
virginity, simplicity, and maidenly sweetness. Like both Priscilla and
Phoebe, Hilda is a transmitter of others' ideas and values, for she is a
copyist of the Great Masters. As a copyist, Hilda has hit on a business
more lucrative than producing original art, as popular as a cent-shop or a
mesmerist's show. Like her counterparts, Hilda offers what the public
will buy. And like the other heroines, Hilda is dangerously blind.

Hilda's blindness is a more deliberate refusal to see than that of the
other two girls, and she is thus more overtly dangerous. Her innocence
appears to be a more consciously assumed armor than that of Priscilla or
Phoebe.[8] Crews says that Hilda's characteristic response to reality is, "It
perplexes me," and, as she shrinks a little, she adds, "neither do I quite
like to think about it" (215). "Her ideals," says Baym, "are based on an
intransigent refusal to know the facts of life" (*Shape* 243). Hilda chooses
to live in a kind of shrine as a kind of vestal virgin, her exaggerated
version of the socially approved role, in a terrified retreat from the
misery around her.

Her armor of desperate innocence makes her cold and cruel. When
Miriam, having sinned, seeks Hilda's compassion, Hilda disdains her,
saying, "Your powerful magnetism would be too much for me. The pure,
white atmosphere, in which I try to discern what things are good and
true, would be discolored." Miriam rightly calls her "merciless," and
notes the danger of the angel: "you are so terribly severe!" (154).

Another person's sin and suffering makes Hilda feel tainted. So she
searches for a new sanctuary, the convent (where, she feels, if she had
only been Catholic, she could have lived happily ever after), and, finally,
the protection of some father-figure. Her first "father" is the priest to
whom she tries to confess. Ironically, she is blind to the sin she should
confess—her heartlessness—and instead tries only to remove her sense

of filth-by-association. As Baym notes, "she can deny evil in herself only by imputing it to others" (*Shape* 244). But Hilda needs a more permanent and Puritan haven from guilt. She needs the shelter of a husband.

When Hilda turns to Kenyon for emotional protection, she turns to the right mate. Although Kenyon evidences some humanity in his sympathy for Miriam and Donatello, at heart he is a prig. When he feebly tries his "Fortunate Fall" theory on Hilda and thus tries to widen his own vision, he doesn't try very hard. Hilda's horrified reaction is enough to stifle his growth. He begs her forgiveness and immediately proposes an alliance of his uncertainty and her invincible innocence. "Were you my guide, my counselor, my inmost friend, with that white wisdom which clothes you as a celestial garment, all would go well. Oh, Hilda, guide me home!" (329).

Hilda, clad in celestial white, is another Veiled Lady, ready to domesticate her Theodore, to take him home to America, where neither he nor she will ever have to question again. Hilda's wisdom can shield the pair from knowledge of their own sin: their denial of their own connection to a world of men, not angels.[9]

With his fondness for tableaux, Hawthorne encapsulates Hilda's story in an early scene in the novel. As in *The Blithedale Romance*, the key scene involves an audience and its perception of an object on view. As in the story of the Veiled Lady, those involved in the tableau are the women whose contrasting characters represent two ways to live. Just as Zenobia offers a key to the mysteries of Blithedale in her story, in this scene, Miriam, another vital, passionate figure, reveals the ambivalence of innocence in her commentary.

In this scene, no person is on display. Instead, the two heroines reflect on the meaning of a painting, the portrait of Beatrice Cenci which Hilda has copied. Hilda and Miriam react to this portrait, with its associations of sexual violation and murder, in opposing ways, and the portrait becomes a central symbol of the novel.

Hawthorne calls this portrait of the girlish and beautiful Beatrice "the very saddest picture ever painted or conceived; it involved an unfathomable depth of sorrow.... It was a sorrow that removed the beautiful girl out of the sphere of humanity," placing her in "a far-off region, the remoteness of which—while yet her face is so close before us—makes us shiver as at a specter" (53).

The portrait is created by Hilda, and it *is* Hilda. Lest we miss this connection, Hawthorne soon tells us that, as the women discuss the painting, Hilda's "expression had become almost exactly that of the portrait" (55). Although it is a portrait associated with a great sin of the past, and as such might be more superficially connected to Miriam, it depicts another sin, the evil of deliberate innocence.

Hilda has painted Beatrice as a ghost, and thus she has mirrored her own lack of humanity. The girl in the painting, like Priscilla, like Phoebe, like Hilda, is spirit, not flesh, so she is untouchable, untouched. Her expression is one of great sorrow, like the face of the Veiled Lady, representing not only her own isolation but the misery that comes to those drawn to her. Such lovers will never bring the specter out of the "far-off region" of innocence; they will, on the contrary, be imprisoned in it themselves. All who choose the angel will be, like her, sad and lonely prisoners of their own fear of life.

When Hilda and Miriam examine the portrait, their words become revealing self-portraits. Hilda thinks of her Beatrice as "a fallen angel— fallen and yet sinless." Her Beatrice is too good for this world, where "only this depth of sorrow...keeps her" (54). To Hilda, Beatrice is tainted only by others' flaws. But Miriam challenges Hilda's analysis, refusing to acquit Beatrice of evil. Hilda replies that Beatrice's miserable expression is caused by sorrow,, not sin, again denying Beatrice's complicity in evil. Miriam's comment, however, forces Hilda to recall the Cenci story, which she claims to have "quite forgotten" (55). Hilda is dismayed. Miriam's mention of sin seems to bring a hidden fear to light. Hilda's reaction is to flee from the subject and from any understanding of evil. She admits that Beatrice did, indeed, sin terribly, and that Beatrice "feels it to be so. Therefore it is that the forlorn creature so longs to elude our eyes, and forever vanish away into nothingness!" (55). In Hilda's polarized judgment, Beatrice must be utterly pure or horribly tainted. There can be no compromise, and the way to deal with sin is to hide it, to run from it.

Miriam's response to Hilda is a judgment itself: "Oh Hilda, your innocence is like a sharp steel sword!" (55). In Hilda's morality, Miriam sees the greatest sin of all: an absence of the tolerance and understanding that can unite all men, all of them sinners, in bonds of love. But Hilda, like any child, is cruel in her simplicity.

In this short scene, Hawthorne includes several significant strains of the novel. There is Hilda the cold and sinless virgin, like Beatrice, remote and non-human. Ironically, this is the untouchable Hilda that Kenyon loves to touch. Then there is the intolerant Hilda who demands that sinners disappear so that her view of life will never be clouded. And, in Miriam's words, there is Hilda the destroyer, an angel with a sword, so obsessed with her own purity that she will cut any human tie that threatens it.

R.W.B. Lewis says that the action of *The Marble Faun* charts "the transformation of the soul in its journey from innocence to conscience: the soul's realization of itself under the impact of an engagement with evil," and he identifies this action as "the New World action (122). But there is a parallel action in this novel, a retreat from experience, and it is equally representative of an American pattern of evasion and fear. In *The Marble Faun*, this retreat is enacted by the American protagonists, Hilda and Kenyon, with Hilda as the central symbol of evasion. As a figure of deliberate innocence, Hilda is the beloved and desired angel, but she is an angel of emptiness. In subsequent American novels, this figure of vacuous purity re-enacts the pattern, attracting lovers who have created her out of their dreams, luring them backwards, to the artificial paradise they desired.

Section Two:
James's Ingenues and Howells's Saint

The Bostonians

Hawthorne's first angel-child, Priscilla, appears, slightly transformed, in Henry James's novel of feminism, reform and rescue, *The Bostonians*. Like Priscilla, Verena Tarrant is the instrument of a shoddy mesmerist, and like Priscilla, she is the center of a group of characters who desire her.

Once again, the pattern of the novel and the child-woman's function in it are dramatized in a theatrical scene. In the initial dramatic scene which introduces all the conflicts, Verena stands apart from an audience, observed and assessed by those who will struggle to win her. Each of these figures sees in Verena what he or she wishes to see, and a major question of the novel emerges: what *is* Verena? As two key figures answer that question, in terms dictated by their own needs and longings, Verena functions to illuminate not only her own nature, but also the hidden natures of those who desire her.

In her first performance before a group of Boston feminists and reformers, Verena confronts a collection of skeptics unsure whether she is to entertain or edify them. Like Priscilla, she does both. It is clear from the beginning that Verena is both actress, in her slightly histrionic dress and manner, and medium. "She has to have her father start her up" (44), a friend explains. Passive, lovely, young, and sweet, Verena exerts a strange power over her audience. If she is acting a role, "she played it with extraordinary simplicity and grace; at the end of ten minutes...the whole audience...were under her charm" (50).

What Verena says does not seem as important as Verena's personal allure. Her words are vague, sentimental phrases "all about the gentleness and goodness of women... how...they had been trampled under the heel of man" (51). Appropriately, the helpless medium speaks sweetly of victimization. When she babbles of women's "day having come at last, about the universal sisterhood" (51), her words echo Westervelt's sales pitch about a future of possibility and brotherhood, and the fantasy being sold is so vague as to allow each observer to create his own dream. Like Priscilla, Verena is a kind of tease, offering her audience spiritual uplift in a physically attractive package—she entices and yet remains inaccessible. As she speaks, she repeatedly reveals and then covers her body with a large red fan.

We first observe Verena's performance through the eyes of Basil Ransom, the young Southerner who has come North to seek his fortune. To Ransom, who likes actresses and little women, Verena appears to be a pure girl sullied by her contact with the commercial and the political. Contemptuous of reformers and feminists, Ransom dismisses Verena's words as "such pretty things," "full of school-girl phrases...childish lapses of logic" (51), and concentrates on Verena's aura of vulnerability. In her submissiveness, Verena appears the perfect bride for an egotist; he can cleanse her of the stain of commercialism and replace that "trash" of ideas "she had been stuffed with" with his own masterful theories. Ransom is sexually attracted to Verena's lack of sexual awareness; to him, Verena is "as innocent as she was lovely," innocent not only of the erotic but also of the political: her speech is merely the "bad music" imposed on "a vocalist of exquisite facility" (51).

Verena's words have a distinctly different effect on the rich feminist Olive Chancellor. To Olive, Verena speaks for all oppressed women, and she does so with a power and composure Olive longs for. To Olive, both Verena's words and music are sweet, and in her desire to appropriate that voice, to train it, amplify it, Olive becomes the adversary of Basil Ransom.

In this first exhibition of Verena, the connections to *The Blithedale Romance* are indisputable, and many critics have noted the parallels. Paul John Eakin, for example, notes the pairing of seedy mesmerists Westervelt and Selah Tarrant and perceives that Tarrant has "got up his daughter in the image of a Zenobia." He notes also the blurring of distinctions between Zenobia's passionate and exotic radicalism and the "meretricious show" of ideas Westervelt elicits from the innocent Priscilla, a blurring that combines in the character of Verena (196). Marius Bewley, too, links Westervelt and Selah Tarrant, Zenobia's pronouncements and Verena's eloquence, and further notes that Olive shares Zenobia's martyrdom and ability to dominate the "weaker" woman (qtd. in Cargill 127). There are other parallels. Ransom, like Hollingsworth, is the protector and rescuer figure; like Hollingsworth, Ransom is cold, hard, egotistic, and obsessed with his own canon of ideas to change the world. Ransom inherits certain qualities from another Blithedale character: like Coverdale, he is a voyeur at heart, afraid of life. And while Verena may babble the words of Zenobia, Olive possesses Zenobia's commitment and drive, and a minor character, Olive's sister Adelaide Luna, possesses Zenobia's flamboyance and frankness.

Far from being even a pale copy of Zenobia, Verena Tarrant is instead a nearly exact reproduction of Priscilla—with one new asset. She can speak. As the conflict of Blithedale is the struggle for Priscilla, the battle of Boston is for Verena. To Ransom, the goal is to possess Verena and, once he owns her, to silence her. He will make her more fully a Priscilla by obliterating any deviation from the feminine ideal. To Olive, the goal is not to own, but to *become* Verena.

As Fetterley recognizes, "the true subject of *The Bostonians* is not love but power" (121). The irony of this struggle for power lies in its object, for both Ransom and Olive seek energy in emptiness. The child-spiritualist Verena is void of spirit and self: this emptiness is her strength. As her father says, power seemed "to flow through her" (46), not from her. Fetterley notes that Verena's power "is seen to derive from those conditions which ultimately make her the most powerless of all. Verena's power is based on her charm, and her charm is based on her desire to please, which in turn is based on an absence of a strongly defined or assertive self." Essentially nothing, Verena can become anything the buyer wants: she can be filled with what Fetterley calls "the projective fantasies" of those who are enticed by her nothingness (141). *The Bostonians*, then, chronicles the struggles of two buyers fighting for the same bargain. Ransom is bidding on a pure bride. If he can get Verena, he will tear off her wrapping of feminism and fame and take sole possession of the trusting girl beneath. Olive Chancellor, however, is investing in an alternative self, for to her, Verena is everything she can never be.

While Olive deceives herself into believing she is rescuing Verena from a mercenary father and a demeaning exhibitionism, Olive is quite clearly buying Verena.[10] Although she couches her purchase in terms of "rescue" and dreams of being Verena's "protectress" and "devotee" (70), in truth Olive wants to find a new self; the more she learned of Verena's life, "the more she wanted to enter it; the more it took her out of herself" (71).

To be taken out of her self and transported into a new one is just what Olive thinks she wants. Olive is a conscientious, sincere, and committed woman. She is firm in her feminist convictions, she is dedicated to improving the world, she is devoted to the cause of the forgotten and abused. She has made an independent life for herself, and she is respected by those she respects. Yet Olive is tormented within; she feels guilt about her money and isolated from the masses she most wants to help. And she is always afraid. As Fetterley says, she is "afraid of being laughed at, she is afraid of not being just, she is afraid of speaking—'Olive had a fear of everything, but her greatest fear was of being afraid!' " (132). She is "subject to fits of tragic shyness, during which she was unable to meet even her own eyes in the mirror" (7). Owning Verena, Olive can evade her own critical glance, and look instead into a new mirror, into the eyes of a soulmate who "had as yet to make acquaintance with the sentiment of fear" (69).

Olive has ideas that she feels can redeem the world, but she is physically stiff, personally awkward, cold, with, to Basil, "absolutely no figure" (15). Verena is adolescent and graceful and lovely and therefore powerful. She can voice the ideas Olive longs to express, and others will listen. And because Verena is so lovely, she is lovable. And Olive, like Zenobia, would like to be loved.

James gives several hints of the underside of Olive's nature. In a kind of aside to the central plot, he comments that when Olive can control her fear and inner torment, she becomes "graceful," with "a tone of softness and sympathy, a gentle dignity, a serenity of wisdom" that link her to Verena in a shared charm (117) and that make others appreciate her. Whether James is implying that the stereotypical female role of charm and softness is Olive's better side is not as significant as the fact that this facet of Olive exists. It is an aspect of Olive that echoes, however faintly, Verena's enormous appeal, and it is not the only sign of the typically "feminine" in Olive. In the earliest pages of the novel, James implies that Olive feels a twinge of romantic interest in her Southern cousin. Meeting Ransom for the first time, Olive, the ostensible man-hater, notes how handsome he is. She quickly represses the thought, however, and replaces it with feminist orthodoxy: "it had already been a comfort to her, on occasions of acute feeling, that she hated men, as a class, anyway" (17-18). For what unfulfilled longing must Olive seek comfort? What acute and sudden feeling must be stifled? How appropriate, then, for Olive to purchase a young and pretty girl, loved by the handsome man she must never consider for herself.

In her power and loveliness, Verena is what Olive can never be or never do. Olive has always dreamed of martyrdom; she habitually thinks of Verena as Joan of Arc. In Verena, Eakin explains, Olive sees "a vicarious fulfillment" (211) and Verena fulfills Olive's acknowledged and hidden dreams. "Everything she [Verena] took up became an illustration of the facility, the 'giftedness,' which Olive, who had so little of it, never ceased to wonder at and prize" (150). And, as the relationship grows, Olive herself becomes more confident; "she had begun to believe in herself to a livelier tune than she had ever listened to before" (138). Olive appears to have bought the right item, a second self that will enact her secret scenario. For a while, anyway, Olive can be less afraid.

Fear remains an undercurrent, however, because Olive's "rival" will not go away. Like Olive, Ransom couches his desire for Verena in terms of rescue, creating a fantasy of Verena that will justify his longing: "She was a touching, ingenuous victim, unconscious of the pernicious forces which were hurrying her to her ruin" (210). The irony of the situation is that, while Ransom dreams of saving Verena from ruin, his true role is to destroy her by reducing her small identity to something even smaller, to stifle and entrap her. Even a casual study of the images related to Ransom and his vision of Verena reveals that Olive is right to consider him Verena's enemy.[11]

Like the philanthropist Hollingsworth, Basil has an ambivalent attitude toward the money he lacks and so desperately needs. Like Hollingsworth, he is a cold and rigid force, violent in his obsessions. Both qualities are revealed in one of James's first descriptions of the man as "very long...he even looked a little hard and discouraging, like a column of figures" (2). The poor Southerner longs for the wealth he claims to disdain, briefly considering a financially rewarding marriage, first, to Olive, and later, and more seriously, to her sister Adelaide. His attitude toward money is similar to his combined scorn and lust for fame. James tells us that Ransom's "expression of bright grimness and hard enthusiasm" gives him a head suitable for a bronze medal, or a judicial bench, or a political platform. We can think of Ransom as the profile on a coin, an image combining his material and political ambitions, but his arrogance prevents him from entering the plebeian fray: he would, James notes, have gone into politics, "if there had been any other way to represent constituencies than by being elected" (160). Too superior to curry the favor of the electorate, Ransom contents himself with expressing his views in articles that are constantly rejected as outdated. To a man so needful of an audience, seeing a mere girl captivate one almost effortlessly, must be frustrating, particularly because Ransom likes women "not to think too much, not to feel any responsibility for the government of the world" (80). The fragile Verena is usurping his role, so it is not surprising that Ransom's love for her is suffused with jealousy and violence.[12]

Ransom's vision of love is thus a vision of destruction. The veneer of Southern manners conceals an anger Nina Auerbach recognizes: "the florid chivalry with which he smothers every woman he meets...is the honey of a universal rage." Auerbach also cites Ransom's reaction to hearing Verena's voice in the night: "Murder, what a lovely voice!" (*Communities* 129), a response that blends fury and admiration. Even in his fantasy of rescue, Ransom's goal is violent. He conceives of Verena's feminist babble as a shabby edifice separating him from the pure girl behind it, a girl who is "made for love." He can save her by making her love him and then "this false, flimsy structure would rattle to her feet" (280). This facade of silly ideas is, in another scene, a glass house imprisoning Verena, and he tells her

he had come to look at her through the glass sides, and if he wasn't afraid of hurting her he would smash them in. He was determined to find the key that would open it...it was tantalising only to be able to talk to her through the keyhole. (270)

Here images of rescue and of sexual violation combine in a curious way. And while the goal of this rescue is communicating, it is one-way communication; Ransom will be able to speak more fully and more loudly. The sexual violation, Ransom perceives, will be a silencing: "If he should become her husband he should know a way to strike her dumb" (271).

What begins, then, as a rescue (ransom?) fantasy evolves into a kidnapping, a deprogramming of the fair maiden that involves sexual and intellectual domination. The more publicity Verena receives, the more successful her speaking engagements, the more infuriated and desperate Ransom becomes, until he "felt almost capable of kidnapping her" (330), and his success is indeed, to him, a capture: "however she might turn and twist in his grasp he held her fast" (338). Ransom's abduction of Verena transports her from what he conceives of as a glass cage to an even smaller prison of male egotism.

Olive thus has reason to fear Ransom, but she fails to see that she, like him, is struggling to appropriate another's self rather than to develop her own. The battle damages both combatants and, James makes clear, is conducted without much regard for the well-being of the prize.

Between them, Olive and Ransom are ready to tear Verena apart; "it was war to the knife, it was a question of which should pull hardest" (322). What makes the war particularly bloody is that the warriors are fighting for what is, essentially, not there—for a being created in their minds, but bearing little resemblance to the inconsequential Verena. The little medium is exactly that, a transmitter of others' ideas, a mirror of others' desires. "Her talent for impersonation," Eakin comments, "her very possession of chameleon identity...raise extremely disturbing questions, both moral and psychological, about the integrity of her personality" (202). Even poor old Miss Birdseye, who supposedly is past any lucid judgment, recognizes Verena's true nature; "she seems to have something for everyone" (184), she says. To her father, Verena is a way to wealth; to her mother, an entry into polite society; to Henry Burrage, a rare and thus valuable collectible; to Matthias Pardon, the greatest public relations gimmick of modern times. Verena is a trick done with mirrors, and behind the glass there is nothing. Whoever gets Verena thus gets what he or she deserves.

In the "awarding" of Verena, the prize of battle, *The Bostonians* differs from *The Blithedale Romance* by providing a slightly happier ending. In James's novel, destruction is not as universal as it is in Blithedale, for in *The Bostonians*, loss of the child bride leads to one recovery and even to one character's development of self. Granted, the victor in this battle, like Hollingsworth, is to be punished for his conquest. When Ransom steals Verena immediately before she is to speak before an enormous crowd, he exults, "You are mine, you are not theirs" (371), but his very appropriation of Verena has diminished her. Without the glittering surface of drama and oration, Verena is reduced to the stature of any helpless girl. As Eakin points out, when Ransom hurries Verena from the music-hall, she is concealed in a cloak and hood. Her face is no longer recognizable (216). And James proposes no bright future for the runaway lovers; while Verena is glad to have chosen Ransom, "beneath her hood, she was in tears. It is to be feared that with the union, so far from brilliant, into which she was about to enter, these were not the last she was destined to shed" (378).

If Verena is, symbolically, dead to the world, her death may have released the woman who lived through her. If Olive can no longer pretend to be Verena, perhaps she may be forced to become herself. In the absence of the lovely, powerful girl, Olive is called on to fill a void. There is an audience waiting at the music hall, an audience enraged at the delay in Verena's appearance and expected to be more enraged at the cancellation of that appearance. Olive is the person who must confront the angry and disappointed crowd, and on the surface it may appear that this thrusting of the fearful, awkward woman into the public arena is a suitable punishment for her selfish manipulations. Yet this very appearance is, on another level, a realization not of Olive's nightmares, but of her dreams. Auerbach rightly perceives that when "Olive flings herself onstage after Verena's defection, her desperate appearance suggests that of the archetypal mousy understudy who becomes a star" (*Communities* 134).

All the elements that Olive fears have come together: a hostile crowd, a duty to speak, alone, and to say what the group does not wish to hear. The situation is the martyrdom Olive has feared and yet longed for, and she herself perceives it as a "fierce expiation" (376). This final tableau will require all of Olive's courage, and she summons the necessary strength. The outcome is not what Olive expects, for, as she faces the loud and unruly audience, "Every sound instantly dropped, the hush was respectable, the great public waited, and whatever she should say to them…it was not apparent that they were likely to hurl the benches at her" (377).

Olive has not yet spoken, but she is a commanding presence. Losing Verena, Olive has somehow duplicated her power and combined it with her own deep conviction to become not merely a transmitter but a source of ideas. Olive's story ends where Verena's began—she is alone, before a skeptical audience, about to speak. But Olive is strong where Verena was weak, defiant where Verena was submissive. Olive truly stands alone, for she lacks the feminine graces which evoked instant, approving support for Verena. "For Olive," Auerbach says, "letting herself go and letting Verena go may be equally therapeutic means of realizing her vision of woman standing alone and 'clinging to a great, vivifying, redemptory idea'—which she spreads over her age" (*Communities* 135). Although Olive can never elicit the patronizing and indulgent approval the crowd bestows on a child entertainer, she can rely on her own beliefs and on the knowledge that she has faced her fears, perhaps faced them down forever.

Thus *The Bostonians* begins and ends with a tableau—but the actors have shifted their positions. In the second tableau, Verena has left the stage; she will now perform for an audience of one. She will have hardly any voice, just a whisper of acquiescence. Ransom, too, has shifted from impotent admirer to theatrical manager, but there is little left for him to control, since his goal is to retire the actress. Replacing Verena onstage is Olive, who, in relinquishing her fantasy self, is forced to act *as* herself, to become someone better and freer than she had ever dreamed possible. Olive has lost the "child" part of herself, with its appealing and dangerous helplessness, and come forward, not to entertain or amuse the crowd, but to confront and even change it.

Olive does not die, as Zenobia did, in an attitude of defiance and despair. The influence of the child bride is, in *The Bostonians*, less pervasive and sinister because one person does escape it. Freed from the lure of the passive role, Olive survives. As she stands by herself she begins a new life. Ransom and Verena, too, begin their life together, but precisely because Ransom has stolen what he wanted—a thing, not a person—he will find himself forever alone with hollowness, Verena's and his own.

The Portrait of a Lady

In *The Bostonians*, the loss of the child heroine leads to the freeing of one woman; in another James novel, *The Portrait of a Lady*, the lure of the child is a repeated enticement to imprisonment and then, in a final reversal, a chance for freedom for the central character.

For Isabel Archer, the role of the innocent is tempting, as it is for Zenobia and Olive Chancellor. Although James's vital American girl would seem likely to scorn the role, Isabel embraces it and thus blindly chooses a life of sorrow. Why she does so and how she lives with that choice are central questions of *The Portrait of a Lady*. Those questions may be answered by examining Isabel and her double, Pansy Osmond.

Isabel, intelligent, energetic and lovely, seems to walk into the world with her arms open wide, eager to embrace life. When Ralph Touchett first meets his cousin, he notices that she "was looking at everything, with an eye that denoted clear perception" (26). That capacity for vision appears, at first, to characterize Isabel and to assure her a genuinely lived future. But Ralph's later, famous assessment of Isabel, "You want to see, but not to feel," is the more telling characterization (134). Isabel's vision is distorted by her terror of feeling.

Dorothy Van Ghent's analysis of the novel identifies its theme as "the informing and strengthening of the eye of the mind" (692), and it is important to note that, when Isabel steps from Gardencourt into the wider world, her vision is clouded by her fears. Although she speaks of a hunger for both freedom and experience, what she truly wants is a freedom from deep emotion, from the adult passion which terrifies her.[13] For Isabel, the surrender to passion is loss of control. To her, to give oneself generously in love could be to give one's self away. And once one began to lose control, there might be no stopping. Isabel's deliberate blindness, then, is a form of control, a shutting out of passion that can, she thinks, protect her from what she most fears. Desirous of seeing but afraid of feeling, Isabel constricts and distorts her vision.[14]

Isabel's fear of losing control causes her to lose the freedom of the adult whose choices are based on clear sight. Shrinking from adult sexuality, Isabel chooses to remain a child, and so she seeks a protector, not a lover. In her terror of losing control through experiencing passion, she surrenders control of her destiny to a passionless, cruel father. And she does so under the illusion that *she* has retained power, even as she is enticed by a perverse image of female powerlessness.

From the outset, it is clear that Isabel's own divided nature will work to damage her. "With all her love of knowledge," James says, Isabel "had a natural shrinking from raising curtains and looking into unlighted corners" (173). Her aversion to the shadows prevents Isabel from fully examining her own motives in rejecting two eligible suitors: Caspar Goodwood and Lord Warburton. Isabel declares that her refusals have to do with her desire for independence, but she will not acknowledge that, for her, any sexual relation threatens to be an imprisoning one. What she prefers are the relationships of an orphan seeking a new family: Daniel Touchett as the indulgent father, Ralph the kind protective older brother, Mrs. Touchett the acerbic mother. In this new family, Isabel finds nurturing and approval, and she need only remain a charming child to receive these rewards. In this new family she also discovers an exciting, alternative mother figure—Madame Merle.

Isabel chatters endlessly to Merle; her stories are all about herself, and, like a child, she assumes her mother will find the stories endlessly interesting. Isabel emulates Madame Merle, admiring her accomplishments, her style, but most of all her control, her ability to keep her "strong impulses" in "admirable order" (154). Fearful of her own impulses, Isabel is drawn to *Serena* Merle and is soon guided by her standards, manipulated by her strategies. Isabel is the adoring daughter who, deep in her nature, has an "unquenchable desire to please" (41), and who, innocently, chooses to please the wrong people.

When Isabel chooses a mate, she remains a child. In Gilbert Osmond, she finds a polished version of her natural father: a man who likes to consume and possess, who does nothing with his life, and who, she thinks, will indulge her. As many have noted, there is something immoral in Isabel's blindness here. Chase talks of "a distortion of self-awareness" that puts Isabel "at the mercy of the perverse and self-destructive inner motives struggling in her for the upper hand" (129). As Dietrichson notes, "a moral attitude to life in James's fiction very often means moral awareness" (143), and Isabel refuses to see.

It is equally troubling that Isabel chooses Osmond not merely so she can remain a child, but, paradoxically, because she thinks she can control him. Rachel Brownstein says Isabel "likes the idea of filling his emptiness" (260),[15] and when Isabel marries she prides herself that "the subtlest manly organism she had ever known had become her property" (358). Just as Isabel is trading a chance at adulthood for a life of imprisonment, she deludes herself into thinking *she* has arranged the deal. The idealistic heroine thinks of the marriage in a characteristically American, mercenary way. James reveals this in a crucial metaphor. When Osmond first proposes, Isabel's reaction is described in images that combine her terror of passion and of losing control with a loss of money. Although Isabel feels "the sense of something...that she supposed to be inspired and trustful passion," the feeling gives her great dread, for it "was there like a large sum stored in a bank—which there was a terror in having to begin to spend. If she touched it, it would all come out" (263).

William Gass calls *The Portrait* James's "first full-dress investigation...of what it means to be a consumer of persons, and of what it means to be a person consumed" (707). Isabel buys and is bought, and such transactions can only dehumanize and, ultimately, destroy. Choosing not to see the nature of the exchanges, Isabel chooses instead a deliberate innocence; she arrests her own development. Her sanctuary becomes a dark prison. Although she is warned repeatedly, Isabel refuses to see the trap that her new parents, Osmond and Merle, have set. Instead, she chooses what she perceives as the safety of a new role, the role of the perpetual child. The trap for Isabel is baited with just such a child—Pansy Osmond, the perverse flower of innocence.

In her decision to marry Osmond, Isabel is greatly influenced by her fascination with Pansy. Before James introduces his heroine to Pansy, he presents Pansy in a nearly gothic scene, as a distorted, unnatural figure. At 15, Pansy is a kind of doll, with a fixed, intensely sweet smile painted on her face, and she is being exhibited to two nuns in the same way Osmond exhibits his watercolors. She is her father's creation. Osmond and the nuns speak of her, in her presence, in the third person, as if she were not there. She is not a person. The nuns, who have raised Pansy, call her perfect, without faults. How, then, can she be human?

With her short muslin gown and small voice, Pansy seems so deliberately ingenuous as to be unreal. And in her programmed obedience to her father and the nuns, we perceive not purity but decadence. The convent training has been devoted not to making an object too good for this world, but, as the nuns frankly acknowledge, one "made *for* the world" (200, emphasis added). Like Priscilla, Pansy is the manufactured item, designed to please.

The decadence of such a process is magnified by the hints of incest. Told she has been made for the world, Pansy, speaking in the presence of the nuns, asks Osmond if she has not, rather, been made for him. Her question amuses her father; he tells he is of the world and thus is one of those who will enjoy her. The entire exchange inspires uneasiness. Are we to perceive the sisters as benevolent caretakers of the motherless girl, or figures in a Protestant nightmare? Is Osmond deliberately evil in his "creation" of his daughter, or merely an ass? And, most troubling of all, are we to believe that a 15-year-old can be so broken in spirit, or are we to suspect a hidden, festering self? However we choose to think about Pansy, we are not likely to accept her as a model of happy, spontaneous adolescence.

Neither, at first, is Isabel. But she soon convinces herself to see only what she would like to see. In two central scenes with Pansy, Isabel is drawn to Pansy, her secret twin.

Osmond's courtship of Isabel begins with an invitation to visit his little daughter, and even Isabel is uneasy with the Osmond family tableau of the dubious Countess Gemini, Madame Merle, Osmond, and the dear little girl in another scant white dress. "Isabel made a rapid induction: perfect simplicity was not the badge of this family." Even Pansy, with her demure posture, looking as if she were about to partake of her first communion, appears to Isabel to have a "kind of finish that was not entirely artless" (219).

Isabel ignores the sense of suffocation that should warn her, "something in the air" that drained her of "all disposition to put herself forward" (219), because she is entranced by the father-child performance staged for her benefit. As she watches father and daughter, Isabel is visualizing herself in Pansy's role, but her vision is colored by her need.

Throughout the visit, Osmond holds Pansy, first between his knees as he sits and Pansy stands, gazing fixedly and blankly at Isabel. Then, as Osmond shows Isabel his "things," he continues to hold Pansy by the hand.

The posture of father/daughter is appropriate to the relationship of a father and a five-year-old child, not a teenage girl. In this sinister scene, however, Isabel sees herself as Pansy, safe in the paternal embrace, as the connoisseur/father shows her selections from the world of culture and art. She will not see that Pansy is one of Osmond's things, and that by marrying him, Isabel, too, will become one of Osmond's pieces.

Isabel takes the bait. Henceforward, her image of Osmond is the image of a distinguished man holding a little girl, and, somewhere in her dreams, Isabel wants to become that little girl.

That this is a dangerous dream is made clear by the images Isabel associates with Pansy. In subsequent encounters with Pansy, Isabel thinks of her as an ingenue, a jeune fille of foreign fiction, figures of artifice, not artlessness. But Isabel will not be warned. Ostensibly, Isabel sees the dowerless girl as possessing a vulnerability and a sweetness Isabel can protect and nourish; in reality, Isabel sees the child she wants to be.

Two related images indicate just how Pansy figures in the entrapment of Isabel. Years after Isabel has married and has suffered for her choice, she acknowledges her husband's evil "hidden like a serpent in a bank of flowers" (360). The sweetness of the clustered flowers tricked Isabel, she thinks. Pansy's sweetness is the greatest trick of all. Being with Pansy, Isabel feels, is like "carrying a nosegay composed of all the same flowers" (341). The snake is in the nosegay. Osmond knows that, to Isabel, Pansy is some kind of living testament to his gentility, preciousness and grace, not a symbol of his ability to stunt growth and retard imagination. When Isabel first refuses Osmond's proposal, Osmond dangles the image of Pansy before her, an image of the "finish" he can give to his bride. And then, in a second scene with Pansy, Isabel again takes the bait.

The scene anticipates the novel's final scene between Isabel and Pansy and, like it, signals a turning point in Isabel's life. Although months pass between this encounter and Isabel's acceptance of Osmond, the novel skims those months, and the extensive description of Isabel's visit to Pansy, followed almost immediately by the information that she has accepted Osmond, indicate a causal relationship. Seeing Pansy, Isabel makes her choice. She decides to become the girl.

In the scene, Pansy is a solitary prisoner in her father's house, forbidden to cross the threshold, spending every moment of her day according to a rigid program dictated by her father. Isabel finds the girl pathetically charming. Again, the images associated with Pansy are ominous. She is a small winged fairy in a pantomime, "soaring by the aid of a dissimulated wire" (267), a picture of artifice and control. She is a deliberately created emptiness, a white flower of "cultivated sweetness," a blank page, "successfully kept so" (267). She is alone in an empty house; the bright summer day denied her, the house deliberately darkened and Pansy forbidden to seek the sun so that her whiteness will not be scorched.

There is further ambiguity in the scene. Pansy's chatter reveals that she knows a great deal about money, about the expense of educating her, about the marriage market and her lack of a dowry. She sweetly confides her wish to marry her father. The pure white page shows faint markings about selling the flesh and about the incestuous nature of the transaction. Isabel hears, and sees, and yet leaves in a charmed state. As she goes, she looks down at Pansy, "almost in envy" (269).

Ostensibly, she envies Pansy's right to speak openly about her love of her father, but there is more here. Isabel is charmed by the image of safety, of a world where order, not passion, rules; where women are protected and, she believes, cherished. Granted, she is charmed by the maternal role she can envision for herself—that of Pansy's loving sponsor, but she is also drawn to the life Pansy lives. And so she buys that life for herself.

Pansy is more astute than Isabel. Hearing the news of Isabel's engagement, she exults, "Oh, then I shall have a beautiful sister!" (298). And, three years after the wedding, Isabel has become Pansy's twin. Trapped in her elegant salon, she wears a painted smile with "something fixed and mechanical" in its serenity (330). She has learned the role assigned her by her new father.

Trapped, Isabel finally recognizes her complicity in the creation of her fate. Because she desired Osmond, she had "effaced herself when he first knew her; she had made herself small, pretending there was less of her than there really was" (337). She had chosen to be Pansy.

The doublings of the characters increase. Pansy's suitor Ned Rosier was Isabel's childhood companion. His dilettante fascination with the Dresden Pansy is a parody of Osmond's romance with Isabel. Isabel and Pansy share a second lover, one they both scorn, Lord Warburton. The women go out together, they are always seen together: The Osmond Collection.

And then there is a curious reversal of roles. When Pansy attracts the rich British lord, Isabel must become the bait used to lure Warburton to the family. She is to be Osmond's instrument, just as Pansy was. But, unlike Pansy, Isabel rebels. She is revulsed by the discovery that Osmond will prostitute her to sell his daughter.[16]

And in another reversal, Isabel again feels envy of Pansy. Seeing the silly Rosier become a committed lover, one willing to sacrifice his precious collection for Pansy, and, above all, seeing the look on Pansy's face when the girl greets Rosier, Isabel sees genuine emotion. Emotion is the thing Isabel most feared. But now, "a wave of envy passed over her soul, as she compared the tremulous longing...of the child with her own dry despair" (440). Isabel, so afraid of passion, has become smaller than her own stepdaughter. The child who tempted her to a diminished life has grown. From Pansy, Isabel begins to learn about passion and, perhaps, about the nature of freedom.

Freedom becomes the central concern for both women, more than ever prisoners of Osmond. A newly rebellious Isabel must free Pansy and herself. First, however, Isabel learns more about passion.

Leaving Osmond to share Ralph's dying moments is an act of defiance, but Isabel is not yet fully free. Although she tries to take Pansy with her, Pansy refuses to disobey her father, remaining a hostage to Isabel's freedom and a prisoner herself. What follows is a sequence of severed ties: repudiation of the evil mother, Madame Merle; a farewell to the beloved brother, Ralph; and a final rejection of Caspar Goodwood. Before this rejection, however, Isabel has one instant of passion, and that moment completes her transition from child to adult. Caspar's kiss is lightning, a flash that "spread, and spread again, and stayed" (489). The famous embrace is, for Isabel, the sexual one she feared for so long. Like lightning, it is terrifying, but "when darkness returned she was free" (489). Isabel has had merely a flash of passion, but she has, however briefly, experienced the thing she most feared. She has relinquished control, and surrender has liberated her. With loss of control comes a loss of fear, and with the light comes the power of a new, adult way of seeing, even in the coming darkness.

Suffering brings Isabel a new knowledge; even before Caspar's kiss she felt herself waking from a "long pernicious dream" (428). Passion completes her education, but she must enter the darkness once more, to rescue her shadow self—Pansy. As she has been throughout the novel, Isabel is drawn to Osmond by Pansy. But this time the connection is less sinister, for Isabel comes to Osmond's dead world not as a blind and vulnerable child. She comes armed with her new knowledge: of Osmond and Merle, but mostly, of herself. And that knowledge is indeed new power. All her life, Isabel's fastidiousness caused her to shrink from the sordidness of human conflict, to evade open confrontation with another. That kind of passion, like sex, frightened her. Now Isabel chooses to involve herself in such a confrontation, to enter the world of disorder and emotion. She has learned the horror of the alternative, a life of imprisonment and arrested development, the life of a child. Isabel must return to Osmond, to fight. Fighting for Pansy, Isabel releases herself from her long pernicious dream.

A Hazard of New Fortunes

In the works of Hawthorne and James, innocent heroines like Priscilla and Pansy figure prominently; while their conflicts are not the only plot of the novels in which they appear, their presence is central to the working out of the story. William Dean Howells employs a minor character in a similar way in one of his greatest works, *A Hazard of New Fortunes*. In Margaret Vance we can see a blending of the elements common to other child-heroines. Like Pansy, Priscilla, and Verena, Margaret is linked to motifs of evasion, self-deception, danger, and death. In her innocence and its consequences, Margaret is a figure of duality, representing an ambivalence that reverberates throughout the novel.

A Hazard of New Fortunes is a novel about connection: it depicts those who are fortunate moving beyond their privileged lives into the lives of the less fortunate. It is also about commitment: it explores the strength of commitment the fortunate must have if they are to help the poor and to change society. In this novel about reform, there are idealists like Conrad Dryfoos, the shy, compassionate son of a millionaire, determined to use his father's money to do good. There are revolutionaries like the stalwart philosopher/teacher Berthold Lindau, and fanatics like the Confederate apologist Colonel Woodburn. And there are cagey pragmatists like Fulkerson, the director who tries to make money out of a magazine, *Every Other Week*, designed to challenge the status quo. Drifting between these figures are the central characters, the well-intentioned but uncommitted Basil and Isabel March, who are repeatedly challenged to connect and to commit.

How closely a person can connect and how deeply a person must commit, in order to change the way things are, is a central concern in this novel. Connection, commitment, and change, however, are linked to one capacity—the capacity to see clearly and honestly. Those who are blinded can be destroyed; those who deliberately limit their vision abdicate their responsibility to reform society. *A Hazard of New Fortunes* is thus another novel about innocence. And its central concerns are embodied in the actions of—and reactions to—another child bride, Margaret Vance.

Margaret is attractive to the well-meaning men who try to live up to her ideals. Her admirers do not see the superficiality of Margaret's principles. And they do not want to see how Margaret's purity is sustained by the very corruption she deplores. Margaret can attract admirers of her soul because the same men can look elsewhere to satisfy the needs of their flesh. Similarly, corruption, in the form of the elder Dryfoos's unprincipled speculation, supports Conrad Dryfoos's charity work. *Every Other Week* is a liberal magazine in thrall to a crass and reactionary owner. The links between worlds in this novel are not all positive, and the ambiguities often focus on Margaret Vance.

Margaret is a rich girl with ideals that take her beyond the money world. She thus lives in two worlds; the socially approved one provides financial security and enables her to enter another world, of poverty, where she dabbles in charity work. To Conrad Dryfoos, who is more genuinely caught between his links to two worlds, Margaret is a kind of saint. In Margaret, Conrad sees the spirit of charity; in his idealism he sees only the "pure" version of Margaret, the angel of pity and comfort. He never sees the angel of destruction. Conrad's loneliness prompts him to see what he needs to see in the girl. Scorned by his father for his refusal to enter a man's career (like speculation), uneasy around the intellectuals his father has "bought" for him at *Every Other Week*, Conrad is looking for someone who shares his commitment to the poor. He wants someone as good as he strives to be, someone to hold him to his ideals. Tragically, he mistakes Margaret for that person.

Isabel March is not so deceived. Isabel's assessment of the bright, lovely, rich girl identifies the mixture of blindness and passivity within such a being and the emptiness of the culture that sustains her. She also questions the ultimate cost of such a creation. Isabel speculates that "city girls" like Margaret, brought up as she has been, are often "the most innocent" of all women. "They never imagine the wickedness of the world, and if they marry happily they go through life as innocent as children. Everything combines to keep them so," Isabel explains, "the very hollowness of society shields them. They are the loveliest of the human race. But perhaps the rest have to pay too much for them" (250).

Isabel March sees the vacuousness within and around Margaret; she does not confuse Margaret's shining emptiness with sanctity. Isabel's husband Basil is entranced by Margaret, just as Conrad is. We couldn't pay too much, he tells his wife, for such an "exquisite creature" as Miss Vance. His comment is interrupted by the cry of a young prostitute pursued by the police. "Ah, but if that's part of the price?" counters Isabel (251).

Margaret's safe world is sustained by the world of the prostitute. In this juxtaposition of the maiden and the whore, the scene exposes the polarities of the city, both extremes essential to the creation of city girls like Margaret. The men who admire the whiteness of Margaret satisfy a different need in the dark city streets. Miss Vance's purity is the luxury of rich girls, and it is expensive to others.

When Margaret sends Conrad on a quest, she kills him. From the shelter of her socially approved role, she can speculate on what she would do if she were a man. Such words are easy and, for Margaret, carry no consequences. She is not a man; she need never do anything at all. But for Conrad, who sees Margaret as the embodiment of every standard he is striving to reach, Margaret's words are directives. If she were a man, Margaret says, she would go among the strikers, the poor men fighting for survival. Her words cost Conrad his life. The young man, torn between the money world and the poor one, chooses to commit himself to the one he believes Margaret has chosen. As he does so, she remains safe in her social enclave. For Margaret, Howells notes, is "the kind of girl that might have fancies for artists and poets, but might end up by marrying a prosperous broker" (254).

Margaret Vance prefers the safety of the status quo to any genuine involvement in an alternative way of living, for such involvement demands too much. Margaret's hobby is a kind of secular sainthood, useful to fill the empty spaces on the social calendar and dangerous only when it is taken seriously. Margaret is not truly a citizen of two worlds, for she need never commit to the dangerous one. However much she may profess the values of charity and sacrifice, she will never be obligated to live by them; for her, the words have no consequences. Words, for her, are never acts. As a creation and not a person, Margaret is expected to choose innocence over experience, to maintain the purity that denies life.

Margaret's innocence permeates the novel. It is related to the selective vision of Fulkerson, the magazine director who can twist his liberal ideas to meet his financial needs. And in Margaret, Howells embodies the fatal innocence of Basil and Isabel March, who eventually deny the terror of their city experiences and retreat to the safety of preconceived ideas. Like Margaret, the Marches dabble in the radical, they talk of the unorthodox. But ultimately, they choose to accept the safe world rather than to challenge it.[17]

Innocence is expensive. Compelled by what he perceives as Margaret's moral superiority, Conrad Dryfoos dies for her words. Lindau, Basil March's friend, dies for his own beliefs, in a commitment freely chosen. But he dies acting on ideals March once learned from him and once supported. Lindau enters the city strife to live his ideals; like Conrad, he engages himself while another chooses to disengage. It is worth noting that, in the scene of Conrad's and Lindau's deaths, March, the detached observer, discovers the bodies. Ironically, he appears to discover very little else about himself or his culture. Like Margaret, he prefers to remain untouched.

Margaret and the Marches are well-intentioned. But innocence has an evil side, a wall of cruel denial. Innocent people do not want to see a shadow world—of street girls who "pay" for Margaret's chastity, of slums where people actually live the lives the Marches label picturesque. Innocence prevents true commitment and change. In Margaret Vance, Howells presents the attitudes of those "good" people who choose to stay within the pure world and thus perpetuate the shadow one.

Section Three:
Sexual Stains

A Lost Lady

Not all innocents remain pure white. All American innocents deny those experiences which threaten their safe attitudes and roles, but some innocents lose the sexual purity which makes them so desirable to men. In novels written in the twentieth century, the child-bride reappears, but she is often sexually tainted. As the figure of the child corrupted, she remains, however, attractive to men, perhaps particularly appealing because she requires rescue and social rehabilitation.

Willa Cather's *A Lost Lady* is the story of such a heroine. Marian Forrester is a far more complex and intriguing heroine than such early innocents as Priscilla or Hilda, and she is a sympathetic figure as well. Her gaiety in the face of sorrow, her vitality and generosity suffuse the account of her "fall." She is at once admirable and deplorable, and her ambiguity is an outgrowth of her role as "lady," or, more precisely, as little girl pretending to be a lady. For, by clinging to that role, Marian Forrester condemns herself and saves herself.

A story about Marian that has become a kind of family legend effectively represents this paradox. When Marian was young, the story goes, she wandered into a meadow to gather wildflowers. She had forgotten that in the meadow was a new bull, and she was chased by the animal. When her husband, Captain Forrester, rescued her, she was "scudding along the edge of the marshes like a hare, beside herself with laughter, and stubbornly clinging to the crimson parasol that had made all the trouble" (12).

This legend has the elements that recur throughout the novel, in all of the stories about Marian that combine to tell of her life. It is about Marian as victim, a hare, running from a male danger. It is about a recklessly gay woman who laughs when she is in danger. Above all, it is about a woman who clings to her feminine role, her red parasol, even when it threatens her life. And it is about how that role is her salvation, for, the Captain says, Marian never looked "more captivating" than on that day, and, of course, the Captain rescued her (12).

We should note that Marian's story is told by a man, and a male perspective is sustained throughout the novel. Marian's story is, in large part, given to us as it is perceived by Niel Herbert, an adolescent fascinated by this "lady." As David Stouck notes, the novel is the story of Niel's initiation as much as it is of Marian's fall (59)[18] and as we learn about Marian, we must differentiate between Niel's version of the story and another story. We must realize that Niel Herbert sees what he needs to see in Marian Forrester.

Niel, once so entranced by Marian, comes to hate her and wish her dead. He says he hates her because she is "lost" in the sense of being confused, off course without her Captain, because she will not remain true to the role Niel has chosen for her. Niel cannot see that Marian does remain true to her assigned role, and that the very qualities of the role itself corrupt her. She clings desperately to the crimson parasol, the identity that has brought her so much and taken so much from her.

Marian Forrester is "lost" in another sense. She represents not merely the pure feminine ideal but, by extension, the vulnerable, untouched land, the virgin territory of the frontier, awaiting the domination of the strong and capable man. She is Sweet Water, the frontier town of promise, the place where Captain Forrester fulfilled his dreams. But that place is gone now, lost. Exploited, tainted by greed and opportunism, Sweet Water has become a source of corruption and misfortune. Marian is like the Sweet Water stream: clear above, but full of mud and water snakes beneath.

Like the dream-land of the frontier, Marian is first taken by the pioneer-claimant, the Captain, and then lost by him.[19] The days of dreams are past. When the Captain dies, his tombstone is his sundial; his time is buried with him. Marian and the land survive, but neither is pure. Cather's novel is filled with animal imagery, and Marian is repeatedly the small and vulnerable animal—the bird, the hare—beset by large predators and small voracious enemies. Her first lover, Frank Ellinger, has "wolfish" eyes (65); her second, Ivy Peters, is a snake (21). The women of the town who exult in Marian's misery invade her house like ants (138). Like the land, Marian is prey to many attackers. What Niel cannot forgive is that Marian surrenders to each one. What Niel cannot understand is that from the beginning, surrender has ensured her survival.

Initially, Niel loves and sees only the image of Marian and the frontier dreams she represents. From his teens, he feeds on the stories of Captain Forrester's frontier triumph, his rise from drover in a freight company to great landowner of "boundless sunny sky, boundless plains of weaving grass" (52). He believes the Captain's philosophy that "a thing that is dreamed of in the way I mean is already an accomplished fact. All our great West has been developed from such dreams" (55). He loves to hear of the Captain's many rescues of Marian, from a scandalous broken romance, from physical injury (she was, curiously, immobilized by two broken legs when he met her), from the bull. Niel admires the Captain's calm strength: "When he laid his fleshy, thick-fingered hand upon a frantic horse, an hysterical woman, an Irish workman out for blood, he brought them peace; something they could not resist" (48). The description is perverse in its depiction of the subjugation of the vulnerable—animals, poor immigrants, women—in the fleshy grasp of one man. It depicts one man's power to re-make others into what he desires.

Niel loves what the Captain has made of Marian. He notices only those details of their marriage that conform to his vision of her role. She calls her husband, 25 years her senior, "Mr. Forrester"; he calls her "Maidy," the virgin maid, the little girl, but also the servant. Niel loves the Forrester dinners, where Marian is the golden hostess to the successful pioneers, railroad kings, politicians, and bankers who have seized the most. He loves to see her decked out in her jewels, about which the Captain had "archaic ideas": "They must be costly, they must show that he was able to buy them, and that she was worthy to wear them" (52-53).

What Niel loves, then, is the image of Marian as an indulged child. He habitually thinks of her as "very, very young" (75). And, above all, Niel loves her in her role as child bride: "her loyalty to him [the Captain]...was quality; something that could never become worn or shabby; steel of Damascus" (78).

Niel refuses to see the innate tawdriness of the child role, but, inevitably, even the dazzled adolescent must acknowledge glimpses of the other side of Marian. He notices her utter dependence on male admiration and her isolation from her own sex: in describing the charms of other women, Marian "always made fun of them a little" (37). The child who lives for masculine approval can perceive members of her own sex only as rivals, and her actions, her dress, her whole life is directed to living her role. Her spontaneity appears calculated. When Marian rushes out to greet visitors, she never stops to pin up her hair; she has even been known to rush out in her dressing gown—actions that appear warm and open and unconventional. But, as Niel notes, Marian creates the effect to display her own charms, for "she was attractive in deshabille, and she knew it" (12). Marian's power is derived from her loveliness. Forbidden to assert her will, she manipulates instead, playing on male infatuation. Niel is dimly aware that Marian uses him to distract a rival, but he prefers not to think about it. He is further troubled by discovering that Mrs. Forrester drinks too much, and that she drinks because she feels trapped and bored and desperate.

Niel does not want to accept the dark side of the fantasy: the loneliness, the petty stratagems of a woman growing older in a role that constricts her. He refuses to acknowledge the hidden power structure of the Forrester marriage. He chooses not to understand that this union of the omnipotent father and the helpless girl is pathetic, if not perverse.

The perversity of the relation is defined not so much by Mrs. Forrester's marriage as by her adultery. Initially, Neil is spared this awareness, but another adolescent, a poor town boy also infatuated with Marian, observes a scene that illuminates Marian's weakness and foreshadows her doom. In her love affair, Marian chooses to replicate the pattern of her marriage, in a grotesquely distorted form. Once chosen by a dominating man, the Captain, Marian now chooses a lover who is a hideous exaggeration of her husband, the powerful, wolfish Frank Ellinger. Marian has a taste for predators. Like a dazed rabbit, Marian is fascinated by what will destroy her. To Marian, sexuality involves assault, possession, destruction. Her eroticism is connected to the masochism so valuable to her in playing a child's role.

The town boy, Adolph, watches the lovers in the woods. He sees Marian wait in the sleigh, smiling, while Ellinger cuts the Christmas tree that provides the excuse for this assignation. As the hatchet falls, Marian waits. "When the strokes of the hatchet rang out from the ravine, he [Adolph] could see her eyelids flutter...soft shivers went through her body" (67). In her lover's destructive act, Marian finds sexual pleasure. As her husband, the first omnipotent possessor, grows old and weak, Marian finds satisfaction with a younger, stronger, more overtly violent version of the same type. After all, the Captain, in his strength, looks like a tree walking, but it is an old tree (115), and the new lover can cut that tree down. Trained only to be "taken" by a man, Marian seeks, in a lover, to repeat the pattern of love she has learned in marriage.

Although Niel never sees the scene in the forest, he soon learns of Marian's infidelity, and he works strenuously to preserve Marian's pure image, before the town, before her husband. Denying the truth to others, Niel may not have to deal with it himself. Ironically, in his efforts at concealment, Niel is aided by the Captain, for he, too, knows, but prefers not to recognize the truth. The conspiracy serves to keep Marian on her pedestal, however precariously, a little longer.

The Captain's death brings several kinds of loss. Marian loses the father, however old and failing, who had given her identity and purpose. During the Captain's long decline, Marian showed courage and strength beyond anything Niel or others expected of her, but her sacrifice and care for the old man are not surprising. Marian was trained to give and please. Without a man to give focus to her life, Marian ceases to exist. She is devastated by her husband's death.

Niel suffers, too. Throughout the novel, he tries to live through the Captain, to imagine himself as the Captain's shadow self, preserver of the old values, guardian of the old ways. Losing the man, Niel attempts to take his place by becoming Marian's new protector. When she rejects him, he loses that precious image of the lady so central to his values, and he loses a clear sense of his own identity.

The man who replaces the Captain embodies all the evils of the modern man who debases the values of the pioneer fathers. Ivy Peters, called "Poison Ivy" by his boyhood companions, is physically repulsive, cold and sadistic. He is also rich and powerful, a nightmare version of Horatio Alger, a poor boy who achieved success through personal viciousness. Ivy Peters takes Marian Forrester not out of passion or even lust, but in hatred and contempt, to demonstrate his triumph over Sweet Water's founding fathers. As a boy, he envied them their property; now he can seize it, in the person of Mrs. Forrester.

Cather uses a particularly horrible childhood incident to foreshadow the relationship of Ivy Peters, Marian Forrester, and Niel Herbert. The incident combines images and conflicts central to the dynamics of the triangle. As a boy, Peters captures and blinds a female woodpecker, then enjoys its pain as it tries to fly and repeatedly hurts itself, with "something wild and desperate about the way the darkened creature beat its wings on the branches, whirling into the sunlight and never seeing it, always thrusting its head up and shaking it" (25). Marian becomes that bird, lost and desperate without her Captain—"like a ship without ballast, driven hither and thither by every wind. She was flighty and perverse" (152). Initially afraid of Peters, she is "caught" by him, and she abdicates her will to his. He becomes her new master, investing her money in dishonest schemes, acting as her lawyer, exulting in his appropriation of the Captain's power. Peters flaunts his control of the woman, using her degradation as a mark of his triumph. He enjoys her misery.

Niel watches Marian's torment, still driven by fantasies of rescue. In a terrible parody of the famous Forrester dinners, Peters attends a dinner at the Forrester home, where Marian, rouged, fatigued, and worn, again plays the gay hostess and Niel sits in the Captain's place. The crude town boys who make up the party do not appreciate Marian's vivacity; Niel perceives that Marian is "going through her old part, but only the stage-hands were left to listen to her." But he cannot relinquish his dream that "the right man could save her, even now" (166). He, of course, must be that savior, rescuing her as the Captain once did.

Niel watches Marian's torment as he watched Peters torture the bird. Then, he wanted to kill the bird, to put it out of its misery. When Marian remains Peters's victim, helplessly dependent on a man who degrades her, when she remains, in other words, *herself*, Niel wishes her dead. As Ellen Moers puts it, to Niel, Marian is despicable because she will not "immolate herself...and die with the pioneer period to which she belonged" (*Literary Women* 238). He feels that she has rejected her proper role, and that she has sullied herself by preferring "life on any terms" (169). He would rather not admit that degradation and defacement have always been the means of Marian's survival.

Marian was, and remains, property. Like the land, she was first taken by the dashing explorer, the Captain, and then lost. Niel's reflection on the loss of the land applies to Marian as well:

The Old West had been settled by dreamers, great-hearted adventurers who were impractical to the point of magnificence...strong in attack but weak in defence, who could conquer but could not hold. Now all the vast territory they had won was to be at the mercy of men like Ivy Peters, who had never dared anything, never risked anything. (106)

Such men devour the land, "as the match factory splinters the primeval forest" (106). The dismal pattern of acquisition traces Marian's life as well, for she is the property taken first by the Captain, who is like a strong, hard, tree, but who lives, as his name suggests, by taking from nature. When the Captain loses his lady, he loses her first to Ellinger, the man with the ax who splits the tree, then, to Peters, who shatters the forest beyond recognition. In this image of deforestation, all three men are linked as exploiters.

The story of the loss of the frontier is one that Niel accepts. But he does not want to know the other story, the one that ties the masterful seizure of the frontier to the dehumanization of women. He prefers to "kill" Marian Forrester, to remove her from his memory and his care. And yet he cannot escape the lesson she has taught him. He dreams of seeing her again, to ask her a question that haunts him, whether "she had really found some ever-blooming...joy, or whether it was all fine play-acting" (172).

In spite of his preference for the comforting fantasy that Marian "fell" from some pioneer Eden, Niel begins to question the nature of that paradise. Was it predicated on a false vision of Eve? Was Marian playing a role she could not escape? Ellen Moers says that Marian teaches Niel: "she brings the whole meaning of his life—too much meaning. For Niel is forced to see how it is done, this womanly mythmaking without which there would be no civilization, no 'taming of the West' " (*Literary Women* 239). Niel is a divided man, torn between his need to condemn Marian and his desire to understand her, between his yearning for the old, lost ways and his awareness that such ways will cripple him in the new world. He is one of Cather's misfits, and as Judith Fryer notes, for such characters, "America is the land of loss" (*Felicitous Space* 206).

By choosing to reject Marian rather than to understand her, Niel chooses not to face himself. He chooses not to come to terms with his own complicity in the system that created her. He remains confused and haunted, while Marian moves on, re-enacting the only scenario she knows. She is taken again, by a rich old man, and every year of her life she sends flowers to the grave of the Captain—homage to her first owner.

Jennie Gerhardt

The concept of owning a woman is most explicitly described in Theodore Dreiser's *Jennie Gerhardt*, whose heroine is the stereotypical, sentimentalized "kept" woman. Donald Pizer notes a significant irony in the novel, the fact that Jennie and Lester Kane's relationship clearly parodies a middle-class marriage but lacks the sanction of a legal tie. Pizer notes the "classic middle-class configuration" of the "businessman husband, the homeloving and matronly wife, the charming child, and the crotchety but inwardly contented grandparent." But he also notes that in reality each relationship within the family constitutes a moral outrage, "for the couple is unmarried, the child is the illegitimate offspring of another man, and the grandfather tacitly sanctions the menage." Pizer interprets this irony as Dreiser's comment on social hypocrisy, on the false values that condemn this "family" merely because it lacks a legal bond (127-28). The parody may be read another way. Jennie and Lester's union truly is a marriage, for, despite the absence of a legal tie, the connection is predicated on the transaction essential to all American marriages, the buying of a wife.

If we view the "marriage" of Jennie and Lester from this perspective, we are led to another indictment, not of social intolerance for the adulterous yet loving union, but of all relationships, socially legitimized or not, based on the economic deal. If this story of the "kept" woman is read as the story of American marriage, it becomes another account of the failure of innocence.

Jennie Gerhardt is purchased for her innocence. In a paean to Jennie, Dreiser calls the quality "wonder":

There are natures born to the inheritance of flesh that come without understanding, and that go again without seeming to have wondered why. Life, so long as they endure it, is a true wonderland, a thing of infinite beauty, which could they but wander into it wonderingly, would be heaven enough. Opening their eyes, they see a conformable and perfect world. Trees, flowers, the world of sound and the world of color. These are the valued inheritance of their state. If no one said to them, "Mine," they would wander radiantly forth, singing the song which all the earth may someday hope to hear. It is the song of gladness. (15)

Dreiser's "wonder" is a response of the senses, not of the mind. It comes "without understanding," that is, without thought, and "wonderers" die without ever thinking. In Dreiser's terms, "wonder" does not mean "question" or "wonder why," but rather "accept," or even "enjoy," "take in." As Blanche Gelfant notes, "this quality is one key attribute of Dreiser's protagonists which he fails to bring to life" (91). While Dreiser praises the ability to "wonder," the word is suspiciously close to "wander," so that an attitude leads to an activity that is actually a passivity, a dazed drift. Lacking the capacity to think, Jennie, the wonderer, seems, as Gelfant says, to lack volition (82). Her deficiencies make her a true innocent.

Apparently, the capacity for this kind of wonder is the most erotic quality a woman can possess, for it makes men mad to own her. Dreiser says that "The hands of the actual are forever reaching towards" such dreamers, "seizing greedily upon them" (16), and two pairs of hands seize Jennie.

Her first lover, Senator Brander, is drawn to Jennie the pure Cinderella. She is his maid, cleaning his hotel room, washing his clothes. Her poor clothes and her dazzled admiration for his exalted rank attract him to her. In her, he sees "a largeness of feeling not altogether squared with intellect, or perhaps better yet, experience, which was worthy of a man's desire" (76). The blanker the mind, apparently, the more irresistible the woman.

Compulsively attracted to such purity, Brander "buys" Jennie, giving money to her family and dresses to her sisters, getting her brother out of jail. Passive, grateful, Jennie allows herself to be taken, and Dreiser makes it clear that such a transaction is the stuff of true romance: "if all beauty were passing, and you were given these things [the beauty of nature distilled in a "perfect maiden"] to hold in your arms...would you give them up?" (77).

Jennie is taken again by Lester Kane, who is drawn to the "sweet little girl" (150) who is both his child and his mirror image. Like Jennie, Lester is not much of a thinker, the dynamic businessman's most significant economic axiom being, "Business is business" (134). Like Jennie, he is essentially a child who wanders in the world, rarely questioning—a reactor, not an actor. But Lester also enjoys the power of owning Jennie, so dependent on his largesse.[20]

Lester fails to see the paradox in his attraction to Jennie. He fails to realize that the very vulnerability that draws him to her has already made her prey to another man. Brander has "branded" her with the mark of the fallen woman; her price has been reduced by her sexual surrender. But even when Lester discovers Jennie's flaw, he can excuse it. Innocence covers a multitude of sins. Jennie's sexual experience was hardly a sin at all, because it was so sexless. It left no mark where the mark would matter—on Jennie's mind. Although Jennie has lost her virginity, "her mind still retained all of the heart-innocence" of the virgin (81), and ultimately, sexual purity is not as important to Lester as intellectual vacuity.

Clearly, Jennie offers her lovers the enticement of the child-bride unsullied by experience, and they both sense that such innocence can best be enjoyed in a world apart from the one they live in. Both Brander and Lester view their mistress as an indulgence; to Brander, Jennie is poetry (51); to Lester, she is the luxury of love (128). Of course, to live in such a world apart is to be irrelevant, so that Brander coldly dismisses Jennie from his chambers when his political battles become intense, and Lester often neglects her for weeks at a time. Jennie's life, then, is miserably split. She has been defined as her man's luxury purchase; when he is absent, what is there to define her? She lives in the world he has constructed; when he returns to the wider world, does she cease to be? Laing defines schizophrenia as a possible result of difficulty "in being a whole person with the other, and with not sharing the common-sense (i.e., the community sense) way of experiencing oneself in the world" (205). This definition of illness is the standard by which Jennie is to live, if she is to please her keeper.

It is an unnatural role because it limits Jennie so severely. Her lover does not want a whole person, and he does not want a woman who defines herself by her action in the world. He wants her in *his* world, a false world where she becomes almost a non-person. Jennie, like so many innocent heroines, is described as a bird, a "wood-dove" (100); she is a caged bird, singing her wondering song of gladness for her jailer only. Repeatedly, Dreiser stresses that Jennie is a creature of the natural world. But she is a social creation, designed to please those in society.

Just like the prostitute in *A Hazard of New Fortunes*, Jennie supports a world denied her. In her role as adoring child, Jennie gives her mate the confidence he needs to sustain him in the wider world; in providing a fantasy of safety and stability, Jennie compensates her man for the anxieties of change he faces elsewhere. Jennie is very much the Victorian angel in the house, and, like her, she is considered angelic because she meets worldly, not spiritual, standards.

Jennie may be the vulnerable girl taken by powerful men, but she is acquiescent in the deals. And the deals bring Jennie the rewards of upward mobility. For all her lack of calculation and guile, Jennie does not give her body to a member of her own class. She has the appetites of any woman who accepts the standards of her culture; she is first dazzled by the Senator's wealth and power, and later by Lester's lavish spending. Even as she perceives her surrender to Lester as a second martyrdom accepted for the good of her family, she is physically drawn to Lester and materially enticed by his money. Pizer notes a hard edge to Jennie's concealment of her illegitimate child and her unconscious attempts to force Lester into marriage by leaving him (114). Her position as "kept" woman is in no way a defiance of social standards; it is merely the closest she can get to the socially approved role she craves. Jennie's lovers choose her because she offers to play the conventional part of the ideal bride, but she does not demand a wedding.

Her exalted generosity is an ambiguous quality. Around such a "soft, yielding, unselfish disposition," Dreiser says, "men swarm naturally" (126). But what does such generosity bring? It brings Jennie uncertainty and desperation. At one point, Jennie is so terrified of losing Lester she expresses a willingness to excuse his infidelity (311). Her generosity is often motivated by fear. Her life is lived in fear of loss, and the loss is inevitable. Lester leaves her, not only because she is a luxury he can no longer afford, but because the role she has learned so well does not entirely satisfy him.

Lester tells Jennie she is "like wine" to him (165), and Lester is a man who drinks too much. When he thinks of her, he perceives Jennie in other destructive images. To live with her is "too much like a bed of down" (222); it suffocates him. The "yielding sweetness of her character both attracted and held him" (198), but Jennie's submission is a kind of dominance. "Jennie was too worshipful," Lester thinks (222); she gives him all her self, but what self is there to give? Throughout her relations with her lovers, Jennie has learned to sacrifice any vestiges of independent identity so that she will remain attractive. She has practiced what Laing calls the basic form of all psychosis: "the denial of being as a means of preserving being" (161). Jennie gives because she needs to be given something in return, but she becomes an emptiness that cannot be filled. It is interesting to note how many deaths surround Jennie: Senator Brander's, her father's, her daughter's, Lester's. These losses, of course, add pathos to her story. But they also point to an image of Jennie as a debilitating figure; those who love her find no vitality in the connection.

Jennie is a figure of loss. She loses all those she loves, and she loses her self. How generous, then, can she be? What can she give?

Jennie Gerhardt's real sin is not her illicit sexual union; it is that selflessness so exalted by society and so destructive of any true relationship. Her common-law marriage is deplorable because it is a model of every legitimate union. Like any conventional bride, Jennie is purchased for her lack of a self. The ideal wife, like Jennie, is to be "kept": kept apart from the world that is so threatening to man, kept "pure" in a safe place constructed for man's consolation. But all the "kept" women, mistresses or wives, live in structures that threaten to collapse. Their foundations—innocence, egotism, and fear—are too weak to sustain them.

Section Four:
The Consumed as Consumer

Sister Carrie

Before there was Jennie Gerhardt, there was Dreiser's Carrie Meeber. Jennie, the later heroine, may be described as Carrie sanitized and sentimentalized. Both are women who trade sex for male protection and material gain, but Carrie does better in the dealing. Perhaps Jennie can be described as a Carrie without Carrie's luck.

The most important link between the two heroines is their innocence. Carrie and Jennie share a blind acceptance of social norms. They want what society has taught them to want and are incapable of independent judgments. Like many other innocents, their incapacity is their great asset, for the lure of both women is the allure of the helpless. No man can be threatened by these girl-women, so passive, so weak. Sheldon Grebstein says that Carrie's sexual allure is composed of "innocence, purity, and helplessness" (545), the same qualities that endear Jennie to the Senator and to Lester Kane.

Like typical innocents, the women are creatures of paradox. Their weakness is a strength; their supposed openness to the fantasies and will of others, which should be a kind of vulnerability, is instead a kind of armor. Jennie and Carrie remain somehow untouched and unchanged by the male dreams and desires imposed on them, frozen in a perpetual virginity even as their physical selves are taken. Sisters in innocence,

Jennie and Carrie are nevertheless different. Jennie, the more conventionally angelic, is the one embued with all the conventionally feminine sentiments: "All her attitude toward sex was bound up with love, tenderness, service" (144). Carrie, by far the more financially successful woman, is *not* generous, sacrificing, or tender. There is no veneer of love to prettify the true nature of Carrie's relationships. Carrie may never have an original thought or an independent judgment, but she does know the price of things. Her affairs are more blatantly economic transactions.

Describing her connection with Drouet, for example, Dreiser makes it clear that Carrie's strength lies in her lack of the conventional emotions:

> She really was not enamored of Drouet. She was more clever than he. In a dim way, she was beginning to see where he lacked. If it had not been for this, if she had not been able to measure and judge him in a way, she would have been worse off than she was. She would have adored him. She would have been utterly wretched in her fear of not gaining his affection, of losing his interest, of being swept away and left without an anchorage. (72)

If Carrie had been "in love," if Carrie had been tender and generous, she would have suffered Jennie's fate.

The difference between Jennie and Carrie illustrates the emergence of a new type in the evolution of the child bride. In *Sister Carrie*, the innocent appears in a crystallized form, stripped of the extraneous and sentimentalized virtues associated with other versions. In Carrie Meeber, the glaze of love and tenderness is gone, revealing the cold, hard being beneath. In its new form, innocence, often characterized as weakness, becomes an almost irresistible force.

Grebstein posits that the novel's flaw is Carrie's flatness (550); it may be the novel's point. Carrie, a crystallized variety of innocence, is more empowered than many heroines whose natures are diluted by tenderness or generosity. Dreiser names the first chapter of the novel, "The Magnet Attracting: A Waif Amid Forces," and he thus introduces the idea of the tremendous lure the city holds for Carrie. Chicago in 1889, he explains, is "a great magnet, drawing to itself...the hopeful and the hopeless—those who had their fortunes yet to make and those whose fortunes and affairs had reached a disastrous climax elsewhere" (11).

Carrie, who has her fortune yet to make, is thus drawn to the city. But she herself can be seen as a magnet, drawing to her Drouet, the man seeking his fortune in Chicago, and Hurstwood, the man whose fortunes will fall in this city and who will flee to another city, in a hopeless effort to begin again.[21]

Like a magnet, Carrie need do nothing but *be* in order to attract. Her passivity stimulates others' activity; "Carrie had little power of initiative; but, nevertheless, she seemed ever capable of getting herself into the tide of change where she would easily be bourne along" (225).[22] Carrie's lack of action is thus a force for action, and this theme of the power of nullity is the dominant one in Carrie's story.

In her role as receptor, open to all experiences yet essentially untouched by them, Carrie becomes terrible. Her lack of emotion becomes a strength, as those attracted to her struggle to fill her emptiness. In her, the gentle longing of other innocents becomes an endless appetite; her "passive and receptive" nature (221) is in reality a capacity to devour her admirers. In her, the child bride's acceptance of social standards becomes an insatiable desire for society's prizes. Carrie is a magnet to men because, like other innocents, she appears to be the delectable item, deliciously consumable. But, created to be consumed, Carrie becomes a frightening image of the consumer—one who never has enough.[23]

At first, Carrie appears to have a more independent vision than most innocents. One of her first statements as she settles in the city is, "I want to *see* something" (42, emphasis added), suggesting that she will widen her vision as her world widens. But in this novel, "to see" means "to desire." Kenneth Lynn says that desire "is the one emotion that exists for Dreiser, once the mind has been exposed to the opium of the city, and the lives of his characters are as narrowly focused as those of so many drug addicts" (517). There is more to see in the city because there is more to desire, and the opposite of sight, blindness, comes only with death. In the luxury of the city, a "craving is set up which, if gratified, shall eternally result in dreams and death....dreams unfulfilled—gnawing, luring idle phantoms which beckon and lead...until death and dissolution remove their power and restore us blind to nature's heart" (214). As this passage indicates, gratification is only momentary, part of the endless cycle of desire. Life is appetite, and consumption is merely the momentary success that leads to new appetites. Carrie is seduced by the promise of seeing (and thus wanting) more. She is initially drawn to Hurstwood because "he had seen this and that" and "made Carrie wish to see similar things" (88). Seeing is both a consumption, a taking in and a feasting of the eyes, and a tantalizing denial of gratification: one sees what he does not have, in order to learn what to desire.

Actually, Carrie doesn't want to see so much as she wants to be seen. If life, in this novel, is desire, then the main component of a successful life is to be desired. More than anything, people long to be seen, for to see something is to desire it. At a turning point in her life, as Carrie is deciding to live with Drouet, she sees her image in the mirror, dressed in new finery, and, seeing the pretty girl others notice, she "felt her first thrill of power" (58). She is developing strength because she is now something to look at. Initially seduced by the image Drouet gives her of herself, she is seduced a second time, in the same way, by Hurstwood, whose "great charm was attentiveness" (72). If desire is the only emotion, and if seeing is desire, then to be noticed is to be the recipient of the only feeling others can have; in a perverse way, it is to be cared for. Carrie begins to reject Hurstwood when he ignores her, thinking he was not "looking after" her at all (242). Carrie sees, she wants, and thus, she believes, when she herself is not "looked at" or "looked after," she is not wanted. To avert one's vision, then, is to deny another life.

Carrie does precisely that when she rejects her lovers. When Drouet first asks Carrie about her attraction to Hurstwood, she will not look at Drouet. She sits in her rocking chair, looking out the window, averting her vision. On the train with Hurstwood, when he tries to persuade her to stay with him, she "seemed not to listen. She only turned her head toward the window" (199). And in Montreal, when Hurstwood asks Carrie if she cares for him at all, she again makes no answer, "but looked steadily toward the window" (205). Not to look, is, to Carrie, a fierce expression of hatred and anger; it is a kind of murder.

Carrie and her lovers share a sense that life is to be viewed, not lived. Each person sees another and thus forms a desire for that other. Action is acquisition of the object viewed; gratification is consumption. There are two possible—and horrible—types of death in this world, the obliteration of identity that comes when a person is not seen, and the physical death that is the only release from endless desire. Carrie fights both types of death, for she is consumed and consumer.

In this world of watcher and watched, one dominant image is windows. The window is both an image of seeing and a part of another important image: the barrier image. *Sister Carrie* is a novel of oppositions and paradoxes. There are viewers and viewed, desires and fulfillments. And there are openings that promise entry to a greater, bigger, more fantastic fulfillment, but the openings are always blocked. They are like windows of unbreakable glass, images that tease and taunt the voyeur with his impotence.

People in the novel perceive life through windows. Windows are openings to new sources of desire or to mysterious alien worlds. On Carrie's first night in Chicago, she sits by the window and looks out on the streets. The next day, she walks the streets, looking in the windows of the factories. She is fascinated and intimidated because she is ignorant of the business world, a place she thinks is composed of "strange mazes which concerned far-off individuals of importance" (13). She wants what she sees in the department store windows and envies the well-dressed shopgirls. After she has been initiated into factory life, she is disappointed and seeks refuge in dreaming by the window all evening.

Windows are a passage to dreams, and thus a kind of promise. When Drouet rescues Carrie from her squalid round of work and slum life, he offers her a window seat in a fine restaurant, so that "the busy rout of the street could be seen." Like Hurstwood, he entices Carrie by widening her vision and thus her desires, and he can do this because he shares her desires: "He loved the changing panorama of the street—to see and be seen as he dined" (44). Commenting on the window images in the novel, Philip Fisher says,

> The window creates a polarized world of insider and outside, actor and spectator, rich and poor that would not occur if what were going on inside were simply unknown. All scenes become opportunities for self-classification in that they seem to invite you in and invite you to imagine being in while strongly reminding you that you are out. (261)

In the restaurant, Carrie and Drouet appear to have achieved fulfillment. Sitting on the inside, by the window, they can inspire the envy of those on the street who see them dining in luxury, and they can observe those on the outside. Even in the restaurant, the pair may be tantalized by what they see outside. The characters in *Sister Carrie* nearly always seem to be on the wrong side of the window; they want to be inside when they are out, and, once inside, they look out again. Because of windows, they can see what to desire, but they never seem able to cross the threshold that divides longing from gratification. There is always some kind of barrier.[24]

Threshold images are important to the novel because the threshold seems so easy to cross, and yet crossing is always impossible. There are many false thresholds, too. When Drouet offers to "protect" Carrie, his words strike her as "the welcome breath of an open door" (52). But she is soon trapped again, separated from the worlds she dreams of. And yet those worlds seem so accessible. Seeing the mansions of the North Side, she "imagined that across those richly carved entrance-ways...was neither care nor unsatisfied desire.... If she could but...cross that rich entrance-way...how quickly would sadness flee" (86).

Many openings are connected to the theater and the stage. The chapter in which Carrie begins rehearsals for her first play is called, "A Glimpse through the Gateway: Hope Lightens the Eye," combining the image of the opening with the theme of seeing as desiring (120). The presentation of the play takes place in a chapter called "Just Over the Border: A Hail and Farewell" (127), as Carrie greets a new and exciting world on the stage, one which will, eventually, enable her to leave both Drouet and Hurstwood behind. In New York, demoralized by her humdrum life with Hurstwood, Carrie clings to her dream of the stage as "a door through which she might enter that gilded state she had so much craved" (270). Driven by Hurstwood's passive acceptance of failure, Carrie seeks theatrical work in a chapter titled, "The Spirit Awakens: New Search for the Gate" (270). Meanwhile, Hurstwood associates his own decline with images of a blocked threshold: to him, New York has a wall around it. "Men were posted at the gate. You could not get in" (241).

The novel teases the characters with openings; some can never cross them at all; others, like Carrie, pass through one gate to find the ultimate entry barred. Why are there always barriers? And what do those barriers represent?

The images of the window, the opening and the threshold are all closely connected to the act of seeing. The barrier itself is connected to vision. It is some blocking of sight. By considering the nature of the novel's three main characters, we can begin to understand that the obstacle to vision is, at least in part, self-created. The barrier is some kind of evasion—an evasion of responsibility, a refusal to act, but mainly, a refusal to see. The members of the triangle in *Sister Carrie* prefer not to widen their vision to include more than objects of desire. And so they never really get inside their desired world, because they cannot or will not get inside themselves.

Sister Carrie is a story of impaired characters. In their perception of themselves and others as objects, in their lack of human connections, their passivity, even in their incessant rocking, they are somehow autistic. They live dissociated from reality, locked in their relentless dreams. And what is so pathetic is that these dreams are not their own; they are the manufactured fantasies they have bought from the culture.

Dreiser calls Carrie's mind "a mirror prepared of her own and the world's opinions" (70), but her opinions are the world's. As Michael Spindler says, Carrie's behavior is "dictated not by principle but by convention" (87) and Mattheissen, too, stresses her conforming nature ("Picture" 485-86). What actually dictates her behavior, "the one stay of her nature," is "her craving for pleasure" (24). Pleasure is narrowly defined for Carrie as clothes, material comfort and social recognition, and her lovers are not much different in their cravings. Drouet loves "fine clothes, good eating," and "the company and acquaintanceship of successful men" (32). Hurstwood shares these values, which significantly exclude any desire for intimate contact. The characters seek "acquaintanceship," an association with socially validated people, or acquisition, possession of socially desired objects (including people), but they do not want any deeper connection.[25] In the first stages of his affair with Carrie, Hurstwood thinks only of "pleasure without responsibility" (98), and the affair languishes when both partners are caught in a net of responsibilities. In New York, when money problems eliminate pleasure from the liaison, Carrie and Hurstwood turn away from each other and turn toward the only source of comfort they know: consumption. Hurstwood spends the last of his money on a fine dinner at a luxury hotel; Carrie, resentful of being forced to support her lover, wants only to buy clothes.

Neither partner can solace the other, for as prisoners of their appetites, they can fill only their own needs. Utterly incapable of empathy, they are utterly alone. Kenneth Lynn says these characters have "almost no real feelings. Beneath the masquerade of saloon manager or gracious lady or happy-go-lucky salesman, there is a terrible coldness" (516). Thus, the characters' typical response to conflict is to protect the self. Driven to live off of his dwindling savings, Hurstwood wants to keep the money for himself, denying Carrie any household allowance. Dimly aware of Hurstwood's bleak financial situation, Carrie can only resent Hurstwood for being an inadequate provider: "what have I got to do with it?...Oh, why should I be made to worry?" (256).

Faced with a misery that threatens them both, Hurstwood and Carrie refuse to share their pain, and they deny the legitimacy of the other's needs. Trapped in discontent, each tries to deny responsibility for creating the conflict or for alleviating it. Berthoff says that Dreiser is the only twentieth century American novelist to have "caught so well...the inner logic of our personal alienation from the behavior we find ourselves committed to; the whole dreamlike way we pass through our lives and days, secretly disclaiming responsibility for them, looking on as we act" (239).

In *Sister Carrie*, preoccupation with the self does not lead to self-awareness. Hurstwood is not "trained to reason or introspect himself" (240), Carrie's mind is a mirror of social opinions, Drouet generally goes along to get along. There are hints that this is a willed shallowness. As the imagery of the novel indicates, the characters seem to choose to live evasively because the choice relieves them of other choices, other actions.

It may be typical of naturalistic novels to minimize the role of individual decision and responsibility in human life, but what emerges in *Sister Carrie* is a sense that a refusal to acknowledge choice, to confront decision, does not preclude such choices. It just countenances them. The sense is most evident in the often-noted inarticulateness of the characters.[26] Granted, the protagonists of the novel are minimally educated, their command of the language may be slight, but they often prefer not to name what they could name, to be silent as a means of condoning their own behavior. The link between evasion and loss of language shows up in Hurstwood's seduction of Carrie. Carrie loves the mimed quality of the transaction because it permits her the freedom to succumb without guilt.

She did not need to tremble at all, because it was invisible; she did not need to worry over what other people would say—what she herself would say—

because it had no tangibility. She was being pleaded with, led into denying old rights and assuming new ones, and yet there were no words to prove it. (88)

Words make actions real; they force one to see what she is doing and to assume responsibility for her actions. This is not the kind of seeing Carrie wants to do in the city. It is not the goal of her lovers, either. There is no direct confrontation in the novel. Hurstwood is silent in his home, refusing to argue with his greedy wife and children; Drouet hints at, but never specifies, the arrangement he offers Carrie; Carrie slides into her affair with Drouet and later sneaks off with Hurstwood, who escapes from his family in the night. No one engages in any dramatic scene, no one verbalizes a conflict. People avoid facing others—and themselves.

No one crosses that threshold within. Instead, everyone lives in a state of frustrated desire, possessed only of what Fisher calls an "anticipatory self," which has "as its emotional substance hope, desire, yearning" (263), and what is hoped for is outside, in a world of appearances, of illusory thresholds, openings to elusive delights.

"The anticipatory world has as its consequence a state of the self preoccupied with what is not," Fisher says (263), and this preoccupation may be with the past, or the future. Or it may be a longing to be the person one is not. In this novel, one is what one has, so the anticipatory state may involve a yearning to own things. In any case, it is a desire for what is not, at the moment, real.

Carrie and her lovers dream consumer dreams, and so they look outside themselves for satisfaction and meaning. Daniel Bell says, "A consumption economy finds its reality in appearances" (68), and the blurring of polarities creates a dangerous fusing of self and other. The city defines being as acquisition and consumption, and things and people live a life of display and sale. The mind is reduced to a mirror, what Spindler calls "a mere reflection of sensory impressions" (86), of the fashion, the stance, one must acquire to be noticed. As Christopher Lasch explains,

Commodity production and consumerism alter perceptions not just of the self but of the world outside the self. They create a world of mirrors, insubstantial images, illusions increasingly indistinguishable from reality. The mirror effect makes the subject an object; at the same time, it makes the world of objects an extension or projection of the self. (30)

Viewer and viewed are in some way the same. How logical, then, that two men who live to be seen, who want, above all, recognition for their power to acquire, should be drawn to Carrie Meeber, the object admired by so many, and filled with a desire so much stronger than theirs? Carrie mirrors and magnifies their dreams, promises to fulfill them, and, in the end, distorts those longings into something grotesque.

In a world of roles, Carrie is all role.[27] She has learned to imitate whatever she sees and wants to be, and she can fill herself with whatever men want in her: innocence, pluck, pertness, style. When Drouet first meets her on the train to Chicago, she reminds him of some popular actress, and there is no higher compliment he can pay her. As Lynn notes, "the characters in *Sister Carrie* are all actors; their personalities are not expressions of themselves, but of the roles they are playing" (515). They prefer life at a distance, acted, not lived. Roles can mimic feeling without the pain of the real thing. And imitation is Carrie's strength. When she falters in her first theatrical appearance, Drouet, in the intermission, advises her, "Act as if you didn't care" (133), encouraging her not to worry about the other actors' nervousness or the audience observing her. His advice is the guiding principle of Carrie's life and success, for she always imitates and never feels.

When Carrie first appears on stage, both her lovers feel more desire for her than they have ever felt before.[28] They are thrilled by an imitation of passion, experiencing an imitation of feeling. Pizer comments that the men "catch fire at the high moralism" of the speeches Carrie recites. Yet, Pizer adds, all these characters—actress and audience—"live by a code of selfish amoralism, a code shaped by the drive to fulfill desire without thought of the consequences to others" (42).

Fulfillment is just what the actress offers, in her new role as exalted object. As Fisher says, the actress flirts with her audience just as merchandise does with the shopper. "In both cases, erotic pampering is the covert promise behind the purchase of tickets and ticketed objects" (268). But neither purchase can deliver on its promise. What Ames recognizes as Carrie's dramatic appeal is her ability to express the world's longing, but she cannot satisfy either another's needs or her own.

Rather than serve as an opening to the realization of dreams, the stage is the final barrier for both Carrie and her audience. The new, scripted roles further separate object and buyer; the buyer sits below, physically cut off from the thing on display. The details of the two theatrical turning points in her life make the separation clear. In her first performance, the amateur theatricals, Carrie's inaccessibility is represented by the way she plays her scenes with the inferior male actor who plays her lover. He cannot meet the demands of the role, but his inadequacy has no effect on Carrie's triumph, for she acts as if she is utterly alone on stage. "She would have done nearly as well with a block of wood. The accessories she needed were within her own imagination. The acting of others could not affect them" (139).

Carrie's first performance defines her progress in the novel and her relationships with her lovers. Like the bad actor, Carrie's lovers are negligible factors in her acting of her own role; she needs someone to play against, but he may as well be a thing, a "block of wood." Carrie, on stage or in life, remains self-absorbed, self-contained. She needs no one for emotional support, for she is only acting emotions.

Carrie again promises the buyer what cannot be delivered when she delivers her first line in the professional theater. As one of a line of harem girls paraded before a potentate, Carrie acts the role of a possession, and her pert improvised line, "I am yours truly" (269), amuses and endears her to the audience. Ostensibly, she charms them because she is an adorable thing, a cute chorus girl open to the advances of any man who can afford her. In her passivity and availability, she seems the perfect commercial product, ready and eager to please by becoming whatever the buyer desires. To her male admirers, she says, "I am yours; I will be whatever you desire." In a sense, she is saying, "I am *you*—your longing, your desire." But Carrie is *no one's* because she is *no one*. She has no self to give. A role is an illusion. Carrie can make no man's illusions real, however well she embodies them. She can only mirror them. She is no one's, truly.

The fantasy world of the stage is also the last barrier to the fulfillment of Carrie's dreams. Carrie dreamed of being an actress, not of living a real life, and she gets illusion as her reward. Acting becomes just another way of living at a distance, like looking out the window. In her dreams, she envisioned the triumph of being looked at. She believed that when she was on stage, others would be observing a fantasy and she would be in one. She wanted the characteristic role of the innocent—enacting another's dream. And just as the role traps others, like Priscilla and Verena Tarrant, it traps Carrie. The role is a one-way fantasy. On stage, Carrie is seen, and she considers that success. But, blinded by the stage lights, she is not able to see her own success. And once she is viewed as successful, she can no longer see what she should want. She is more alone than ever, separated from her admirers and divorced from new sources of desire. What is she to want now?

Seeking to fulfill her longings by becoming the object of others' longing, Carrie disappoints herself and damages others. She learns to imitate but not to be a person; "She did not grow in knowledge so much as she awakened in the matter of desire" (85). Completely passive and relentlessly demanding, she draws strength from those who desire her. When her lovers cannot satisfy her appetite for things, she casts them aside. She dooms herself to an endless cycle of disappointment.[29] The much-discussed encounter with Ames at the end of the novel only supplies Carrie with a new source of discontent; like earlier men in her life, Ames gives Carrie the attention she craves but also frustrates her with a glimpse of what she does not have.

And so Carrie grieves for what she does not have, and the novel ends where it begins—in desire. There has been movement for Carrie: upward mobility, financial success, but no inner growth. As Tanner says, desire, "by its very nature, tends toward a self-perpetuating stasis" (*Adultery* 87). And so Carrie remains frozen in discontent.

Carrie never gets what she wants, and that is sad. Sadder still is the nature of her dreams. As mistress and actress, Carrie tries to satisfy her own hunger by becoming what others want. She becomes a magnifying, distorting reflection of what a whole culture wants. She and her lovers are enticed by the impersonal attraction of things, "large forces which allure with all the soulfulness of expression possible in the most cultured human" (1). Pizer says that, in representing this allure, Dreiser is attempting to convey the pathetic theme that "the desiring imagination has the ability to create beauty out of the tawdry" (54) but the fact remains that the tawdry is not beautiful, and the imagination that attempts such a feat is a small one.[30]

This imagination dreams such limited dreams, of life without love or compassion or any other human link to people or to nature. In *Sister Carrie*, people dream only of things, and to get them, they become things. Carrie's power derives from her ability to transform herself into a thing; her triumph, from her genius at expressing others' hunger. Her ultimate failure derives from the same source, from the stunted imagination that substitutes the manufactured article for the human self.

Chapter Two:
Destroyers

She once said to herself...that it was always her fate to find out just too late about the "something beyond."

Edith Wharton, *The Custom of the Country* (54)

The most destructive force in life is the power of insatiable youth, of youth that has never known wisdom, of innocence that devours.

Ellen Glasgow, *In This Our Life* (291)

He took out a pile of shirts and began throwing them, one by one, before us, shirts of sheer linen and thick silk and fine flannel, which lost their folds as they fell and covered the table in many colored disarray.... Suddenly, with a strained sound, Daisy bent her head into the shirts and began to cry stormily.

F. Scott Fitzgerald, *The Great Gatsby* (99)

Section One:
The Trader

The Custom of the Country
"*Diverse et ondoyante*—so he had seen her from the first." So Ralph Marvell, the second husband of Undine Spragg Moffatt Marvell de Chelles Moffatt, envisions his bride-to-be. Ralph convinces himself that he is "not blind" to "Undine's crudity and her limitations," but can consider them "a part of her grace and persuasion" (83).

Undine, heroine of Edith Wharton's *The Custom of the Country*, is a persuasive woman indeed, and Ralph's assessment of her charm is one of the many ironies, contrasts, paradoxes and incongruities in this bleakly comic novel. At the center of the contradictions is Undine herself, dramatically, almost garishly, beautiful—writhing, preening, undulating. To Ralph, she "might have been some fabled creature whose home was in a beam of light" (21). Is she a mermaid? She is named after a hair product her grandfather put on the market the week she was born, yet she can devastate two continents with her red-gold hair and her pure, red and white complexion. But above the vivid, crude beauty of Undine's face and her sinuous figure, there are her black eyebrows—fixed, straight, like a black bar—threatening, even masculine. What is Undine? In essence, she is a snake.

Wharton creates a new metamorphosis for the child bride, the most poisonous form of all. Blake Nevius calls Undine "the most egocentric and dehumanized female in American fiction....the perfect flowering of the new materialism" (148). This embodiment of the darkest facet of innocence is most comfortable in light; for her "no radiance was too strong" (105). She is a dark angel that dazzles, and her function is to cast light on things evaded, on values, goals and attitudes more comfortably concealed. When Undine first enters the world of "old money," with its reticences and reserve, she is puzzled by this place of "half-lights, half-tones, illuminations and abbreviations; and she felt a violent longing to brush away the cobwebs and assert herself as the dominant figure of the scene" (37).

Undine will satisfy this longing. *The Custom of the Country* tracks her progress through the social classes and exposes each class caught in (and by) the light of Undine's beauty. As each world embraces her, its vices are captured in the glare: society is revealed in its passion for the tawdry and its capacity for self-deception.[1]

Like Carrie Meeber, Undine Spragg is a young girl from the provinces seeking her fortune in the city. But Undine is a Carrie with boundless energy. Cynthia Griffin Wolff says that there is only one thing fixed in this novel—a "preoccupation with energy" (232)[2] and Undine is a vortex of vitality. She is the child bride who not only sells but buys. She is the innocent as financial genius, the consummate trader in human flesh. As Elizabeth Ammons notes, "Undine Spragg is no more exploitive than the culture which produced her. She just accepts marriage for the speculative economic institution it obviously is." But this enterprising heroine does not settle for a restrictive bond. Instead, Ammons notes, like an ambitious young man changing jobs until he finds the right one, Undine "regards marriage as a commercial enterprise and...goes the system one better by viewing men as *her* possessions

("Business" 338). As she trades her way up the social ladder, Undine mirrors the evil within every social class.[3] "Her success," Louis Auchincloss remarks, "speaks more for the weakness of the patient than for the virulence of the microbe" (102).

In her amazing career, the relationship between the marriage world and the money world is most explicitly defined.[4] Undine is the "monstrously perfect result of the system" (208) that lives by and for the deal. In her, the passivity of earlier child brides is replaced by a boundless energy, a fury of desire, and the subtle destructiveness of the earlier women becomes overt and far-reaching. Like a Midwestern tornado, Undine brings widespread devastation, but she is not a force of nature. She is the creation of the very men she threatens, at once their enemy and their darling, the viper in their hearts.

Differences in this latest edition of the innocent are most obvious when Undine is compared to Carrie Meeber. Undine, like Carrie, is a role player, an actress who can become whatever the role demands: "it was instinctive with her to become, for the moment, the person she thought her interlocutors expected her to be" (386).[5] Some of Undine's most personally dramatic moments take place in theaters: sulking in her opera box when New York society has not noticed her, blazing in triumph at the theater as her engagement to Ralph becomes public. Twisting and preening, she is characterized by "youthful flexibility" (6), for she is "passionately imitative" (19) and can learn almost any role. The guiding principle of her career is, "It's better to watch than to ask questions" (65); like Carrie, Undine sees what she wants to be and then imitates it.

Like Carrie, she wants what others want. She can assess the value of things only by their value to others. For Undine, people and things appreciate in value when someone else wants them. Thus, Ralph Marvell becomes attractive to her because Clare Van Degen loves him, Faubourg Paris becomes a fortress to be conquered because her rival, Nettie Wincher, has entered it. The poverty of her desires for fashionable clothes, showy entertainments, and flashy display only reflects the desires of those she looks to for consumer guidance.

Undine shares Carrie's lack of an independent self, for not only her values, but her whole identity, are externally defined. And validation of self must come, like an actress's reward, from a full house. Undine seeks "admiration, not love." Her dream of pleasure is a fantasy of "publicity...the crowd, the close contact of covetous impulses, and the sense of walking among them in cool security." Any "personal entanglement might mean 'bother' " (223-24). Because the "image of herself in other minds...was her only notion of self-seeing" (401), her moment of pure success comes with the unveiling of her portrait. When Claude Walsingham Popple, the society painter who can "do" pearls so well, fashions Undine's image, and when that image is viewed and approved by the New York *nouveaux riches*, Undine knows that she *is* what she wants to be. Like Carrie, she is truly theirs, their creation.

Such victories, unfortunately, are countered by a seemingly endless discontent: there is always something new and better to want. Like a child, Undine is fascinated by the plaything of the moment, has a very short attention span, and wants every new desire gratified instantly. "Undine never wanted anything long, but she wanted it 'right off' " (43), her parents note. She is a prisoner of her own dissatisfaction.

Like Carrie, Undine is essentially sexless. Things, not people, cause her blood to race. And she has learned to use her coolness as a weapon, just as she uses the child role more skillfully and more openly than any of her predecessors.

Undine differs from Carrie in that she flagrantly manipulates her status to get what she wants. At times, she even finds society's adherence to the standards of her role amusing: when the Marvells invite Undine to dine but address the invitation to her mother, Undine finds it silly that "the best society" pretends that young women cannot do anything without their mothers' permission. She will, on the other hand, play society's game, concealing her first marriage from the Marvells, so that they will "think she's right out of kindergarten" (133), assuming the aura of virginity they expect.

The most significant modification of the child role apparent in Undine is that she is an *unruly* child. Undine wants paternal financial support, from a father or a father/husband, but she is infuriated by any attempt at paternal control. She is a child who will not submit; her tantrums are a weapon she uses with her parents, husbands and lovers, as are the "nervous breakdowns" that can only be cured by surrender to her demands. Her father Abner dreads her anger, fearing the darkening eyes, the cold glance, the straight brows and narrowed lips. Husband Ralph finds her sinister when crossed, when she becomes "inaccessible, inplacable," with eyes "like the eyes of an enemy" (165). Undine, the

badly behaved child, blames her guardians for her little upsets. "If only
everyone would do as she wished she would never be unreasonable"
(266).

The energy in Undine's recalcitrance is missing in Carrie's subdued
rebellions against her keepers. Energy is Undine's distinctive
contribution to her role; she is her father's daughter in the endless vigor
which she applies to trading on the domestic market and in her financial
acumen. Even as she blithely expects her male providers to supply her
needs, she is the practical child, knowing the price of everything, loving
"to bargain, pare down prices, evade fees" (181), not for love of
economy but for love of the deal. She is a pragmatist, knowing whether
one more dollar can be squeezed out of her indulgent parents, or her in-
laws, or out of her ex-husband frantic to keep their child. As Wolff
notes, she has the skills to be another financial baron, another Elmer
Moffatt, but that arena has been denied to her (*Feast* 245). And so she
calculates, estimates and trades in the only arena open to her, the
marriage market.

Undine trades herself in two ways. Ostensibly, she sells her body
and whatever soul she has, to a male provider. But less obviously, she
buys her "self," for each man she becomes involved with is, to a great
degree, *like* Undine. Undine, "passionately and persistently," wants only
two things: "amusement and respectability" (354). Of course, both these
things take money, so Undine really wants three things. The conflicts of
the novel arise not from a disparity of values among Undine and her
men, but from a difference in definitions of amusement and
respectability, in strategies for obtaining them, and in ways to enjoy
them.

Much of the bitter comedy derives from the question why such
supposedly superior men as Ralph Marvell and Raymond de Chelles are
drawn to Undine in the first place. She is ignorant and crude. Her beauty
is a loud beauty, too loud for the reticences of old New York or
Faubourg France. What, then, is the attraction? The men who select
Undine choose a hidden part of themselves.

Ralph Marvell, Undine's first big-city conquest, appears
ludicrously wrong for Undine, even physically. Although Undine is
described as slender, she is also described as somehow larger-than-life,
and she has a tendency to put on flesh. She is a "big" woman, but Ralph,
the quiet, refined, and studious young man, first appears as the "little

friend" (21) of a mutual acquaintance. The scion of an old family, he appears to have nothing intellectual or cultural to share with Undine, either.

But Ralph has long been fascinated by the Invaders, the crude new money entering New York society. Like Undine, he wants what others want: the value of Undine appreciates for him when he senses that the prince of the Invaders, Peter Van Degen, is attracted to her. His courtship of Undine is like a bidding war: he cannot offer the amusements of the new rich, but he can offer the respectability of the old.

In entering the competition for the acquisition of Undine, Ralph is deluded by his egotism. Undine's vulgarity and ignorance appeal to him as an unfinished product which he, with his superior ability, can refine. Ralph is happiest living in "the world of wonders within him" (75)[6] and he dreams of initiating Undine into the delights of that world. He will open "new windows in her mind" (148) as he exposes her to the glories of *his* mind; he will mold her to his dilettante tastes. The foolish and fatuous attitude Ralph has toward Undine is best described by his vision of her hand: "small...soft, a mere featherweight, a puff-ball of a hand,...one to be fondled and dressed in rings" (141). Taking Undine's hand in marriage, Ralph thinks he is buying a malleable child he can form to suit his whims.

His illusions are immense. Ralph has been bought, and bought by someone very like him. Both husband and wife seek a provider; both look to "Daddy," Abner Spragg, to supply them with the funds to live a life of amusement and respectability. Ralph has no scruples about accepting an allowance from his father-in-law, but he is appalled when Undine suggests his family might supply a little cash. His reaction is only one sign that Ralph knows, somewhere inside himself, that he has been bought.

Ralph's professed disdain for the money-grubbing of the Invader class is also a pose he abandons. He soon becomes, like Undine, fascinated by the intricacies of the deal. But while she is learning the rudiments of trading up in marriage, Ralph is an adoring trainee at the feet of the master, Abner Moffatt, assisting his mentor in transactions that are not quite ethical. Ralph, like his wife, is drawn to Moffatt's boldness and intelligence; unlike his wife, he does not have the talent to become Moffatt. Instead, he dreams of corrupting what talent he does have, of writing a potboiler for the money.

The Marvell marriage fails because of conflicts of money and amusement. Both partners expect money to come from some source other than themselves. And when Ralph is driven to earn some money, he proves pathetically inadequate to Undine's demands. Both partners expected the marriage to provide a great deal of amusement, but the relationship founders when they cannot agree on the nature of that amusement. On the honeymoon, Ralph seeks the reclusive, exclusive pleasure of roaming the Italian countryside, meditating on his planned novel (or poem, he is not sure). Undine is thwarted in her longings for the glitter of trendy resorts and fashionable crowds. Back home in New York, Undine is further disappointed when the fossilized social set of the Marvells provides a scant backdrop for displaying her charms. As Ralph sinks deeper into a sense of personal failure and misery, Undine counters with a vigorous campaign to get what she wants: more money, more freedom to spend it, more pleasure.

Ralph remains caught in his own delusions. Even as Undine leaves him to seek a better deal with Peter Van Degen, Ralph is dreaming of her as his child, "still in the toy age," and fantasizing that "when she came back he would know how to lift her to the height of his experience" (309). Ralph has been duped by his own foolishness. Seeking a child bride, he has gotten one, with a vengeance. Undine is so purely infantile that she is empty: void of passion, void of ideas, void of compassion. None of these deficiencies had seemed to matter to Ralph, for he had deceived himself into thinking he could fill those spaces. Only when Ralph must confront the emptiness within himself, when he feels himself "miserably diminished by the smallness of what had filled *his* world" (449, emphasis added), does he begin to fall apart.[7] This confrontation with self begins when Ralph must face the true nature of the woman he has chosen. When Undine tries to trade her child for money, Ralph must recognize her monstrous manipulations. But even this recognition, and the corresponding inner scrutiny it provokes, do not break Ralph. What finally prompts his suicide is the revelation that shatters his final illusion, the discovery that his fair bride was sullied in the way that seems to matter most—she was previously married. Discovering that he had, in essence, been denied Undine's maidenhood, Ralph puts the gun to his head. It seems that he can countenance her inner emptiness and his own, but he cannot live knowing that he did not get what he so dearly paid for.

Undine's next lover, Peter Van Degen, appears to be the ideal mate for her. Van Degen, with his "grotesque saurian head" (49) and his large hunger "for primitive satisfactions" and his "sturdy belief in his intrinsic right to them" (228), appears to be of the same species as Undine. He lives only for pleasure and pays for it extravagantly, buying everything from an "Aboriginal" princess (Ralph's old New Yorker cousin, Clare), to more temporary companions, to yachts and lavish holidays. Van Degen is physically repulsive, stupid, and gross. But he is immensely rich and committed to a life spent flaunting the power of his money.

Undine fails in this venture because she miscalculates. In a bold move, she becomes Van Degen's mistress before either he or she has obtained a divorce. Like any ambitious entrepreneur, she seizes the moment when it comes, but, having given her body without a written guarantee, Undine finds Van Degen has reneged on his side of the deal. Like her, he is a shrewd bargainer and sees no need to pay for what he has already enjoyed. And, like everyone else in the novel, Van Degen wants not just amusement but respectability as well. Undine threatens his respectability with her demands for his divorce, her divorce, and the ensuing period of social ostracism. For all his flamboyance, Van Degen prefers to play safely within the social limits.

In reality, Van Degen is not Undine's "type." Although she is impressed by his "contempt for everything he did not understand or could not buy" (192), she is developing a kind of finesse that is far more polished than her lover's reptilian ways. She is becoming a consumer with taste, not an independently formed taste, but one that mirrors the aesthetics of the Marvell family and of the international set she meets in Paris. She is learning to want things she had never dreamed of back home in Apex, and she now wants a husband who can help her to continue to learn. An aesthete, perhaps. Someone like Ralph.

Thus her marriage to Count Raymond de Chelles is as incongruous as her previous one. Chelles, like Ralph, seems a physical mismatch. With his aura of lassitude, his "lean, fatigued and finished" (275) look, he seems dwarfed by the red-haired beauty who dominates the international scene. Again, the question of motives arises, for, like Ralph, Chelles finds his wife in an environment he pretends to disdain.

Chelles first encounters Undine at the Nouveau Luxe, a gaudy hotel where a gaudy set of Americans and Europeans meets to play. The place is, to Chelles, a refreshing change from French institutions, which are, he acknowledges, "the necessary foundations for society" (274), but are nevertheless somewhat boring. He compares a brief indulgence in the pleasures of the Nouveau Luxe to the vagaries of a married man seeking an extramarital adventure. Paradoxically, it is at the Nouveau Luxe that Chelles, representative of European tradition, meets Undine, who could quite fittingly become his mistress, and whom he makes his wife.

Like Ralph, Chelles is entranced by the promiscuous world where Undine reigns, and, like Ralph, Chelles is trapped by his own illusions and desires. He is bested in the sexual trade, for Undine has learned from her failure with Van Degen. In her new role, she assumes a renewed virginity; with Chelles she becomes "the incorruptible but fearless American woman who cannot even conceive of love outside of marriage" (404), and the pose keeps Chelles frustrated but interested. Undine will not agree to become Chelle's mistress, but she *is* willing to buy *him*. Chelles, like Ralph, thinks he is acquiring a bride, but in reality he is himself acquired.

Initially, Undine lacks the assets to make *her* an attractive purchase, and the Chelles family's attitude toward her indicates the financial basis of this French "romance." When Undine is merely a divorced American, living on whatever her parents can send her, her beauty and charm are perceived as a threat to Chelles; his family fears that his infatuation with her is "spoiling his other chances" for a lucrative marriage (410). But when Undine becomes a rich widow, trustee of the considerable estate Ralph left to his son, the Chelles family perceives in Undine "the moral and financial merits necessary" (483) to permit her to buy into the family concern. And so Raymond de Chelles is bought, just as surely as his younger brother is bought by an American heiress appropriately named Miss Looty Arlington.

The courtship of Undine and Chelles, then, is a series of financial maneuvers, and the marriage is a series of money battles. As in the case of Ralph, Chelles can give Undine large quantities of respectability but not much fun. And they fight constantly over how to spend their money. Undine is appalled to discover that not only is Chelles as inadequate a provider as Ralph, but also he is not at all indulgent of her whims. In Chelles she finds a new Daddy, willing to assume responsibility for his child-bride, to nurture and form her, but she finds him a strict disciplinarian.

Money, amusement and control—Undine chafes and wriggles when all three are wrested from her. Chelles is as money-conscious as she is, but in a different way. Her new husband, she soon learns, thinks of money not as a way to individual gratification, but as something "binding together whole groups of interests" (495); as Abner Moffatt shrewdly observes, ancestors are Chelles's business, his life devoted to supporting the family and upholding its interests. When Undine refuses to understand this puzzling monetary policy, Chelles merely ignores her. And he not only ignores her whining and her tantrums, he restricts her movements, calling her to account for her time, severing her connections with the world of the Nouveau Luxe. Undine is expected to languish in the family chateau, trapped in an incessant round of prayers and family meals, eternally dressed in mourning for the most lately deceased Chelles. Like an impatient child, she writhes under the watchful eye of her mother-in-law, who perpetually disapproves of her deportment.

The Chelles establishment, significantly called Saint Desert, is a cold and sterile place, and Chelles, for all his refinement and grace, is a cold keeper. And it is clear that he and his family are somewhat spurious in their professed allegiance to a rigid moral code. Enacting the scenario he had earlier described, Chelles soon tires of his wife and indulges in extramarital adventures. His dalliances and the far more blatant but accepted exploits of his cousin, the blithely amoral Princess Estradina, reveal a side of the family they would prefer to conceal.

Even Undine senses that Chelles is something of a *poseur*. During their courtship, while Undine enacts the part of the virtuous and vulnerable young American, Chelles plays the role of ardent suitor, and he plays it with flair. His gift for "looking and saying all the desperate and devoted things a pretty woman likes to think she inspires" is, to Undine, a wonderful performance, giving her "the thrilling sense of breathing the very air of French fiction" (404). And when the marriage is nearly over, and Chelles delivers an impassioned tirade about the corrupting influence of Americans upon sacred French values, his fine words are undercut by his stance, that of "an extremely distinguished actor in a fine part" (546). Finally, Undine must leave Chelles because he has proven a disappointment. Not only has he failed to give her the fun and finances she wants, but he may not even be the genuine item she paid for.

And so Undine's final union is with her twin, Abner Moffatt, the upstart from Apex, her first husband, who, like Undine, early demonstrated "the capacity to develop into any character he might care to assume" (108). He has transformed himself into the multimillionaire, the man who can confidently say, "Nobody can stop me now if I want anything" (534). In his energy, in his appetites, Moffatt is Undine. Her attraction to him is, in a sense, a passion for herself.

Moffatt is the amoral but omnipotent collector; he makes no pretense of judging a thing but likes to own pretty objects. He can now afford to buy Undine. And he has the power to make her the supreme consumer. Moffatt's material reach wakes in Undine the closest thing to passion she can feel. Gary Lindberg describes the marriage as the union of "endless erratic desire...with boundless means for gratification" (76), and Moffatt's enormous fortune ensures that, at last, Undine has found a good provider. The man who can handle his business affairs "like a snake-charmer spinning the deadly reptiles about his head" (563) should be well-equipped to handle this charming serpent.

But this match, like the others, brings its dissatisfactions. Again there is the incongruity of the partners, for while Moffatt has become rich and confident, he remains vulgar and unpolished. And Undine, once the equally rough product of Apex, has evolved into a finished, finely glazed collectible, formed by her experiences in old New York, parvenue society and Faubourg France. And, in a further incongruity, Undine, in spite of all her finish, proves to be the less changed of the pair. While Undine has been trading and adapting and learning, Moffatt, the collector, has been learning, too. He has learned a deep appreciation for those aesthetic values represented in the art he buys. He has learned to love beauty, with a disinterested and abiding love. Moffatt has moved beyond Undine, widening his vision to include satisfactions she will never comprehend. She cannot understand the things he collects; she is simply one of those things.

While Undine only dimly senses this failing in herself, she is quite conscious of her husband's shortcomings. Moffatt may be a generous provider, he may supply endless amusement, but he can never give her enough respectability. Moffatt is not Ralph or Chelles, and, ironically, those unsatisfactory spouses gave Undine the polish, the manners, the aura of distinction Moffatt will never provide. And so Undine, having worked so hard, is still left to yearn, pitifully, for that elusive, perfect deal.

Undine does deserve some credit for all her hard work, and some sympathy for all her thwarted desires. Like Carrie, she is caught in a pattern of unsatisfied longing, each triumph quickly superseded by emptiness and disillusion with the object of desire. Repeatedly, Wharton makes it clear that Undine's greatest punishment comes from the terrifying loss of self she suffers when she loses the approval or recognition of others. Perceiving herself as an object whose value is the current market price, Undine dreads being left "on the shelf," unnoticed. Thus, she chafes at the injustice of being beautiful in obscurity in her early New York days and feels duped when she marries into the Marvell set, only to find she has allied herself with "the exclusive and the dowdy when the future belonged to the showy and the promiscuous" (193). Undine correctly assumes that society will value her according to how much some man will be willing to pay for her; thus, when she is divorced from Ralph and abandoned by Van Degen, her new visiting card, with her maiden name on it, "was like the coin of a debased currency," testifying to her diminished capacity to trade (361). "Wharton's point is important," Ammons says. "As a single woman, Undine is unrecognized, even ostracized; and she consequently grows spiritless and insecure. She *must* marry again in order to have identity itself" ("Business" 334).

Since Undine can define herself only in others' eyes, her marriage to Raymond de Chelles is the most painful of all. When Undine crosses Chelles, she ceases to exist for him. His attitude fills Undine with terror, and she retreats to compulsive efforts to define herself through acquisition. She buys more clothes, and she tries to acquire an improved self, investing in beauty regimens, make up, rejuvenation creams, massage. The chief horror of St. Desert is, for Undine, the possibility of being left alone with herself.

Undine's remarriage to Moffatt is another source of great pain because it promises so much and then delivers such frustration. She expects the union to bring her the recognition she craves, the recognition that will confirm her desired image of herself. The wedding makes the society pages of every newspaper; the groom's gifts to his beloved and their residences and exploits are lavishly reported. After a brief period of ritualized disapproval, international society embraces the prodigal Undine, "forgiving" her divorce from Chelles. Undine appears to have transformed herself into the glittering and admired object she so wanted to be. Even the vulgarity she deplores in Moffatt can be a useful backdrop, a contrast to her sophistication and refinement. With Midwestern hard work and ingenuity, Undine has formed herself; from the worlds of each lover and husband she has acquired a veneer of style. Yet the self she has wrested from all the marital battles, the only heritage of so much romantic discord, is flawed. Without the polish acquired from the worlds of her former husbands, Undine would not be the treasure Moffatt chooses. But because of those husbands, Undine is left unsatisfied. She will never fill the one role she now believes she has been made for—that of Ambassadress. An Ambassadress cannot be a divorced woman. Undine's marriages have made her and damaged her. And so she remains, to the end, the object seeking the perfect, unattainable, setting.

Forever looking to others to define her, perceiving them only as part of the setting of her life, Undine is isolated by her selfishness. She perceives others only in terms of what she seeks. Most often, she is looking for a mirror. "At the center of Undine's being is a void:," Wolff says, "she has none of the 'softer' emotions, no capacity to feel sympathy for others" (*Feast* 241). Ralph discovers that Undine has only a social self, that she thinks of all interaction as performance; she regards intimacy as a rest period, a time to escape from conversation "into a total absence of expression" (151). Thus, her marriage to Ralph becomes the kind of mute connection typical of Carrie Meeber. When Undine is challenged in her demands, as in her marriage to Chelles, she perceives the conflict not as a personal disagreement, but as open warfare. There are no human relationships for Undine, even in her non-sexual relationships. With other women, she forges business alliances. She negotiates a non-aggression pact with Indiana Rolliver, pledging not to exert her charms upon Mr. Rolliver in return for certain favors. With Nettie Wincher de Trezac, she establishes the detente of two invaders on European soil, both seeking entry into aristocratic circles. As for Undine's connection to her child, it is never characterized by maternal feeling. To Undine, Paul is most often a pawn (to be sold in return for cash), an extra (in the St. Desert scenario, she realizes that a true French mother has her child by her side), or a doll (separated from Paul, Undine is haunted by the thought that others may be dressing him in clothes she would hate). Really, Undine is neither mother, nor friend, nor wife. She is a monster, but she is lonely and empty in her monstrousness.

Undine is the American girl gone bad. Like her male counterpart, the young man seeking new territory to explore, new worlds to conquer, she embodies those cherished American values of initiative and drive. She is a dreamer of big dreams, forever challenging herself to find "something still better beyond...more luxurious, more exciting, more worthy of her!" (54). Unlike the young man, Undine's battles are limited to the domestic front. It is "the custom of the country" to limit women to such an arena, and so the country must pay.

Every social group, every fortress falls before Undine Spragg, because she preys on its weakness. Entering new territory, she watches and learns. She adapts each group's protective coloration, its manners, its proprieties. And so in choosing her, each world chooses an imitation of itself, a distorted yet recognizable image of its own follies and flaws. Undine is no more calculating, materialistic and empty than those who are drawn to her, and that is Wharton's point. Those characters who are most willing to deceive themselves about Undine—and thus about their own natures—are most damaged by her. Undine's beauty casts a frightening glare. That light is too strong for those who prefer the evasions of their class. Others, caught in the blaze, are forced to face their own false values, their "passion for the factitious,"[8] their hunger for the imitation.

Section Two:
Insatiable Girls

The Great Gatsby

Undine Spragg is only one in a series of girls whose appetite mirrors a nation's desire. In four novels that followed The *Custom of the Country—The Great Gatsby, Twilight Sleep, The Sheltered Life* and *In This Our Life*—versions of the insatiable girl appear, and so, too, does a recognizable pattern. The desiring/desired girl stands at the center of a vortex. Around her swirl instances of failed marriages, blocked communications, social disorder and decay. Like *The Custom of the Country*, each of these four novels is set in a world of deception, where illusion and role-playing supersede reality and emotion. But a new element appears in the pattern: a crime. In these novels, there are two shootings and two car "accidents" (hit-and-run). In each case, the innocent heroine is either the culprit or is indirectly responsible, and, in each case, society helps to cover up the deed.

These conspiracies of evasion are the logical outcomes of the crimes, as those around the heroine are her accomplices. They have created the atmosphere in which the child bride flourishes; they have, in essence, created her. And those around her perceive that she cannot be held responsible for her actions, for she embodies the pure freedom of endless choice without consequences. She is the consumer who need never pay.

She is an icon of desire and damnation. Like Undine Spragg, she is what men want, and she is full of discontent: forever attracted to a new amusement, a new toy, a new man, and forever bored, disappointed, seeking a new deal. Men strive to pay for her, and they pay twice. They work to acquire her, and they assume the responsibility of owning a delinquent child, one who smashes things and people with the petulance of a spoiled little girl.

The price of the child bride never seems to be too high. In these novels, even when the beloved child is revealed as a manipulator, betrayer, or murderer, she is carefully shielded from the consequences of her desires. This icon of longing must not be shattered, for if she is gone, what is left? Only the Valley of Ashes that created her.

In the middle of *The Great Gatsby*, Meyer Wolfsheim, who has ingeniously transformed human molars into jewelry and the dirty deal into a corporate empire, offers Nick Carraway a business connection. His offer encapsulates most of the relationships of the novel, for F. Scott Fitzgerald's book is largely about deals. Tom Buchanan has bought his wife, and Jay Gatsby wants to exercise his prior option on the merchandise. Nick, the novel's moral center, is learning to trade in stocks and bonds. Gatsby sells liquor in the guise of medicine, Tom Buchanan and George Wilson dicker over the sale of a car, Myrtle Wilson sells herself, and Meyer Wolfsheim bought the World Series.

At the center of the trading is, of course, the golden girl, or more accurately, as Michael Millgate notes, the gold and white girl. Daisy is the golden girl in the white palace, the "Daisy" with a gold center and white petals, the princess dressed in white, driving a white roadster. She is, then, the color of money but also the color of the "absence of all desire." The white palace is remote and inaccessible, Millgate says, and Daisy's white innocence is life-denying (111). Daisy wants things and people, but she feels no true sexual desire, and thus there is no space inside her that can be filled, no unfinished part of her that can be completed by another. She is a trick of blankness. Even her golden color, the color of money, is also the color of brass, the imitation. It is the color of the brass buttons on her dress the day she reunites with Gatsby, himself resplendent in a silver shirt and golden tie.

At the center of all the deals, then, is a bad bargain. Daisy is the meretricious beauty to which Gatsby consecrates his life.

It is fitting that a book about buying and selling should center on a woman who does not give full value for the money. Most trades involve some deception, or at least some illusion, on the part of buyer and/or seller. And so *The Great Gatsby* is a novel of lies, filled with open secrets, evasions, deceit, and betrayal. It begins with the open secret of Tom's infidelity and Daisy's dramatic enactment of the role of long-suffering, beautiful fool. The scenario entertains Jordan, a professional golfer who is a liar and a cheat. The first scenes introduce the keynote of deception that continues throughout. Tom lies to his mistress about his wife's refusal to divorce him; Myrtle and her sister deceive Myrtle's husband, poor George; everyone suspects Gatsby is lying about his genteel past; and a series of deceptions lead to Gatsby's murder.

As the Houyhnhms said, a lie is "the thing that is not," and this is a novel about the love of "what is not." In *The Great Gatsby*, appearances are worshipped as if they were real, things are substituted for emotions, things provoke emotion, and people become things.[9]

The central characters, Daisy and Gatsby, drift from role to role, almost as if they were searching for the most appropriate one. Daisy is first seen in an elaborate tableau of elegance and lassitude, posed on her sofa, gazing motionless at some invisible object, a figurine in a cool, lush setting. In the space of a few hours, she attempts two new roles: the injured wife and the adoring young mother. Her lover, trying to explain his past to Nick, also posits a series of roles, from which Nick can chose the one he finds most plausible: war hero of Montenegro, white hunter in the colonies, Oxford man. Daisy is drawn to Gatsby's flair for drama. As Marius Bewley notes, what Daisy likes best at Gatsby's party is the empty gesture of and actress and her director (278), slowly moving toward one another in a pantomime of love, a parody of her own slow movement back to the lover who wants to dominate her life.

And the love that supposedly binds these two is frequently represented as an uncontrollable feeling prompted by an object. Gatsby beseeches Daisy's green light in the darkness; she is where the light is, but somehow the light evokes the feeling. Daisy loses control and weeps, not on first re-encountering her lost love, but when she sees the piles of pastel-colored shirts he flings, like tribute, into her lap. Betrayal is also revealed by a thing: George Wilson discovers his wife's adultery when he finds a jeweled dog leash in her room.

The lines dividing people, images and things become increasingly blurred. Daisy's little girl, charmingly dressed and adorably (but briefly) exhibited to Nick, seems like her mother's doll, or a prop in Daisy's drama of marital virtue wronged and affronted. Daisy's attitude towards Gatsby is most tellingly revealed in the words of passion that give the game away. Tom is certain that Daisy has been unfaithful when she lovingly compares Gatsby, so fresh and clean and beautifully dressed, to the image of a man in a shirt advertisement. There seems to be no higher tribute in this world of illusion than to compare one's beloved to an advertisement.

It is a dead world, a place dominated by a pair of eyes on a billboard, eyes that are sightless but forever peer out, looking for something. Like the eyes of Dr. Eckleburg, the innocents of the novel keep looking for something, something new and better, for they are bored with the things they have already bought. Daisy wonders what they'll do each day, and the next day, identifying the dilemma of people who can have whatever they want, as soon as they want it. Tom, too, is bored, seeking excitement first in sport, then in infidelity, seeking identity in a book of racist political philosophy. Myrtle is bored with her husband and looking for a better deal; George, too, dreams of moving to a new place where business will be better.

Gatsby, more than anyone else, is eternally hopeful, confident that one more purchase will save him. Malcolm Bradbury says Gatsby aims "to transform money into love" (65) by buying Daisy. For, as Fetterley says, Daisy has become the embodiment of the things Gatsby has craved for so long. Her family's rich house in Alabama, where he first sees her, is "the house of romance which he can only enter through her," and she is "the ultimate object in it. It is she for whom men compete, and possessing her is the clearest sign that one has made it into that magical world" (74).

Fitzgerald's comment on his relationship to his wife Zelda is relevant to Gatsby's motives. In his notebooks, Fitzgerald discussed his marriage to Zelda, a dream fulfilled only after much frustration. Zelda had broken their engagement because Fitzgerald had no money, and she married him only after he had become rich and famous, with the publication of his first novel. Fitzgerald describes the bitter lesson learned from both denial and subsequent gratification of his longing:

The man with the jingle of money in his pocket who married the girl a year later would always cherish an abiding distrust, an animosity, toward the leisure class—not the conviction of the revolutionist but the smouldering hatred of a peasant. In the years since then I have never been able to stop wondering where my friends' money came from, nor to stop thinking that at one time a sort of *droit de seigneur* might have been exercised to give one of them my girl. (Qtd. in Spindler 152)

His fear describes the plot of *The Great Gatsby*, and Spindler says the statement reveals Fitzgerald's awareness that "money was the dynamo which powered the bright lights of the leader class" (152). But the comment also reveals Fitzgerald's understanding that women are property, prizes to be won. And so his greatest character, Jay Gatsby, perceives Daisy as "that which money exists to buy," as Fetterley says. To own her "both indicates the fact of money and gives point to its possession" (74).

Fitzgerald seems to say that Daisy is the source of Gatsby's doom, that she brings him down. Critics of the novel generally agree that Daisy's destructive power is not willed or conscious, that Gatsby has simply invested too much in a property that cannot appreciate in value. Nevertheless, our general sense of Gatsby's story links his fall to his choice of the golden girl. Perhaps if he had found some other embodiment of his dreams, if he had purchased something else, his life might have been otherwise. The being who created himself, this Son of God, is incarnated, made fallible and vulnerable, when he makes the wrong consumer decision.

As Gatsby remembers it, the fatal choice is his decision to commit himself to Daisy. On that autumn night, as he and Daisy walked on a sidewalk "white with moonlight," he turned to Daisy and noticed that "the blocks of the sidewalk really formed a ladder and mounted to a secret place above the trees." The moment of choice arrives, for Gatsby can reach the secret place

> if he climbed alone, and once there he could suck on the pap of life, gulp down the incomparable milk of wonder.
>
> His heart beat faster and faster as Daisy's white face came up to his own. He knew that when he kissed this girl, and forever wed his unutterable visions to her perishable breath, his mind would never romp again like the mind of God. So he waited.... Then he kissed her...and the incarnation was complete. (112)

Gatsby has bought the definitive item; given the choice between the stars and the earth, between a secret place of endless wonder and the blank, white face of mortality with its "perishable breath," Gatsby comes down to Daisy, who must lift her face to reach him. God has been made man; anticipation, infinite promise have been reduced to a limiting realization. It seems that God has become man not by *becoming* a child, but by *loving* one.

The passage is not so straightforward. For the alternatives of Gatsby's choice are not clear. From what heights did Gatsby fall? And to what has he been reduced?

Without Daisy, Gatsby thinks, he could climb that white ladder to the sky and be safe in a solitary spot, free to suck the milk of wonder, to romp. This choice is a child's choice, a consumer choice. Gatsby perceives this secret world as a place of dependency and drift, where the maternal breast of dreams is ever-available, where he can suck the milk of wonder endlessly as he romps in innocence. To get there, he must take a white sidewalk and climb a white ladder to live on the white liquid of dreams. In a novel filled with negative images of the white princess in her white world, the world relinquished by Gatsby seems remarkably similar to the world he chooses.

Gatsby's "fall" into Daisy's perishable world is no Fortunate one. There is no moment of transition from that secret world of play to the mature world of guilt, sorrow, and perhaps redemption. If Daisy indeed brings Gatsby down, she brings him down to reality. The fallen Gatsby is not so much diminished as revealed. He has chosen Daisy not as an alternative to that playful world of wonderful white dreams, but as an embodiment of it.

As Fitzgerald points out, Gatsby makes himself, and he creates his own destiny as well. Like that first self-made man, Ben Franklin, Gatsby methodically and systematically designs his regimen of self-improvement. His diary, like Franklin's, allocates each moment of the day for one more step on the way to wealth. Gatsby learns and studies under a more modern version of the self-made man, the predator/pioneer Dan Cody. Gatsby learns to believe in his mentor's values of power, possession and control. He becomes exactly what he wanted to be—the latest incarnation of an old American dream. By Gatsby's time, the self-made man is no longer creative and inventive like Franklin, nor rapacious and atavistic, like Cody. He is polished and charming, a con man. But Gatsby's misfortune is to be the con man duped by his own yearnings.

Gatsby is brought down by his refusal to see the nature of his own dreams, and that is why he must remain faithful to Daisy until he dies. As Fetterley says, Gatsby has invested himself in Daisy (76-77), so to recognize her emptiness is to recognize his own. It is easier to remain in a world of lies, to die waiting for a call that will never come, a declaration of love from a girl who cannot love. The dream must be sustained by deception, of others and of oneself, so that identity can be sustained.

It is easier for all those in Gatsby's world to go on as they began than to confront the evil inside their dreams. When the golden girl kills, her crime must be concealed, and Gatsby, Tom, and even Nick conspire to cover up the truth. And so the novel ends as it began. It ends in falsehood, from Gatsby's lie to save Daisy, to Jordan's lie to save her pride. It ends in deception, from George Wilson's tragic mistake, to the revelation of Gatsby's real name, to the Buchanans' re-assumption of the role of united married couple.

And, most of all, it ends with a final picture of the power of money. Money can buy the innocent bride, and enough money can keep her safe in a white palace. Money can sustain the illusion that, somewhere, there is one new thing, one new pleasure or one new person that, purchased, will fill the emptiness inside. And so the story of the Buchanans ends with two more purchases, as Tom buys jewelry to adorn his new mistress, his latest acquisition. Business continues as usual.

Twilight Sleep

In *The Great Gatsby*, Daisy stands alone as a representative child-heroine; she is peerless in her ability to represent what men want. Edith Wharton, in *Twilight Sleep*, employs two innocent heroines, one young, one middle-aged, linking the innocence of the past to a new, more virulent form of the disease. The young innocent is Lita Wyant, beautiful, amoral, irresponsible, narcissistic. All she wants, another character notes, "was to keep on finding herself, immeasurably magnified, in every pair of eyes she met!" (285). Lita wants admiration, amusement, and, most of all, a life without pain. Whenever Lita is thwarted in her desires, whenever discomfort threatens, she demands "a new deal" (230), and throughout the novel she manipulates those around her like so many items she can trade, in a quest for a better bargain.

Her double is her mother-in-law, Pauline Manford, the innocent grown old, who shares Lita's values but is losing her power as she loses her youth and beauty. Although Pauline disguises her selfishness under a mask of benevolence, she, too, is a ruthless user of persons, ready to eliminate anyone from her world if he threatens her serenity. For Pauline, even more than Lita, is terrified of pain.

"Twilight sleep" is the name of a process that takes much of the pain from childbirth, but in Wharton's novel of the 1920s the term can be seen as a metaphor for making the transition into adulthood without knowing it. When Lita gives birth to her baby, she merely goes to sleep, drifting into motherhood "lightly and unperceivingly," to awaken to the presence of a baby, a "wax doll" in the cradle by her bed (19). Adult experience does not make Lita an adult. Similarly, the characters of the novel are all physically mature, yet they remain trapped in infantile behavior. Because the one secret goal of their lives is to avoid suffering, they deny their experiences and thus deny themselves growth. Even when they must confront the rare, inescapable painful situation, they manage to evade it.

Pauline, the rich, smiling society matron, is the character most overtly afraid of being hurt, perhaps because her safe haven is the most under siege. "Her whole life...had been a long uninterrupted struggle against the encroachment of every form of pain. The first step, always, was to conjure it, bribe it away, by every possible expenditure—except of one's self" (306). As in the case of many child brides, Pauline uses money to buy protection, and to that end, she buys her first husband,

Arthur Wyant, a son of old New York. This marriage is Pauline's first deal: when Pauline wants to marry the ineffectual but genteel Arthur, her father consents, saying, "Better just regard him as a piece of jewelry: I guess we can afford it" (24). When the acquisition proves disappointing, Pauline "trades up" and marries the self-made, wildly successful businessman Dexter Manford. But no matter how rich Pauline is, and no matter how hard she searches for the right partner, she cannot find what she wants, a life without pain. Pain seems to be everywhere, and she often finds herself "agitated by the incessant effort to be calm" (47). Her children, Jim Wyant and Nona Manford, are constant sources of potential unpleasantness, for they come to her with their problems. To protect herself, she must eliminate all but superficial contact with them. When a devoted servant's mother is dying of cancer, Pauline must flee from this source of discomfort; she simply cannot visit hospitals. But pain keeps threatening her, especially as she grows older and loses the look of the child.

Still a child inside, Pauline desperately struggles to stave off the physical signs of age and the misery that seems to loom nearer every moment. She tries to buy the appearance of innocence with massage, wrinkle remover, and with quack doctors who promise her a firm body and a smooth face. She tries to buy inner peace from a series of trendy spiritual guides, forever looking for a new Messiah. And she fills every minute, day and night, with an activity, for nothing terrifies her more than a moment alone.

Wharton emphasizes that Pauline is not alone in her terrors and in her responses to them. When Pauline drives through New York on her way to another function, she passes dozens of women just like her, safe in their limousines, the New Women, the committee women, the club women, all as paralyzed by innocence as Pauline. Denied adult roles in the male world of business, these women deceive themselves into believing that their clubs and causes and charities matter. In reality, their busy benevolence is a trivialized version of genuine commitment; it is an incessant playtime, for the women have no convictions.[10] These are women who can enthusiastically support birth control and a national mothers' association on the same day, and see no disparity. They simply do not see because they do not want to see. All their civic and philanthropic activity is merely another form of buying, of purchasing something to kill time, to fend off the empty hour.

The society women are not the only ones who fight the unpleasant. The men of the novel are equally caught in a fear of suffering and a secret recognition that all their evasions cannot keep darkness at bay. Pauline's husband Dexter lives in two worlds, the daily round of business, with its "great sense of pressure, importance, and authority," and the cycle of leisure, the "drop at the close [of day] into staleness and futility" (56). As he looks around him, Dexter realizes that all the men he knows—bankers, brokers, lawyers—are "cheating their inner emptiness" with work as "futile as [the activities of] the women they went home to" (189). When Dexter finally consults a doctor about his ever-present malaise, the doctor recommends travel, and Dexter recognizes the prescription as "the perpetual evasion, moral, mental, physical, which he heard preached, and saw practised, everywhere about him, except where money-making was concerned!" (56). Money, in this rich world, provides various means of evasion, but none of them seems to satisfy. People are troubled and confused. Dexter's stepson, Jim, is a sensitive young man, unhappily married to the childish Lita, and about to lose her; Jim's father Arthur Wyant takes refuge from his sorrows in alcohol and hypochondria and a nostalgic yearning for the more genteel evasions of old New York. Everywhere there are unhappy marriages, infidelity, lies, discontent.

And everywhere there is a constant search for something *new*, some external change that can substitute for inner growth: an improved complexion, a better physique, a redecorated house, a trip abroad, a new lover, a new marriage. There is sex, but there is no real sexuality. And nothing satisfies.

The young innocent, Lita Wyant, is in some ways admirable because she most frankly expresses what everyone feels. "I'm a fake," she states (231), and she is, because she is sexually enticing without being sexual, lovely on the outside and shallow within. But she is more honest about the values of her world than anyone else in it. To Dexter, she is "the one person in the whole group to whom its catchwords meant absolutely nothing," the one person who does not dress up her "selfish cravings" in "wordy altruism" (190). When Lita openly and aggressively acts to satisfy those cravings, she becomes the enemy of her group—because she exposes it.

Lita is Wharton's recreation of Undine Spragg as flapper. Like Undine, she is a red-gold beauty, sinuous in her charms, always in motion. Like Undine, she is a mirror. She most closely mirrors Pauline. Pauline bought her first husband and cast him aside; Lita was bought by her husband but now wants to break the contract, either by infidelity or divorce. Pauline is obsessed with keeping her face and body young; Lita longs to display her charms in the movies. Pauline seeks a new guru, the Mahatma, to find a way to slim her hips; Lita becomes his devotee and poses, semi-nude, for his brochure. Lita's chaotic schedule, in which nothing has an appointed time and punctuality does not exist, is the flip side of Pauline's over-scheduled day. Both women are playing at life; both fill the hours with meaningless activity.

Lita mirrors everyone around her, not just Pauline. Her perpetual cry, "Oh, children, but I'm bored!" (129) correctly labels her peers and identifies the outcome of all this expensive serenity—perpetual boredom. Lita hates being bored, so much so that, as her husband says, she grows to hate the things, places and people that don't amuse her. And so, like everyone else in the novel, Lita is looking for a better deal.

Lita's affair with her father-in-law Dexter is the alliance that can smash all the other precarious relationships in the book. Lita draws Dexter with her innocence. His own child bride is growing old; he wants a younger version. And he can afford to pay Lita's exacting terms, to indulge her whims. Pauline at least subconsciously recognizes Lita as her replacement, and so her search for rejuvenation becomes more frantic. Jim Wyant clings to Lita, ready to excuse almost anything if he can keep her.

The adultery precipitates a crime and brings the unpleasant perilously close to all the characters. When Jim's father, Arthur Wyant, tries to shoot Dexter, who is in bed with Lita at the time, the whole carefully constructed house of evasion comes close to toppling. But it doesn't fall. The elaborate system of repression prevails, and every member of the Manford-Wyant family works to cover the crime. The attempted shooting becomes a "burglary," and much money is spent to restore life to what it was. There are no divorces. There is no open suffering. Everyone merely travels to a new place, Dexter and Pauline to the Far East, Arthur Wyant to a private inebriate asylum, Lita and Jim to Paris, where it is hoped Lita will find some new amusements. Lita's misbehavior must be suppressed and contained, just as the misery in everyone must be kept below the surface of "pleasant" lives. Money is spent, once again, to buy off pain. And money keeps the bad child, Lita, safe within the family, with new purchases to distract her from her gnawing discontent.

The Sheltered Life

Like Edith Wharton in *Twilight Sleep*, Ellen Glasgow focuses on two generations of innocents in The *Sheltered Life*. But her focus is the education of one girl as she learns her role from an older woman. Both heroines are, in their different ways, destroyers, yet Glasgow describes, with sympathy and understanding, how the innocent role damages self as well as others. Alfred Kazin says of Glasgow, "The great quality of the life she saw all about her was a simple and astonishing refusal to admit reality," a quality that Glasgow can sometimes find charming, but that is ultimately ridiculous and even tragic (193). In this story of decaying Virginia aristocrats, those sheltered from the truth learn to live lives that are lies. In so doing, they bring tragedy to themselves and others.

For Jenny Blair Archbold at age nine, the adult world is fascinating and forbidden. Her mother warns her that she sees too much, but she keeps looking into the forbidden world, and she learns its secrets. She learns the most from observing the marriage of George and Eva Birdsong.

Eva Birdsong is the quintessential belle, what Frederick McDowell calls "a sacrificial victim to the inflexible ideals of her role" (188). She is another graceful, red-haired beauty who, everyone says, married a man unworthy of her, George Birdsong, a penniless, extravagant lawyer. To the young Jenny, Eva is pure beauty and serene elegance. Jenny's mother comments that Eva's radiance is so "imperishable" that "it might have been painted" (20). Jenny's grandfather General Archbold adores Eva, as do all the men in Queenborough.

As Jenny watches Eva, she learns that Eva's marriage and her identity are lies. George repeatedly betrays Eva, with a mulatto mistress, with younger belles. Eva, aware of the infidelities, conceals her obsessive jealousy behind her painted gaiety, her pretense trapping her in a kind of living death. "Nobody will ever find out what regrets Eva has had," Jenny's mother Mrs. Archbold says, "Not even if he takes the trouble to unscrew the lid of her coffin" (20). As belle, Eva must never really see what is happening around her. When George becomes ill at the house of one of his lovers, even when he must be dressed before his distraught wife arrives, Eva pretends that he was there to give the woman legal advice.

Watching Eva and George, Jenny learns their secrets; she sees how the game is played. She watches Eva suppress her fury at George's flirtation and feign illness to separate him from a rival. She admires Eva's mask of innocence and dimly understands that "Always...the glow of her [Eva's] loveliness would come...between her and life" (72). Jenny learns that George, too, is a child, "that it was nursing he craved, the maternal sort of nursing she gave her doll after she dropped it" (74), and she realizes that he cannot find what he wants in marriage to the childlike Eva.

When Jenny encounters George leaving the home of his mistress, she learns another secret, one that initiates her into "that mysterious world where grown-up persons hide the things they do not wish children to know" (68). With the nine-year-old child, George shares the guilt he cannot reveal to his wife, and Jenny uses the secret to forge a hidden bond between them. For the child Jenny wants George, and she wants to be Eva—a stronger, more successful Eva, one who can keep what Eva is losing.

The rest of the novel charts Jenny's growing power and Eva's loss of it. As Jenny grows up, she becomes aware that everyone around her is lying: her mother lives in that "smiling region" where she can "believe anything and nothing" (24), her grandfather devotes his whole life to keeping up appearances. She perceives that reality is like the "bad smell" of the neighboring factories, something always there, but always ignored (195).

An emblem of denied reality is the now middle-aged Eva, ill and wasted with pain, refusing medical treatment because George has a horror of "maimed women" (130). But once again, weakness allows Eva to hold George. When she finally does enter the hospital, George plays the role of devoted spouse. Hidden, for a little longer, is George's discontent, his realization that Eva expects too much of him: "I sometimes wish...that she didn't believe in me. If she saw me as I am, I might be able to measure up better" (250). Who can live with an ideal woman? And who can measure up to her ideals? "She has never been happy. It was all too big for me...what she is, what she feels, what she thinks, what she expects—everything" (251). George, doomed never to meet Eva's demands, continues to lie to her, but he shares this new secret with Jenny.

Jenny, at 17, has become what she wanted to be, a younger, more ruthless version of Eva. Frederick McDowell links her sheltered upbringing to her amorality, saying that her protected existence "has encouraged an idle hedonism and a compulsive desire to satisfy her instincts."[11] Like so many innocents, Jenny wants "everything before I am too old" (336). Yet she is not sure exactly what to want—perhaps a career on the stage, perhaps travel. She is restless and unhappy. All she knows, for certain, is that she wants to be in Eva Birdsong's world, to be adored and admired, like Eva. And so Jenny takes George.

Raised in a world of lies, Jenny knows that things are not real if they are kept hidden, and so she feels no real guilt about her affair with George. As long as it is a secret, it cannot harm Eva. What is not acknowledged simply does not exist. Eva returns from the hospital, broken, her eyes "veiled and remote," with "the flicker of some deep hostility in the blue fire of her gaze" (277). But Eva does not tell what she sees; in fact, she will not admit that she sees it. Ever.

Even when Eva discovers the lovers in an embrace, she "smiled through them and beyond them to the empty horizon" (391). She will not see. She simply takes George's gun and kills him.

And then no one else will see, either. The forces of Queenborough are marshalled to conceal reality. General Archbold declares that George died accidentally, by shooting himself. Only Jenny cries hysterically, and the General admonishes the family to be kind to her, to remember how young she is, and how innocent.

Jenny's cry is, "I didn't mean anything!" (395), and indeed she didn't. Her seduction of George was a whim, a fantasy, an innocent amusement devoid of true emotion. She did not mean to hurt anyone because she does not understand pain. As McDowell says, Jenny has been raised so that she will have no knowledge of suffering (190). How, then, can she understand it? Jenny has seen only lies, lies that cover suffering, and she has been taught that pain does not exist if it is not confronted. Her betrayal of Eva was not supposed to hurt because it was never to be acknowledged; it was to be like the secrets of all the adults who taught her how to live. From Eva, more than anyone, Jenny learned how to live the sheltered life, and now, like Eva and all the others, Jenny must remain in the world of deception.

In this Our Life

The Great Gatsby, *Twilight Sleep* and *The Sheltered* Life all end in the suppression of an unpleasant reality and a resumption of life-as-lies. In all three, the terrible energy of the child-woman, her seemingly endless power of destruction, is contained within the boundaries of the society that adores her, and this containment allows for a continuation of the status quo. In Glasgow's later novel, *In This Our Life*, there is actually a brief moment when the true nature of the innocent must be acknowledged and when the lying stops. The moment of truth, however, is *very* brief, and it does not seem to matter.[12]

In a central scene, the innocent girl, Stanley Kingsmill, is exposed by her father, Asa Timberlake, as a killer. Driving recklessly, Stanley has hit a little girl holding a bunch of flowers, smashed the child beyond recognition, and driven off.[13] When Asa, who loves his daughter, feels bound to reveal the truth of the crime, when he forces his family to put the truth into words, he "felt the whole carefully built surface of pretense ring hollow and give way underneath" (383). The moment, ironically, does not set anyone free, for Asa realizes that what the family feels is "fear of the truth, fear of certainty, and, most of all, fear of action" (412). Even when the police are summoned to hear Stanley's confession, they, like the family, prefer not to see reality: by the time they have finished questioning the lovely, helpless Stanley, "the three men had confused Stanley with the dead little girl" (421). The killer becomes the victim, for she so much looks the part.

Symbolically, the death of the little girl may be read as the death of Stanley's innocence, the act that precipitates a general realization that Stanley is no longer a child. Glasgow, however, makes it clear that, while the little girl with the pink flowers can never be resurrected, Stanley's innocence can be restored. If enough people wish for it, blindness can make it so.

The outcome of this encounter with the truth is particularly shocking because Stanley is perhaps the most vicious of the innocents. McDowell calls her the most forceful person in the novel, and the personification of "the forces of death and destruction which Miss Glasgow felt to be at the center of modern life" (219). More than other innocents, Stanley seems directly responsible for much of the chaos around her. She steals her sister's husband, Peter Kingsmill, and then drives him to suicide with her demands. She kills a white child and attempts to frame a poor black boy for the crime. Stanley knows and sees nothing but her own appetites, and in her drive to satisfy them she considers no one but herself.

And yet she is adored by her family and by her lovers, even her ex-lovers. She is the favorite niece of her rich uncle William Fitzroy, who can deny her nothing: expensive schools, European tours, a luxury sports car. Her mother, a sour hypochondriac, lives through her child, "serenely centered in her own egoism, which embraced her dream-life in Stanley" (53). Even her father, who knows what Stanley is, cannot help making excuses for her, for he still sees her as the little girl she once was. Her sister Roy, brighter, morally superior, defers to her power and beauty. And her lovers wait, like helpless adolescents, to be picked or rejected by her. The final move to shield Stanley from the consequences of her crime is, then, consistent with Stanley's relationships to others throughout the novel. She exists to be taken care of, to be indulged, because she represents some universal weakness in the hearts of those around her.

In This Our Life is set in Queenborough, in the same world as *The Sheltered Life*, but the later novel demonstrates that time has only further damaged that world. Now, people can openly admit that "the bottom has dropped out of everything" (44), and everyone is more deeply trapped in a cycle of longing, frustration, and pain.[14] In the Timberlake family, no one has achieved what he wants, but everyone keeps longing and languishing. In the midst of all this surrender to disappointment, Stanley has a terrible energy that sets her apart. She says her generation knows what it wants and believes in "going after it" (96), or else how could anyone get it? It is her only tenet of faith, and she lives by it. Stanley's face is the face of "a disappointed baby"; her mouth "had a trick of never quite closing, and in moments of anger or excitement her thrust-out lower lip would give to her face a vacant and hungry look" (22). Infantile, insatiable, Stanley lives to get what she wants, and what she wants, above all, is the admiration of others, for "she has no real existence apart from her effect on other people" (243).

Her incredible energy is used to bring others to her so that she can define herself by her conquests. In return, her hunger mirrors the endless neediness of her victims. One by one, the inhabitants of Stanley's world betray their own weaknesses as they are drawn by the strength of her demands. Her sensitive father, broken by a life of sacrifice, is bullied by

Stanley as he is bullied by his wife. Her sister Roy, parroting the modern jargon of self-expression and self-fulfillment, allows herself to become her sister's victim. Stanley can exploit Roy because Roy finds her identity in masochism, taking her father's way out of conflict. Uncle William, ridden with cancer and fearful of dying, has lived for money, believing in it because "there was nothing else to believe in" (353). His "gluttonous love" (128) for Stanley, his one extravagance, is worship of another emptiness; he comes to admit that he loved her because 'she was as innocent of moral judgment as she was untroubled by convictions" (177). Stanley's men, Peter Kingsmill and Craig Fleming, share a surface success and charm, but they need something in Stanley that appeals to their worst selves. For Peter, Stanley's attraction is her recklessness, the same recklessness that makes him abandon his wife, spend too much, and drink too much. Craig Fleming, on the other hand, is seduced by Stanley's lack of conviction. The same emptiness that draws Uncle William exerts its power on Craig, the socially conscious lawyer, as well. Given the choice between Stanley and his social ideals, Craig shows where his loyalties lie. Stanley's need for him is far stronger than Craig's principles.

In a book layered with ironies, one of the greatest ironies of all is that the nature of Stanley's relationships ensures that neither she nor those she attracts will ever get what they want. Stanley's mother Lavinia astutely defines the dynamics of each relationship in recognizing that her daughter is "parasitic by nature, and would instinctively cling to the victor" in any conflict (142). Unfortunately for Stanley, *she* is always the victor, and she despises those she conquers. And so she must cast them off, continually seeking the strength she lacks, damned by her weakness, betrayed by her victories. "Stanley, who worshipped power, could never forgive where she dominated" (208).

Her sister, thinking of Stanley's power, asks, "Isn't she what men want her to be?" and affirms that the world where Stanley flourished is a man's world. In that place, Stanley's weakness is her power, for it makes men want to take care of her at the same time that it reflects their own failings. Stanley's father knows that "She would always win in the end ... not through strength, but through some inner weakness, whether her own or another's" (366).

In This Our Life ends with Stanley winning. All around her rally to take care of her; even her discarded lover, Craig Fleming, hastens to her, compelled by Stanley's look of "lost and abandoned innocence" (417). That look, however sullied, continues to empower the child-woman, with a dark power.

Stanley is a very dark version of that first ghost-child, Priscilla, but she is nonetheless her descendant. She shares those negative qualities - passivity, frailty, dependency, vacuity—which, when they appear in an American woman, become positives in male eyes. She, like Priscilla, is a dream-child. As men's dreams darkened, so did the child bride. Thus Stanley and her peers, Undine Spragg, Lita Wyant, Daisy Buchanan, Jenny Archbold, continue to represent men's dreams. They are the girls in a wilder, wider, dream, of endless possession and perpetual pleasure, a dream that very easily slips into a nightmare of unsatisfied, unsatisfiable desire. These later child brides embody the dream gone sour, the awful fate men discover when they wed the Veiled Lady, owning and using her as they use all the things they can buy. Yet, even when men discover this horrid surprise, they cling to their purchase, preferring any dream, even a dark one, to reality.

Chapter Three:
Daughters and Sisters in Love

The strongest guard is placed at the gateway to nothing.... Maybe because the condition of emptiness is too shameful to be divulged.

F. Scott Fitzgerald, *Tender Is the Night* (70)

Section One:
Father/Daughter Incest

The Golden Bowl

The American "love" stories explored so far have all, to a greater or lesser extent, been tales of incest.[1] In the pairing of a dependent and vulnerable girl with a man who will give her protection, moral values, and identity, we see the union of father and child. The disparity in ages of many of the partners—Priscilla and Hollingsworth, Marian Forrester and her captain, Carrie and Hurstwood, Jenny and George Birdsong— underscores the character of the relationships. The innocent girl is bought by a man who is her superior economically, intellectually, or morally. In his new role as parent, the father-lover may become uxorious or neglectful, permissive or stern; he may relish his child's eagerness to please or deplore her recalcitrance. In any case, he is part of a patriarchal relationship, predicated on the dynamics of the trade, where the power to initiate the deal is in male hands.[2] Nowhere is the nature of the relationship more overt than in Henry James's *The Golden Bowl*.

"In this novel," Mary Suzanne Schriber says, "*a priori* ideas of all sorts are not simply exposed; they are overturned" (139).[3] James does indeed turn things upside down in *The Golden Bowl*, for he does not give us a marriage that is incestuous; he presents a father-daughter bond that imitates marriage. In so doing, James slyly exposes the characteristics of the conventional American marriage. The great love story of the novel

111

recounts the all-encompassing love of Maggie and Adam Verver, a tie that marriage, adultery, and physical separation cannot break. As Adam's wife Charlotte says of her stepdaughter, "Maggie thinks more...of fathers than of husbands" (I, 157), and neither marriage nor motherhood elicits the depth of feeling that Maggie lavishes on her father. Even though Maggie has her handsome Prince, she is still truly wed to her father, the King. Her child has a second nursery in Adam Verver's house; her own happiest moments are spent in that realm where "she would still always...be irremediably Maggie Verver" (I, 323), queen of a bigger domain than the Prince can ever provide.

The union of father and daughter is founded in and nourished by innocence; the Prince, about to marry Maggie, characterizes the life of father and child as one of "innocent pleasures, pleasures without penalties" (I, 11). But that innocence is *very* expensive, and its pleasures do not come without consequences. The dazzle of such pleasures is the flash of money; it gives the sheen of the fairy tale to another money story. The King and his princess, for all their glamour, are merely extremely big spenders; their much-vaunted virtues—generosity, tolerance, simplicity—are mainly by-products of the luxury of never having to think about money. When Fanny Assingham extols at length the virtues of Maggie, her husband Bob, the pragmatist, replies, "She's very nice, but she always seems to me more than anything else the young woman who has a million a year" (I, 77). One need not sacrifice niceness for personal gratification, when one is very rich.

But pleasure, innocent pleasure, does not come without penalties. R.W.B. Lewis speaks of the "aggressive innocence" described in *The Golden Bowl*, identifying James as the first American writer to see that "innocence could be cruel as well as vulnerable; that the condition prior to conscience might have insidious undertones of the amoral" (116). The innocence of the Ververs is an evil force.⁴ When Adam Verver uses his millions to buy his child a sanctuary from the world, he fills that world with people he has also bought. Commodifying human beings, Adam and Maggie Verver reduce them to the level of accessories in the fairy tale they substitute for life. Others pay for the Ververs' pleasures, in the degradation and dehumanization that result whenever the Ververs shop.

The so-called goodness of the Ververs is, at best, an absence: a lack of conscious malice, yes, but at worst it is also a lack of awareness of others, of their needs, their fears, their flaws. Maggie, describing her father's style, his "form," explains, "It's his goodness that has brought him out." But the Prince disagrees, countering that "goodness...never brought anyone out. Goodness...rather keeps people *in*" (I, 7). The Ververs' money can buy them all the goodness they desire—innocent pleasures, without ostensible penalties. But such goodness keeps people "in," for it keeps them exactly where they want to be, safe from all human contact except their own incestuous romance. And it imprisons those it pleases them to buy. It traps others in cages made of a cold, hard, unbreakable substance, perhaps the perfect crystal innocence so valued by the Ververs, a crystal dome gilded with money.

James explores the nature of the Ververs and their possessions through metaphor. This is a method that Tony Tanner, in *Adultery and the Novel*, finds appropriate to a modern account of romantic transgression. According to Tanner, adultery not only threatens to break the marital contract, but it imperils the particular economic system that sustains marriage. Tanner makes one further connection, perceiving a systematic interdependence among "rules of marriage, economic rules, and linguistic rules" (85-86).[5] *The Golden Bowl* tells its tale of money and love in metaphor, challenging us to explore the language of image, the linguistic transgression that speaks of both economic and romantic crime. When the Prince and Charlotte sin, their fall poses no real threat to the pseudo-marriages they share with their spouses. Instead, their adultery threatens to break the incestuous bond formed and sustained by all the innocence money can buy. Charlotte and the Prince thus imperil not only a powerful love but the power of money, the power of an entire world of money. In depicting this rebellion, one that affronts the deepest American dreams, James, like the lovers, is subtle. He embeds his tale of incest and adultery in images that connect, very quietly, innocence, imprisonment, deception and control.

The novel is famous for its images of buying. Adam Verver is the great American collector, acquiring treasure to be exhibited in that great museum in American City, "a monument to the religion he wished to propagate, the exemplary passion, the passion for perfection at any price" (I, 146). The goal of opening the doors of his treasure house to the public may be a noble one, provided we can ignore the plundering of continents needed to fill the structure, and the fact that the entire world is, to Adam and Maggie, a museum filled with human plunder. Maggie calls the Prince a part of Adam's collection, "a *morceau de museé*," bought for her (II, 91). And Charlotte rightly identifies her own role as a "remunerated office." Her talent for the "worldly" has been purchased so that the Ververs can retreat further into innocence; Charlotte performs so efficiently that they have "renounced" reality "even more than they had originally intended" (II, 318). All the buying, then, creates and maintains the safe haven, the museum-world of father and child, and strengthens their mutual love. For the Prince is purchased as Adam's "gift" to Maggie, an expression of his love, and Charlotte is selected as a kind of consolation prize for Adam.

The perverse nature of the Ververs' buying is also seen in a small contrast between the parallel "shopping scenes" that involve the golden bowl. When Charlotte tries to buy the bowl, she does so in one last, extravagant act performed for the Prince. She is indiscreet and perhaps even immoral and manipulative in this last declaration of love for Amerigo, a man who is about to marry someone else. But whether she is in fact "Giving myself...away—and perfectly willing to do it for nothing" (I, 98), or making one last attempt to figure in the Prince's life, she is buying for, and giving to, the man who matters most in her life. Years later, when Maggie finds the bowl, she, too, is looking for a special gift for the person she loves most in the world. She is buying a birthday gift for her father.

Adam Verver and his daughter want to buy rare and perfect objects, but perfection implies stasis, even death. There is the chill of death around the Ververs, for all their emotion is lavished on the family romance. Essentially, they are cold and hard as ice. Maggie is like a 'little pointed diamond" (II, 145), glittering, but the color of ice, and the hardest of substances. Her father thinks of her as a statue, one that can move, yes, but that retains "the blurred absent eyes,...the impersonal flit of a creature lost in an alien age" (I, 187), a statue with the qualities of an antiquity. The image underscores both the innocence and the coldness of the "creature."[6] Verver himself is so cold that what he remembers most about his dead wife is her deplorable taste. He is grateful that her demise spared him from "the enormities, the depravities of decoration" of which she was so fond, and enabled him to scale the "vertiginous Peak" (I, 143) of aesthetic excellence.

The most terrifying image of the cold innocence of father and child comes via the Prince, who, as he completes the details of his marriage contract, suddenly remembers the story of Arthur Gordon Pym he had read as a child, when Pym

drifting in a small boat further toward the North Pole...than any one had ever done, found at a given moment before him a thickness of white air that was like a dazzling curtain of light, concealing as darkness conceals, yet of the color of milk or of snow. There were moments when he felt his own boat move upon some such mystery. The state of mind of his new friends...had resemblances to a great white curtain. He had never known curtains but as purple even to blackness—but as producing where they hung a darkness intended and ominous. When they were so disposed as to shelter surprises the surprises were apt to be ominous. (I, 22-23)

The Prince has indeed drifted into a mystery, a region of blankness and ice, where the white curtain conceals things as horrid as any dark one. The thick white air of the Pole, the color of milk, so cold, is like that distant place of wonder that summons Gatsby, and like that place, it is the color of the void. In this image of air, which sustains life, become obstruction, there are hints of living death, and there is also the lure of concealment, the attraction of whatever is behind the white barrier. The explorer longs to penetrate the white curtain, so much like a heavy veil, perhaps a wedding veil. The curtain creates an intended whiteness, a shelter that is as ominous as any dark place. Once behind the curtain, the Prince is forever a prisoner.[7]

The innocence that reduces people to the status of objects diminishes human life as it imprisons and controls. The Ververs' habit of treating people "like works of art," Adelaide Tintner says, ignores certain human needs "which will eventually assert themselves" (250). In the Ververs' world, strong guards protect against such assertion; the museum pieces are, as Adam himself calls them, "fixed" (II, 90). And so the Prince, discussing the details of the marriage contract, associates the moment with "the grimness of a crunched key in the strongest lock that could be made" (I, 5). And so Charlotte describes the serenity of her marriage as entrapment: "I'm...fixed as fast as a pin stuck up to its head in a cushion" (I, 256). When Charlotte and the Prince assert their flawed humanness by committing adultery, Charlotte finds herself caught in a new cage of innocence. Because no one will speak of the sin that preoccupies them all, Charlotte is locked into a "spacious but suspended cage" of "baffled consciousness." And Maggie, "having known delusion," is avenged (II, 229).

Maggie deliberately chose delusion, chose not to see, as a way of life. Charlotte's innocence is imposed on her like a cage. Both kinds of blindness are pernicious, as the imagery of imprisonment makes clear. As Maggie moves toward an unwelcome realization of the truth about her husband, James describes her mind as a locked room full of objects that represent the unanswered questions she fears. "She passed it [the room] when she could without opening the door; then, on occasion, she turned the key to throw in a fresh contribution." By this process, she is "getting things out of the way" (II, 14). The description is strikingly like the famous one of the ivory pagoda, the description that opens Book Two, in which the intruding, inescapable knowledge that is threatening Maggie's routine is described as a strange tall tower rearing itself in her lovely garden. It is a beautiful pagoda, armored in "hard bright porcelain," and Maggie circles it, knocks at it, but cannot figure out how she could enter it, "had she wished" (II, 4). This is another locked enclosure, and to Maggie, it seems to represent the bargain she and her father have struck, the deal by which she "had been able to marry without breaking...with her past" (II, 5). This deal is the contract of incest, that past tie that need not be broken, at which she has never really looked before.

The cold bright pagoda can be many other things. It can be the prison of innocence which the Ververs have created for their spouses, never acknowledging the crime for which they are being punished. Or it may embody the Ververs' own safe haven, the place of blind serenity no longer accessible to the troubled Maggie. The structure may also represent the intimacy building between Charlotte and the Prince, a love which excludes Maggie. The inaccessible and mysterious house is another place like that locked room in Maggie's mind, a place she avoids but which is always *there*. If it, like the locked room, stands for self-deception, it is another image that links innocence to confinement.

With confinement comes control. The Ververs are decidedly in charge. Maggie is the author of her own play, she thinks; the others are her characters (II, 235). But it is really her father who pulls the strings like a puppet-master. In one of the most gruesome images of the book, Adam ties his errant wife to a silken leash, and his power is so great that he can slacken the cord, he need not even twitch it or drag Charlotte, "but she came" (II, 287). The master manipulator of the novel is the funny little man in the straw hat, silent, simple, soft—rich beyond measure, acquisitive beyond imagination. His money makes him so powerful that he need never even state his wishes; his "good" life is an absence, the absence of ever needing to express desire. Adam, not Maggie, is the author of this fictive world because he has bought the setting, the characters, the plot: "Everything that touches you," his daughter acknowledges, "everything that surrounds you, goes on—by your splendid indifference and your incredible permission—at your expense" (II, 267).

Adam's control is described as subtle and covert; it is a "permission," an absence of demands. When his power is used to chastise, it is equally an absence, for Adam and his daughter use denial, repression, and refusal, the tools of deliberate innocence, to punish their spouses. By withholding knowledge from the lovers, the Ververs trap and hold them.

The evasion that supports the Ververs' world also transforms it into a place of deception.[8] One kind of lie is the assumption that what is never confronted is not actually happening, a lie that enables all four main characters to indulge in pleasures seemingly without penalties. It permits the adulterers to commit adultery, as the Prince can pretend that his intimacy with Charlotte is based on the honorable pledge "never consciously to wound" (I, 325). Since consciousness in this milieu is so deliberately restricted, the pledge is fairly easy to uphold. Thus Charlotte can propose that she and the Prince "make the best of our circumstances" because such quiet, hidden activity will allow their mates "the life they prefer" (I, 338). If the adulterers can merely play quietly, they will not disturb the games of the others but will, by their absence, encourage the family love affair.

Adam and Maggie use various forms of deception even more astutely than their partners. They "handle" the adultery without ever once naming it to one another, and the tissue of lies and evasions tightens their emotional connection. One of Maggie's proudest moments occurs when her father tells her he and Charlotte will leave Europe. Maggie exults that her father has thus solved the problem of the adultery, has done it "*all* for her," and that she has made him do it "without naming her husband" (II, 272). In victory, Maggie, more than ever, identifies with her father: "his strength was her strength, her pride was his" (ii, 274-75). Lies and evasions bring both pairs of lovers closer.

On the other hand, deception can be an effective punishment—when deception is in the right hands. When they are crossed, the Ververs know how to use denial of the truth as a weapon. Their method is, appropriately, to manipulate by withholding. They seldom lie outright; they simply deny others knowledge. Thus, Maggie baffles and breaks the Prince by changing her behavior without an explanation, but she never directly tells him what she knows of his transgression. Although the Ververs seldom tell a direct lie, they manipulate those in their power into overt lying. The Prince lies to Charlotte about Maggie's discovery of the adultery and thus severs their illegal tie, doing precisely what the Ververs wish. Charlotte, too, lies, calling the move to American City her idea, again merely acquiescing in what the Ververs have determined. Denied knowledge, the adulterers cannot determine what choices of action are available to them. And so they become afraid, and their fear divides them. Again, absence is the source of the Ververs' power. Fanny Assingham rightly sees that innocence is to be the Prince and Charlotte's nemesis: "They'll be mystified, confounded, tormented. But they won't *know*.... That...will be their punishment" (II, 135).

The greatest lie of all may be Maggie's blithe denial of responsibility for anything that has happened, the ultimate denial of knowledge. Although *The Golden Bowl* is typically read as the story of Maggie's painful entry into the adult world of knowledge, the novel ends in innocence. Maggie, who, we can assume, speaks for herself and her father, refuses to see the Ververs' role in the conflicts that have changed at least two lives. She sees the separation she and Adam have imposed on their spouses as salvation for the Prince and Charlotte; "for them it's just, it's right, it's deserved"; it is a cleansing punishment that saves them from further sin. But for her and her father, "it's only sad and strange and not caused by our fault" (II, 333).

So the novel ends with a retreat into a righteous innocence, a victory of lies. The Ververs remain essentially untouched and unchanged by their own actions and the actions of others, and thus they remain untouchable, inhuman. They have conquered by refusing to see others as persons. The sad farewell of parent and child is played out in front of all their possessions: the antiques Adam has bought for Maggie, and the partners they have acquired. Those partners have been reduced to "the kind of human furniture required aesthetically by such a scene....concrete attestations of a rare power of purchase" (II, 360). Adam's last loving words to his daughter are his highest praise, *"Le compte y est.* You've got some good things" (II, 360).

There is really no sad, strange separation for the father and daughter. Distance will not break this bond, for it is the only connection of which the pair is capable, and it is founded on the most solid of all supports. The father has bought his beloved all the good *things* of the world, and neither parent nor child need ever acknowledge the power of their money to change people into things, into the human furniture of the Verver's museum-life.

The Ververs live behind the white curtain, and, like other curtains, this one shelters surprises. And the surprises, for those who dare to enter the dazzling white region, are apt to be shocks. Explorers of the Ververs' world will be as mystified and horrified as Arthur Gordon Pym, because the icy bond of innocence is as dangerous as any darkness.

Section Two:
From Father to Brother

A Modern Instance

In his limitless power to purchase and control, Adam Verver is a strong father, but in his deliberate refusal of experience and growth, Adam Verver is as much a child as his daughter. Although the parental side of Verver is most apparent because his power dominates the characters and events of the novel, Henry James recognizes the other, infantile side of the man. This aspect of his personality emerges most clearly in Verver's relationship with Maggie, as the two of them "play" at life. Thus James identifies a change in the role of the father: he becomes more of a child by living with one.

In other novels, the father-lover has fallen so far that marriage is transformed into a new type of incestuous relationship—the marriage of brother and sister. Two novels, one published earlier than The *Golden Bowl*, and one later, trace the transformation in more detail, depicting heroes who are both parent and child and exploring the conflicts of the dual roles. William Dean Howells's *A Modern Instance* and F. Scott Fitzgerald's *Tender Is the Night* are transitional novels, describing an intermediate stage in the regression of father to child, a stage when the father begins to fall but is not yet fully a child.

The moral center of A *Modern Instance* is Squire Gaylord, a strong, outspoken, natural leader, a lawyer and thus a defender of those limits set by custom, religion, and reason. The Squire is a respected man in his small Maine community; he could have been a successful politician had he not so vigorously and frequently spoken his mind.

Gaylord is an indulgent and doting father to his child Marcia; he tries to protect her when she falls in love with Bartley Hubbard, a man the Squire feels is unworthy of her. But he has little authority over his impulsive child. After Marcia's marriage to Bartley, the Squire can merely repeat his harsh judgment of the man he considers a scoundrel and try to protect Marcia from the disappointment he foresees. In his old age, the Squire is called to his daughter's aid one last time. When she fights her husband's attempt to divorce her, Marcia calls on her father to speak for her. As her attorney, he defends her honor and her rights as an outraged woman; he is the voice of tradition and authority.[9]

Defending his daughter, he is stricken; as a result of the stroke, he is as helpless as a child. Mercifully, the Squire does not live long in this reduced state.

The death of Squire Gaylord may be read as the end of the old ways in America. With the Squire go honor and reason and integrity. But the Squire's demise may be seen in another light as well. His fall in the courtroom as he battles for his daughter involves a shift in identity. it is the transformation of father into child as he struggles to meet his responsibilities *to* a child.

A *Modern Instance* is not primarily a novel about the Squire, but it is about the transformation he undergoes. The conflict embodied in the Squire's fall is the same conflict experienced by Bartley Hubbard, one of the major characters in the book. He, like the Squire, is required to be a father and degenerates to the level of a child.

A *Modern Instance* is one of the earliest American novels about divorce. George N. Bennett says that, in this novel, Howells developed his perception that the question of divorce "involved the spiritual health of the nation. It was a symptom of a general slackening of the force of religious sanctions" (xv).[10] The world of A *Modern Instance* is a world without religion. There are still churches, but most can only survive by "providing for the social needs of the community" (24). When Marcia

Gaylord Hubbard, the novel's heroine, gives birth to a daughter and decides to choose a church for the baby, she looks for one "where most of the good people belong" (247), so that her child can make the right social contacts. Hardly anyone in the novel possesses any firm religious beliefs; neither of Marcia's parents does, Bartley doesn't, and when Marcia herself is troubled, she considers praying, but "what would be the use?" (93).

Religious commitment demands self-discipline and posits a delayed, uncertain reward at best. Those in the world of *A Modern Instance* want immediate gratification, and so churches, like all other institutions, must be designed to give people what they want.

A theater manager brags that he gives the public "what it wants. I don't pretend to be any better than the public" (267). A newspaper owner, justifying his commitment to making money, compares his paper to a church. No church, he says, can do any good "till it's on a paying basis." A church without cash cannot buy "the best talent for the pulpit or the choir," and so the members feel "discouraged and out of heart" at the inferior entertainment value (194). Conscience has become an outdated concept; now "nobody sins" (261), now "you couldn't get hell-fire—not the pure, old-fashioned brimstone article—out of a popular preacher" (268). Sin doesn't pay because people don't want to hear about it any more. The theater, the press, the church have all become sources of pleasure, not ideas or values. All are reduced to the level of a paying concern.

As religious values disappear, the business ethic permeates everywhere, so that there is a confusion of purpose and role associated with all institutions. The growing faith in money as a means of providing what the individual wants and of assessing the worth of institutions (does the church pay?) is a new, bad religion with many converts.

There are other kinds of bad faith. The times seem to discourage conviction and commitment and to replace them with some form of self-deception, so that the publisher who panders to the lowest public taste can justify his greed, or so the minister without vocation can ignore his emptiness. The most admirable characters of Howells's book are those who do have convictions and faith, even though their beliefs may be unorthodox. Thus the Squire, who professes no religion, is nevertheless a staunch upholder of an ethical system that, ironically, goes back to the Puritans. And Olive Halleck, who rejected the staid, establishment churchgoing of her parents and who rebelled against convention by remaining unmarried, is a strong Unitarian and a perceptive observer of the foolishness around her.

But such characters remain anomalies, surrounded by those who have created religion-substitutes, beliefs that seem to demand less and promise more. The most common of these false systems involves the fantasy romance, the creation of a new religion of love.

In this new religion, love promises a more immediate gratification in an earthly paradise, and the beloved offers entry to that place. The love between the sexes is elevated to an adoration, creating impossible images of the loved one and endless demands on the relationship. And since this new heaven can be attained only through union with the beloved, expectations merely escalate after marriage. Love and marriage have replaced traditional religious beliefs as the primary source of meaning and fulfillment in life, assuming a terrible burden of demands. Howells signals the substitution of love for religious belief in one unmarried character's statement that "Married life is as much a mystery to us outsiders as the life to come.... The ordinary motives don't seem to count; it's the realm of unreason" (287).

Love is elevated to the status of a religious mystery that must be taken on faith, and this faith is never supported by reason. Modern marriage becomes a union of self-deceived, deluded partners, both doomed to be disappointed when their bad faith is tested.

The false conceptions of both male and female damn the marriage from the start. Each husband elevates his bride to the level of sainthood; she is, like the Victorian angel, repository of all virtue, including *his* better nature. As such, she is, of course, charged with keeping him on the straight and narrow; when he strays, she may be blamed. Thus, like a child, the husband is absolved of responsibility for his actions. Or, if the husband so chooses, he may find a woman's virtue a reason to leave her, using her high standards against her. "You're too good for me," the husband may say, as he bids farewell to the model wife.

Paradoxically, the sainted wife is also considered a child in need of protection; if she is a monitoring angel, she is a very young one. The wife is both archangel, fighting for her husband's soul against the temptations of the world, and cherub, too sweet to know the world. The conflicting roles make the wife at once demanding and dependent, adoring and reproving.

Her roles and behavior are the obverse of those assigned to the male in this religion of love. Schriber rightly notes that Howells links the culture's gender expectations to the decline in religious values. In the conventional marriage, wives were to be subject to their husbands, who were to be subject to God. But in this new world, where religion is dying, Schriber says, "belief in God is no longer a viable force. Therefore a husband does not simply speak for God; he *is* God" (102-03).

As God, the husband is morally superior even to his angelic wife, but the adoration of the male has the somewhat unexpected effect of reducing him to child status. The watchful wife is expected to monitor the behavior of her spouse, so that he is forever true to the god in him. But her continuous adoration tends to dilute her disciplinary powers. That is, such worship encourages the wife to excuse or ignore her husband's misbehavior, so that, like a child, the husband need never become responsible. If the wife attributes her husband's failings to her own inability to fulfill her role, he is further absolved and further diminished.

On the other hand, if the wife holds her man to the standards of a god, if she insists that he meet these impossible demands, the woman will be confronted with rebellion. The rebellion is apt to be immature, the act of a stubborn child whose will has been thwarted.

The fantasy romance, then, results in the wedding of two partners, both of whom seek a parent and resent the demands of adult life. The bride, denied a Father in heaven, wants paradise on earth with a flawless mate, one who can master the world and shield her from it. The husband, having dreamed of the pristine child on the pedestal, secretly wants that child to indulge, excuse and approve of him as a doting mother would. Both husband and wife seek, in marriage, an unconditional, exclusive, endless love. Since even the strongest and most deeply desired self-deception cannot sustain this fantasy for long, the partners are doomed to disappointment. And since it was a marriage founded not on religious truth but on bad faith, the tie is easy to break. Thus, *A Modern Instance* is a novel about marriage—and divorce.

"I've thought a great deal about it, and I think my worst trouble is that I've been left too free in everything," says the wife in this marriage, Marcia. "I've never had anyone to control me, and now I can't control myself at the very times when I need to do it the most.... And Bartley is just so, too" (253). Marcia has had a strong father, but he has left her to her whims. And Bartley, her husband, never had a father. An orphan, he learned to manipulate his dependence and his charm to get whatever he wanted. The lack of inner discipline that results from the lack of external control freezes the couple in childhood.[11] Marcia is the traditional child bride. "Sometimes she *scares* me with her innocence," says Olive Halleck (356), for she is utterly blind to what she does not want to see. And she refuses to see the flaws in Bartley, a good-natured opportunist "with no more moral nature than a baseball," his rival for Marcia's affections, Ben Halleck, claims (213). During their courtship, Marcia adores her man, simultaneously assigning him the role of the new god and damning him with its expectations: "I care for you because you know a great deal more than I do, and because I respect you. I know that everybody expects you to be something great, and I do too" (44). Bartley sees only the flattery and not the implied demand in Marcia's declaration; as the Squire notes, "her adoration flatters his self-love to the same passionate intensity...of her worship" (55). And so, Bartley, too, converts to the new religion of love, paying homage to his beloved, canonizing her: "your influence upon me has been ennobling and elevating" (15). Yet Bartley retains his allegiance to another faith, the business ethic.[12] Even as he enjoys Marcia's praises, he considers the relationship a deal, one in which he has the upper hand, for he has not said "a word ...that anyone could hold him to" (19). He can break the contract without penalty, for he has never made a firm offer of marriage.

Love and money combine again when the pair, only recently separated by Bartley's flirtation and Marcia's jealousy, suddenly decide to elope. The minister they summon at night, dazed by the peremptoriness of their demand, feels "as if there were something else" that should be in the ceremony, but he cannot think what it is. Perhaps, Bartley suggests, it is cash, and he hands the still-perplexed reverend a five-dollar bill (133).

The wedding night hints at what might truly be missing: adult partners. Bartley fondly calls Marcia a child and pledges to try never to betray her childlike trust. As he thus assumes the parental role, he assigns a similar one to Marcia, warning her, "if you want me to be good, you must be kind" (37). Bartley wants to be the spoiled, petted darling Marcia was when her father raised her. Marcia expects Bartley to be like the Squire, only better. Living "in him and for him" (208),

Marcia looks to Bartley for vindication of the most important choice of her life. Only by Bartley's enormous success can Marcia disprove the Squire's suspicions of her husband.

Like the children they are, Marcia and Bartley live irresponsibly, a fact made most evident in their response to the family finances. When Bartley, a journalist, fails to become the good provider Marcia expected, she becomes frightened of not having enough income. She reacts with economies that were "frantic child's plays—methodless, inexperienced, fitful." These are soon followed by remorse at her implied judgment of Bartley's inadequacy and by a renewed commitment to Bartley, when she abets him "in some wanton excess" of expenditure (188).[13]

Love turns suffocating for Bartley and bitter for Marcia. Feeling trapped by Marcia's obsessive jealousy and bored by domestic bliss, Bartley begins to drink and gamble, to avoid going home. Money creates different problems. Bartley's deepest allegiance, to the values of the marketplace, emerges when he joins the staff of a purely-for-profit newspaper and sells a friend's stories as his own.[14] Marcia, the idealist, is forced to recognize Bartley's corruption. As the marriage decays, it becomes more like a corporate merger. Marcia's outbursts and tears are replaced by silence; "there was now what might be called a perfect business amity between them" (330).

Neither partner, however, has relinquished the fantasy romance. Each uses it as a weapon against the other. Bartley, deprived of the glow of Marcia's approval now that he can no longer meet her standards, realizes he really doesn't feel the loss. He is prosperous and successful and feels little desire to change. Instead, he excuses his betrayal of Marcia's ideals by declaring them impossible to meet. Remembering her loyalty to his best interests, he is amused when he realizes "he himself preferred his second-best interests" (332). Marcia, the bride he placed on the pedestal, is *too* good. Her devotion brings rather irritating exactions. She fulfills her role too well to suit her husband.

Rather than criticize her own dream of love, Marcia retreats within it. Having begun by worshipping an illusion rather than loving a man, Marcia prefers to cling to the fantasy that defines her. Although she knows that Bartley is "not her young dream of him," she feels she cannot "forgo that dream and live." Rationalizing that perhaps her unkindness has made Bartley misbehave, she vows that "hereafter, no matter what happened, she must show perfect faith in him by perfect patience" (341).

As Schriber says, "Marcia's burden of responsibility for Bartley's conduct reaches masochistic proportions" (102).

Bartley finds it hard to live with a sainted woman who treats him like a precious but errant child. His desertion of Marcia is a child's whim, a half-hearted "running away from home" that, almost accidentally, becomes the real thing. Bartley just gets on a train one day, thinking about not coming back. Only when he loses his wallet on the trip does Bartley consciously decide to leave his wife. Having lost money loaned to him by a friend and having quarreled with Marcia, Bartley finds it less complicated to leave than to confront the problems waiting at home.

Howells's original title for this novel was *The New Medea* (Bennett xi), and Marcia, the woman abandoned, becomes terrible in her revenge. Her vengeance is a constant love, a perversity of illusion. She simply refuses to accept the fact of her abandonment; Bartley, she asserts, must have been taken ill, perhaps he has suffered a loss of memory; at any rate, he will come back. Marcia refuses to leave her home because it must be forever accessible to the returning husband. That house becomes a shrine to Bartley, now canonized in Marcia's memory. There is a fury of self-deception in Marcia's actions, a lying so blatant and so fierce it frightens observers like Olive Halleck: "She's so undisciplined, that she couldn't get any good out of her misfortunes—she's only got harm; they've made her selfish" (401). Because Marcia's sense of self is so dependent on her fantasy,[15] she must cling to that dream, even when her motive is hatred instead of love.

Notice of Bartley's intent to divorce Marcia, on the grounds of her desertion of him, merely stresses the facility for lying the partners share. Bartley, established in the Midwest, thinks the newspaper announcement, a legal formality, a safe if blatant lie. He never expects Marcia, back in Boston, to see it. But she does. And, seeing only what she wants to see, she perceives the notice as further evidence that Bartley has lost his reason and truly feels abandoned by his loving wife. Her anger and her obsessive jealousy are disguised as beatific concern as she rushes to her husband's side to contest the divorce, to "save" him. She is accompanied by her father, who, Eakin says, perceives himself as "an angel of retribution" waging a "holy war" against the villainous husband (114-15). Marcia, even when she is abandoned by her husband, is never without at least one protector.

One of the bitterest ironies of this novel is that the more disagreeable the main characters become, the more beloved they become to certain others. Thus, Bartley's callous desertion of his wife provokes her crazed adoration. Similarly, the more obsessive Marcia becomes, the more she is worshipped by her long-standing admirer, Ben Halleck.

Halleck figures significantly in the plot when Bartley runs away from the divorce hearing and is later killed by an irate reader of the newspaper he has established, in a town aptly named Whited Sepulchre. Marcia is finally available to the man who is as fixated on her as she has been on Bartley. Halleck, an idealized version of Bartley, longs to be Marcia's protector. As a longtime witness to Marcia's frenzied fidelity to her husband, Halleck wants that worshipful gaze directed his way.

Although some readers perceive a curious similarity between Ben Halleck and Bartley Hubbard,[16] there is also a similarity between Halleck and Marcia. They are linked in their devotion to the fantasy romance.

When Bartley was alive, Halleck was so tormented by his love for the married Marcia that it broke him. The temptation to adultery so frightened him that he ran away to South America. He returns, beaten by an obsession he could not conquer, without hope, without faith, without commitment to a career. He enters the ministry not out of conviction but in despair. As the novel ends, Halleck is contemplating marriage to the woman he has deified, and the pattern of the fantasy romance is about to begin again.

The new father—of the church and quite possibly of Marcia—is an empty, weak man, believing in one thing: female innocence. The projected marriage of Halleck and the widowed Marcia represents the diminished nature of both father and child. Halleck is a man of the church defeated by his adulterous longings, but, even more significant, he is an adult reduced to childish dependence by his deluded love for a child. In the final pages of the novel, Eakin says, "The twin flames, domestic and religious, on the altars of New England have burned out."[17] The new marriage promises to be another modern instance of self-deception and discontent.

Tender Is the Night

When Dick Diver, hero of this novel, is about to begin his career as a psychiatrist, he is a divided man. He wants to be the greatest psychiatrist that ever lived, but he disdains the slow, plodding progress of his friend Franz Gregorovius. During World War I and immediately after, Dick has seen that there may be another, more exciting way to get what he wants. He has observed the effect of his charm on others and he has been privy to the "American splendor" (133) of postwar celebration and lavish spending. Although he finds the one world superficial, he finds the other dull. And so he lies awake at night, planning an alternate role for himself, tormented by the question, "God, am I like the rest after all?" (133).

It does not matter whether Dick most wants to dissociate himself from the shallow or from the slow. What matters is that he badly wants to be different. The question that keeps him awake in these early years haunts him throughout his later ones. And the conclusive answer to this question is, "Yes." Dick Diver *is* like the rest, after all.

Even more than he wants to be loved, Dick wants to be superior. He seeks a moral, psychological, and intellectual advantage over those around him. In so doing, he assumes three paternal roles: as a priest, as a father/lover, as a doctor. He sees himself as a source of values, direction, and healing. In each role, Dick seeks to be loved not as an equal but as a benevolent, godlike figure.

Tender Is the Night demonstrates that Dick is not truly above the others in any of these roles. He is a failed priest of the new religion of pleasure. He is a doctor tainted by his own desires. And Dick is a child, arrested in his own development by his own choices, choices that reveal that what Dick wants is very much like what the rest want, that he is, after all, not so very different.

The point is demonstrated repeatedly in a series of reverberations and reversals throughout the novel. *Tender Is the Night* is a rich, textured book in which images multiply and echo and reappear, and the traits of one character are replicated in another, or in several others. There are mirror images and doublings and triplings, and images that cluster around these multiplications in significant ways. And at the center of all the rippling of image and character is Dick Diver, master manipulator of image and role.

The reversals that fill the book also center on Dick. In this novel almost all relationships are some version of a parent-child configuration: Rosemary and her mother, Abe and Mary North, Devereaux Warren and Nicole, Rosemary and Dick, Nicole and Dick. The plot of the novel begins in an incestuous parent-child relationship, and then the incestuous tie is itself reversed, so that Nicole, victim of one parent, becomes, ostensibly, the victimizer of the man who serves as her surrogate father. And yet that reversal is repeatedly reversed, so that we are never sure exactly who is parent to whom, and we begin to understand that Dick Diver is as much a child as a parent.

Dick's childish innocence is an outgrowth of his need to be superior. This need is so extreme that Dick lives in fear of challenge to his authority and designs his life so that he need never take risks. Afraid of the threat to his stature that marriage to an adult would entail, he marries a child he thinks he can control.[18] When the child bride proves unsatisfying, he chooses another child as his mistress. And, because it is easier to feel superior there, Dick chooses to live among the rich, in their infantile world, the "psychological Eden" of the expatriates.[19] Avoiding the risks that all adult relationships pose, Dick chooses to remain a child.[20] He is only a pseudo-father. Defining himself by the approval of those he pretends to despise, Dick uses their neediness to fill his own needs.

The women in this novel come in for a great deal of open hostility and contempt. Dick, for example, consigns responsibility for the decline of the West to the American woman, who had "broken the moral back of a race and made a nursery out of a continent" (232). The women are at the center of this empty place, but it is not so certain that they created it. If we consider the pattern of images and the multiplication of character traits in the novel, we discover a subtle balancing of the indictment, another complex reversal in which many share the responsibility for this creation.

The setting of the novel is indeed a nursery run by children, a chaos. All distinctions of custom and gentility have been discarded, a point implied by Tommy Barban's horrified recitation of the guest list of the Hotel Palace in Vevey. Tommy himself, with his perpetual look of faint disgust and his inability to endure boredom, is the typical spoiled and dissatisfied child of his milieu. Childish misbehavior characterizes those within and outside the Diver set, but this is behavior with a cruel and violent edge to it, so that within the early pages of the novel the nursery world is disrupted by a duel, by Nicole's breakdown, by a murder precipitated by a racist prank, and by another murder, a crime of passion. With his boredom and with his solution to boredom—killing for pay—Tommy Barban truly represents both sides of this society.

Of course, the true emblems of this world are the twins of innocence, Nicole Diver and Rosemary Hoyt.[21] Nicole is the typically blind child; her eyes do not see her rival, either on the beach (6), or in Cannes (14). Her delicate mouth is "expectantly half open to the world" (67), hungry for what no man can give. She is the child bride who cannot grow up to be a mother; thus she bears and rears two "guided orphans" (180). Rosemary is "Daddy's Girl," the child star. On screen, she is utterly lovely but has an "empty harlot's mind" (89). Her body is her fortune, for it offers the promise of innocence, "calculated to a millimeter to suggest a bud but yet guarantee a flower" (104).

Together, the two women represent America's desires. Rosemary acts out society's fantasies of beauty, glamour and love; Nicole lives them. And together, the women represent the dream as nightmare.

They are women of destruction. Rosemary's role as Daddy's girl shows her to be the child of chaos: "Before her tiny fist...the very march of destiny stopped; inevitable became evitable, syllogism, dialectic, all rationality fell away" (89). Nicole is the child as consumer, and her consumption buys cataclysms. Behind her reckless spending is a whole world of misery and exploitation; before her, "the whole system swayed" (55) and her face glows in the inferno of her buying. Nicole can buy anything, even a doctor, and Rosemary tries to imitate her.

Nicole and Rosemary are also the golden girls of incest. Nicole is the victim of her father's lust; Rosemary, in her popular movie, enacts a sanitized and sentimentalized version of the same lust. Dick's women both have three lovers: the father-seducer of reality or film, from whom Dick appropriates them; Dick himself, the father-substitute; and the dark and unworthy rival to Dick (Tommy Barban or Nicotera), each representing Dick's fear of losing control of his woman.

The corruption that shadows Nicole and Rosemary mirrors the sickness of a whole society. Sexuality, for example, is often tainted by its association with the sale of the body. The initial scene of Nicole's adultery is played out against a backdrop of prostitutes and their sailor lovers, so that Nicole becomes another whore with her soldier. Then there is the casual polygamy of Hossain (Mary North's second husband), who "buys" her with his endless riches so that she becomes another whore, who then amuses herself buying prostitutes, replicating her husband's purchase in her disguise as a male. The illness of society, whether it is sexual, spiritual, or psychological, is not limited to the clinics and asylums that fill the novel, for the parents who send their troubled children to such places are sicker than their own children, and the best hotels are filled with rich ruins, drugged nobility listening eternally to "the coarse melodies of old sins" (248).

Here is a world that needs a doctor to cure its ills, a priest to restore lost values, a father to impose order in the nursery. But Dick cannot meet these demands. He is infected with the same disease that weakens all around him, an addiction to the easy life, the good time, the perpetual playtime. His delusion is that, in living with children, he can remain distanced and superior. But by marrying a child, he demonstrates that what his heart most values is an emptiness that matches his own.[22]

In all his actions, Dick evidences a need to distance himself from what he pretends to despise and yet secretly needs. He is repeatedly caught between his own assumption of moral superiority and a deeper self-hatred that threatens the superior stance. He prefers to live in a nursery world because he feels he can control it. Within that world, however, he is as much a conformist as a controller. As a doctor, he is famous for his ability to simplify, not to innovate. His claim to fame is a little book called A *Psychology for Psychologists*, and a psychologist warns him that "Soon you will be writing little books called 'Deep Thoughts for the Layman,' so simplified that they are practically guaranteed not to cause thinking" (138). His talent, then, is for reduction, for the adaptation of ideas to suit the audience. His dream is to establish a center for billionaires whose money can protect them from all the discomfort of difficult ideas. Thus Dick's success will be measured by his ability to satisfy the very rich; he will depend on them to validate his efforts. Long before he meets Nicole, Dick is planning to let the rich buy themselves a doctor.

Dick controls through others' weaknesses, not through his own strength. Lacking the power of great wealth, Dick seeks other means of domination, and, like everyone else, he envisions human relationships as some version of a trade. Whether he is playing doctor or lover, he offers the security of parental love in return for childlike submission. He is drawn to those who are vulnerable or maimed, yet they mirror his own dependency and need. More than once, he finds some version of love in a clinic: he is strangely attracted to a woman severely disfigured by eczema, he casually kisses the daughter of a patient. And, of course, he makes his former patient his wife.

Ostensibly, Dick's marriage fails because he cannot reconcile Nicole's demands that be both doctor and husband, that he be, therefore, a *very* powerful father. On the other hand, it is quite possible that the lure of such power is what attracted Dick to Nicole in the first place.

Even if we assume that Nicole's money bought Dick, that the Warren millions devoured a sensitive and intelligent man who was no match for such financial control, we cannot explain away the fact that, when Dick is not under the influence of so much cash and can choose nearly anyone as his mistress, he chooses a replica of his wife. Rosemary is a less threatening, and therefore perhaps more desirable, version of Dick's wife. Possibly, as John F. Callahan says, Dick seeks in Rosemary a more pristine innocence than was available in Nicole (123). A Hollywood imitation of Nicole, Rosemary is younger and less sophisticated, and therefore more vulnerable to Dick's charms. Although she is a celebrity, she is not rich and thus is not terribly powerful. It is particularly revealing that, when Dick chooses a lover, he chooses one as vapid and vacuous as Rosemary, truly a cheap copy of his wife, who is already a diminished and damaged person. But in selecting a mistress whose idea of an intellectual is a Hollywood director, Dick can most certainly feel superior. He can feel he is "taking" her rather than being "taken." With her, he can play the lover, father, and doctor roles again—only better. "I'm going to save your reason," are his first words to Rosemary as he offers her a hat to protect her from the sun (28). From the beginning of this romance, Dick reprises the roles that worked so well with Nicole and then proved so disappointing. Unfortunately, the revival of an old performance does nothing to improve it.

In both relationships, Dick and Nicole's and Dick and Rosemary's, there are reversals of the parent/child paradigm that hint at Dick's dependence on what he supposedly dominates. In both cases, the reversals also create a kind of twinning of the lovers. Although there are repeated descriptions of Nicole as parasite, there is one curious commentary on the nature of her relationship to Dick. When she begins to assert herself and question Dick's authority, the change is described as follows:

the long years of sheer being had had an enlivening effect on the parts of her nature that early illness had killed, that Dick had not reached—through no fault of his own but simply because no one nature can extend entirely inside another. (280)

The puzzle of this description is that it may be read so that Dick is the parasite, a kind of evil embryo growing inside Nicole, blotting her out, so that she becomes the larger, nurturing vessel and he the child. A similar ambiguity concerns the explanation of Dick's fall; his destruction is a consequence of his having "chosen Ophelia," of selecting and drinking a sweet poison (302). The obvious connection here is to the love of a mad girl, but Ophelia descended into madness and death because of Hamlet's rejection of her. Is Nicole, then, an Ophelia with power? Nicole demonstrates the power of a parent when Dick's charisma begins to fade and his self-hatred becomes more blatant. Reacting to Dick's episodes of drunken misbehavior and bravado, Nicole "indulged him as she might have indulged Lanier [her son]" (280).

Obviously, Dick needs his child-wife; he feeds on her, whether the sustenance is or is not a sweet poison. Similarly, the attraction of Daddy for his new girl evolves into a reversal of dependency when Dick falls in love with Rosemary. By the time the affair is finally consummated, Dick needs Rosemary to shore up his eroding self-esteem. Dick's choices of wife and mistress reveal him. As each relationship develops, Dick is exposed as dependent and desperate.

The fact that both Dick's romances are models of incest helps explain these power shifts. The father in such relationships needs his child; he cannot find what he wants in a connection to an adult, for he is unsure of his own status. Ironically, the shameful nature of the relationship reduces the father, so that both Nicole and Rosemary become Dick's doubles, reflectors of his own dependence. And, as the father-seducer, Dick is like the sinister and pathetic Devereaux Warren. Fitzgerald's description of this man foreshadows what Dick is to become at forty: "strikingly handsome," "a fine American type in every way," with a "special air about him of having known the best of this world" and "whiskey on his breath" (125).

As much as anyone in this novel, Dick is part of a world where there is something wrong with the sexual relationships. This point is made repeatedly, through the imagery, from the opening scene where Dick clowns in black lace drawers, to the scene of Dick's arrest in Rome, where he is mistaken for the rapist/murderer of a five-year-old. Most typically, Dick is linked to a love of children, to the "ickle durls" who distract him when he talks clinic business with Franz and whom Nicole teases him about (172). Dick associates sex with childish behavior. Rebuffed in an attempted flirtation, Dick can only think that "Strange children should smile at each other and say, 'Let's play' " (202). In a nursery world, children play at sex.

Dick is not a particularly successful parent in his role as spiritual father, either. Perhaps he is too demanding of the congregation, for he requires total faith in his power to create an "amusing world." If anyone begins to doubt the creation, to see the magic as a magic trick, Dick "evaporated before their eyes" (28). As the priest of pleasure, Dick's power is mainly to diminish, even eradicate, and to conceal the loss with empty ritual. Only Dick can reduce a World War I battlefield to an amusement like "one of his own parties" (59)[23] while simultaneously mourning the loss of traditional values. If Dick is a priest, he is a priest in one of Howells's new American churches designed to give the people what they want. Although Dick thinks he is teaching the rich the ABCs of morality, he is in fact learning from them. He must learn what they want so that he can supply it, for he needs their approval, their friendship, their love. Just as he feeds on Nicole, he feeds on this entire world of wealth.

And so Dick has another double, the seedy American veteran Dick meets on the Paris streets, making a profit off rich expatriates, dreaming of being an actor. Dick is at once salesman, con-man, actor.[24] He is, in fact, mistaken for an actor on the set of Rosemary's movie, and she is right to offer him a screen test. Dick's ceremonies of serenity, his superior rituals, the cleansing of the beach, the blessing of the beach, the elegant and understated parties, are all performances. And all are designed to act out a falsehood, to give meaning to the meaningless.

Moreover, Dick can design scenes as well as scenarios. His insane asylum looks like a country club; his lush Riviera house, like a string of peasant farms. Simplicity and serenity cost a great deal to manufacture, and so Dick, the master illusionist, is a good man to have around. He can restore a mad, violated girl to innocence. He can make empty lives into seemingly full ones merely by imposing a nursery-like regimen and routine: the sun, the swim, the taking of the meal. Even the writing of a check can become a lovely little ritual, a way to stave off the empty minutes. Dick can sell the rich a spurious peace and bring the appearance of order to their lives.

The greatest victim of Dick's con games is Dick himself. He must continually assert his superiority and seek external sources of his failure because to look within would be so terrifying. When he arrogantly blesses the beach as he takes leave of the Riviera, his gesture is the blind and bitter statement of a man who has not looked inside. He has denied the truth of Mary North's final advice: "All people want is to have a good time and if you make them unhappy you cut yourself off from nourishment" (313). It is easy for Dick to accept her words as an indictment of others, but he does not see that he has been feeding on the very people he despises.

Dick, like his wife, is a consumer. Even if he can think of Rosemary as a drug, as "blinding belladona...caffeine....mandragora" (164), and Nicole as a sweet poison, he will not see that they have been his drugs of choice. He has lived on the hedonism around him, feeding his own insatiable hungers. He has drawn his strength from the sad sick world of perpetual innocence, but he cannot accept that he has become a part of it. By looking to children for the nourishment he craves, he has demonstrated that he is like all the rest—just another child, after all.

Section Three:
Sibling Sweethearts

The Age of Innocence
From the beginning, the child-heroine subverts the patriarchal power of her lover, if only because, like Priscilla, her dependency saps men's strength, and her emptiness reflects a larger cultural void. As differing versions of the child bride appear in Priscilla's successors, patriarchal power diminishes further, and the heroine of the modern American novel appears to be more a threat to her lover. Thus, as the father falls, it seems as if the child rises.

Those who study the interrelationships of history and literature frequently make such a connection. Kate Millet, for example, links twentieth century literature's frequent expressions of hostility between the sexes to the "animus toward women which their gains in this century have provoked from jealous patriarchal sentiment" (336). Similarly, Sandra Gilbert and Susan Gubar note that in the modern period the rise of women helped to weaken "the ideological and theological underpinnings of the patriarchal culture" (*War* 89),[25] at least in part attributing man's fall to woman's rise. But even if we acknowledge woman's political gains in this century, we must consider her status (and man's) in terms of economic as well as political change, and we must look at those representative novels produced during the time of change for depictions of the change.

The three novels which most explicitly describe the lover of the child bride as a child himself are all products of the 1920s, a time of political change for women. None of these novels contrast the fall of man with a concurrent rise for woman. Even though one of these books, *The Age of Innocence*, is set in an earlier historical period, it can reasonably be expected to reflect at least some of the spirit of the age in which it was written. And it does. All three representative novels, *The Age of Innocence*, *The Beautiful and* Damned, and *An American Tragedy*, depict both partners in romance as children, dependent on their culture for their values and their personal validation. In these books, there has indeed been a redirection of power, but it has not been in the direction of women. Power has shifted, instead, to a new father.

The novels were published at a time when the American economy most noticeably shifted from being production-oriented to being consumption-oriented.[26] As mass production fostered by new technology eliminated the small merchant, the independent farmer, and the craftsman, and as it replaced them with the corporation, the agribusiness conglomerate, and the assembly line, there was a shift in power—from the many to the few. The average man could no longer claim an identity based on his ability to produce, for in his new role on the assembly line or in his corporate cubicle, he was rarely linked to a completed or tangible product. Male identity was now derived vicariously, from affiliation with an employer, the huge, impersonal, unseen but omnipotent father.

An economy based on mass production of commodities to be consumed immediately can best be sustained by people trained to remain children. If an entire culture is to want what others want, to want it now, and then to be almost instantly dissatisfied, it must be an infantile culture. As Lasch says, a culture organized around mass consumption makes people "weak and dependent":

It undermines their confidence in their capacity to understand and shape the world and to provide for their own needs. The consumer feels that he lives in a world that defies practical understanding and control, a world of giant bureaucracies, "information overload," and complex, interlocking technological systems vulnerable to sudden breakdown. (33)

The power is elsewhere, out of man's control, in the hands of the new patriarchs, those enormous and remote sources of control which cannot be challenged and cannot be understood. In his relation to this power, man is doubly reduced. As Lasch says, "The social arrangements that support a system of mass production and mass consumption tend to discourage initiative and self-reliance and to promote dependence, passivity, and a spectatorial state of mind both at work and at play" (27). The reward for work is no longer a feeling of accomplishment earned through an exercise of discipline, creativity, or skill. The reward is, simply, the money that can give man the only identity still open to him: that of the consumer. Lasch says that in the twentieth century culture of mass consumption the individual regresses to the oral stage of childhood, when the child is utterly dependent on the breast (34). Rather, it is that stage of childhood where women have been for years— dependent not on a nurturing mother but on a great, controlling father whose approval brings identity and whose largesse brings the gratification of consumption.

If we consider the economic power shifts of the modern age, we can perhaps better understand the loss of power within modern romance. It may be that male power has not been allocated to women. Women may not be getting stronger; men may simply be getting weaker as their patriarchal role within the nuclear family is appropriated by the money powers of the corporate state. Women seem more subversive of male power because there is so little of it left within the family—only the power to buy things that never seem to satisfy.

If we consider those novels that trace the transition of man from father to child, we can see the increasing emphasis on consumption and the disappearance of meaningful work. Thus, we can see the marriage of Marcia and Bartley Hubbard jeopardized by their reckless spending and by Bartley's preference for easy money, however dubiously acquired, over honest work. We can trace the disintegration of Dick Diver's personality as he abandons the discipline of study and work and assumes the role of big spender. We perceive that all those caught in the crystal cage of *The Golden* Bowl exist to buy or to be bought. American City is to be a monument to consumption, a place where the things that money can buy are to be exhibited for the edification of less powerful consumers. Even the princesses of great wealth, Maggie Verver and Nicole Warren, are princesses, not queens, vicarious spenders of male fortunes, of the father-King's bounty. There are no women at the top of the pyramid. Males still occupy the peak. There are merely fewer of them.

As the money power becomes more concentrated and inaccessible, the more typical male role is thus a duplicate of the female one: the child role. The union of the sexes in *The Age of Innocence*, *The Beautiful and Damned* and *An American Tragedy* reflects the change in male status by depicting romance as the love of two children, brother and sister in their shared immaturity. If there is a father, he is a distant power—an old man like Mr. van der Luyden, the power of convention and old money in *The Age of Innocence*, the wealthy grandfather Patch of *The Beautiful and Damned,* or industrial founding fathers like Mr. Griffiths and Mr. Finchley in *An American Tragedy*. These old men, remote as gods, are the true fathers of entire societies, whether the place is old New York or Lycurgus, New York.

Although *The Age of Innocence* is set in the New York City of the 1870s, it may be read as a study of the kind of child lovers that populate a later time. The novel anticipates the themes and conflicts of the modern period because it is about old New York, a group that, earlier than any other group, possessed the means to live like children. The upper class of the novel does not have to work, and in its preoccupation with pleasure and its fear of unpleasantness, it establishes values that will later be adopted by classes below. As Thorstein Veblen says, the effect of such a class upon the community "is of the nature of an arrested spiritual development" (213), and that effect will spread as each lower class appropriates the morality and behavior of the rich. That Wharton was aware of these shared values (or vices) is apparent by her employment of the same triangular conflict pitting innocence against maturity in a novel set in pre-World War I Europe, *The Reef,* one set in the Jazz Age, *The Children,* and in her famous portrait of old New York, *The Age of Innocence*.[27] In all three novels, it is a conflict embodied in a little fairy tale Wharton wrote very early in her career, a story called "The Valley of Childish Things." The story is about a little girl who grew up in this valley, playing a number of delightful games with her peers, but who decides to leave the valley to see something of the world. None of the other children want to leave their games, so she goes alone.

Her travels bring her hardship and pain, but the little girl learns a great deal and "in so doing grew to be a woman." One day she decides to leave the bleak, cold land of her apprenticeship and return to the Valley of Childish Things, to work with her old companions. On her difficult journey back, she meets a man who helps her over the roughest places. She recognizes him as one of her former playmates, once a very dull boy, but now an engineer with great dreams of improving the Valley. As the woman and her fellow traveler share their ambitions, she is encouraged, for if "he has grown into such a fine fellow, what splendid men and women" her other playmates must be.

Unfortunately, her expectations are all disappointed, for upon returning to the Valley, she discovers that her former playmates have "remained little children," "playing the same old games," or pretending to work at such tasks as "building mudpies and sailing paper boats." At first, the children seem happy to have her back, but soon she realizes that "her presence interfered with their games." They are not interested in her stories of the world beyond the Valley.

As for her fellow traveler, he has found "a dear little girl" to worship and to play with. When the woman asks him if he would like to join her in the work of improving the Valley, he replies that he is much too busy. And, comparing the woman's weatherbeaten face with the soft skin of his new beloved, he adds, "Really, my dear, you ought to have taken better care of your complexion" ("Valley" 58-59).

This little parable outlines the story of Ellen Olenska, the woman; May Welland, the little girl; and Newland Archer, the man caught between them, in The *Age of Innocence*. It is an outline of the conflicts of *The Reef* and *The Children* as well, but since *The Age of Innocence* gives the most detailed indictment of innocence, it is the most relevant here. It defines innocence and its effects in describing the courtship and marriage of Archer and May. And it most obviously damns innocence by contrasting it with the maturity of the woman who has moved beyond the child-world, Ellen Olenska.

Ellen Olenska functions as an alternative way of seeing and of being, and she is thus a threat to innocence. Her subversive role as an intruder in this child's paradise will be discussed later. The love affair of Archer and May, however, provides the most openly critical description of innocence in American literature, as that innocence forms—and deforms—a male.

The Valley of Childish Things that is old New York is a money world. Old money built this place, where unpleasant reality may not trespass, and parvenue money buys entry into the region. Old New York is composed of "two great fundamental groups" of consumers: one, the Mingott and Manson branch, cares about "eating and clothes and money"; the other, the Archer-Newland-van der Luyden set, is dedicated to "travel, horticulture, and the best fiction" and scorns "the grosser forms of pleasure" (Wharton, *Age of Innocence* 34). The Invader group, with its new money, is initially rebuffed, but when the new rich like Julius Beaufort and Mrs. Lemuel Struthers can supply enough money to provide better entertainments, they penetrate the enclave. Very little work is done in this world; Newland Archer, for example, is a lawyer, but his profession occupies very little of his time. When a writer friend suggests that Archer find meaning and purpose by entering politics, Archer must decline, for gentlemen do not do such things; "decent people had to fall back on sport or culture" (126). Even those activities, taken seriously, can prove suspect; a member of the old money tribe who becomes an anthropologist appalls his family with this dangerous eccentricity. Writers, artists, and musicians are never part of the social circle, for they have strange ideas.

New York is particularly afraid of ideas, for it is "a society wholly absorbed in barricading itself against the unpleasant" (99). The terror of the unpleasant is so great that communication is limited to that which does not disturb. Archer and his mother never even allude to what is "uppermost in their thoughts" (38) if indeed they should entertain an idea. Generally, everyone lives in "a kind of hieroglyphic world, where the real thing was never said or done or even thought, but only represented by a set of arbitrary signs" (45).

Innocent worlds are worlds of appearances, and this one is no exception. At some time, New York may have had some deeper values and may have lived by them. At present, society professes these values but repeatedly violates them. The severe business probity of old money is exposed as a sham by New York's embrace of the unscrupulous speculator, Julius Beaufort. The sanctity of the family is regularly challenged by the infidelity of its members. The family is important not as a model of virtue but as an enforcer of the code of appearances, a conveyer of signs. It is the great moneyed families, particularly old families with elderly patriarchs, which retain the power to deny reality and thus protect the child-world.[28] As aged Mr. van der Luyden explains, it does not matter what the individual does, as long as the group refuses to see it: "as long as a member of a well-known family is backed up by that family it [the family's decision to support the individual] should be considered—final" (57). Thus, not only is communication severely restricted, so is vision. What one sees is not reality; reality is what the family acknowledges. This is truly a kind of innocence "that seals the mind against imagination and the heart against experience!" (145).

Newland Archer, raised in this world, feels superior to it in many ways. And, in some ways, he is. He is a sensitive, intelligent man, able to distance himself from his milieu by travel, reading, study. He has compassion and generosity and enough insight to know that a great deal is missing from the lives of his companions. And yet he is damned by the "thrill of possessorship" (7) he feels when he looks at May Welland. In his acquisition of the innocent girl, Archer sells himself to the tribe.

May, submissive in her white dresses, delights Archer most in her "resolute determination to carry to its utmost limit that ritual of ignoring the 'unpleasant' in which they had both been brought up" (26). Her wide eyes are empty, for she knows nothing and expects everything. That vacancy entices Archer, who dreams of sexually and intellectually initiating the girl. But he also knows that she is a "creation of factitious purity" manufactured to provide the "lordly pleasure" he will experience in owning her (46). Repeatedly, May's innocence both attracts and repulses Archer, reflecting his own divided attitudes toward his world. May is physically perfect, good at games, beautifully formed, but so pure she is sexless. Archer dreams of marriage to May as a passionate and tender comradeship but in a moment of insight admits that such a union would demand the very qualities May has been "carefully trained not to possess": "experience...versatility...freedom of judgment" (44).

The image most connected to May is that of Diana, and, as Irving Jacobson notes, it is an image of both innocence and death (76). Before the wedding, May looks like, "a Diana just alight from the chase" (66), and of course May is hunting Archer. On his round of betrothal visits with May, Archer feels exhibited "like a wild animal cunningly trapped" (69). In her most famous incarnation as Diana, May competes in an archery contest at Newport, utterly beautiful, physically flawless. As she is poised to shoot, an admirer exclaims, "God...not one of the lot holds the bow as she." The notorious libertine Julius Beaufort replies, "Yes, but that's the only target she'll ever hit" (211).

Beaufort is right but not entirely so. As Jacobson says, Diana's arrows can bring sudden death, and May has indeed caught her prey in Archer. She has hit a target. What is particularly important about this scene is that it depicts the *married* May, ironically, now named May Archer, but more than ever the virginal goddess. In one sense, then, Beaufort tells the truth. There is no passion in May; even as a wife, she is forever the child playing games. She will not strike passion in men's hearts.

Before the wedding, May's face "wore the vacant serenity of a young marble athlete" (142). After the wedding, May remains what she was designed to be—a statue, a goddess, a symbol of innocence rather than a person. Her eyes are the blind eyes of a statue; she is as cold as a chaste goddess or a marble figure. As Archer overhears Beaufort's scornful dismissal of May, he realizes he has selected a bride designed never to change, and he is afraid: "What if niceness...were only a negation, the white curtain dropped before an emptiness? As he looked at May...he had the feeling that he had never yet lifted that curtain" (211). Like Theodore and his Veiled Lady,[29] Archer, confronted with the implications of the innocence he desired, is afraid to see too much. He is afraid to see death.

However, this is an inescapable recognition for Archer. He has irrevocably linked himself to the child world, and his awareness of his fate grows as the boundaries of that world constrict. On his wedding day, he feels caught in "a nursery parody of life" (182), and his honeymoon is no tender scene of lordly initiation. For May, it is merely a new "lark," an adventure in playing house, "like a grown-up person." To Archer, May looks more than ever "a type rather than a person"; "she might have been chosen to pose for a Civic Virtue or a Greek goddess" (188). Nearly two years after the wedding, May most appropriately wears her wedding dress, for she is the same pure icon.

Archer is perceptive enough to see that the women of his world most blatantly express the dead quality of perpetual serenity. They move from youth to age, changed in body but not in mind or heart. They grow old but they do not grow. To Archer, they are all virgins become old maids (86), so that he perceives his mother and May's mother as middle-aged images "of invincible ignorance" (145), and the elderly women at a dinner party seem "curiously immature" (63). Mrs. van der Luyden, the patriarch's wife, is a living corpse: she seems "gruesomely preserved in the airless atmosphere of a perfectly irreproachable existence," like a body trapped in a glacier, preserving "a rosy life-in-death" (53).

But Archer cannot ignore his own imprisonment in that same frozen world. Women are not the only ones who age but do not change; thus, all who refuse to be "so much as brushed by the wing-tip of Reality" are, in Archer's terms, old maids (86). Images of dying without living, of never being fully alive, proliferate and describe both sexes. The van der Luyden house is a mausoleum (131), the summer games of Newport are filled with "children playing in a graveyard" (207), a description juxtaposing the infantile quality of this world with its deadliness. The people of old New York are like interchangeable pieces in the great game of evasion. To Archer, he and his companions are as alike "as paper dolls cut out of the same folded paper" (83). Like paper dolls, each inhabitant is linked forever to a chain of children, all afraid of pain. Their fears arrest their development so severely that they die without having ever lived. Archer's misfortune is the fact that, possessing the potential for adult growth, he chooses the eternal childhood he both desires and despises.

He does so for many reasons. Archer is very much a part of his society, aware of its forms and accepting of its rituals: "the young man cherished his old New York even while he smiled at it" (62). Perhaps Archer's feeling of superiority to the other inhabitants of his world creates a false sense of security, a reassuring feeling that he can move within society without committing to it.

Ironically, Archer's reluctance to commit leads him to his imprisonment. He is a dilettante and observer, and old New York has trained him in all the tactics of evasion—passivity, withdrawal, repression—as the means of avoiding decision or commitment. Archer's choice may not be a choice at all, but merely a series of small retreats to the safety of the role he knows best.

There is a further irony in that Archer's denial of his own opportunity to grow stifles the potential growth of his wife. Within May there is a capacity to learn and change and even to rebel against society's dictates,[30] but, as Archer realizes, "her courage and initiative were all for others" (150). May can relinquish her role only for another's sake and with another's help. But Archer's response to May is the characteristic old New York one—a refusal to respond at all.[31] Before his marriage, Archer recognized his responsibility to "take the bandage" from May's eyes (83), and he flattered himself that he would show her the world outside their limited one. Once married, Archer decides it is "less trouble" to "treat May exactly as all his friends treated their wives" than to challenge the status quo (193). And so, long after the wedding, May remains trapped behind her curtain of niceness.

The archery contest at Newport reveals Archer's complicity in a double entrapment, his own and May's. Patricia Meyer Spacks notes that Wharton, in her memoir *A Backward Glance*, recalls the women of her childhood competing in such contests. Wharton remembers the thick veils the women wore to protect their complexions—hot, uncomfortable, suffocating veils. When the veil was lifted, however, a dazzling beauty appeared (243). Gilbert and Gubar discuss the motif of the veil as it is used by both male and female writers. For the male writer, they say, the "veiled woman reflects male dread of women." For the woman writer, that veil is "a symbol...of [women's] diminishment into spectral remains of what they might have been" (*Madwoman* 472). To Archer, May's veil is an easy focus for his own discontent; it is that layer of niceness that tricked him into marriage. Yet he will not lift it, for he lacks the initiative and the courage to face uncertainty, to risk the pain of changing himself, much less of changing May. And so May's potential self diminishes. The veil was designed to keep her pristine, but she remains confined behind it. The dazzling beauty of a grown-up wife is lost to Archer because, like everyone around him, he prefers not to act.

Like the fellow traveler of "The Valley of Childish Things," Archer makes the occasional foray out of the playground. He dabbles in politics, in philanthropy, in civic works. As he grows old, he may console himself with the thought that "there is good in the old ways" (341), yet he ignores the fact that the old ways, of financial integrity and marital fidelity, have been reduced to slogans. People no longer act in accordance with these old ways; they are merely arbitrary signs used to conceal the common practice of fraud and avarice and adultery. Archer is by no means the worst of the inhabitants of his world. He is a good citizen and a loving father. He adjusts to the limits of his marriage, playing the part expected of him and relegating May to her role as well.

But because he has been so afraid to change, to act, to risk, Archer has chosen a life of sameness.

Shortly before his wedding, Archer envisions his nightmare self: "the dwindling figure of a man to whom nothing was ever to happen" (227).[32] His worst dream does, in part, come true. Evading pain, he evades life. Most specifically, he denies himself adult life. Archer never becomes a man, just a very sad boy.

The Beautiful and Damned

An earlier book than *Tender Is the Night, The Beautiful and Damned* is also a much simpler one. Brian Way calls it "an unfortunate aberration" in Fitzgerald's development as a novelist and says it took Fitzgerald "clear out of the path that appeared to be leading directly to the creative climax of 1924-26" (64). While *The Beautiful and Damned* may not contain the best of Fitzgerald's writing, it does encapsulate the themes and images of later, better work, particularly of *Tender Is the Night*.

If one of Fitzgerald's major concerns is the fall of the hero, then it is useful to study *Tender Is the Night* and *The Beautiful and Damned* out of chronological order. The later book traces the stages in the fall of a protagonist; the early one merely describes failure without fall. it begins, in one sense, where *Tender Is the Night* ends: with a hero who is a child. If Dick Diver initially possesses the capacity to live as a grown-up, Anthony Patch begins and ends in immaturity. What passes for a decline in *The Beautiful and Damned* is just Anthony's growing realization of the dark side of innocence. Anthony, unlike Dick, cannot fall, because he has never attempted to reach beyond himself.

The Beautiful and Damned is thus a simpler novel because there is no real conflict in it. There is, instead, a pattern of desire, fulfillment, and instant discontent. And each repetition of the pattern deepens the discontent and provokes a new desire. Only after endless repetitions of the same futile cycle does Anthony Patch realize that "nothing grew stale so soon as pleasure" (418). The sense of a downward movement in the novel is derived more from the pathos of watching children grow old and nasty, but not up, than from any genuine fall. Because the book is structured as a series of re-enactments of the same scenario of desire, it, like *Tender Is the Night*, employs reverberation and repetition of image, here to underscore the futility of desire. And, like its successor, it relies on a twinning of hero and heroine to reveal the essence of the hero and his world.

Anthony Patch and Gloria Gilbert are more obviously twins than Dick Diver and Nicole Warren even though the novel contains several passages which appear to differentiate between the lovers and to assign Anthony the superior status. He is sporadically portrayed as the sensitive, special talent destroyed by his love for a crude and selfish woman. At the end of the novel, for instance, Anthony muses, "All the distress he had ever known, the sorrow and the pain, had been because of women." Sensing, perhaps, that he is "tender-minded," the women "killed the things in him that menaced their absolute sway" (444). Anthony even tells his wife, "I think that if I hadn't met you I *would* have done something" (211). Such passages are consistently undercut, however, by early descriptions of Anthony as a fatuous dilettante, a man who dreams of becoming a Renaissance scholar but who is bored by books on the Renaissance, who justifies his inactivity by envisioning himself as "a man knowing too much for his talent to express" (36). Anthony introduces himself to Gloria by explaining, " I do nothing, for there's nothing I can do that's worth doing" (65), and even in this early self-portrait we see Anthony's capacity for self-deception.

Thus the motto of the book, "The victor belongs to the spoils," poses a series of questions. Ostensibly, Gloria is the spoils, the prize which Anthony desires, the woman-as-thing. To own her is to fulfill desire, but, as Anthony learns, "desire just cheats you" (341). In this reading, it is Gloria, the "spoiled" child, both pampered and tainted, who comes to own the man who won her. If so, she is as much the victor in this battle of love, and Anthony is "spoiled," infected, by the disease beneath her beauty. Yet in another sense, Anthony comes to Gloria already tainted; he is the "spoiled" boy ruined by the money that protects him from life and growth. Who, then, is the victor? Who the spoils? Because these characters are twins, they are both victors, winning the objects of their desire, and both spoiled, because in the long run, desire is a cheat.

Tainting both Anthony and Gloria is a fear of life. Although he visits the world, Anthony is afraid to live in it. Thus, after a night on the town in New York, he hurries back to his apartment: "he was safe in here from all the threat of life...safe, safe!" (27). The fear intensifies into "a longing to be emotionally undisturbed" (284), a need to be safe:

from the world and from himself" (286). Shutting himself in safety, Anthony imprisons himself in "an enclosed life of infinite dreariness" (300).

What exactly "the world" or "life" contains that so terrifies Anthony is clarified in a central scene. The night before his wedding to Gloria, his last night alone, safe in his apartment, Anthony listens to the sounds of the city and dreams of being part of that vitality. But then he hears a woman's coarse laughter, and it "aroused his old aversion and horror toward all the business of life.... He wanted to be out in some cool and bitter breeze, miles above the cities, and to live serene and detached back in the corners of his mind. Life was that sound out there, that ghastly reiterated female sound" (147).

"Life" is a woman's voice. Life, so terrible, is related to sex,[33] the business of life. In this passage, Anthony's fear links sex to coarseness and to spontaneity of feeling at the same time that it associates safety with superiority, withdrawal and coldness. Anthony's moment of fear comes directly before he is to marry, when he will be expected to take on "the business of life" as he takes sexual possession of his bride. However, his choice of Gloria both reflects and calms his fears. He has chosen an ice maiden, a girl, not a woman, and thus he has evaded life.

"I'm a solid block of ice," Gloria says, and her gray eyes are so cold Anthony thinks of them as blue-white (57). Her "strongest appeal," Anthony recognizes, is her "indifference" (135), her distance from emotion. Gloria is exactly what Anthony wants, a great void, and he longs "to find rest in her great immobility" (107). Later, he blames her for lulling his mind to sleep: "She...hung like a brilliant curtain across his doorways, shutting out the light of the sun.... he saw the sun always through the pattern of the curtain" (191). But Gloria does what she was expected to do. She helps her mate escape from life; she is his buffer, the veil that separates him from the life-giving sun, providing him with the cool retreat he desires. Anthony has chosen the Veiled Lady as modern bride, and she shelters him from the business of life. Yet he deplores the curtain as he cowers behind it.

Marrying the cold and changeless Gloria, Anthony selects the negation of all he fears: the vulgarity of sex, spontaneity, energy. But because Gloria is female, she remains a threatening presence nevertheless. And she is more dangerous because she is Anthony's mirror image.

Maxwell Geismar calls Anthony and Gloria "ecstatic 'twins,' mirrors of each others' glitter," and he identifies a kind of sexual role reversal that develops in their marriage, so that Gloria, the "Nordic Ganymede," emerges as a hard, cold, masculine temperament while Anthony clings to her and takes on the role of "volatile, uneasy, and even perhaps betrayed, un-Nordic woman." Geismar defines their relationship as a "pathological interdependence" (291, 300-01),[34] and although he defines the bond as a reversal of the traditional masculine-dominant, feminine-submissive one, it may also be described as an amalgam of androgynous traits in both characters. Both Anthony and Gloria are essentially presexual because Gloria shares Anthony's fear of adult sexuality.

At several points in the book, Gloria emphasizes her unwillingness to have children, initially explaining that she does not want the responsibility of children or the damage to her lovely body that pregnancy would cause. Another reason for her reluctance to bear children, however, is that she is appalled by the "reality, the earthiness, the intolerable sentiment of childbearing" (392). Like Anthony, Gloria associates certain natural parts of living, particularly sexuality and parenthood, with grossness. For both twins, spontaneous emotion is somehow feeling gone out of control, "intolerable sentiment" or "coarse laughter." Anthony fears the coarse woman; it seems that Gloria fears becoming that woman.

In both characters, the fear of life also takes another form, a feeling of revulsion toward the lower classes. Anthony and Gloria need to distance themselves from that dirty element beneath them, constantly impinging on their private world. Their hatred of the poor is obsessive; when Gloria is ill and delirious, for example, she cries, "Millions of people...swarming like rats.... For one really exquisite palace...I'd sacrifice a hundred thousand...a million of them" (394). She and Anthony attempt to distance themselves from the masses by maintaining a kind of feudal fantasy; in the fantasy, the lord Anthony may casually take and just as casually discard his peasant mistress, Dorothy Raycroft. He is the Chevalier O'Keefe of his little tale,[35] and he is most distressed when his army career forces him into "constant personal contact" with waiters, chauffeurs and other subordinates "who had previously been remarkable only in the subservience of their professional genuflections" (329-30). Deprived of his aristocratic fantasy, Anthony removes himself from coarse contact with subordinates, refusing to engage in even ten minutes' of conversation with a single man, for two months.

Anthony and Gloria, isolated by fear of human emotion, come together because there is nothing else to do. Shortly before he meets Gloria, Anthony is troubled by "a growing lack of color" in his days (53), an increasing sense of "horror and loneliness" (54). He does not work, he cannot write, there is nothing or no one to put color in his days. Detachment is his chosen stance but, "It seemed a tragedy to want nothing—and yet he wanted something, something" (55). Perceiving existence as desire, he does not know what to want, and he knows that desire cheats. And so he chooses what others have wanted, "Coast-to-Coast Gloria" (61), desired by men across the continent, herself burned out by conquest, "suddenly anaesthetic" to her own triumphs (81). Their union of icy desire translates all relationships into the language of things. When Anthony dreams of Gloria, he dreams of her shopping, surrounded by shopgirls "like courtiers" bringing her booty; he perceives his function as her husband as "giving her many things...clothes and jewels and friends and excitement" (150). To Gloria, the focus of the wedding is the wedding presents; she tears each one from the tissue paper "with the rapaciousness of a dog digging for a bone," her face, unsmiling, shows "rapt interest" as she critically examines each tribute (143).

It is to be a marriage of horror, although it begins as a kind of play. This part of the book reverberates with the multiple meanings of "play," with the word's associations with the worlds of the theater and of childhood. During their engagement, for instance, the lovers repeatedly quarrel and make up; "They were stars on this stage, each playing to an audience of two: the passion of their pretense created the actuality" (132). They are actors and also children playing at love. They are playacting and also playing at acting, pretending to be involved in the activities of lovers—quarreling, kissing, reconciling. In her diary, right before her wedding, Gloria writes that her marriage will be "the performance," and "the world shall be the scenery" (147). The world, then, will be her playhouse, but she will be playing house, pretending to be a grown-up, assuming what she knows to be a role.

If the lovers are to live in a play (and Anthony talks of writing one for Gloria), it will be set in children's theater. As Gloria herself recognizes, they play a children's game in pretending to love: "Blowing bubbles...and they'll explode and we'll blow more and more...until all the soap and water is used up" (147). Sooner or later, the games will stop, and real life, that dirty, coarse, vulgar element lurking outside the play-house, will come inside. There will be no more soap-and-water to remove the coarseness; there will be no more juvenile roles. In her diary, on her wedding day, Gloria fortells the moment when she and Anthony will become "like players who had lost their costumes" (405), or, perhaps, children with no new games.

It all begins as a lark. When they are married, Gloria tells Anthony, "there'll be no good nights...and we can do just as we want" (136). But, as it did before marriage, the problem of what to want looms large. There is nothing to do but consume—gumdrops, alcohol, excitement, travel—and nothing satisfies. Like her successor, Daisy Buchanan, Gloria is bored; the "eternal monotone" of their conversation is "What then? Oh, what'll we do then?" (179). "I wish somebody'd take care of us," Gloria cries (171), and the focus of their marriage becomes the distant, omnipotent Adam Patch, the multimillionaire grandfather whose death will bring them endless wealth. Adam Patch will "take care" of them by dying. This father will release them to the endless freedom of endless spending as they remain dependent on his gift. And so their lives are directed toward this moment of delayed but supreme gratification. And while they wait, they rehearse the great role to come, buying, consuming, in the pattern of inescapable discontent.

Each cycle of desire-fulfillment-satiation-despair further erodes the marriage. Mutual contempt is doubly painful because the spouses are mirrors. Anthony grows to hate being alone, and he dreads being alone with Gloria, for, in either case, he is forced to confront his failings. Painful as this union has become, it cannot be broken, for the narcissists need their audience, and there is nothing else—only life.

The death of the great rich father does not bring a long-delayed adulthood.[36] At the end of this final cycle, there is only more horror. Anthony has played his child role to madness. The day he becomes heir to millions is the day he retreats to the safety of unreason. He learns of his inheritance as he sits on the floor, playing with his stamp albums. The stamps he tosses in the air drift around him like leaves. To the broken Anthony, they are just pieces of paper, like the money that was the last thing he wanted, the final desire that cheats like the rest.

An American Tragedy

Twenty-five years after Dreiser's controversial Carrie first appeared, she reappeared. *She* becomes a *he* in Clyde Griffiths, the hero who possesses all of the heroine's salient traits, the male equivalent of the endless longing and endless discontent that carried the heroine so far. What was for Carrie a source of strength becomes, in this novel, a disease that devours. As a male, Clyde cannot use his childish nature to the same advantage.

Elizabeth Hardwick calls Clyde a trusting girl (190), and the phrase captures Clyde's passivity, dependency, and blind faith in consumer values. Clyde has "a soul that was not destined to grow up" (169), and all his life he is a prisoner of his adolescent longings and actions. From his days at the street mission, through his hotel work and his struggles in Lycurgus, Clyde wants the things that attract a child: glitter, glamour, excitement, and, most of all, the freedom of a succession of pleasures enjoyed without consequences. And he wants them with "a feverish, urgent disposition" that "could ill brook the delay or disappointments that are the chief and outstanding characteristics of the ambitions of men" (297). What differentiates the childish Clyde from men is not only his inability to delay gratification but his passivity; as Hardwick notes, he is "seduced" by the Green-Davidson hotel (190), the word connoting the trusting, malleable nature of a young girl. When Clyde dreams, he never considers his own actions an avenue to his goals; more typically, he fantasizes that someone else will initiate his success, will discover him or smile down upon him and reward him. Like a child bride, he wants to be "taken up," and taken care of. Clyde never envisions himself a success at any specific kind of work but rather dreams of the rewards of work—money, prestige, leisure.[37] Since he cannot imagine any connection between his own efforts and his dreams, Clyde is a masculine version of Cinderella, languishing in a corner, waiting for something to happen. He feels, as Carrie does, forever thwarted, forever outside of that place where people are happy. He waits for someone to open the door to the paradise-of-the-moment but is repeatedly confronted by another closed door.

Like Carrie, Clyde is pure conformist in his values. Spindler calls him "a waxen seal of the society in which he lives and dies" (148), and each group Clyde enters imprints its standards on his soul. From the soda fountain to Lycurgus society, he watches and learns new things to want. One value, however, never changes, for it is the most basic principle of all the groups. It is the supreme importance assigned to the deal. In every stage of Clyde's journey, he learns to buy and sell human flesh.

This is the same principle that worked so well for Carrie, but it cannot succeed for Clyde because he is male. As such, he has nothing to sell, and so he is excluded from the role of prostitute. And because he is a poor male, he cannot buy what he desires, either. With his powerful longings but with his feminine passivity, Clyde is doomed to be irrelevant in the marketplace because he has nothing to trade.

He learns the lessons of the marketplace by dealing with girls who cost too much. In *An American Tragedy*, the roles of the child bride are split, so that certain characters become exaggerated versions of the child bride as victim, while others represent the child bride as bitch. Both types are equally dangerous to Clyde and effectively convince him that all human connections are some form of trade.

In the first version of the split, Clyde learns that both the dependent woman and the aggressively demanding one expect him to pay. When his sister Esta becomes pregnant, Clyde is pushed toward a role he fears, that of the adult provider, the responsible man. This is a terrible role for Clyde not only because it will cost him money, but also because it deprives him of the child role he finds so comfortable. While Esta is being seduced and abandoned, Clyde is being seduced by the pleasures of the childish consumer world of Hortense Briggs, with its parties and drinking and promiscuity. Hortense speaks loving baby talk to the object of her desire: "you pity sing!" she coos to the fur jacket displayed enticingly in a store window (103). She can manipulate Clyde and stimulate his desire with the same language, "Giddap, horsey.... my horsey has to skate me now on the ice," she calls flirtatiously when she needs to reassure Clyde of her regard (131). Thus, while Esta is teaching Clyde about the financial consequences of sex, Hortense is educating him in the financial prerequisites. The sexual bargain Hortense proposes stipulates a fee—up front—before surrender. In any case, with either the pathetic Esta or the calculating Hortense, Clyde is learning to view relationships as deals. Thus, as he reflects on Esta's predicament, he blames her for her bad business sense. In her affair, Esta should have been shrewder, more like Hortense: "She ought, as he saw it, to have been able to manage better" (100).

Sex, then, must be "managed"; that is, all relationships demand some kind of strategy that will permit one to retain control of what is, in essence, a trade. Clyde learns further lessons from his early encounters. One is that sex brings trouble. Esta's fall brings misery to her and Mrs. Griffiths and irritation to Clyde. Clyde's own sexual obsession with Hortense leads him down a path to serious problems with the law and a flight from Kansas City. Thus, sex costs a lot, perhaps too much. When Clyde works at the all-male Union League, he begins to wonder if sexuality might cost a man success. "Probably one could not attain to or retain one's place in so remarkable a world as this unless one were indifferent to sex, a disgraceful passion, of course" (169). Sex has deprived Clyde's sister of all status and reduced her to beggary. It may destroy a man's chances for recognition and respect. To deal in the sexual market, then, is very risky. But Clyde has the adolescent's strong sexual urges. He wants what he considers evil. Out of this conflict emerges Clyde's worship of a certain kind of power, the power of denial.

For Clyde, a thing (or a person's) value is merely its price; most definitely, the best in life is not free. Thus, Esta was a fool and has become a worthless person because she didn't manage well, and Hortense is to be respected for her shrewdness. What Clyde finds so fascinating in Hortense is really her shrewd denial of his desires, a denial which enhances her value in his eyes. The lesson of Clyde's first encounter with two child-heroines establishes the pattern of Clyde's behavior in the central triangle of the book involving Clyde, Roberta Alden and Sondra Finchley.[38]

Roberta Alden is, to Clyde, the embodiment of the victim-as-destroyer. Her power is her powerlessness. More than anything, Roberta is the girl who can't: she can't dance, she can't swim, she can't afford nice clothes, she can't rise without someone to raise her. Her sweet helplessness draws Clyde, but "his thought was not that he had ever wanted to marry her, but rather just to play with her happily in love" (382). Roberta becomes an enemy when her pregnancy dictates an adult response to what was initiated so playfully. The blind trust that encouraged Roberta to give herself away now threatens to imprison Clyde in darkness. Roberta's helplessness, her overwhelming need for Clyde is, to him, "her power—or that of life to restrain him," and he wants only to "free himself of her—her touch—her pleading—consoling sympathy" (492). Clyde perceives the strength in Roberta's weakness, the stranglehold of her embrace. Roberta's feminine submission is a hard mastery, reflected in the many variations on her name, all of them masculine: "Bob" or "Bobbie" to her parents; "Bert" to her lover. Initially drawn to Roberta, Clyde has not foreseen the suffocating power of the despoiled and desperate Bert. He has not "managed" well. He feels cheated, having envisioned a different transaction. He does not see why he must pay so much for what Roberta did not hold dear.

In contrast, there is Sondra, who promises so much simply because she denies all fulfillment. To Clyde, the choice is between "Sondra with everything offering all—asking nothing of him; Roberta, with nothing, asking all" (472). But Clyde evades the real terms of this bargain even as he fulfills them. Sondra demands more than Roberta ever will. The heiress, aptly enough, to a vacuum-cleaner company, Sondra sucks up adulation and demands Clyde's total devotion. Ultimately, she demands life itself. To Clyde, her voraciousness establishes her value. Vain and hungry, Sondra lives in the child world at its best; she enjoys the most expensive version of infantile pleasures Clyde has ever seen. Clyde thinks of Sondra as the princess of this world, his "baby-talking girl" whose patter "had an almost electric, if sweetly tormenting effect on him" (429). The key phrase in the description is the paradoxical "sweetly tormenting" which establishes the nature of Clyde's longing. His attraction to Sondra is founded on, and sustained by, gratification refused, for anything worth possessing, Clyde knows, must cost a great deal. It must, then, be beyond his means. Thus Clyde's first reaction to Sondra encapsulates what their relationship will always be:

her effect on him was electric...arousing in him a curious stinging sense of what it was to want and not to have—to wish to win and yet to feel, almost agonizingly that he was destined not even to win a glance from her. It tortured and flustered him. At one moment he had a keen desire to close his eyes and shut her out—at another to look only at her constantly—. (219-20)

Sondra is initially valuable because Clyde cannot have her. Roberta, it is true, will threaten to cost a great deal, but Clyde is able to meet her price; he just doesn't want to pay it. With Sondra, on the other hand, Clyde feels the lure of something so far beyond what he had ever believed possible that the magical, the miraculous must happen to him if he is to possess it. Perhaps that is why, as Pizer notes, the imagery of

Clyde's response to Sondra is so heavily religious (252). For Clyde, to whom sex is so clearly allied with money, Sondra represents the realization of both physical and economic fantasies. She is as close as he will ever get to an icon.

A dreamer, Clyde believes in miracles. And he is drawn further into this dream of paradise by small but significant signs of Sondra's acquiescence—a dance, a touch, a kiss. At the same time, he is sustained in his endless longing by constant denial, frustrated desire. Sondra must be valuable because she is expensive. In the end, Clyde convinces himself that he can afford her, after all. He is willing to pay for her with whatever it takes, even murder.

Clyde trades Roberta's life (and his own) so that he will never have to enter adult life. When he thinks of being rich, he thinks of being able "to do in life exactly as you wished" (266), and the marriage he plans for himself and Sondra would merely give him a secure place in Sondra's circle of playmates. It is interesting that Clyde's conflict reaches a crisis in the summer, when Sondra's milieu is the extended summer camp full of athletic pleasures. There Sondra is, like May Welland, the athletic goddess. In contrast to Roberta, she is physically capable, good at swimming and tennis and all the camp games. Marrying Sondra, it appears, would put Clyde on perpetual holiday. Such a marriage would not so much make Clyde a husband as it would make him an adopted child of Sondra's father. Pizer identifies the motif of "a search for a father of strength and guidance" in the novel (283), and for Clyde, the perfect father must also be rich and generous. At first, Clyde hopes that his uncle Samuel will become the powerful parent who will take care of him. Emotionally and economically still an orphan when Samuel ignores him, Clyde continues to search for a father. The romance with Sondra has the additional benefit of supplying that parent, the benevolent protector more commonly associated with the child bride than with a son-in-law.

Clyde's dream of submitting, like an adopted son, to a powerful surrogate father, is only one of the sex role shifts of the novel. Clyde's entire affair with Sondra is based on a reversing of the typical economic underpinnings of romance. That is, she has the money and she controls the spending of it. Sondra takes Clyde up, in both senses of the phrase. She amuses herself with him, as if he were a fad, a new hobby, and she also carries him upward into a consumer's heaven beyond his imagining.

Controlling the cash, she initiates the courtship: she issues the invitations, places the phone calls to her beau, even, in a reversal of the all-American "date," picks Clyde up in her automobile. And yet we are not for a moment to assume that Sondra has become Clyde's surrogate mother. She is a reckless spender, it is true, but she is a vicarious one, totally dependent on her father, head of the Finchley Electric Sweeper Company. In a sense, as a testament to her father's money power, Sondra is as much an employee of the family firm (in the public relations department) as any factory hand.

The economic role reversal implicit in this revised Cinderella story underscores the financial base of many of the relationships in the novel. Characters seek to get ahead, economically or socially, through romantic involvement. Clyde's earliest experience of sex is the bellboys' visit to a whorehouse, and the experience is a warning that he never fully heeds. Everyone is dealing. Hortense is selling her body as astutely as she can; Roberta, as many have noted, envisions a connection to Clyde as a step up from poverty, just as he perceives his relationship to Sondra. Dillard is a crude version of Clyde's social climbing, and the Finchleys themselves feel precariously positioned at the top of society. Mrs. Finchley can only countenance Clyde's presence in her home when others in her set have invited him; she is afraid that Sondra will make the wrong contacts. Sondra herself is using Clyde to connect to his rich cousin Gilbert; at first, she introduces Clyde into society to spite Gilbert for snubbing her. Later, as she considers reasons to marry Clyde, she is moved by the thought that marriage would make Gilbert "related to her in spite of him" and would connect her to "the Griffiths, too, whom her mother and father so much admired" (449).

All her vanity does not make Sondra a fool. She is her businessman father's daughter, "persistently characterized" by "a marked trace of the practical and the material" (449), and she knows the value of the right connection. Sondra knows and lives by the money rules, the rules of the deal. They are rules that can disqualify Clyde, for he is poor. As Clyde is about to enter his dream world of Lycurgus, he is again warned that the game is not for him. Even though he is handsome and charming, his looks are not negotiable. "People like money even more than they do looks," a plain but rich girl, a Lycurgus insider, admonishes. His look of longing is not a magnet attracting protectors and providers. As a male, he is required to act and to plan, not to dream and to wait. He is expected to buy.

Clyde is a failed Carrie, and both the similarities and differences are apparent in his talent for evasion. Even in his thoughts, he can never articulate the price he will pay for Sondra, for, like Carrie, he knows that naming can force recognition and action. Even as he plans to kill Roberta, he thinks that "it did not mean that he was going to attempt to kill her. Never once did he honestly, or to put it more accurately, forthrightly and courageously or coldly face the thought of committing so grim a crime" (467). Carrie's refusal to identify her "crimes," her seduction by Drouet and then by Hurstwood, her abandonment of Hurstwood, allows her to proceed and succeed in a blissful and deliberate blindness. Clyde's comparable evasions make him ineffectual and impractical; his selective vision makes him a poor manager.

The reluctance to see is, of course, tied to Clyde's refusal to act. As Pizer notes, a jury finds Clyde guilty of murder because of what he did *not* do. He did not save Roberta; he did not take her up from the water. He is dammed for the same passivity and inaction that elevates Carrie (272), who is taken up into a new life, rescued from a deadly existence precisely because her helplessness is so appealing. Clyde, a child himself, cannot carry the burden of a child-wife and the child to come. He has never visualized an adult role for himself, and when the time comes to assume one, he is paralyzed.

Roberta, dead, strikes the coroner as "just a child" (506), and it is interesting to note how *An American Tragedy* keeps coming back to the killing of a child. The two most significant romantic conflicts in Clyde's life are ended by the killing of a child. He is separated from Hortense by the hit-and-run killing of a little girl. He loses his dream girl, Sondra, when he is arrested for the murder of Roberta, who is carrying his baby. Clyde himself remains a child until death, in his last days comforted by his mother and his new father, the Reverend McMillan. And, as the novel ends, another child, torn by the same dreams that haunted Clyde, is growing up, perhaps to die with the same tormented desires.

Children play a curious role in many American novels. Often, when the novel presents a world of adult-children, of incestuous lovers safe in a fantasy romance, a biological child becomes a threat to that world. There is a great deal of hatred directed at children in certain American novels, perhaps because innocents cannot accept a child and remain children themselves. Gloria Patch is revulsed by the idea of childbirth and the attendant responsibilities of parenthood. In *A Farewell to Arms,* the idyll of love in snowy Switzerland must end because the baby brings death to Catherine. The child is an invader of her body (she must drink beer to keep the baby small) and, as a killer, an emissary of that terrible "world" out there that breaks everyone, an intruder in paradise.

More recent fiction is also concerned with married children and their offspring. John Updike's Rabbit Angstrom (of *Rabbit, Run*) is forced to relinquish the glory days of basketball because Janice traps him with her pregnancy; refusing to grow up, the couple shares a rare moment of serenity as they watch The *Mickey Mouse Club* together. The baby, source of so much misery, drowns, bringing guilt to intensify the misery. In John Cheever's *Bullet Park*, the suburban haven of Eliot Nailles is under siege by his teenage son, Tony. This world of endless barbecues and cocktail parties, where pain and suffering "would never be on [Nailles's] itinerary" (48) is disrupted when Tony calls it a house "made of cards" (45) and refuses to accept its evasions. The challenge to his dream of life prompts the father to try to kill his son with a golf club, and later, Eliot Nailles's alter ego, Paul Hammer, also tries to kill the boy. Only after two attempted acts of violence and after Eliot has become a drug addict, is tranquillity restored to Bullet Park, and "everything was as wonderful, wonderful, wonderful, wonderful, wonderful as it had been" before (243).

Children disrupt things. Granted, parenthood is often a source of conflict, and depiction of that conflict is not limited to American fiction. We think of the fearful consequences of pregnancy in *Adam Bede* or *Anna Karenina,* or the parent-child conflicts in many novels of initiation and growth. But the conflict, as depicted in American literature, repeatedly takes a curious form. It is not so much a conflict of parent vs. child as it is a war in which all the participants are children. In this struggle, the biological parent fights not to keep his mature authority, but to protect his turf. He is defending the shelter of his immaturity, the child's paradise of activity without purpose, choice without consequence, the place where lovers can do just as they want and never say good night. In this war, the parent is fighting to retain the American dream, to remain forever a child, greedy for pleasure and terrified of pain.

Part Two:

Intruders

Chapter Four:
Hester as First Rebel

You see...it's worth everything, isn't it, to keep one's intellectual liberty, not to enslave one's powers of appreciation, one's critical independence?.... to be able to look life in the face: that's worth living in a garret for, isn't it?

Edith Wharton, *The Age of Innocence* (200)

...she gained from many people the reverence due to an angel, but, I should imagine, was looked upon by others as an intruder and a nuisance.

Nathaniel Hawthorne, *The Scarlet Letter* (28)

The Scarlet Letter

The first intruder heroine, like the first innocent one, makes a dramatic entrance. Like Priscilla, Hester Prynne stands above the crowd, but she is on a scaffold, and her audience finds her at once repellent and compelling. Hester is no white dream of a bride but the dark reality of a wife who broke the marriage contract. Her emblem is no gauzy veil, refracting experience and deflecting human contact, but the letter "A" that signals her experience and secretly links her to the experiences of others.

R.W.B. Lewis calls Hester's first appearance "the paradigm dramatic image in American literature," "the tableau of the solitary figure set over against the inimical society, in a village which hovers on the edge of the inviting and perilous wilderness." As she stands alone, confronting the hostile crowd in "silence and pride," she appears, Lewis says, "as a disturber of the moral structure of the universe, and yet she is a life-giving force, an incarnation of "those rights of personality that society is inclined to trample upon" (111-12). For Lewis, she is the classic American hero, the American Adam, her story the account of a "moral engagement with the alien tribe" (85).[1] If so, the classic American Adam is Eve.

161

It is precisely because Hester is female that she cannot fully meet the criteria of the American hero. Lewis defines such a person as "springing from nowhere, outside time, at home only in the presence of nature and God,...thrust by circumstances into an actual world and an actual age" (89). This is the "hero in space," beginning not only outside the constraints of time but in "space as spaciousness, as the unbounded, the area of total possibility" (91). But Hester Prynne, the first of many such heroines, is characterized by containment, not space. She is a prisoner of her past; her sin has put her on the scaffold. She is defined by her connections to others—she is the scarlet woman because of her relationships to her husband and lover and because she has become a mother. From what we know of Hester, there has never been a time in her life when she was permitted communion, free of social constraints, with either nature or God.

Hester is, as the first scene indicates, the heroine as prisoner. She is a captive not merely of the Boston jail but of the society she has never escaped. She has never dwelt in the area of total possibility, for her role has been narrow and rigidly defined by society. Like the Adamic hero, Hester is the individual in conflict with the alien tribe. But until Hester directly confronts that group, she cannot release herself into a new realm of wider possibility.

The intruder heroine is the woman born inside and caught inside and yet forever an outsider. Carolyn Heilbrun defines an outsider as one excluded from the "cultural patterns of bonding at the heart of society, at its centers of power" (*Reinventing Womanhood* 37). According to this definition, both male and female characters may be outsiders, but the crucial difference is one of choice. A male character may choose to remain outside the centers of power and may even opt for the forest, the river, the territory. But in the society depicted in American novels, females have no such choices; they are forever outside because they are not allowed in: into the church, the governor's house, the marketplace. They are irrelevant and excluded. And they are denied another choice. They cannot escape to nature, to a new place. Their rebellion must take place *within* the very walls that confine them.[2]

People who must live within an environment that defaces and perhaps even obliterates their identity have little allegiance to the values of that environment. For the weak, the only response to such treatment may be a conformity to prison standards, an acquiescence born of fear, but for others, confinement brings rebellion. Daniel Hoffman describes rebellion as the "crucial American experience" in American literature, and he defines that rebellion as a declaration of independence "from family, from social class, from church and God, from history (357). Usually, the American hero demonstrates that independence by moving away. The American heroine, however, cannot or will not, and so she rebels within, openly challenging the values that limit her and accepting the social consequences of her rebellion. In this kind of rebellion, the heroine becomes doubly intrusive, not only because she is outside of mainstream power centers, but also because she challenges them. And because her rebellion takes place inside society, it poses far greater dangers to society than the personal rebellion of the hero, safe and far away in the forest or on the frontier.

The intruder is subversive because she remains linked to family, social class, church, God, and history. Her rebellion is a form of civil disobedience that, like Hester's presence among the Puritans, compels attention. Nina Auerbach rightly calls Hester a "defiant icon, unapologetic in its self-presentation, its purity and subversion" (*Woman and the Demon* 165).

There are intruder heroines whose rebellion is less dramatic than Hester's and evolves more from circumstance than from conscious choice. Such women move only gradually toward defiance, and their declaration of independence may be fragmented into a series of small steps toward autonomy. Not all intruders enjoy (or suffer) the clear separation of self from society that Hester experiences on the scaffold. Nevertheless, all these women share a critical stance, a challenging of the values that confine them. This stance makes them women, not children.

For Hester, the pain of direct confrontation and social condemnation is a release. "The scarlet letter was her passport into regions where other women dared not tread" (142). This new territory is the region of free, mature thought; as an outlaw Hester looks "from an estranged point of view at human institutions," at "the clerical band, the judicial robe, the gallows, the fireside...the church" (142). Isolated from and punished by those male centers of power, Hester is free to abandon the child role such institutions assign to her, and to become fully adult. As Auerbach says, "Hester's spiritual strength does not transcend her fall but arises from it"; it is the avenue of her growth (*Woman and the Demon* 166).

In the causal relationship between a socially defined sin, punishment and growth, the intruder heroine is again differentiated from the American hero. For she emerges as a heroine *in time*, her past a determiner of her future growth; her present, often, the moment of confrontation and pain that releases her potential for growth. Thus, the intruder's story is predicated on experience, not innocence. When Hester mounts the scaffold, she carries her past with her, but it is precisely that past which precipitates the forward movement of her character and of the novel itself. Thus, while Hawthorne's innocent child, Priscilla, of *The Blithedale Romance*, may be advertised as the instrument that can link present and future (and who has no past), Hester, Hawthorne's intruder, is the legitimate sign of connection and continuity. Only an adult, formed by experience, can truly deliver on America's dreams of possibility and potentiality, linking events in a positive chain, an upward movement. Priscilla, the child, can offer only an endless but fragmented series of dreams feeding on themselves—isolated moments of fantasy.

Hester is a connector figure in another sense as well. As an alien within a crowd, she threatens division, but she also offers the possibility of new, humane bonds. Battered but not broken by society, Hester appeals to the outsider within each conformist, to the potential adult within each fearful child. As Hester ascends the scaffold, there are those who are incensed by her wickedness, but there is already one young woman who seems to feel what Hester feels and is moved to express her sympathy. The bond of compassion between Hester and this young woman begins a network of connections that spread into the Puritan world as Hester herself grows. Her adult presence indeed threatens to divide society, for she constructs a *community within* the existing community, a counter-world formed by positive values. The bonds she offers are not predicated on the power structure of master and slave, of the patriarch and his dependents. She has disassociated herself from such ties and offers instead a communion of sinners linked in understanding. She posits an egalitarian world that can subvert existing hierarchies.

Heilbrun says that Hester turns the apparent waste of her life "into a tremendous source of androgynous energy" (*Androgyny* 65). If the child bride can be characterized by passivity, then the intruder may be recognized by the vitality that sets Hester apart. The "feminine" virtues that are associated with the child-bride—submission, dependence, frailty—are, in the intruder, replaced by the more traditionally "masculine" quality of energy. And yet this heroine is indisputably a woman. Hester's lush dark beauty and bold vigor disturb the easy sexual polarities that sustain the Puritan centers of power. In her, the categorizations that sustain the status quo become meaningless. Seeing her, the Puritans see a different way to be. And seeing her, the Puritans see the power of a new kind of vision.

Walter Allen says that the great theme of European and English novels is "man's life in society," specifically, "the education of men and women, in the sense of their learning to distinguish, through their inescapable involvement in society, the true from the false both in themselves and in the world about them" (qtd. in Pratt 167). This theme may also be the theme of *The Scarlet Letter*, for it is a story about ways of seeing in society. Although its heroine is an outsider, her conflicts are with insiders, with society itself. Only by living within the Puritan world does Hester learn to distinguish "the true from the false" in herself and in others. She learns to see, and as she looks around her, her vision widens and sharpens.

In one way, intruder heroines are like children. They are childlike but never childish in their open-eyed approach to experience, their receptivity to it. They will take in what the world presents, not blind themselves to it. They are not evaders who shrink from unpleasant experience, but adventurers who risk pain for the opportunity to grow. Their capacity to see is not limited by society's definitions of what may be seen; thus, they are not dependent on social definitions of reality or on the facile categories that prescribe and proscribe vision. As outsiders, they see more and they see differently. Often, they see beneath or beyond appearances. With the letter on her heart, Hester sees what is hidden. She perceives the secret failings of others, but, unlike the cold Puritans, she sees with "a sympathetic knowledge" (66) that links her to others.

Hester Prynne ascends the scaffold and looks. She faces the crowd with "a glance that would not be abashed," and "looked around at her townspeople and neighbors" (43). Hester will not evade the stares of their hatred, just as she never evades responsibility for her sin. But she is not humble or demure. She looks back at her accusers. She will not lower her eyes like a child under discipline. If the townspeople are to examine her and thus to judge her, her scrutiny is also a kind of judgment. Spiritually honest, Hester looks around her and within.

She seems to challenge her punishment even as she accepts it. Her stance before the group makes her deviance a virtue. She is brave—refusing the assistance of the beadle, who seems to pull her from the prison door, stepping out into the open air and moving above the spectators, alone.

Hester is to be used to teach a lesson in Puritan values. She is to be displayed in the marketplace, the center of religious and financial activity. She is an object of scorn because she is damaged goods, no longer saleable. Above her stand the men who have "marked her down," "old males," Baym says, a patriarchy that "surrounds itself with displays of power" (*Shape* 126) like this one. She is to be displayed as "the figure, the body, the reality of sin" (61).

Therein lies the irony of this Puritan morality play. As a figure of sin, Hester has become Everyman. All humans sin, and so Hester's function in this play is dependent upon the perception of the audience. Those who see truth, who acknowledge that they, too, are sinners, are linked to the woman above them. They share her humanity. Those who refuse this vision and deny their own flaws prefer to perceive themselves as the elect, the superhuman. Thus they are blind to that part of Hester that is like them. Deluded by their desire for perfection, they become inhuman, less than the reality, the figure, of acknowledged sin.

Emerging from the prison into the open air, Hester truly becomes herself. That prison may represent the prison of Puritan values, for, having violated those standards and having been marked as an outcast, Hester has been cut loose from such values. Outcast, she is legally free to leave this world forever, but she cannot. Her ties are not the bonds of Puritan law but of a lover to whom she feels responsible, a child who must be reared near her father. These ties force Hester to rebel from within the walls of her enemies' territory.

Initially, that rebellion is mainly an inner transformation. As she makes her rounds on the fringes of Boston, Hester is outwardly humble and self-effacing, appropriately submissive. She survives by concealing the critical spirit hinted at in her elaborate "A." If there is a deception here, it is performed out of love for others. The pragmatic part of Hester knows that, if she is to be permitted to live near her lover and to raise her child, she must be seen as what the Puritans expect to see.[3] And yet she never confuses her assumed identity with her inner self. No prisoner of self-deception, Hester consistently sees what she is doing, acknowledges that vision and accepts responsibility for her actions. Reborn with powerful vision, Hester never shrinks from the power to see. And, as her power grows within, she sheds the covering of submission, appearing to others as "able," capable of widening their vision as well as her own.

At first, Hester's new life must be devoted to protecting Pearl, and in a sense to protect the child is to protect the emerging self. The new Hester seems reborn in her child. "There is no law, nor reverence for authority, no regard for human ordinances or opinions...mixed up with that child's composition" (99), Chillingworth says of Pearl. "The child could not be made amenable to rules" (68), and in her utter disregard for authority, Pearl represents that part of Hester released into intellectual freedom by open acknowledgment of her sin. Carried within Hester's body, Pearl is a human representation of the self behind the submissive self, and many parallels between mother and child emphasize the connection. Pearl's relationship to the Puritan children mirrors her mother's conflict. Pearl, at age three, must fight the children who want to throw mud at her and Hester; in her fierce posture, Pearl resembled "a half-fledged angel of judgement,—whose mission was to punish the sins of the rising generation" (76). Like Pearl, Hester is to evolve, in Puritan consciousness, into a type of angel; meanwhile, her presence is an inescapable reminder of Puritan shortcomings. Like her mother, Pearl is the outsider; in all her games, her imaginary playmates are her enemies. Pearl's words to the continually babbling and melancholy brook are a parody of Hester's famous exhortation to Dimmesdale: "0 foolish and tiresome little brook!... Why art thou so sad? Pluck up a spirit, and do not be all the time sighing and murmuring!" (134). The child's advice undercuts the pathos of Dimmesdale's melancholy, reducing it to a perpetual whining. Pearl's remedy for such sorrowful lassitude is close to her mother's "Preach! Write! Act! Do anything, save to lie down and die!" (142) directed at her lover.

What characterizes mother and daughter, and what is missing from Dimmesdale, is energy. Dimmesdale feels this "tumultuous rush of new life" (111) in the second scaffold scene when he takes Pearl's hand, for both "the mother and the child were communicating their vital warmth to his half-torpid system" (111). In this novel, life-giving energy is associated with rebellion, so much so that Hester's new identity appears to have been created by defiance. Pearl, conceived in a violation of all the rules, acts out the feelings her mother, conscious of Puritan scrutiny, does not fully reveal.

There is another significant similarity between Hester and Pearl. Just as Pearl's "unflinching courage...uncontrollable will...and sturdy pride" are extreme versions of the same qualities in her mother, Pearl, like Hester, has the gift of vision: "a bitter scorn of many things, which, when examined, might be found to have the taint of falsehood in them" (130). Hester's ability to distinguish truth from falsehood is tempered by her charity: she does not seek the false or the wicked, and when she finds them, she is tolerant. Pearl, again, is an extreme image of her mother. Her talent for detecting falsehood makes her her father's harshest critic and cruelest judge; she, not Hester, repeatedly challenges the man. Bereft of any reason to love the minister, Pearl sees him in the cold light of truth, and she conveys that vision to her mother. Once, looking into Pearl's eyes, Hester sees the shadow side of her lover, she confronts what he has become: "a face, fiend-like, full of smiling malice, yet bearing the semblance of features that she had known full well, though seldom with a smile, and never with malice, in them" (73).

The contrast between Hester and Dimmesdale is the disparity between the discerning outsider and the evasive insider. If Hester can be said to be developing an emerging self, Dimmesdale, throughout the novel, can be seen to be protecting a highly developed egotism. Even in the first scene in the novel, Dimmesdale, witness to the public torment of his lover, manages to shift his compassion within. His plea to the woman in pain implies that he is actually suffering more than she and that it is her fault that he is denied the bliss of public repentance. Her "open ignominy" becomes a grant from heaven of which he has been deprived; her refusal to name her lover, then, is selfish (53). Dimmesdale's self-pity is countered by Hester's declaration that she is willing to suffer the pain due to them both. Hester, suffering, perceives another's pain; Dimmesdale is conscious only of his own.

Dimmesdale nourishes his ego with approval.[4] He finds the prison bars of Puritan society a necessary support: "it would always be essential to his peace to feel the pressure of a faith about him, supporting, while it confined him within its iron framework" (91). Dimmesdale flourishes inside the bars; for him, they are a shelter. To be within their confines is to be safe from external threats to the self and confirmed in his chosen identity. Dimmesdale perceives his prison as a center of male power, so he is willing to trade his liberty for such safety.

The minister relies on external authority to define him, and he is willing to sell whatever autonomous part of him remains for such external validation of self. In Hester's visit to Governor Bellingham's house, there is an interesting description that hints at Dimmesdale's bargain. Hester comes to the governor's mansion to plead for continued custody of her child; when she arrives, she finds the father of her child among the political and clerical leaders in the house. Before she does so, she is greeted by "one of the Governor's bond-servants, a free-born Englishman, but now a seven years' slave. During that term he was to be the property of his master, and as much a commodity of bargain and sale as an ox, or a joint-stool" (77).

The bond-servant's term of servitude matches the seven years during which Dimmesdale hides his sin. In this encounter, Hester, the alien, must beg entry into the world of the patriarchs, where she meets a bondsman who is safely inside. He is within, however, because he has sold his freedom, his very self, to a powerful Puritan and, in so doing, has reduced himself to the level of a thing. He has denied his humanity in the transaction. For seven years he must remain within the governor's world, unless, at the governor's pleasure, he is traded, like a piece of furniture, to another owner.

In the bonded servant, Hester meets Dimmesdale's counterpart. For Dimmesdale, too, has traded self for security. And in so doing, he has relinquished his humanity. If Hester, the emblem of sin, is also the emblem of all the fallen, for Dimmesdale to deny his connection to her is to deny his human nature. And that is precisely what Dimmesdale does, for seven years. Hester is freed in the marketplace when she is devalued on the scaffold. Her "fall" is a sign that she is no longer a negotiable item. Having no "value" in the Puritan economic/religious system, she is released from its values. Dimmesdale, in contrast, sells himself into bondage so that his worth, in the fathers' eyes, will not be questioned. He becomes a commodity of the old men, his owners.

To remain valuable, Dimmesdale must remain innocent. That is, he must be a child, dependent on the fathers, and he must be deliberately blind. As Baym says, Dimmesdale "requires authority over him" (*Shape* 136). The congregation considers him an angel because he "kept himself simple and childlike" (52), and his simplicity is the deliberate innocence of the man who refuses to differentiate between falsehood and truth. Repeatedly, Dimmesdale either limits his vision or refuses to look at all. Caught in his own fear of exposure, Dimmesdale "seldom...looked straightforth at any object, whether human or inanimate" (96). He is also afraid to see what words can show him: "He had a ready faculty...of escaping from any topic that agitated his too sensitive and nervous temperament" (98). When he is forced to look on, at Hester's sad pleading to keep her child, his reaction reveals his egotism and innocence. Asked if he did not notice Hester's suffering, Dimmesdale replies, "There was a look of pain in her face, which I would gladly have been spared the sight of" (99). As in the first scaffold episode, Dimmesdale has managed to convert this scene of Hester's misery into a testimony to his own greater anguish. He desires, not that the scene had never occurred, but that he had not witnessed it. What Dimmesdale need not look at has never, for him, actually happened. Thus, to refuse to see is to remain safe.

The pain of perpetual concealment and fear supposedly makes Dimmesdale a more effective minister, giving him "sympathies...intimate with the sinful brotherhood of mankind" (104), but the mask of innocence blocks genuine intimacy. Unable to reveal himself as a member of the sinful brotherhood, Dimmesdale cowers behind his role at the top of the hierarchy. Thus, others are merely confused and damaged by their minister. He sends "a throb of [his] pain through a thousand other hearts," but, since he cannot acknowledge the source of his suffering, "people knew not of the power that moved them thus." Its effect is to widen the gap between sinners and saint: "They deemed the young clergyman," in his power to transmit pain, "a miracle of holiness" (104-05).

Dimmesdale's conception of his ministerial role is another evasion, for he prefers to deal with abstractions instead of with people. He is filled with "high aspirations for the welfare of his race, warm love of souls... natural piety, strengthened by thought and study and illuminated by revelation" (96). The description is noteworthy for its loftiness. Dimmesdale loves souls, not individual people; he cares for the race. His piety is strengthened by retreat to his study, not by contact with his congregation. Like the characteristic American hero of so many Romantic novels, Dimmesdale seeks answers in the large world of abstraction or in the small, personal haven of the solitary self.[5]

Either place provides a cowardly retreat from the kind of seeing that can distinguish truth from falsehood. Such vision is, of course, abhorrent to Dimmesdale because Dimmesdale's true crime is self-deception.[6] In his notebooks, Hawthorne considers writing about "a man who, in himself and in his external circumstances, shall be equally and totally false....making the whole universe, heaven and earth alike an insubstantial mockery to him" ("Hawthorne's Notebooks" 194-95). Dimmesdale is such a man, and his ability to deceive himself condemns him to live in an insubstantial universe, where he can no longer differentiate between falsehood and reality.

Dimmesdale is the solipsistic hero who will not see the truth of himself. His agony is that, in the retreat within, he is left alone with that which he most fears. On his long vigils, he spends entire nights "viewing his own face in a looking-glass, by the most powerful light which he could throw upon it. He thus typified the constant introspection wherewith he tortured, but could not purify, himself" (106).[7] No light, no matter how powerful, can substitute for the inner vision he avoids. Dimmesdale cannot purify himself because he will not acknowledge his true failings. He identifies his error as his adulterous love. He is thus most penitent for the one action in his life that enabled him to be fully human. Loving Hester, Dimmesdale might have experienced a Fortunate Fall—into the community of sinners. Choosing to live, instead, among the Puritan saints, Dimmesdale imprisons himself in their falsehood and his own.

To maintain his innocence, Dimmesdale must increasingly limit his vision and deny himself any intimacy with others, who might see beyond his role. And so he is left alone, in darkness, with the mirror image which can give him only falsity. Tormented by deception within, Dimmesdale perceives the taint of falsehood everywhere. Denying that inner vision which could reveal him to himself, Dimmesdale is also deprived of the capacity to see beyond himself. "It is the unspeakable misery of a life so false as his, that it steals the pith and substance out of whatever realities there are around us, and which were meant by Heaven to be the spirit's joy and nutriment" (107). Dimmesdale's carefully chosen innocence starves his soul. Severing his connection to the realities of earth, he loses the realities of heaven as well. "To the untrue man, the whole universe is false,—it is impalpable,—it shrinks to nothing within his grasp" (107). By refusing to see his own humanity, Dimmesdale, in the end, can distinguish nothing at all.

From that small prison of the false self, Dimmesdale looks out upon distortion. He cannot recognize Chillingworth as his enemy; he cannot be sure if a meteor is a mark of his sin. Even his final moment of "truth" involves a sequence of lies. There is the initial self-deception that Hester has "tempted" Dimmesdale to run away, when in reality she had merely "spoken what he vaguely hinted at, but dared not speak" (143).[8] After this lie, the minister is truly in a maze of deception, for he lies again in declaring his motive for delivering the election sermon to be duty, not pride. No wonder that, on returning to society, every familiar object seems strange!

Election day brings further falsity. As he begins to deliver his sermon, Dimmesdale retreats into total self-absorption: "he saw nothing, heard nothing, knew nothing, of what was around him" (169). He remains oblivious to Hester's agony, replicated in the agitation of Pearl. As Hester endures the cruel gaze of strangers and of the matrons who condemned her seven years earlier, Dimmesdale enjoys his moment of supreme glory. His sermon is a paean to Puritan values, predicting "a high and glorious destiny for the...people of the Lord" (176). According to Joel Porte, "What he actually—and incredibly—does in his last utterance is to apply the sermon's prophetic message of a high and glorious destiny for the people of New England to himself" (411-12). Exalting his congregation, Dimmesdale exalts himself, in a clear exchange of delusions. Dimmesdale can find the approval he craves by telling the people what they want to hear. He is again selling the values of the group, thereby acquiring public esteem.

Dimmesdale encases himself in a tissue of lies that separates him from his lover. And although Dimmesdale leans on Hester as he ascends the scaffold, his words on the platform dissociate him from her forever. For Dimmesdale again manages a curious transformation: his confession becomes his own eulogy. His final words confirm his sanctity and repudiate his bond to Hester. When she asks him if they might meet again in a new union in heaven, Dimmesdale evades any commitment to Hester and retreats to the safety of Puritan doctrine. It may be, he postulates, "vain to hope that we could meet hereafter, in an everlasting and pure reunion." However, "God knows; and He is merciful" (181). In what Crews calls this "egocentric confession" (151) Dimmesdale has apparently appropriated that mercy for himself. Having dismissed Hester's appeal, he focuses on the certainty of his own final destination; he tells the crowd that the pain in his heart and the tortures of Chillingworth have been signs of God's favor, bringing him to the "triumphant ignominy" of this moment of salvation (181). And so, although he dies in Hester's arms, Dimmesdale expires, in essence, in what Gross the calls "the spiritual embrace of his orthodoxy" (364).

Dying is the only thing left for Dimmesdale to do. It is the supreme evasion of responsibility, the final negation. Having confessed without confessing, he can exit without care for the consequences of his act. His death is symbolically appropriate. Stripped of his veil of innocence, the minister appears as he is—living death. His self-deception has reduced his life to nothing. Without the veil that was all that remained of him, Dimmesdale is exposed as a nullity.

Perhaps that is why so many of the crowd claim to have seen nothing on the scaffold. They are careful to deny a connection between the dead saint and the living sinner. Like Dimmesdale, they look away from what disturbs them. But in a sense, they see clearly, for the tie between Dimmesdale and Hester was broken long before, when Dimmesdale, like the crowd, chose not to see.

Innocence is death. Rebellion is life. And so Hester is left to live alone, again surrounded by a hostile crowd, protecting her child. The insider and the outsider[9] cannot unite because Hester has long ago rejected her assigned place in the static world of marketplace and prison. And for Dimmesdale, what happened in the forest is too frightening to be acknowledged. His one venture into that world must be forever denied, or, better yet, converted into a parable of Puritan virtue. He dies an insider, his legacy to his child the taint of conformity, the kiss that will enable her to move within society.

At the end, there is only Hester. With Pearl safe within the old world, Hester, still the intruder, returns to play out her drama to the end. By again wearing the letter, the sign of her separateness, Hester, as Baym says, "brings the community to accept that letter on her terms rather than its own" (*Shape* 6). She completes the task begun on the day she left the prison, her function as what Charles Feidelson calls "an agent of transvaluation for her contemporaries" (397). She constructs a new community within the old one. Because she does not retreat from confrontation with the crowd, she proposes a "transcendental ideal of positive freedom," as Frederic Carpenter describes it, "instead of the romantic ideal of mere escape" (316). She carries rebellion—and thus vitality—where it is needed, inside.

Hester's Boston is a place where religious and financial power are inextricably linked and where both are sustained by lies. Hester's crime against the elders is a religious crime punished in the marketplace, and rightly so, because it is a defacement of her husband's property. Pearl's outcast status as a product of sin is quickly transformed when she becomes an heiress (of a truly sinful man) and thus a highly suitable bride for any Boston boy. As Feidelson notes, the jail and the burial ground are the proper meeting-houses in the place: "Not once in the book is a church physically described or a scene actually staged within it" (393).

The second center of power, the governor's mansion, is a house characterized by simulation, where shards of broken glass embedded in the stucco can pass for diamonds in the momentary dazzle of the sun. What is outside, what appears to be, is all that matters, for Governor Bellingham makes people, like his bonded servant, into things. "Puritan institutions," says Baym, "define the human being as all surface, all public" (*Shape* 141). Boston, both a Puritan and a money society, is doubly dedicated to appearance. Thus Hester, who redefines her own appearance to reflect an inner strength, threatens the centers of power.

The letter is designed to devalue the woman. Wearing it, Hester is to be a living signpost. Her appearance is meant to remind others of the penalties for deviance; thus she is to serve as an enforcer of the Puritan code. But Hester's assigned public self is transformed by her private rebellion. The "A" that is meant to signify wantonness becomes, instead, a sign of transcendence. When society declares that Hester has failed in her feminine role, Hester suggests that she has moved beyond the role. She recreates her private self and modifies appearances to reflect the change. Assuming a "studied austerity" of dress and "a lack of demonstration in her manners," she casts off the stereotype like "the fragments of a broken chain" (119). The letter which was to limit her to a sexually defined position has the effect of "a cross on a nun's bosom" (118). The letter protects her from the dangers of life as a female object; it keeps her secure "amid all peril" (118). Because she is no longer perceived as the standardized sexual possession, Hester can move freely in the forest, safe from Indians and thieves, and in the town, where she is eventually re-valued, not devalued.

Hester's widening perception enables her to recognize the dangers of accepting appearance as reality. By assuming the role of child bride in a loveless marriage, she committed the original sin that led to so much sorrow. Her "crime most to be repented of," she sees, was her innocent acceptance of "the marble image of happiness" as a substitute for the "warm reality" of a different kind of relationship (127). Recognizing the falseness of this patriarchal bond, Hester speculates about alternatives, ways to "establish the whole relation between man and woman on a sure ground of mutual happiness" (185).

Hester's incipient feminism subverts the Puritan power structure, but that feminism is part of an even greater danger. By speculating about alternative relationships, Hester threatens to break every chain in the hierarchy. Offering connections based on the inner life and not the public one, Hester can shatter the facade of appearances. She can expose diamonds as shards of glass and release the prisoners of the public self.

"Little accustomed, in her long seclusion from society, to measure her ideas of right and wrong by any standard external to herself" (116), Hester develops a new moral code.[10] Remaining within Puritan society but not of it, she proposes an ethics of compassion and generosity, of concrete action, not abstraction. Because Hester is a woman, Hawthorne compares her to a nun, but, in terms of her effect on the Puritan community, Hester is more a minister than Dimmesdale.

Dimmesdale couches his spiritual goals in abstractions, conceiving of people as "the race," or as "souls," and his consciousness of universal suffering brings only pain and puzzlement to the needy. Terrified of revealing his private self, Dimmesdale remains the minister as spiritual superior, the isolated judge. Hester, on the other hand, "was quick to acknowledge her sisterhood with the race of man," not by accusing others of wrongdoing, but by sharing "her little substance" with the poor, by nursing the sick, by practical actions "in all seasons of calamity" (116). "In such emergencies, Hester's nature showed itself warm and rich; a well-spring of human tenderness, unfailing to every real demand, and inexhaustible by the largest" (117).

The people of Boston worry constantly about their beloved Dimmesdale, for he seems weak and frail, debilitated by his sanctity. Hester's ministry reveals her vitality; her capacity to give is boundless, her energy immense. In her, others see not only the "power to sympathize," but the "power to do" (117); she offers no sermon or personal exhortation, no words, just deeds. "She totally challenges the abstract city of their [the Puritans'] abstract God," says Feidelson (395).

And she challenges the dominion of appearances as well, substituting an inner reality that is positive and rich. Her "power to do" transforms the letter, so that it comes to mean "Able," but it is also the symbol of Amor, the love that conquers all, the light that comforts the darkest hours of a dying man (117). As a symbol of Hester's inexhaustible "power to sympathize," it marks her as an angel.

Dimmesdale, too, is considered an angel. But his people define him as such because he appears too good for the earth, above sinners and thus beyond human concerns. They see only the appearance of the man and feel estranged from its perfection; it is a hard, cold surface deflecting sympathy while demanding respect. Like the glass on the Governor's house, he shines with simulated value. If he is an angel, he is a spirit of despair, for his carefully maintained purity signifies an impossible ideal. Accepting the public man as a superior spirit, the people see no connection between him and themselves. His perfection is, instead, a reproach for their failings, a reminder of their flaws.

Hester was to have been a reminder of sin, and yet she becomes an angel of hope. In her fall and subsequent rise, others see the possibility of their own redemption and renewal. Because she reveals the inner self, first, in her adultery, and later, in her charity, she exposes the community to a new vision. This is the vision of the integrated self, joined to others by bonds of care and yet free to question, to think, and to grow alone. Remaining within the community that reviled her, Hester transforms it. Her power is the power to widen vision, to propose a new world within the old, based on principles of inclusion, not exclusion. Hester brings the American dream of possibility within the walls of her enemies and, at least in a small way, conquers. After some years, Hester, the outsider on the scaffold, becomes known in Boston as "our Hester" (118). Accepting the intruder, the community embraces its own sin—and its own regeneration.

Chapter Five:
Rebels Defeated and Compromised

The bird that would soar above the level plain of tradition and prejudice must have strong wings. It is a sad spectacle to see the weaklings bruised, exhausted, fluttering back to earth.

Kate Chopin, The Awakening (82)

Section One:
Division and Death

The Awakening

In *The Scarlet Letter*, society's punishment of Hester Prynne illuminates its brutality in suppressing female rebellion. In three subsequent novels, Kate Chopin's *The Awakening*, Edith Wharton's *The House of Mirth*, and Willa Cather's *Lucy Gayheart*, the fate of the heroines is equally revealing. In each case, a woman struggles to construct an adult, autonomous self, and her conflicts in that struggle are a vehicle for social criticism. As the heroines try to grow, they battle an entire culture designed to arrest their development.[1]

Even as they begin the conflict, these heroines, like Hester Prynne, are already at a disadvantage, for they are markedly different from their peers. "She is not one of us," a Creole woman says of Chopin's Edna Pontellier (21), for Edna drifts through everyday duties while she lives in her dreams. Lily Bart, of *The House of Mirth*, is at the same time chameleon-like in her adaptability and unique: even her appearance, so calculated to please, has "an external rarity, an air of being impossible to match" (229-30). And Lucy Gayheart, Cather's heroine, becomes a kind of legend in her town because she is so alive. To her lover, she seems "gathered up and sustained by something that never let her drop into the common world" (215). All three are women who are in some way unorthodox and are therefore both attractive and threatening to others. They defy easy categorization, for they are involved in the process of creating a new self even as they cling to the old one. And, in each novel, the heroine's ongoing conflict with society is most fully reflected in her romantic relationships, in her interaction with a husband and/or with her lovers. As in *The Scarlet Letter*, the novels become the stories of outsider heroines involved with insiders, with men who are safely accepted by society and reluctant to join the heroine outside of it. In the interaction of insider/outsider there is thus a double plot, one part tracing the effect of conventional masculine standards on the unconventional heroine, the other exploring the heroine's impact on male sensibilities. The books are doubly novels of education because both sexes, representative of widely divergent ways of being and thinking, teach and learn.

Duality is the motif of all three novels; all are studies of the divided self, of the woman who needs to be free of social definitions that debase her, and, at the same time, needs to feel linked to another person. The heroines are tormented by the ambiguous nature of solitude, and their dilemma is expressed most effectively in *The Awakening*, when Edna Pontellier listens to a song she particularly likes and which, in her fantasies, she calls "Solitude." "When she heard it there came before her imagination the figure of a man standing beside a desolate rock on the seashore. He was naked. His attitude was one of hopeless resignation as he looked toward a distant bird winging its flight away from him" (27). The dream evoked by the music is exciting but bleak. Edna envisions a man, perhaps her concealed, energized self, alone and naked, perhaps like her desired self, released from social roles and social disguises. But the solitary figure is looking toward a creature that eludes him—the bird soaring out of view. Solitude, as imagined by Edna, brings discontent, a yearning for something so elusive it is hardly visible.

The duality of the three novels emanates from the central puzzle of solitude. To re-create the self, the heroines learn, one must move away from those social ties that have formed the old self. And yet solitude is terrifying to women who have been formed to conform and to live in others' eyes. Edna, Lily, and Lucy are vital and young, but they are afraid. They fear isolation, but they scorn the constraints of the conventional love affair or marriage. They want some new and different union to relieve the pain of being alone. But it is difficult to create such a union within a hostile world. To do so, one must be very strong, with a strength that can only be acquired by suffering and by transcending the misery of solitude.

The novels focus on heroines caught in this double bind. Each book is rich with the imagery of division and polarities, and with all the gradations between the extremes. Each involves an outsider heroine and insider men, and there is a further, complex interaction of external and inner self. The language of polarities centers on images of freedom and suffocation, heat and cold, up and down, stimulant and narcotic, sleeping and waking, decision and drift. Such imagery reflects the confusion of the heroines as they move between extreme versions of the self, assuming tentative identities or resisting those imposed by others. These are novels filled with movement: Edna Pontellier's erratic escapes from convention and her puzzled returns, Lily Bart's social fall and her simultaneous moral climb, and Lucy Gayheart's brave steps into the wider worlds of the city, of art, and of romance.[2]

Much of this movement, however, is not a conscious step forward; it is a drift that ends in death. Edna exults in her swimming, but she dies in water; Lily travels into new social sets, but each new milieu diminishes her social status; Lucy escapes from the small town that limits her, only to return to it in despair.

The ambiguity of this movement and the heroine's inability to control her fate are reflected in the pervasive water imagery of the novels. Two of these heroines die in water; the third, Lily, is repeatedly associated with images of drifting and drowning. Even as these women sever their connections with society, they realize they cannot survive alone; they are engulfed by solitude. And so they regress, back to conventional roles and relationships, until these structures again become too confining. The heroines are compelled to repeat the futile pattern of disconnection and reconnection because they cannot maintain their rebellious selves in isolation, and thus, on re-entering society, cannot maintain a new connection to the group.

Presenting the new, emergent and vulnerable self to society, each heroine encounters rejection. There is no one within who desires the transformed female self, and there is no one within who will support further change. In all three of these novels, the death of the heroine is closely preceded by an encounter with a lover and a failed attempt at union. The final confrontation of intruder and social insider is precisely that, a confrontation, because it involves such divergent interests and needs. In the classic American novel involving the traditional American hero, isolation would be considered triumph, a moral if not a material victory over the hostile forces of society. As recent studies by Carol Gilligan suggest, the moment of separation is, for the male in modern American culture, the moment at which maturity is achieved. For the female, however, maturity is equated with attachment, an ideal that is very threatening to men (171).

The final scene between the lovers in each of the three novels describes the sexes at cross-purposes, the male attempting to preserve his isolation, the female to alleviate hers. Each heroine is searching for some bond that can nurture the embryo self. Each heroine learns to despair of such a radical union.[3]

Subsequently, there is no completed transformation of the self. Edna, Lily, and Lucy are not Hester Prynne; they cannot travel as far as she. Discarding their conventional identities, they become, like Hester, aliens within the conventional world. Like her, they redefine themselves from within and conceive a new way to be. They suffer the misery of solitude and discover another kind of loneliness in society's rejection of their recreated selves. But unlike Hester, they are weak: they are unable to remain in the isolation that could bring its own bitter strength, and they cannot confront a hostile world alone.[4] They cannot move from empowering isolation to a genuine human bond, the step Kate Chopin described in her own life as one of "emerging from the vast solitude in which I had been making my own acquaintance" ("Confidences" I, 700). The embryo self will not survive in society, and so, in these three novels, it is preserved another way—in death. For two of the three heroines, who die in the water, the fragile self surrounded by water seems like a baby in the womb. The third woman dies dreaming of a sleeping infant who must not wake up.

These women die to preserve life, to prevent the destruction of the new identity that living would entail. Awakened to a vision of an alternative way to be, they cannot convince others to share that view. Their stories illustrate Baym's words about earlier American heroines: "a sense of self-worth is fragile, and it is not the end but the beginning of change" (*Women's Fiction* 104). Edna Pontellier, Lily Bart, and Lucy Gayheart acquire that sense, but they are not capable of sustaining the new self. They find no person who will join them to effect change. Their conflicting needs for autonomy and acceptance divide their energies and confuse their actions. They die because there is simply no place for them in the world as it is, and because they are defeated by their own dual natures.

Edna Pontellier is the most mysterious of the three heroines. Externally she is the most successful: she is the indulged wife of a well-to-do man, a mother who cares for her children, a secure member of a social group that is less restrictive than most. The Creole society of *The Awakening* pampers its women; they have their servants, their amusements, their harmless flirtations, and more latitude in their behavior than, say, old New York would give them. Edna appears to enjoy what she has, but she is not truly a part of it, nor is she sufficiently amused by it. She married rather casually because Léonce Pontellier's devotion flattered her; she is fond of her husband but feels no passion for him. She is fond of her children, too, "in an uneven, impulsive way" (2), but feels they are a responsibility for which she is not suited. She is a Protestant among Catholics, and she does not understand the Creole women's flirting, their off-color remarks, and their corresponding chastity. Edna moves among the members of her group, but she is not really there. A "mantle of reserve" envelops her (15). From childhood on, she has lived "her own small life all within herself. At a very early period she had apprehended instinctively the dual life—that outward existence which conforms, the inward life which questions" (15).

What makes Edna so puzzling can, in large part, be explained by her retreat within. The capacity to withdraw frees Edna from many of the daily irritations of the feminine role. Confronted by the trivial concerns of marriage and motherhood, Edna merely moves back, inside, behind the mantle of reserve. Her ability to do so is a clear sign that Edna is in many ways like a hero, not a heroine.

Patricia Meyer Spacks notes that all Edna's "connections with the outside world are arbitrary and temporary; the focus of her real interest is entirely within" (75). Retreating to the small world of the inner self, Edna resembles the classic American hero seeking similar sanctuary. There are many others ways in which she is like a male. She tries to read Emerson, that spokesman for the male American dream, and like an American hero, she feels dissociated from time. "The past was nothing to her; offered no lesson which she was willing to heed. The future was a mystery" (46). Free of the constraints of the past and of considerations for the future, she wants a similar freedom in her human relationships. Like a man, she wants marriage to be a part of her life, but not its focus; she wants sex without consequences, children without the heavy burden of parenthood. "Although she does not wish to be the possession of another," Spacks says, "she yearns to possess" (75-76),⁵ in other words, to enjoy a male privilege.

Nonetheless, Edna is a woman. And the traditionally masculine qualities she exhibits damage her not only because she is a woman and thus is not expected to assume a male role, but also because the traits are equally destructive of either sex. In her desire for pleasure without consequences, in her denial of the responsibilities of human relationships, and particularly in her retreat to dreams, Edna represents the American innocent, the child in the child-world.

Edna's ability to dream is simultaneously a source of strength and the cause of her destruction. For Edna, the life within has always been the life of fantasy. Her concept of love, for example, has always emanated from her dreams, and thus Edna has trouble distinguishing love from infatuation. She had married because she wanted to free herself from dreams: as a wife, she felt, "she would take her place with a certain dignity in the world of reality, closing the portals forever behind her upon the realms of romance and dreams." Léonce's worship of Edna, she felt, would release her from her infatuation with a great tragedian whose picture had come to "haunt her imagination and stir her senses. The persistence of the infatuation lent it an aspect of genuineness" (19).

The episode encapsulates Edna's confusion of dream and reality, a confusion exacerbated by her childish longing to make her dreams real. Driven by the needs her dreams define, Edna mistakes role for reality, so that Robert LeBrun's summer romance becomes, for Edna, the passion of her life. "Let Mrs Pontellier alone," Edna's friend warns Robert. "She is not one of us; she is not like us. She might make the unfortunate blunder of taking you seriously" (21). Infatuated with Robert, Edna becomes again the child who had a crush on a cavalry officer; not only can she live her dream, she can return to a childhood of dreaming. Much of Edna's rebellion, then, is regression, for it is an attempt to fill a child's needs. Edna's confidante, Adèle Ratignolle, scolds her, "In some way you seem to me like a child.... You seem to act without a certain amount of reflection which is necessary in this life" (95).

A creature of impulse and whim, Edna is criticized for her childish behavior, yet others want her to be childish. The problem is that Edna is not the right kind of child: she is too assertive, too full of her own fancies to be the perfect child-wife. And the problem is compounded by the fact that Edna is trying to grow up, "daily casting aside that fictitious self which we assume like a garment with which to appear before the world" (57). Edna is trying to learn to distinguish role from reality. "She began to look with her own eyes; to see and to apprehend the deeper undercurrents of life" (93). But as she looks around her for a new way to be, she learns a new lesson. She begins to understand that a social self is a useful garment, and that, without it, one can feel very cold.

The people around Edna present her with a variety of roles, most of them socially defined and therefore socially acceptable.[6] Léonce Pontellier, an ambitious businessman, considers his wife a possession. When Edna swims in the heat of the day and becomes sunburnt, Léonce is upset, "looking at his wife as one looks at a valuable piece of personal property which has suffered some damage" (4). Committed above all to "*les convenances*" (51), Léonce expects Edna to behave conventionally: to be a committed mother to his sons, a gracious hostess to his business associates, and an efficient manager of his household. Léonce enjoys spending money and thus appearing successful, and he expects his wife to shine, for she is one of his acquisitions. But one of Edna's first acts in the novel is to remove her wedding rings.

Adèle Ratignolle proposes another way for Edna to be; she is the mother-woman, pregnant every two years, preoccupied with childbirth and child-rearing, encased in an aura of domestic and maternal bliss. Her relationship to her husband is the close union of two people deeply involved in the home and desiring nothing else. Adèle lives the Creole ideal of womanhood, and her nurturing personality draws everyone, including Edna, to her. But she is not what Edna wants to be.

Edna's lovers appear to offer her more exciting images of herself, but these images, too, prove unsatisfactory. Both Robert LeBrun and Alcée Arobin propose conventional escapes from the tedium of marriage and motherhood.

Although Robert is briefly drawn into Edna's fantasy of love, he is unwilling to risk his place in society to retain that love. Even when he discovers that he cannot escape his feelings for Edna by running to another country, he can imagine only a social solution to their problems, "a wild dream of your some way becoming my wife" (106), he tells Edna, offering her a role she is unwilling to resume, even for a new man. And for Robert, the vision is merely a dream, because, as a conformist, he is unwilling to accept the social consequences of such a marriage. Unable to consider Edna as another of his seasonal amusements, and unwilling to make her more, Robert does not know how to think of her, and so Edna is not certain what she is supposed to be.

Alcée Arobin knows exactly what he expects of Edna. The stereotypical, almost comic seducer of other men's wives, Arobin views Edna as one of many dalliances, and she, too, assesses their affair as superficial. In the Creole world, Arobin functions as a safety valve for bored housewives, as a conventional sinner who may actually help to preserve marriages rather than to disrupt them. In Arobin's arms, Edna is a recalcitrant wife, but a wife nevertheless.

Each of these characters, safely established in society, emphasizes one version of Edna to the exclusion of all others. To Léonce and Robert, Edna is a valuable possession; to Arobin, she is a sensuous animal. To Adèle, she is a mother who needs to be reminded of her duty. Only Mademoiselle Reisz envisions a radically new way for Edna to be, for Mademoiselle Reisz lives that role. A spinster and artist, Reisz is self-centered, "disagreeable," with a "temper which was self-assertive and a disposition to trample upon the rights of others" (26). As disagreeable as she may be, she is in constant social contact with most of the major characters of the novel, visited and visiting frequently. She is a very good musician. And she lives, quite successfully, alone.

Reisz presents an image of a new self; "by her divine art," she "seemed to reach Edna's spirit and set it free" (78). She is not liked, but she is respected, consulted, confided in. She is not rich or pampered, but her life is filled with the pleasure of her art.[7] In isolation, she has achieved strength; she has re-connected to society on her own terms. She warns Edna, who fancies herself an artist, that "The bird that would soar above the level plain of tradition and prejudice must have strong wings" (82). But Edna is not strong; she does not want to live alone, to be a middle-aged lone woman, without much money, forced to fight for herself because no one else will fight for her. If Edna is a bird, she is the caged parrot whose cries open the novel, or the domestic pigeon of her pigeon-house, or the bird with the broken wing of the novel's ending.

She cannot become the image Reisz proposes, for it is as elusive as the bird in Edna's dream of "Solitude."[8]

"One of these days," Edna says, "I'm going to pull myself together for a while and think—try to determine what character of a woman I am; for, candidly, I don't know" (82). Edna rarely thinks; thus, she often behaves like a child.[9] In her initial rebellion against her husband, she is "blindly following whatever impulse moved her," placing herself "in alien hands for direction," freeing "her soul of responsibility" (33). Returning from the summer at Grand Isle to the more restrictive routine of New Orleans, she continues to drift, "lending herself to any passing caprice" (57), petulantly waiting for "something to happen—something, anything, she did not know what" (75). Edna feels, acts, and reacts, but she rarely thinks. The doctor Léonce calls in to diagnose the "disease" of Edna's rebellion sees an energized being, free of repression, but he thinks of her as a "beautiful, sleeping animal waking up in the sun" (70). Edna releases her sensuous self, but she is still a creature, not fully human in mind or spirit.

Without a conscious purpose or a self-defined image of what she wants to be, Edna repeats a futile pattern. It is important to note that Edna never makes a clean break with society. Even as she learns to swim alone on Grand Isle, she enjoys her trysts with Robert, maintains a cordial relationship with her indulgent husband, and participates in the group activities of the summer residents. On her return to New Orleans, she stops her social calls and retreats to her studio, but she also spends a great deal of time visiting—seeking maternal affection from the cheerful Adèle, and discipline and direction from the irascible Reisz. Losing one romantic fantasy when Robert leaves, she settles for a more conventional affair with Arobin.

Rejecting the social set of her husband's business connections, Edna merely enters a new, less respectable group, the Merriman/Highcamp set, a cheap imitation of her earlier friends. As Spacks says, Edna's "fantasy of freedom depends on another human being" (75),[10] and so the pleasures of solitude soon become, for Edna, the miseries of isolation, and she repeatedly moves outside society and then inside again.

The imagery of the novel emphasizes the confused nature of Edna's rebellion. Polarized water images and other contrasts of conscious/unconscious, inside/outside explore the conflicts of the divided self. Chopin's language increases the distance between the rigidly defined roles that imprison Edna and Edna's amorphous dreams of something better.

During the summer when she learns to swim, Edna feels "as if she were being borne away from some anchorage which had held her fast...leaving her free to drift whithersoever she chose to set her sails" (35). She feels at once free (cut loose of a restricting anchor) and in control, for she can decide to "set her sails." But there is also a sense of passivity in the drift that comes with freedom. Edna is moving, as she desired, but is she setting her own course or being "borne away" by whim? Swimming, she feels "exultation," but the farther she swims, the more she endangers her life: "the stretch of water behind her assumed the aspect of a barrier which her unaided strength would never be able to overcome." The reckless power of movement gives way to a "quick vision of death" that "smote her soul" (28-29). Moving beyond society, Edna fears she can never get back; she has cut herself loose of social restrictions but also cut herself off from the social approval that nourished her for so long.[11]

There is a similar ambivalence in the language of awakening that fills the book. One of the first references to this awakening characterizes it as a source of conflict, not release: "A certain light was beginning to dawn dimly within her,—the light which, showing the way, forbids it" (14). Edna is beginning to widen her vision, but what she sees and how it will help her are questionable. As early as 1909, Percival Pollard asked whether Edna was waking up or drugged (160-62), and the question is a valid one. For every reference to Edna's heightened consciousness there is another to a dulled one. That first reference to a dawning light, for example, is rapidly followed by the results of such enlightenment: "It moved her to dreams" and to "thoughtfulness" (14). Light brings thought, but also fantasy. Edna sleeps a great deal in the novel, and her waking moments are often deliberate attempts to evade consciousness. She gambles, caught by "the fever of the game" which gets "into her blood and...brain like an intoxicant" (74). Her love for Robert is "the spell of her infatuation" (54); the presence of Arobin, who is "absolutely nothing to her," acts "like a narcotic upon her" (77). Forced to choose between the two men, she "stayed alone in a sort of stupor" (101). Drifting between a manic excitement and a waking sleep, Edna bruises herself as she brushes against the extremes.

Whatever the nature of her awakening, it results in a perpetual displacement. Edna cannot find comfort inside or out. On Grand Isle, where she quarrels with her husband, she chooses to rebel by refusing to sleep inside the cottage, but when Léonce joins her on the porch, she decides to retreat to the bedroom. Back in the city, she finds the familiar streets "an alien world which had suddenly become antagonist" (54). Buildings threaten; Mrs. Lebrun's house, with barred doors and windows, is a prison (59), yet Edna's declaration of independence from her husband's domain involves her move to a smaller interior, a "pigeon-house." Only Mademoiselle Reisz seems to reconcile inside and outside, to create a space to protect but not imprison the free self. In her house, the windows are always open. They thus admit a good deal of smoke and dirt, but "at the same time all the light and air that there was" enters, as well (61). Reisz's home is thus open to all that life offers: the filth and the unpleasantness (that Edna fears), the light (that Edna sees only dimly), and the air (that Edna craves). There is no such place for Edna. She cannot be the solitary soul she admires.

And there is no one to share Edna's isolation and thus to ease it. Robert, far more terrified of ostracism than Edna, leaves her—twice. He can connect to Edna only when she remains within a conventional context; he is unwilling to imagine, much less enter, a different relationship. Robert is like Arobin in that he will violate the rules of his world only in ways that world will tolerate. On Grand Isle, Edna's awakened sensuality evokes a genuine response from Robert. In this summer retreat, however, there is little risk in Robert's passion. He can break the rules without fear of reprisal, for the tolerant Creoles do not take his flirtations seriously. But when Edna does take Robert seriously, when she assumes that his love for her is more important than the sanctions against it, she frightens him. When the summer is over, Robert wants to retreat to the safe, structured world of convention. In that world is his "real" life—his business, his ambitions. In that world, women are easily categorized—there are the wives of other businessmen he can amuse but not possess, and the lower class women he can seduce and discard. Edna challenges Robert to look beyond such categories. But he prefers to remember her as an idealized but inaccessible love rather than to live with her in scandal. Having awakened Edna to a dream of love, he abandons her to a reality of isolation. What she teaches him, then, is the depth of his conformity.

And so Edna remains divided. Dissatisfied within society, she leaves it, only to find the loneliness unbearable. For her, there is to be no reconciliation of inner desires and external demands, no emergence of a new being who can confront society and create a new place within it. In Adèle's labor and delivery, Adèle cries out, "think of the children!" and her words express the two poles of Edna's dilemma (109). When Adèle exhorts her friend to remember her sons, she is reminding Edna of her social responsibilities, of the self she repeatedly rejected. But to re-enter society is to face a double danger. To become again the imprisoned wife and mother is, for Edna, to obliterate the awakening self, and to be tempted to new corruptions as well. Edna fears a life so purposeless that soon one lover will mean nothing more than another, when the conventional roles and her conventional rebellions will have made her into something monstrous. To live for the children, then, could be a living death.

Adèle's words may hold a second meaning for Edna. As Adèle suffers, Edna feels "a vague dread" and she remembers the birth of her children: "an ecstasy of pain, the heavy odor of chloroform, a stupor which had deadened sensation, and an awakening to find a new little life to which she had given being" (108). Edna's memories chart not only her deliveries but also the pain of her present isolation, the drugged stupor of her confused sensuality, and a final, frightening awakening. Witnessing this delivery, Edna realizes that she cannot give birth to herself; she cannot be re-born as the strong figure who can survive alone. The birth would be too painful. The new being would not live. Edna awakens, then, to a decision to die.

Cynthia Griffin Wolff calls Edna's awakening a realization of her separation, a recognition of "the hopelessness of ever satisfying the dream of total fusion." She describes Edna's suicide as a regression, an infantile retreat ("Thanatos" 217). And, in moving back to the site of her initial rebellion, Edna does retreat to her dream of a freedom sustained by love, as a swimmer is buoyed by the sea or a child is carried in the womb. As Spacks notes, the suicide is voluptuous; it is an "ironic sexual consummation: she has found an illusory physical fulfillment without the pain of relationship" (76). Dying, Edna is again the child, remembering the meadow, the endless ocean of grass near her father's house. And she is again the infatuated young girl, for, in her last moments of consciousness, the cavalry officer, her first fantasy of romance, appears. Death is a lover who will not forsake her.

But death is also the only means of preserving Edna's new self.[12] The water is the womb in which that fragile creation can be protected; there is no other place where it will not be damaged and destroyed. Feeling powerless to change her future, Edna chooses to stop time in the only way possible. In her final swim she is forever the "new-born creature" of hope (113).

Edna is destroyed by forces inside and out. She is not a model of maturity; she has learned to see, but her vision is limited and blurred. The inner failings that arrest Edna's growth are the social values she has internalized. Her inability to plan, to think, and to discipline herself are the very qualities expected of the child bride who submits to another's control and lives by another's standards. Edna's misfortune is her inability to play the role well—or to abandon it fully. Her conflict reveals the power of her world to deface women, whether they remain inside that world or try to move beyond it.

The House of Mirth

Edith Wharton explores the power of another, similar world in describing the struggles of Lily Bart in *The House of Mirth*. Discussing the novel, Wharton said that she faced a problem in attempting to inject human significance into a story of "irresponsible pleasure-seekers," another group like those in "The Valley of Childish Things." She solved the problem, she said, by concluding that "a frivolous society can acquire dramatic significance only through what its frivolity destroys. Its tragic implication lies in its power of debasing people and ideas" (*A Backward Glance* 207). In depicting the social fall and simultaneous moral climb of her heroine,[13] Wharton reveals the dehumanization of a whole culture and proposes an alternative network of human connection.

Beginning with an intruder who becomes increasingly threatening to the group, Wharton charts that woman's movement through a series of social confrontations to social ostracism. Each step beyond the rich New York society of the turn of the century brings Lily closer to a moral ideal and widens her vision of herself and others. The tragedy of the novel, however, is Lily's incapacity to reconstruct herself and to repair the damage that living in society has already inflicted.[14] Like Edna

Pontellier, Lily Bart relinquishes her place in the old world only to suffer a loneliness and confusion that overwhelm her. Cast out of society, Lily can see it more clearly, and she can understand why she must never return to it. Isolation frees Lily to think and to see for herself, but it also locks her into a solitary confinement that is the worst punishment of all. Formed to decorate a social setting, the lone woman is "an organism as helpless out of its narrow range as the sea-anemone torn from the rock" (301). When Lily fails to form a new connection, she, like Edna, is too weak to survive alone.

Her predicament is presented, like Hester Prynne's, in a tableau. This is the famous *tableaux vivantes*, an entertainment staged for the rich by the rich, in which fashionable women exhibit themselves in a series of pictures. While the other women are applauded for their ability to transform themselves into replicas of famous paintings, Lily takes a different approach. She presents "a picture which was simply and undisguisedly the portrait of Miss Bart":

> Here there could be no mistaking the predominance of a personality—the unanimous "Oh!" of the spectators was a tribute, not to the brush-work of Reynolds' "Mrs. Lloyd," but to the flesh and blood loveliness of Miss Bart.... The impulse to show herself in a splendid setting...had yielded to the truer instinct of trusting to her unarrested beauty, and she had purposely chosen a picture without distracting accessories of dress or surroundings. (134)

Lily's appearance is a dramatic representation of her central conflict. Her initial impulse is to display herself in a "splendid setting," for this is what Lily has been trained to do. The child of extravagant and improvident parents, she has been bred to trade her beauty for the sumptuous environment of a wealthy marriage. To this end, Lily has learned to become a chameleon, to play whatever role the buyer desires. And yet she is the victim of a deeper instinct, the desire to be "simply and undisguisedly" herself. Thus her appearance in the tableau becomes symbolic of her greatest virtue and her fatal flaw.

What Lily displays in the scene is what both saves and damns her throughout the novel—her difference. From the beginning of the novel, Lily is an outsider. Although she desperately wants the social prize she so carefully works for, she repeatedly sabotages her own best efforts to marry a rich man. It is as if, a friend says, "at heart, she despises the things she's trying for" (189). Craving a secure place in the world of the wealthy, Lily cannot help perceiving that place as a prison. Unlike the other women of her group, she cannot fully efface her personality and blend into her surroundings. Her inability to do so makes her more admirable than others, but it also makes her more vulnerable.

There is more than one parallel to Hester Prynne's appearance on the scaffold in Lily's appearance in the tableau. Like Hester, Lily is above those who observe and judge her. And like the adulterous woman, Lily is condemned for her difference from the crowd. Although she does not fully realize it, Lily faces a gathering of her enemies.

There is a Dimmesdale in the group—a conventional, weak lover who speaks with the voice of an assumed moral authority. This is Lawrence Selden. Gus Trenor is the Chillingworth figure, the man who feels he has property rights in the woman displayed. And there is the hostile crowd who can only see Lily in terms of the stereotypes that destroy her.

Lily interprets the reaction of the crowd as a tribute and perceives the moment as a personal triumph. She is not aware that others see her in the only role she is allowed to play: as a thing. To them, she is a kind of prostitute up for bid. The men in the audience are initially titillated by the scantiness of her draperies ("Deuced bold thing to show herself in that get-up" [135]) and then hypocritically censorious about her "standing up there as if she was up at auction" (157). Attempting to be herself, Lily has shown her audience to itself; instead of the beauty of a woman, the crowd sees only the sale of flesh that is the essence of all their relationships. Lily, like Hester, threatens the values of her group. Standing above the crowd, she is at once superior and despised.

Lily's movement in the novel is erratic. She steps outside the group, then moves back within, repeatedly. The overall effect of such oscillation, however, is to make her more and more of an outsider. As she encounters the disapproval and subsequent disciplinary action of society, she is cast further beyond its boundaries. Her progress is contrasted to the parallel journey of her lover, Lawrence Selden, within the confines of the same society. As Lily moves (and is pushed) outside of society, she learns to see beyond appearances, even beneath her self-deceptions. At crucial moments in her travels, she encounters Selden, and the two share significant but brief attempts at union. But Selden is far more deeply involved in the world he professes to disdain than he will admit. The further Lily falls from social grace, the more Selden retreats into the safety of social attitudes.

As the conflicts of the novel develop, Selden becomes, as Wolff calls him, "the unthinking mouthpiece for the worst of society's prejudices" (*Feast* 111), or, as Louis Auchincloss says, "a sort of Ward McAllister posing as a Thoreau" (348).[15] The parallel but opposing movements of these characters—Lily beyond society and Selden within it—provide an ironic commentary on the price of acceptance in this world.

Ostensibly Lily's mentor, proposing a finer way for her to be, Selden is an agent of division. He upholds an ideal of behavior that is largely negative: he teaches Lily to disdain the social prizes she has been trained to seek, but he offers no realistic alternative for a woman dependent on society. Thus Selden can tempt Lily with his vision of a "republic of the spirit" that she can aspire to, just as she is working assiduously to win material security. Challenged to define this republic, Selden says that it offers freedom "from everything—from money, from poverty, from ease and anxiety, from all the material accidents" (68). The lesson of his lecture is fraught with irony, for he expounds his doctrine as he enjoys the luxuries of the Bellomont estate, a guest of the very rich friends who have invited him at the request of his equally rich mistress. Selden warns Lily that very few of the wealthy can ever enter his republic, and he cautions her that she will forfeit her own membership if she makes a wealthy marriage. Merely by meeting with Selden, Lily has already jeopardized her chances for marriage to the rich and boring Percy Gryce, but Selden is free to pontificate without consequences. "It seems to me," Lily tells Selden, "that you spend a great deal of time in the element you disapprove of" (70), and she is right.

Selden is teaching Lily to despise what he enjoys, and he appears unaware that freedom from "the material elements" implies a certain material security. There is no way for Lily to gain such security without a male provider.

Selden is unwilling to become that provider. He pleads his inadequate income as an excuse, but in reality, his conception of freedom includes a freedom from the demands of marriage. When the pair play at the idea of their union, Selden is shaken by Lily's readiness to enter the game. Her banter about a love match is not entirely a joke, and Selden senses that, by even discussing the possibility of marriage, he and Lily have "climbed to a forbidden height from which they discover a new world" (73). This world is not Selden's republic, however, for the republic has only one citizen.

Selden does not want to consider Lily as anything but an adventuress, much as he likes to deplore her adventures. She identifies his double game by asking, "Why do you make the things I have chosen seem hateful to me, if you have nothing to give me instead ?" (72).

Clearly, travel to Selden's republic involves a safe retreat within society, a movement that costs him very little. The encounter at Bellomont, on the other hand, is expensive for Lily. It destroys her chances for Percy Gryce and makes a permanent enemy of Selden's mistress, Bertha Dorset. Having lost what Lily considers her last good marital prospect, she is desperate for money. To free herself of the "material accident" of debt, she sells herself, allowing Gus Trenor to "invest" money for her in return for an unspecified dividend he expects her to pay. To remain within society, Lily must have the money that will make her look expensive; she must debase herself to maintain her social status.

Knowing the importance of appearances in her world, Lily works to become the illusion others desire. And yet she is often careless of appearances, flaunting her violations of the code, her recklessness a kind of testing of the social limits. At other times, she continues to be exactly what the occasion demands, demure and admiring to Percy Gryce, cheerful and helpful to her hostess Judy Trenor. Appearances, however, repeatedly work against Lily.

Nowhere is this more obvious than in the *tableaux vivants*. The evening and its consequences are a series of multiple misreadings. Lily's admirer, Selden, first misreads her appearance and then judges her on the basis of his misperception. As Wolff notes, Selden sees Lily almost entirely in terms of externals, "willing at every point to accept the appearance for reality" (*Feast* 122). He is the "connoisseur" who regards her as a "moral aesthetic object" (*Feast* 125), and this attitude is particularly in evidence as he views Lily in her tableau. Selden thinks he sees "the real Lily Bart, divested of the trivialities of her little world," a vision of "soaring grace," "eternal harmony" (134). He interprets her pose as an emblem of "the whole tragedy of her life" and decides that only he can rescue her beauty from "all that cheapened and vulgarized it" (135). To Selden, this new Lily is Miranda, and the crowd that ogles her is Caliban (135).

Selden is caught in his own fantasy here, for his vision of the "real" Lily elevates her to an impossible purity. It also reduces her to the level of a child, a helpless Miranda who needs the paternal supervision of Prospero to keep her safe. Selden's new version of Lily, then, is the stereotypical model of the child bride—utterly pure, submissive, and vulnerable. In his imagination, the stage has become a pedestal, a precarious place for any woman.

Selden's faith in Lily is so slight that it takes very little to shatter his image of her. When appearances seem to confirm the nasty rumors about Lily's affair with Gus Trenor, Selden again misreads the scene. He can no longer believe in Lily as innocent; therefore she must be guilty. He finds it less threatening to his peace to categorize the woman than to confront her. And so he runs away.

Selden rejects Lily because he perceives her as tainted by her social ties. Ironically, he dissociates himself from her just as his set begins to push her out. At the same time, the Lily of the tableau is becoming more "herself" as she corrects her own misreading of her place within the group.

For one day, Lily deludes herself with memories of her triumph in the tableau, excited by the admiration of the crowd and by Selden's tentative commitment. But when Gus Trenor demands a return on his investment, Lily must face the fact that, by taking his money, she has become a kind of dishonest prostitute. Presenting herself as an image of inaccessible beauty, Lily now recognizes that what the crowd saw in her is what she has become: one of them, a dealer in her own flesh: "I've taken what they take, and not paid as they pay!" (166). Lily identifies her inner division, recognizing the self "she had always known and a new abhorrent being" (146). This hated being is the socially defined self that has deformed the woman within. The realization of her divided nature precipitates a change in Lily. As she moves away from society, she sheds that social self, becoming the "real" Lily, different from society's (and Selden's) perception of her.

Her new self appears again in an unlikely place, when Lily returns to society in a new role. Again, she is paying her way in the money world, in a dubious fashion. She is to distract the suspicious George Dorset while his wife Bertha enjoys her new lover. Again, Selden is an observer who misreads the scene. He accurately perceives that Lily is a finer ornament than the other women, "her grace cheapening the other women's smartness" (215), but he concludes that Lily has become a lifetime member of this tawdry group, "where conspicuousness passed for distinction" (216), and where the food is stupidly expensive, the talk dull, and the freedom merely promiscuous. Condemning Lily for her allegiance to this set, Selden never speculates on his own presence at the dinner table, his own contributions to the dull talk and vulgar ostentation.

In his eyes, Lily is doubly damned. As a supposed insider, she is to be condemned; when she is publicly cast out of Bertha's circle, she is again condemned. Selden now judges Lily as society does. He knows that Bertha, his former mistress, is using Lily's expulsion to distract attention from her own adultery. But he feels that Lily must have done something to deserve such treatment, wondering "what weakness had placed her so abominably at her enemies' mercy" (219).

Lily's latest humiliation is a result of inner division. Her role in the Dorset marriage is ignoble; her reaction to Bertha's viciousness is admirable. Lily has the power to retaliate, to destroy her enemy and assume Bertha's place merely by using Bertha's love letters against her. But she will not battle this group in the only way that ensures victory, by using its own weapons with its own savagery, for she is not, ever, fully a part of the group. Refusing to save herself by becoming as brutal as Bertha, Lily moves further from that abhorrent being she feared she was becoming and further away from society.

She moves toward isolation, not toward union. Cast out of the highest reaches of society, Lily falls more rapidly than before. Although she finds new groups to accept her, she remains an alien. Somehow, the "real" Lily, who despises the things she craves, defeats the abhorred self. But this new Lily is not the woman Selden sees or wants.

Lily's final visit to Selden resolves her inner division in a curious way. Exhausted and broken, Lily comes to him on an impulse. She addresses him like a penitent would address a priest; she confesses that she has been unable to live up to his standards but that they haunt her nevertheless. She asks Selden if he will take custody of "the Lily Bart you knew" (309), so that someone will remember that ideal. She is relinquishing her good self, she feels, because she is about to re-enter the social world in the only way she can, through blackmail. When she leaves Selden's rooms, she feels, she will have become what Selden cautioned her against, and she asks him to understand her failure.

The meeting is no meeting at all. Lily has changed so much that she is frightening to Selden: "her presence was becoming an embarrassment to him" (306). He is uneasy with her tears and her physical exhaustion. He shields himself behind a barrier of words and wit: "it seemed incredible to her that anyone should think it necessary to linger in the conventional outskirts of word play and evasion" (306). Selden is uneasy with the woman who wants a human, open, contact; he prefers the sophisticated, self-possessed Lily she used to be. Selden is only comfortable with the woman in her social role, and thus the scene provides the sharpest contrast of the two characters. He has become completely enmeshed in the world he warned against; she has become increasingly estranged from it. Having once dreamed of rescuing Lily from society, Selden now shrinks from helping her when she is outcast.

She comes to Selden in despair of meeting his expectations; when she leaves, she has far surpassed his standards. Burning the letters that could bring her social rehabilitation, Lily destroys her social self. She leaves all traces of that being with Selden, who consistently preferred to judge the external woman rather than to love the one beneath.[16]

Lily's next encounter, with Nettie Struther, heightens the irony of Lily's sad overture to Selden. Nettie's story, like Lily's, begins in shame but, unlike Lily's, ends in a marriage based on understanding, acceptance, and trust. The sentimental tale of seduction and abandonment ends in a rescue and redemption. Nettie, having borne another man's child, marries a man who, she explains, knew all about her and "cared for me enough to have me as I was" (315). As Wolff notes, there is a blatant contrast here to Selden's declared admiration for the "real Lily Bart" and his inability to commit to her (*Feast* 132). And there is another element to this counter-tale. In Nettie Struther's slum kitchen, Lily finds something she never found in any of the homes of the rich. She sees a "central truth of existence" in this struggling family; a "solidarity of life" (319) in this love. Nettie, cast out, has created a new place for herself. Granted, it has "the frail audacious permanence of a bird's nest built on the edge of a cliff" (320) because it is subject to all the material accidents of poverty. But, Lily realizes, this home is "so put together that the lives entrusted to it may hang safely over the abyss" (320).

In contrast, there is Lily's terrible solitude, and her realization that she has never enjoyed any true connection to another. "All the men and women she knew were like atoms whirling away from each other" (319), dissociated from each other, and from themselves.

The alternatives for Lily are the isolation of the pariah or the equally terrible isolation of the social insider, all role, all disguise. Lily knows that she does not have what she admires in Nettie Struther, "strength to gather up the fragments of her life, and build herself a shelter" (319). Lily has developed the courage to recognize the moral debasement that is the price of social success. But she does not have the power to construct an alternative life. She has formed a new self, but it is beset by the demands of the old life. Her sense of duality, her confused movement between dangerous alternatives, are repeated in the images of the novel.

There is no safe place for Lily. Her seal of a flying ship with the motto "Beyond" (154) conveys a sense of adventure and freedom. But the language of the novel indicates that there is danger for Lily both within society and beyond it. Initially, Lily believes she can navigate a course to a triumphant destination—marriage to a millionaire. Wharton, however, makes it clear that society is a treacherous ocean, ready to drown the weak. Each season, the *arrivistes* fight this sea; they "rose to the surface with each recurring tide, and were either submerged beneath its rush or landed triumphantly beyond the reach of envious breakers" (120). Lily cannot survive in this sea without a social anchor; without such security, she is "like a water plant in the flux of the tides" (55). The rhythm of the tides repeats Lily's cycle of rebellion/return. Each time she challenges the standards of her set, she panics at her own impulsiveness, and, penitent, tries to regain her membership in the group. But each movement outside brings her back inside, on a lower level. Isolated from her rich friends, she feels "stranded in a backwater of the great current of pleasure" (235); openly "cut" by them, she is in more danger still, experiencing "the doomed sense of the castaway who has signalled in vain to fleeing sails" (225).

There is no clear choice between life inside and out. Both are dangerous to the individual and threaten to engulf or isolate. Thus Lily repeatedly swings between the extremes: she makes no definitive break with society, but cuts one tie, only to try to re-establish it or to seek a new tie. Lily is afraid of being alone. In the first chapters of the novel, for instance, she risks her reputation by visiting Selden, largely because she dreads an empty hour by herself. Her first action on her subsequent train ride is to look for an acquaintance to share the journey. And yet she dreams of a refuge, like Selden's study, where she can be alone and be herself.

The language of space in the novel, of inside/outside, is equally ambivalent. As Lily moves out of society, the perimeters of her environment narrow and oppress. Her fall begins in the expanses of Bellomont; then Lily travels to the airless Penniston townhouse, and finally to one room in a claustrophobic boarding house. Judith Fryer notes that in the world of the rich, "space is money, and more space means less human contact" (*Felicitous Space* 91). Lily is initially fastidious; she shrinks from the touch of a scrubwoman and from Gus Trenor's advances, and she despises the close quarters of Gerty Farish's tiny flat. Unlike a hero, Lily does not find the movement away from society a step into the endless space of a new frontier; instead, isolation implies a series of shrinking boundaries, walls that move ever nearer.

To move outside, then, is to lose a certain mobility, but, for a heroine, it also brings the human touch once feared and now desired. When the American hero moves to the world outside, he moves alone, shedding the restraints of relationships. Lily's most genuine connections, characterized by openness, compassion, and honesty, take place in the smaller world of the outcast. Only when Lily moves beyond the money circle does she find the pity and generosity in Rosedale, the beauty in Gerty Farish, the solicitude in Carry Fisher, the strength in Nettie Struther—all of them, to some degree, outsiders themselves. Perhaps the point of such encounters is that, outside the world of the rich, people can be touched, not taken. At any rate, being outside is as dangerous—and rewarding—as being inside.

The contrasts of rise and fall, of the real Lily and the false one, of life inside and out, are accompanied by continual references to Lily's emotional states, to mood swings that shift erratically between manic highs and black depressions.[17] The constant in the descriptions is a reference to an unnatural high or low, to drink or drugs. Thus, when Lily feels triumphant in her tableau, she experiences a "moment of self-intoxication" (137); the evening brings her "happy dreams" (139) but the subsequent encounter with Trenor leads to a new and terrible cycle of insomnia and daytime exhaustion, to waking nightmares, "horrors"

(265). Strong tea in the afternoon and chloral at night are Lily's remedies, aggravating the stimulant/narcotic, up/down cycle of her misery. "Her craving for keen stimulant was forever conflicting with that other craving for sleep" (288), for "an escape into depths of dreamless annihilation" (295). High or low, Lily exists in an artificial state suited to one who is afraid to see things as they are. "Her personal fastidiousness had a moral equivalent, and when she made a tour of inspection in her own mind there were certain doors she did not open" (82). There is a prison outside society, in those small spaces where others impinge, and there is a similar place within the mind. Both places can bring release: to new relationships with others, to a new vision of oneself. But Lily, trained in innocence, shrinks from seeing new things or touching strange people.

Lily's moral climb is difficult. Each step outside the perimeters of society is followed by another retreat, each widening of her vision is accompanied by an aversion to the sight. Ever reluctant to open that closed door of her psyche, Lily must repeatedly draw on very small reserves of courage. Her impulses are sometimes self-defeating, sometimes empowering. By the time she visits Nettie Struther, she has become debilitated by her difficult journey, and she cannot go any farther.

She does not want to go back to the world of the rich, where all women compete to sell themselves.[18] Rosedale tempts her to make such a return by offering her an alliance based on sound financial principles: extortion of their enemies. To accept Rosedale's offer would be, for Lily, to become a more powerful version of Bertha Dorset, a monstrous product of society.

The alternative is for Lily to remain alone, outside, and to continue her struggle for moral development and against the social Furies. Lily's friend Carry Fisher warns her that the money world is "not a pretty place" and that the only way to survive its enmity is "to fight it on its own terms—and above all...not alone!" (252). But there is no one willing to join Lily in her battles. Her isolation grows just as she needs allies, and freedom becomes a heavy burden. The demands of the new, free self are represented in the scene in Nettie Struther's kitchen. Lily holds Nettie's baby, a new, weak, being, all vulnerability and possibility. At first, the baby feels "as light as a pink cloud," but soon its "weight increased, sinking deeper, and penetrating her with a strange sense of weakness, as though the child entered into her and became a part of herself" (316). In a reversal of childbirth, the new being returns within, to the only place it can be safe.

The image of the child persists. After Lily takes her last dose of chloral, she dreams of the baby. The child is in her bed, and Lily senses she must protect and comfort it.

No sound must awaken the sleeping baby. Lily's final act is her way of protecting her new identity, of securing it in an endless sleep, for an awakening into life would destroy it. Lily dies at a moral pinnacle—she has consciously rejected the money world by burning the Dorset letters and paying her debts to Trenor; she has found different values both within herself and in other outsiders. For a moment, she has defeated the money world, on her terms. But she cannot sustain the moment—or the new self—alone. And so she dies, to freeze the victory in timelessness. It is a kind of tableau.

The "heart of fools is in the house of mirth," the Bible says, and Lily has painfully acquired a wisdom that excludes her from this house. Her capacity to please, to gauge her effect on others, to know what others want, has developed into the ability to feel what others feel. Moving "behind the social tapestry" (276), Lily has entered a place of wisdom. But that new world is the "house of mourning" (Ecclesiastes 7:34), and it is hard to live there alone.

Unwilling to go back, unable to move forward, Lily dies, "simply and undisguisedly," herself.

Lucy Gayheart
At the beginning of this novel, Cather's heroine appears to be deliberately and successfully extricating herself from the conventional roles and ties that bind Lily Bart and Edna Pontellier. She is 21 years old, unmarried, boldly exploring the city, free from the confines of the small town of her childhood. She is characterized by vitality, energy, and movement. Stouck calls her "an embodiment of Life with all its energy and desires" (220), and O'Brien categorizes her, with Marie Shabata of *O Pioneers!*, as one of Cather's romantic heroines, "vital, gay, intense, a figure always in motion." But O'Brien also notes that Lucy's energy and drive are always juxtaposed to "a stationary and ultimately confining background" (373). This contrast of freedom and confinement, of movement and stasis, reveals what Fryer identifies as a central subject in

Cather's work, the divided self: "often presented in her early works as a conflict between woman and artist, and developed with an interest, finally, not so much in reconciliation as in creating a new context in which the force, passion, and energy of the creative self can be preserved" (*Felicitous Space* 217).

As a student of music, Lucy can loosely be identified as an artist, but her struggle is a wider one, to sustain not only the vitality of the creative artist, but also the very life of the independent being. If she embodies force, passion, and energy, they are expressed not only in her music but in the wide range of actions and attitudes she demonstrates in all facets of her life. And while the novel tentatively proposes a new context in which the free, creative self can be sustained, it ultimately denies that place to its heroine. Lucy remains divided—unto death—by her irreconcilable needs for autonomy and support.

Stouck notes that *Lucy Gayheart* has received more negative criticism than any of Cather's other novels, and he cites its "dime-store" romantic plot as a possible reason. But he rightly points out that the book's "mannered simplicity is deceptive" and calls the novel perhaps Cather's most philosophically complex work (214). The complexity of the novel is reflected in its imagery, not its plot. The constant oppositions of freedom/suffocation, protection/exposure, heat/cold, fire/water, and, most notably, up/down, add meaning to what might otherwise be perceived as the confused movement of the plot.[19] Like its counterparts, *The House of Mirth* and *The Awakening*, *Lucy Gayheart* is a novel about the frenzied movements of a woman defeated by external demands and inner weakness. Her vitality is not her salvation, for her energy is often misdirected and self-destructive. "Life seemed to lie very near the surface" in Lucy (5), and the description, in the very first scene of the book, encapsulates the heroine's weakness and strength as it introduces the up/down image that characterizes Lucy's career. Imbued with a power that sets her apart and above, Lucy thinks she can skate across the cold, snowy surfaces of life, as she did in childhood winters in Haverford, Nebraska.[20] Unafraid and thus incautious, she believes she can make cold into warmth and find fire in the icy breath of the snow. O'Brien says that the underground rivers that pervade Cather's work are the author's recurrent metaphors for unconscious energies (391).[21] But what is below the surface for Lucy is the ever-present pull of death.

Against the early descriptions of Lucy running through the snowstorms, "giving her body to the wind," embracing the winter cold and the summer sun, 'direct and unhesitating and joyous" (4) in her movement, we must consider the later descriptions of the broken girl who seeks protection from the elements and who is afraid to move alone. In her quest for a protector, Lucy is looking for a reduction of self. Like Lily Bart and Edna Pontellier, Lucy both craves independence and fears it. Her movements toward freedom are repeatedly negated by her longing for a father/lover, someone who will move her, not through passion, but by appropriating her energy and thus divesting her of herself.

The social criticism of this book is embedded in the images of Lucy's lovers, the lover from the money world, Harry Gordon, and the lover from the music world, Clement Sebastian. Both men offer tempting opportunities to get rid of the loneliness that shadows Lucy's independence, and both take from the heroine that energy that makes her unique. Because she misreads her own submission as a sign of their support, Lucy is pulled down by her own needs. Her lovers are drawn to her fire, but they offer her no corresponding heat. She cannot kindle their energies because they are locked into cultures that have made them cold. Neither culture—business or art—can accommodate her as she is. To enter such places, Lucy herself must accommodate by forfeiting those very qualities that attract and challenge her lovers. She cannot live in a world where lovers are fathers and domination substitutes for passion. But she is afraid to live in the alternative world she would have to create, daily, for herself and by herself: "you couldn't, after all, live above your level" (118), and death is waiting just below.

Lucy's story is a spare tale, almost a fairy tale, that reverberates through metaphor, not plot. The imagery that permeates the novel is introduced in the description of Lucy's relationship to her home town, where, as a young girl, she had felt lonely and trapped, "looking up at the moon from the bottom of a well" (135). There, she suffocates because there is no passion to match her own; loving her home is "heartbreaking...like loving the dead who cannot answer back" (136). She is drawn to the one superior man of Haverford, sensing his energy. Harry Gordon, rich, self-possessed, enjoying life, seems, to Lucy, to "set her up" with his vitality (18). Harry, she thinks, can pull her up, toward the moon, and he is drawn to the world of deep feeling, idealism, and vulnerability that Lucy seems to represent. "There was a part of himself that Harry was ashamed to live out in the open (he hated a sentimental man) but he could live it through Lucy" (107).

A core of feeling is deep within Harry, and he has the capacity to nourish that self, but in his relationship to Lucy there is more than a hint of the exploitive and the possessive. He cannot help perceiving his connection to Lucy in conventional terms; for this rich businessman to marry her, he thinks, would be "the supreme extravagance," for she is only a watchmaker's daughter. Nevertheless, Harry intends to stoop, to raise the beautiful girl above her station, "to have a wife other men would envy" (23).

In Harry and Lucy's eyes, the romance is a Cinderella story, one of rescue and elevation for the heroine. In return for his largesse, Lucy will supply the emotion for two. Money will buy love. Harry is essentially a shrewd businessman, one said to be "hard" and to take advantage of people "in a tight place" (18). He perceives Lucy as his weakness, his indulgence, the one aberration in his conventionally successful life. Marrying Harry, Lucy would be, at the same time, owned by an insider and valued for her irrelevance to his hard commercial life.

Lucy's escape to Chicago is thus an escape from both her conventional town and her conventional lover. She enjoys her years as a music student, revelling in her independence, free, for the first time in her life, to "come and go like a boy" (26). The icy lakefront wind and snow seem to buoy her. Breathing the air is "like drinking fire" (97), and she can "make an overcoat of the cold" (37) and feel her own heat within it.

Wrapping herself in ice kills her own fire when she finds a new lover in the concert singer, Clement Sebastian. From the first moment Lucy hears him sing, it is evident that below the surface of Lucy's new fantasy, there is death, not love. Hearing his song, Lucy senses a "passion that drowns, like black water" (31); rather than experiencing the warm protection of love, Lucy hears Sebastian sing and feels that "some protecting barrier was gone—a window had been broken that let in the cold and darkness of the night" (32). The window shatters, and the dividing line between hot and cold, independence and suffocation, is gone. What has always lurked beneath the surface is no longer safely contained. Lucy cannot skate above the dark water; the ice, like glass, shatters, pulling her to her death.

Sebastian, middle-aged, married, brings nothing to the affair. Stouck calls the song that lures Lucy "nihilistic" (216); beneath its surface is a "cold, inhuman void" (218). When Sebastian first embraces Lucy, he "took her secret" of energy and joy, and he gave her his own: "he had renounced life" (87). Like Lawrence Selden, Sebastian lives in a safe and sterile republic of the spirit, without a country, a home, friends, and without the "deepest of all companionships, a relation with the earth itself" (78). Enjoying insider status in a world he claims to disdain, Sebastian survives by retreating—from challenge, from commitment, from life itself. He lacks even that core of feeling that draws Lucy to Harry Gordon.

Why, then, does Lucy fall into the blackness of this passion? Their romance is a tragedy of Lucy's misreadings. Sebastian is Lucy's master, teacher, artistic ideal, and father. He is never, even physically, her lover. She mistakes his talent for artistic commitment, his amused tolerance of her infatuation for emotional engagement. She is grateful she can give him joy. She becomes, appropriately, his accompanist for rehearsals *only*, since a male must appear with him on stage. In her roles as student, servant, daughter, devotee, Lucy finds a safe identity and a channel for all that fierce generosity of energy and fire. Loving Sebastian, Lucy loves the dead who cannot answer back. And then Sebastian dies, by drowning.

His death does not free Lucy, for she thinks of it as an abandonment, not a release. Drained of the energy that once allowed her to come and go like a boy, she does not resume her own music studies in the city. She retreats to the suffocating world of Haverford, living on her fantasy of love, able to "breathe only in the world she brought back through memory" (156). Her regression takes her further back, to a desperate attempt to cling to her former protector, Harry. She wants to be "taken up" again, to have him "put his hand on her" and "start the machinery going to carry her along" (175). An alien in her home town, beset by rumors of her failure in art and love, she is simultaneously suffocated by convention and anxious to become the conventional product. Lucy looks for her redemption in an equally divided man. Harry wants her but is offended by her loss of innocence. He has become cold and impersonal, regarding her as if "through thick glasses" (149), separated from his feelings by a barrier of his own creation.

Then, Lucy's confused fall into dependency is reversed. When an aging soprano performs in Haverford, Lucy witnesses a passion that is not sustained by any one lover. Unlike Sebastian, this woman is committed to her art and to something even wider.[22] Singing old, tired songs in a small town opera house, the singer is, to Lucy, supremely *alive*. Like Edna Pontellier's mentor, Mademoiselle Reisz, this woman has confronted the world alone and embraced its joy and pain. She is the catalyst for Lucy's moment of insight: "What if Life itself were the sweetheart?" Lucy wonders (184). Experience has shown Lucy that life is not all fire and light and passion. But she now begins to understand that she, all alone, must connect to all of life if she is to be reborn. "She must have it, she couldn't run away from it" (184). "She...stretched out her arms to the storm, to whatever might lie behind it... Let it all come back to her again! Let it betray her and mark her and break her heart, she must have it!" (185).

Through the lone woman artist, Lucy has envisioned a new way to be. Lily Bart discovered a new life in Nettie Struther's kitchen, and Edna Pontellier saw a potential self in Mademoiselle Reisz. All three heroines are challenged by women living, however precariously, beyond social norms. All three are stimulated by such visions of an alternative life, but they cannot re-create themselves and make the vision real.

Even as Lucy awakens to a renewed embrace of all of life, she retreats to her dream of protection and support. On her way to skate, she meets Harry and asks him for a ride. She wants to be carried, taken up on her journey, to move under another's power. Harry's refusal to carry her, his scorn for her, stimulates Lucy to a final, angry rebellion against those who stifle her with their judgments and righteousness: "she would show them they couldn't crush her. She would get away from these people who were cruel and stupid—" (198). Skating alone, she falls. She drowns in the icy water.

In a strange way, Lucy's uniqueness is preserved by the ice. The final section of the novel, narrated from Harry's point of view, depicts the impact of the outsider heroine on the insider who cannot forget her. Harry has become a warmer, generous and more compassionate man, a close friend of Lucy's father and a caring husband to a cold wife. Lucy's death has released that part of Harry he was once ashamed of, and his life (which he perceives as a life sentence) is colored by memories of Lucy. Ironically, he regards her as superior even in her lowest times. Even when she retreated to Haverford, grieving for Sebastian, Harry saw her as "gathered up and sustained by something that would never let her drop into the common world" (213). He had planned to reconcile with her, after he had "punished" her for her romance with Sebastian. He tells himself he had planned to "break with this town and all the guarantees of his future" (217), to join the outsider in her free world. But Lucy drowned, falling "like a bird being shot down when it rises in its morning flight to the sun" (207). She could not live above her level; her wings were not strong. Dying, Lucy remains the one important thing in Harry's memory; she seems untainted by the compromises of the conventional life, unscarred by the struggles of a solitary one.

The fallen bird, the bird with the broken wing, the sea anemone torn from the rock—there is an aura of melodrama and martyrdom in these novels of heroines dying young and misunderstood. But the aura of the dime-store is avoided by the ambiguity of the conflicts and of the heroines themselves. Edna, Lily, and Lucy are simultaneously foolish and wise, perceptive and self-deceiving, timid and bold. Their stories cannot be used as sentimental tracts recounting the vicissitudes of virtue unrecognized by a heartless world. For these women act in ways that are clearly self-defeating, and they repeatedly violate the same standards they have so painfully and independently conceived.

What makes their stories noteworthy is not the dramatic endings. It is the ambivalence of their struggles and the nature of the battle. The heroines must fight an external force that demands an extreme distortion of self. And they must also battle an inner longing for the social rewards of such distortion. Their deaths do not glorify their virtues. They reveal the impossibility of victory for women so divided.

Section Two:
Living Death

The Golden Bowl

Dying may be preferable to the fate of another intruder, who is sentenced to a living death. Charlotte Stant of *The Golden Bowl* is one of many intruders whose deviance is juxtaposed with the conformity of an idealized woman and whose fate is somehow determined by the juxtaposition. Charlotte's fate is the slow strangulation of the vitality that makes her so threatening to the conventional world.

As mentioned earlier, Edith Wharton employs the triangular structure of one man divided by his attraction to both an innocent and an intruder in *The Age of Innocence*, *The Reef*, and *The Children*, but her use of the contrasting heroines is not unique. Many American novels place two contrasting heroines at the center of the conflict, and the women are not the stereotypical fair angel/dark temptress twins of Fiedler's mythology. The innocent is no angel but an evolving bitch, each work presenting her in a different phase of that evolution; the other woman does, in fact, tempt others, but towards their liberation, not their damnation. Schriber notes that, in *The Golden Bowl*, "the underpinnings of fair and dark ladies and virtue and vice have been dismantled and reconstructed" (139), and a similar challenge to the familiar dichotomy occurs elsewhere.

Hawthorne balances the ghostly and sinister Priscilla with the passionate and zealous Zenobia. The dreamlike Hilda, who evades reality, is paired with Miriam, who *is* that reality. In James's *The Bostonians*, Verena Tarrant's sweet femininity is countered by the tart feminism of Olive Chancellor; in Glasgow's *In This Our Life*, the baby-bitch Stanley is sister to the grown-up, independent Roy.

In each pairing, the idealized heroine somehow "wins" a significant conflict, and the unorthodox woman is somehow punished. Those novels by women authors seem to spare the deviants the harshest penalties and deny the innocents complete triumph. In all three of Wharton's triangle novels, for example, the intruder is separated from her lover, but the separation is partly her choice. And the innocents of these books are not truly victorious: May Welland clings to an empty marriage, Anna Leath of *The Reef* gets her man but also develops an all-consuming jealousy, and Rose Sellars of *The Children* is left to savour her exquisite perceptions—alone. Ellen Glasgow also blurs the lines of victory and defeat: Roy loses both husband and lover to her sister Stanley, but Stanley is reduced to a contemptible (if secure) position, in the end. Hawthorne, however, metes out a more polarized kind of justice.

Priscilla gets her man, the money, and control; her sister Zenobia drowns herself. Hilda finds the love of Kenyon and a permanent sanctuary from adult life; Miriam is reduced to abject penitence and a pariah's wanderings. As for James, he gives Verena a teary wedding, but a wedding nonetheless, and he leaves Olive, after a string of losses and humiliations, to seek a new identity by facing what she most fears. And, in *The Golden Bowl*, he crushes Charlotte Stant under the power of her rival, Maggie Verver.

While there is considerable ambiguity in characterizing these opposing heroines, there is a clear division in resolving their stories: innocents get something; intruders lose something.[23] In each pairing, the intruder is the more interesting of the two women. Breaking the rules, stretching the boundaries, she makes others seem timid or dull or petty. Sometimes she seems the only person who is awake among a somnambulist group, the only adult in the nursery. She seems powerful and alive. And perhaps these qualities are reasons why, in so many instances, this heroine suffers a loss. Her power invites others to seize their own power, but the liberation she offers threatens to take power from those already in control. "The role breaker," Janeway says, "threatens the order of the universe not just by his own challenge to it but by disturbing the accustomed connection with this order which is felt by other people" (124-25). By moving past the one acceptable role of innocent, the intruder becomes disturbing, disruptive. And so her presence must be nullified. Charlotte Stant, wicked but fascinating, must be strangled with a silken cord.

Even on a halter, Charlotte seems wild and snarling, still untamed. She is worth watching, even admirable. Long before she appears in the novel, she is introduced with sympathy and admiration. She is "extraordinarily alone" (I, 39) both in her lack of family and in her personal qualities. Like Lily Bart, she is a rare and special item (I, 53), clever, speaking many languages, knowing all of London, of Rome, possessing a "curious world-quality" (I, 99). She conveys a sense of adventure and of movement; she has the aura of Hawthorne's intruders: like Miriam, she belongs nowhere but grew up in Italy; the Prince associates her with far places and "winds and waves and custom-houses" (I, 45), and her sins will be like Hester's.

Charlotte sees things, and she is not afraid. Mrs. Assingham characterizes her early affair with the Prince as romantic precisely because the couple had the courage to, "look the facts in the face" (I, 70). They chose to love each other in spite of the poverty that denied them any hope of marriage. Mrs. Assingham deplores that same quality when Charlotte returns for her lover's wedding: her visit is a "perversity" (I, 69). "She needn't have looked it all so in the face" (I, 70). But Charlotte cannot help seeing everything. "Her own vision acted for every relation" (I, 105); she notices things the others never see: servants, cabmen, the beauty in the children of the poor. She notices life. Maggie calls her "Great in nature," in "character...spirit. Great in life" (I, 180).

It is brave to see everything without averting one's eyes. "She's not afraid—not of anything," Maggie says (I, 181). And again, there is sympathy for the woman who, utterly alone, must be brave. Her lack of family, home, and money make her vulnerable. She can be hurt and used, and no one will jump to help her. Such vulnerability makes her attractive. What the Prince calls "her want of ramifications" is "a sort of small social capital" (I, 54), for she can be taken without consequences for the taker. She can be bought cheaply, and there will be no one to negotiate on her behalf.

The Ververs buy her because she brings them life. To their country home, Fawns, which is "out of the world," Charlotte gives the "pulse of life" (I, 211, 212), and Adam is entertained by her "free range of observation" (I, 213). He can buy, but she can see. She *is* the world, life, come to Fawns. But if she is great in life, she is great—or greatly wicked—in love as well.

The Prince plays his role in their renewed romance, but Charlotte instigates the renewal. She sets the scene and writes the script. A central scene of the novel plays cleverly against another famous tableau, as Charlotte emerges as a new version of Hester Prynne—before her fall.

Two years after her marriage, Charlotte stands, alone, on a grand staircase at a grand party in a London house. She has come to this place without her husband, and she is waiting for her former lover, the Prince, to join her on the stairs, above the crowd. The Prince must first escort his wife to the carriage that will take her to her favorite place, her father's house. Meanwhile, Charlotte stands, alone, above the crowd, in full view of society but untouched by the crush of people who move up and down. She waits for the man who must move away from his wife and move up to reach his lover, to attain her level. She seems frozen in the moment, magnificently dressed and jeweled, "exposed little to the public," "a bit brazen" (I, 247), she thinks, but utterly in control. When Hester stood alone on the scaffold for the first time, her adultery was over. Charlotte has chosen to begin hers. "She knew how she should work it, and what she was doing there made already a beginning" (I, 247).

Charlotte is on her stage, awaiting the entrance of the hero. She has written the scenario that is about to be played out, and she is ready to establish motives for the actors' conduct. To Mrs. Assingham, she will provide the exposition: two loyal spouses have been rejected by a father and daughter. The Ververs, according to the script, prefer the parental to the matrimonial bond and encourage their mates to amuse one another. Charlotte will define the affair for the Prince in a way that makes it seem justifiable. Their intimacy is to be a bond of honor; they are "never rashly to forget and never consciously to wound" (I, 325). Charlotte is bold, brave, even brazen as she initiates the adultery. And, like Hester, she is fascinating—even admirable.

Charlotte shares many of Hester's attributes. Hester's passion, revealed in her forest encounter with Dimmesdale, revives and liberates him. To the Prince, one day alone in the country with Charlotte brings a freedom as perfect as a perfect pearl (I, 358), a fair compensation for years of a stifling marriage. And, of course, there is the ever-present contrast of Charlotte and Maggie to create sympathy for Charlotte. Their rivalry is not a fair fight. Behind Maggie stands the enormous power of her father, the money power that conquers all because it owns all. In this struggle, Charlotte may feel empowered, and she may feel the strength of the Prince behind her. But she and the Prince are possessions of the Ververs, and the Ververs can do whatever they want with what they own: they can sell their things, or divide them, or discard them. Charlotte fights a hopeless fight, alone. Like Hester, she evokes sympathy because she fights so hopelessly.

And, like Hester, she fights out of love. Naomi Lebowitz says that James's "supreme ethical concern" is one's commitment "to human relationship, morally sanctioned not necessarily by the laws of society but by the measure of its own strength and depth" (18), and she explains our sympathy for Charlotte as a recognition that her sin is founded on a "desire to be true to a relationship of long duration" (16). Cargill, too, stresses Charlotte's greatness in love: "she is mastered by her blind affection for her former lover and not ridden by any other motive" (394). At the core of her terrible betrayal, then, is a true commitment. The honesty of her passion shines brighter when it is juxtaposed with Maggie's marriage, a relationship sustained by the Ververs' ability to manipulate and evade. Maggie's fantasy of the "Perfect" Prince requires that Amerigo be as tightly locked away as any museum piece. Maggie's version of love is a withholding: withholding power, withholding intimacy, withholding information, withholding reality, so that Amerigo remains baffled and dependent. Never knowing where he stands, Amerigo fears to move.

Maggie is the child-heroine who must manipulate all the figures in her play-house; her only version of love is a form of control, replicating the quiet but absolute domination of her father. Maggie's love, like her father's, is a love of beauty that expresses itself in the purchase of the beautiful object. Charlotte, on the other hand, is a reckless, fearless gambler. The one day of freedom that the Prince perceives as a priceless pearl, is, for Charlotte, that infamous great gold cup. When the Prince, more cautious than Charlotte, wonders if perhaps this day conceals its crack, Charlotte warns, "Don't you think too much of 'cracks' and aren't you too afraid of them? I risk the cracks" (I, 359). But the Prince is unconvinced; be reckless for yourself, he admonishes Charlotte; as for him, "I go...by my superstitions." "I go but by one thing," Charlotte counters, "I go by you" (I, 360). Because she is willing to risk the flaw to savor the golden beauty, because she is willing to risk everything to give everything, Charlotte is herself a flawed yet dazzling character. But she is doomed to lose all she gambles for in this dirty game.

Cruelty can be justified when its victim can be labeled non-human. Thus, when Maggie proceeds to punish Charlotte, Maggie thinks of her as "the creature" (II, 239), and when Adam decides to transport her to his new museum in American City, he thinks of her as a "dark, doomed *thing*" (II, 271, emphasis added). The Ververs deal with the rebel in their characteristic way of withholding and silence, and they demand a new betrayal as an atonement for the first.

Charlotte, great in love, must lose her lover—not merely through a physical separation, but fully and finally. The Prince must be made a man of double dishonor. Having betrayed his wife, Amerigo, to prove his penitence, must now betray his mistress. Charlotte may be beautiful and wonderful, the Prince confides to Maggie, but "I feel somehow as if she were dying...for you and me" (II, 346). Amerigo recites his Act of Contrition as Charlotte, so disruptive of the peace of the innocent, is obliterated.

Charlotte must cease to exist as anything but the submissive wife of the great collector. Forced to remain within society, in the confines of such a role, Charlotte is indeed dying. The sense of movement and of adventure that characterized her is gone now. So is her knack for seeing, for she is to be forever denied the free range of observation that once characterized her. Now, she is baffled by a conspiracy of lies, lies so powerful they are never spoken even as they dictate the actions of the Ververs and their Prince. Surrounded by the silence, Charlotte cannot confirm her own vision, her own version of truth. Her role now is not to see, but to be seen. As her husband's greatest museum piece, she has become a rare item, subject to constant surveillance.

Section Three:
Marriage and Compromise

Vein of Iron

Death by drowning, drugs, or psychic obliteration—these are dramatic ends for the intruders, but there are other outcomes when a strong, unorthodox woman confronts a disapproving society. One such outcome is the compromise within the marriage, the accommodation to societal norms, the partial acceptance of the expected role. The compromise may involve such a distortion of self that a woman becomes grotesque, as in the case of Ada Fincastle in Ellen Glasgow's *Vein of Iron*. Or, in the case of Grace Breen of Howells's *Dr. Breen's Practice*, it may merely impose certain limits on the wife's freedom within an otherwise happy marriage. In both novels, however, the very presence of compromise underscores the powerful pull of the traditional female role.

Ada Fincastle does not seem born to accommodate to others' standards. When she is in her teens, her father warns her that "There are only two ways of meeting life—...to yield to it,...to retreat from it" (149). But Ada sees another way—to fight hard, for she has that "vein of iron...in her secret self" that "could not yield, could not be broken" (135). Her grandmother admonishes her, "Bend your will before it is broken!" (170), and ultimately, this is what Ada must do. Ada is one of several strong women in a novel about strength, the vein of iron. It is mainly the story of strength diverted into a lifetime of sacrifice, and of how such diversion becomes a perversion of force. When the vein of iron is turned against itself, there are two results: deformed women and diminished men.

Warner Berthoff says that one of Glasgow's major themes is waste: social, moral, psychological" (254), and the channelling of female strength into female martyrdom ends in both waste and horror. The iron will bent to submission remains a kind of terrible power. Submission, Patricia Meyer Spacks notes, provides one with the power to control "by taking care of others." The woman who lives to sacrifice herself becomes twisted into grotesqueness; the saint becomes witchlike and endlessly powerful. Her giving is directed at her man, and he suffers from her generosity. "Women," Spacks says, "doggedly taking care of their men, form men who need to be taken care of" (103). Marriage becomes a union of a male child and his mother, the male controlled by his wife's sacrifices, the female dependent on male weakness for her identity. Trained to yield to life but born to fight it, the strong woman becomes doubly controlling, suppressing her own desires and rigidly denying herself, then dominating the man who receives her boundless sacrifice. In marriage, such a woman is an ever-generous mother to her husband, indulging his weakness, forgiving his failings, sustaining, nurturing, encouraging him no matter how far he falls or how cruelly he transgresses. And thus the martyr-wife reduces her man to the status of child, and the husband, hating his life, chooses to escape.[24]

One central image in the novel defines the conflict between female self-expression and conventional repression. It involves Ada's china doll. When Ada was small, she badly wanted a doll with real hair. All summer, she worked and saved her money so that her father, John Fincastle, could buy her the doll on one of his trips to town. On the day of her father's trip, Ada is in an ecstasy of expectation. But Fincastle brings her a china doll instead. It is one of her first lessons in disappointment, and the women in her family provide specific directions on handling it. Her maiden aunt Meggie counsels her not to "give way to disappointment," for the world would be so "sad if we all gave way" (31). Her mother advises her to think of her father. "Try not to let him see how much this has meant to you" (32). Ada is taught to suppress her own pain so that she can create a world of cheer and spare another's feelings. It is a lesson she will hear, and see enacted, over and over again, until she learns to develop an appropriate substitute self. That self must be strong enough to conquer its own longings, and yet it must

appear weak and empty and helpless. Ada must train herself to become
the china doll, and to pretend to prefer it. Suppression must become
repression and denial, and finally, a nearly complete self-deception. But
the irony is that Ada is never really good enough at imitating the china
doll, and that men prefer "real" china dolls to her imitation, anyway.

Vein of Iron begins by describing the pattern Ada must learn to
imitate. At the center of this elaborate configuration is Ada's father, John
Fincastle, a consummate evader of life. Fincastle is almost a parody of
the American philosopher-hero, a man intimate only with ideas:
"Persons and objects...had a way of stepping out of his vision" (109).
Once a minister, now a full-time philosopher, Fincastle's radical books
have lost him two pulpits, and he is reduced to working as a country
schoolteacher, having retreated to the family home in Ironside, Virginia.

Fincastle counts his happiest years as the two he spent alone,
studying in the British Museum, for he has an "otherworldliness of the
mind" and feels content only when he is reaching for "something beyond
life" (49). He characterizes his love for his wife as a kind of unfortunate
distraction from his true vocation. Marriage forced him to consider such
mundane things as a ministerial career and to relinquish a life of pure
scholarship. In fact, women make Fincastle "recoil" sometimes, for they
demand too much. "He would have given all he was for [his wife], but
he could not give what he was not, he could not make himself over"
(50).

But to make herself over is precisely what his daughter learns to
do, from every generation of the Fincastle women. Ada's father escapes
to what Glasgow, in a telling reference to Wharton, calls a "bloodless
republic of the spirit" (253), while his child learns to yield to life. She is
raised on the tale of her frontier ancestor, a girl captured by Indians and
wed to a chief at age sixteen. "Rescued" at 17, weeping, the girl was
wed to a church elder and became what she was supposed to be. Bearing
her husband's 11 children, living to be 100, she spent her life longing for
the forest but forever concealing that longing.

Later generations of Fincastle women demonstrate the same
strength—and the same perversion of their natures. Aunt Meggie,
Fincastle's old maid sister, has learned to find her happiness in little
things. Ada's grandmother has an "intense relish for life" (115) and a
rigid adherence to a severe Presbyterianism. Mary Evelyn, Ada's
mother, is a Tidewater belle with a thrilling voice always on the verge of

breaking. She is dying, but she is beautiful and brave and gay. All three women have vitality and a courage that enables them to make light of their poverty. And all three live for John Fincastle.

The Fincastle women spare John Fincastle the trouble of looking at (or after) people and things. Gaily and bravely, they minimize their poverty. Gaily and bravely, Mary Evelyn slips into her last illness. John's staunch Presbyterian mother forgives him his heresy, denying her deepest beliefs for her boy. And all these women teach Ada to be strong and to survive, but they also teach her to deny herself, and to choose a man to be strong *for*.

Quite naturally, then, when Ada falls in love, she chooses a near replica of her father.[25] If John Fincastle is a dreaming child, Ralph McBride is a spiteful one. Reared by a widowed and sacrificing mother, Ralph is Fincastle's star pupil. When Ada, at 20, falls in love with him, she is already suppressing her own forebodings about the relationship. She has no fear of the poverty her marriage to a poor law student would entail, for she has been trained for sacrifice. She can be happy, she thinks, if she can have Ralph, "and no one could be easier to make happy than Ralph" (80). When the image of the china doll suddenly flashes into her fantasy, Ada does not heed its warning. Ralph wants a doll-wife, and Ada tries to be that doll. But the "stubborn willfulness, the periods of introspection and irresolution,...the recklessness for the sake of recklessness, the disbelief for the sake of disbelieving" (102) that characterize Ralph make it clear that he needs a mother-wife. What is Ada to be? She is drawn to "something childlike and helpless in his defiance. She felt the wish to protect him in the very moment when she surrendered" (104). Ada's happiness is to be predicated on making Ralph happy, but she is torn between becoming what he wants and supplying what he needs. And she cannot fully suppress her will to become something entirely different from either role.

Ralph is, by turns, an evader and a yielder, never a fighter. When his peers taunt him about his abstemiousness, he joins them in drinking. But Ada is too willful to join the party: "something...the vein of iron...could not yield, could not bend, could not be broken" (135). Ada loses Ralph to Janet Rowan, who has the flaxen hair, blue eyes, and vacant expression of a genuine china doll. When Ralph marries the conventional and manipulative Janet, Ada learns another lesson about what she must not be. For Ralph soon grows to hate his wife; his new responsibilities force him to give up law school and get a job selling cars. Ada's double bind is obvious: her strength lost her her man, but Ralph resents the helplessness that once attracted him.

Ada must develop her skill for channelling her power into an acceptable role. She must learn to be simultaneously submissive and strong, to rebel by acquiescing, and to be ready to pay the price for such rebellion—alone. Three years after Ralph's marriage, Ada defies the conventions by sleeping with a married man. In the encounter and its aftermath, Ada must both fight and yield, but Ralph need only retreat.

The affair takes place in a male world: in the woods, in the mountains where the little girl Ada was forbidden to roam. Even as she exults in this "island of happiness," Ada knows it isn't real, that around it is "the ebb and flow of a treacherous universe" (217). A dream to her, the affair, to Ralph, is "the only thing that seems true" (218). Back in that treacherous universe, Ralph soon leaves for war, another male world, while Ada remains behind. There is no retreat for Ada when, pregnant, she faces social condemnation and fights self-pity. Like her grandmother and her mother, she endures a double dose of pain. Her mission is to "spare" Ralph the news of her pregnancy, for he is already terribly sickened by the war.

Ada's pregnancy is characterized by terrible denials. She will not permit herself any open expression of her loneliness and anguish. She denies herself the solace of sharing her pain with Ralph. And she denies Ralph adult status by "protecting" him from the knowledge of her circumstances. Asking nothing of her lover, Ada is doomed never to receive. But she is also spared the disappointment of asking for something and not receiving it, like the little girl who asked for a special doll.

When Ralph returns from the war and is able to marry Ada, the marriage is as horrible as can be expected. There is no cabin in the woods for an eternal retreat; instead, Ada, Ralph, their son Ranny, and John and Meggie Fincastle all move to the city. Once a troubled child, Ralph is now an obnoxious one; Ada cannot be happy because nothing makes Ralph happy. He prefers her father's company to hers. He finds another china doll, Minna Bergen, and consoles himself in flirtation.

Only in disaster—repeated disaster—does Ada find joy. When Ralph, on an illicit afternoon drive with Minna, is severely injured, Ada is faced with his illness and unemployment as well as his petty betrayals. But she is in control, and power brings its own reward. "As long as he depended upon her, she could face anything"; a "strange happiness...flared up suddenly" (356). Ada's demeaning work in a department store, Ralph's alcoholism, the bank failures of the Depression seem to feed Ada's sense of purpose. Soon she is not only a martyr, but a patronizing one, dedicated to supplying what Ralph has lost, "his pride in himself and his masculine vanity." To her, this is a near-religious mission, an "act of faith...that affirmation which was more to him than the thing it affirmed" (366).

How fitting that a novel filled with ambiguous sacrifice should end with the most dubious sacrifice of all. John Fincastle slowly starves himself so that his family will inherit the insurance money and the chance to return to the family home at Ironside. The death of a man who was never interested in life but only reaching beyond it is, perhaps, his final retreat. The quality of this last gift is somewhat undercut by Fincastle's dying vision—he can recall his childhood perfectly, and he is aware of the moment of death. But, as far as the years in between, there is nothing but loneliness. He sees his mother but cannot remember his wife. It is as if John Fincastle had had no adult life, for he recoiled from the contact with people and things that constitutes maturity.

And so Ada returns to Ironside with her children, Ranny and Ralph. Reflecting on her situation, Ada admits that she is married to a man with an "incurable hostility to life" (462). But, like the generations of women before her, Ada has learned to adapt. Her vitality will sustain Ralph. Never, she realizes, has her life been "so perfect as this" (462).

Ada has conquered and destroyed. And she has been destroyed. The energy that could have made her into something has become the source of her unmaking. It has been used to stifle all spontaneous emotion—disappointment, fear, even rage—so that Ada can make her man happy. Ironically, such manufactured nobility is poisonous. Once, when Ada disapproved of Ralph's joining the other boys to buy moonshine, he excused himself by saying, "It's easy to be noble in the woods, but among other people, it makes you a killjoy" (129). In the context of the scene, the words are Ralph's justification for his conformity; in the context of the entire novel, they represent Ada's plight. There are no woods to which Ada can escape; those republics of the spirit where one can be safe with one's noble thoughts are reserved for men like John Fincastle and Ralph McBride. And so, attempting nobility outside the woods, among people, Ada destroys.

The pervasive china doll imagery of *Vein of Iron* is matched by imagery of the idiot. As the novel opens, the children of Ironside, Ada among them, are chasing Toby Waters, an idiot boy. Ada is enjoying the wildness of the pursuit until, suddenly, she becomes Toby, terrified and hurt. She cannot play the game any more. Compassionate and empathetic, the child Ada is different from others; she will not be part of the group.

Toby Waters is a touchstone to the character of Ralph McBride, too. As a child, he chooses to play with Toby, but not out of compassion. He does so because his mother forbids it. To rebel against her helps him to define himself, so Ralph uses Toby for his own purposes.

Later, Ada *becomes* the idiot. Shortly after she bears her illegitimate child, Ada must run to the village to get a doctor for her grandmother. The village children chase her and pelt her with stones; she is the pariah, again outside the group. In both of Ada's links to Toby, the association is positive, for it reveals the generosity and courage that separate her from others. But when the image reappears later, it marks the change in Ada. When Ada and Ralph, during the Depression, are beset by troubles, Ada permits herself a moment of fear: "her identity twisted and doubled upon her....was she an idiot fleeing over a twisted path?" (396). This time Ada is, in a new sense, Toby Waters. She has twisted her identity against herself. Her courage and generosity have become grotesque, so that Ada is both alien to those around her and a stranger to herself. Denying her fear, her anger, her own need, Ada is a freak. Her sacrifice provokes revulsion.

No one loves what Ada has become. Given two ways to deal with life, to escape or to yield, Ada has been unable to do either. Unable to relinquish the vein of iron, she twisted it into something that feeds on others' needs.

The men she lives for, husband and father, have chosen to escape life. John Fincastle dies in a dream of idiots. He dreams that he is surrounded by a whole world of idiots and that he must get away from them. In his last moments, Fincastle dreams a version of his life: the escape from the material world into the world of ideas, the revulsion for those who could not understand his philosophy, the desire for something above and beyond. For the philosopher, those grounded in the mundane, those who keep him from his quest are alien and repulsive—idiots. In his dream, Fincastle saw his mother among the idiots, helping them. This is a woman's role. She is trained to help, not to lead, to surrender self to survive. A woman is to remain behind, to yield to the world, not to escape it to something beyond. Her role is to serve the noble thinker and the society he disdains. But when a strong woman like Ada Fincastle cannot shed her strength, her compromise becomes horrible. Trying to play the role, she becomes disfigured. Thus, the noble abstractions of the woods are sustained by generations of women turned against themselves. For the sacrifice required of such women kills joy.

Dr. Breen's Practice

Vein of Iron presents a bleak view of marriage, a picture of the disastrous union of a strong woman caught by convention and a weak man sustained by that convention. The novel implies that in marriage, the wife will have to yield and compromise while the husband can simply escape from conflict. As a result, the strong woman is repeatedly damaged by the marriage, as she sacrifices more and more of herself to maintain the very bond that hurts her. For Grace Breen, heroine of Howells's *Dr. Breen's Practice*, there is another compromise, combining goodness and pleasure, submission and a modicum of freedom.[26] What is missing from the amalgam is duty.

Grace Breen, like Ada Fincastle, is severely tempted by the lure of the stereotype. She would dearly like to be a martyr, and, at the beginning of the novel, is in rehearsal for a lifetime of saintly performances. Granted, in choosing to become a physician, Grace selects an unconventional profession, and she believes herself prepared "to encounter anything in the application of her science" (12). Yet as Schriber notes, "Grace's awareness of the world's attitude makes her pursuit of medicine courageous—while at the same time it reinforces her self-sacrificial nature and stringent conscience" (94).[27] What can be more noble than to assume a burden at once personally difficult and socially unacceptable, to dedicate oneself to solitary, unappreciated service? There is something of the killjoy in Grace Breen, reflected in the stiff, almost cardboard characterization of the humorless woman. She is all conscience and no charm.

Defying convention in her choice of career, Grace seems to have simultaneously deferred to conventional strictures. The plot of the novel is worked out in a world of women, the spinsters, widows and wives at a summer hotel, a chorus of female judges who, like Ada Fincastle's female relatives, assess the heroine's every action and influence her behavior. And Grace herself appears quite stereotypical: jilted by her lover, she has chosen medicine "in the spirit in which other women enter convents" (12); she dreams of the traditional woman's role, of doctoring children while sharing a practice with an experienced older man. She denies any allegiance to feminism and seems driven by guilt. That guilt is repeatedly exacerbated by the circle of women who repeatedly try to press her into the mold, by her mother, who advises her never to wed but to do her *duty*, by those women who have a "fine distrust" (22) of a woman doctor and who find Grace's pursuit of the profession "scandalous" (30).²⁸

The greatest stereotype of all is that a man must extricate Grace from this tangle of duty and sacrifice and guilt—by marrying her. Thus the central metaphor of the novel is a scene in which Grace is, literally, entangled in thread. She is sewing, and her husband-to-be, Walter Libby, has to cut her out of the mess. Fryer calls this scene "a symbol of the way in which he will later rescue her through marriage" (*Faces of Eve* 236). But it can also be read as a symbol of the compromises that resolve Grace's dilemma.

Grace is caught in a web of thread because she has been sewing, doing traditionally woman's work, and her predicament indicates that she is not good at it, but it traps her. True, a man must free her, but she hands him the means to do so. "She extended him the scissors with the stern passivity of a fate. 'Cut it,' she commanded, and Mr. Libby knelt before her and obeyed" (34). The language of this vignette indicates that both the scissors and Mr. Libby are instruments of Grace's liberation and that she controls them both. Libby gets her out of the tangle, but she at least helps, if not directs, his action. The scene depicts a distribution of power and represents the movement of the novel, a progress towards Grace's crucial choice.

Schriber says that Howells's preoccupation with gentility led him to create interesting women characters. Because he avoided the subject of sexuality, she says, Howells "created heroines as heroes are most often imagined, as fictional human beings with a range of aspirations and difficulties, with marriage and sexuality being but two" (88). Eakin notes that *Dr. Breen's Practice* is Howells's first novel told from the point of view of a woman, "casting her more nearly as the dominant center of consciousness, no longer the mirror but the lamp" (97). Grace

Breen is interesting because she has more options than the typical young, single woman of fiction, and her choices are more complex. Placing her at the center of the novel, Howells directs attention to Grace's complicated circumstances and her confused inner life. And then, it seems, he resolves her conflict in a hackneyed way—by marriage.

"Although we get a sense of Dr. Breen's self-doubt," says Fryer, "we get a greater sense of her as a lovely woman; although she struggles with self-definition throughout the book, she is really defined in every case by her relationship with men" (*Faces of Eve* 235). All the complexities of Grace Breen's career and personality seem to have been reduced, in the end, to a choice of husbands, and thus, it appears, the novel is one more variation on the same old theme. Or so it seems. But in considering Grace Breen's marriage, we must note that she chooses, rather than is chosen, and that her selection implies a personal growth beyond the limits of the stereotype. Howells appears to be using Grace's suitors symbolically, to represent the warring parts of her personality, and to dramatize her inner struggle between conformity and freedom. In choosing a husband, Grace does not so much find a man who will give her identity as liberate the healthy part of her own personality.

One suitor represents Grace's dark side—the temptation to surrender to a father/husband, to give up the struggle for self. Dr. Mulbridge, the excellent and revered physician, is the potential Daddy. He finds Grace's assumption of professional status amusing and refuses to share a case with her. Grace becomes his nurse, not his colleague, and she likes the role. Under his scrutiny, "she felt herself dwindling away to the merest femininity" (96), and she interprets his directions, and even intentions, with a "perfection" of submission (119). Mulbridge offers her safety; Grace need never worry about who or what to be. Mulbridge asks only that Grace destroy herself. He is a killer of women; he brags of his women patients that "There is not one of them...that I don't believe I could have for the turn of my hand, especially if it was doubled into a fist. They like force" (205). He wants to break Grace's will, to convince her to give up her practice. She will fail, he tells her, because she is herself—because she is a woman. "You can't do anything by yourself, but we could do anything together" (228). This is the great temptation: to be at once a martyr and a dependent, to do good deeds in submission to another.[29] The chorus of women swoon at Mulbridge's sexual mastery and advise Grace to accept it; even her mother speculates that it is Grace's duty to marry this man.

The alternative is Walter Libby—Grace's light side. Initially, she avoids him because he seems a lightweight. He lacks her seriousness of purpose; to Grace, he seems to have no purpose at all. Initially, he stands in the same relation to Grace as she does to Mulbridge, "always doing little things for her with a divination of her unexpressed desires" (125). A helpmate, he is a more androgynous figure than the hypermasculine doctor. He is a friend to Grace, who reminds him of his best male friend. Soon, she comes to depend on him, to rely on that "prompt common sense that made him very useful in emergencies, and a sympathy and an insight that was quick in suggestions and expedients" (125).

Libby gives Grace strength, and he is moved by her energy to assume a position as manager of a cotton mill, to take on serious work. He is attracted to her by her difference from other women and perceives her as a comrade, a colleague. "I shouldn't keep anything back from you," he tells her, "because you would be equal to it, whatever it was" (125). And Libby is funny, and charming, and fun. But that sense of "fun" is precisely what frightens Grace, so steeped in duty, so stiff with guilt.

Tempted by martyrdom, Grace must resist—and choose pleasure. She sins against her best self in rejecting Libby's proposal and moves toward self-destruction in considering Mulbridge's. But when her mother pushes her toward duty, Grace saves herself: "I have had enough of conscience,—of my own, and of yours, too.... There is such a thing as having too much conscience, and of getting stupefied by it" (235).

Grace turns from Ada Fincastle's way, the idiocy of martyrdom, the noxious role of the killjoy/saint. Freeing herself, she is free to choose. She calls Libby back to her; she takes the initiative so that he can renew his offer—and she can submit.

After they marry, they spend a frivolous year on pleasure: travel in Europe, souvenir-hunting, visits to theaters and operas and museums. When they return to America, Libby settles into work at the mill, becoming a reformer of energy and intelligence. And Grace, who is learning to love life, embraces pleasure. She abandons her medical career until her husband, with "a shrewder knowledge of her nature than she had herself" (270), convinces her to open a practice for the children of the mill workers.

The ending of the novel, then, is a kind of "happily-ever-after" that fails to satisfy. For the father/husband, the mill manager, must manage his wife's career, a position where "Dr. Breen's Practice" is really Libby's, since he controls the mill from which her patients come. And the doctor is still, in essence, a very feminine doctor, caring for children, like a mother. It seems as if it was Libby who opened all the doors for Grace, leading her to culture and pleasure and sexuality and meaningful work. It seems as if the ending of the novel is the same old story.

And yet there are several significant deviations from that story. Dr. Breen may have become Mrs. Libby, but she still has her practice. In some, however small, part of her life, she is still Dr. Breen. Choosing to become Mrs. Libby, Grace Breen rejected the enticements of duty. She chose the man who would keep her out of the net of custom. "Mr. Libby cut me loose," she said of her early entanglement in thread. "I could have done it myself, but it seemed right that he should do it" (43). Grace Breen has compromised, but she has not effaced herself.

Chapter Six:
Surviving Alone

She wanted to see with her own eyes the action of primary forces; to touch with her own hand the massive machinery of society; to measure with her own mind the capacity of the motive power.

Henry Adams, Democracy (10)[1]

What good comes of lying about things? People used to believe in lying, but we don't any longer.

Ellen Glasgow, They Stooped to Folly (26)

Section One:
Facing the Gorgon

The Age of Innocence

Some of the strongest heroines in American literature are, like their predecessor Hester Prynne, solitary. Ellen Olenska of Wharton's *The Age of Innocence*, Milly Burden of Glasgow's *They Stooped to Folly*, and Madeleine Lee of Adams's *Democracy* are loner figures of power. Their power derives from their position as isolates within society; their ability to remain independent in the face of group pressure is an enormously subversive force.

Clearly, the heroines are not like the typical American boy-heroes who run away to discover themselves in a social vacuum. Not only are they confined to society, they are intimately connected to it, specifically, by a past sexual relationship. Unlike adolescent males or child-brides, these heroines are sexually experienced: Ellen Olenska is married, Milly Burden has had a lover, Madeleine Lee is widowed. In each case, the heroine enters the novel with a history, trailing clouds of scandal; she is labeled a fallen woman or an adventuress. Socially defined by such past ties, the intruder heroine becomes more threatening because she can no longer be defined by them. Since all acceptable roles for women are predicated on connection to a man—a father, a husband—these loners, defying categorization, are suspect in their solitude.

Standing alone, they stand out, and their bold vision makes them even more conspicuous. The one quality that characterizes the loners is their hunger to see. Repeatedly, these women talk about seeing things as they are, getting to the bottom of things, looking for something bigger or better. They emphasize a need to see or to widen their vision, challenging those who would prefer to limit or distort it. The meaningful life, it appears to them, is largely a life of critical vision.

The critical stance, not the wide-eyed one of the innocent girl or the wondering boy, threatens but also entices others. Questioning the supposedly unquestionable, challenging the previously sacrosanct, the intruders attract admirers and inspire imitators. Living within the group, they provoke its members to look again, at accepted verities, and even to look beyond, for newer truths. The process begins within society and thus can be initiated only by a figure in the group but not of it: the intruder. Each lone intruder participates in the learning process she initiates for others, for her perception stimulates her personal growth. The intruder is thus both a pupil (largely self-educated) and a teacher.

These heroines draw others to them, but they do not connect. For, to connect within society, this kind of heroine would have to compromise by assuming a role that restricts her vision and her self. And to form a connection beyond such roles would require a partner of rare imagination and courage, a man willing to sacrifice those values that have created and sustained his identity. True to her vision—and to herself—the woman remains alone. She remains a living alternative to the reduced beings around her.

Ellen Olenska, the solitary figure in *The Age of Innocence*, is frequently defined by contrast to the socially constricted group she enters. Since the novel is presented through the eyes of Newland Archer, social insider, our understanding of Ellen develops through his repeated comparison of Ellen to his conformist fiancée, May Welland. The novel opens as Archer observes the pair at the opera, May, in virginal white with her white flowers, blushing at the love scenes on stage; Ellen, in an unusual dark blue dress, exposing "a little more shoulder and bosom

than New York was accustomed to seeing" (15). Shortly after, there is
the contrast of their houses. Ellen's drawing room is full of strange
items, eclectically chosen and eccentrically placed, and of Italian-
looking paintings Archer cannot understand. The room is "so different"
that Archer experiences a "sense of adventure" and a revulsion for the
purple satin and gilt that passes for style in May's (and his) set (71).[2]

And then, to underscore the nature of the contrast, there are the
flowers. Archer, like every old New York beau, sends flowers to his
betrothed, daily. Most men, he knows, merely establish a standing order
at the florist, but he makes a point of buying the flowers each day, in a
renewal of his commitment and a declaration of his difference from his
peers. The flowers he sends, however, are the standard lilies-of-the-
valley deemed appropriate for all the brides-to-be. On one of his visits to
order the daily tribute, he sees some yellow roses and thinks of sending
them, instead of the white flowers, to May. But they are not right for
May—"there was something too rich, too strong, in their fiery beauty"
(80). And so he reverts to the habitual. May gets the lilies-of-the-valley.
And Ellen gets the gold roses.

Such juxtapositions illuminate the natures of both women and the
nature of Archer's dilemma as well. To Archer, May embodies the world
he is used to, a little dull, perhaps, but comfortable in its predictability.
Ellen, on the other hand, embodies difference, for she is socially,
sexually, culturally opposed to May and to Archer himself.[3] *The Age of
Innocence* is divided into two books, and the structure of both is the
same. Each section begins with Archer in relative complacency; then
Ellen intrudes upon that tranquillity, disturbing and enticing the hero.[4]
There are repeated attempts, by Archer and by his social set, to limit and
confine the intruder by stereotyping her, by appealing to her moral
values, by pressuring her financially. Ultimately, in each book, Archer
retreats from Ellen, and she remains free and alone. Although the novel
tantalizes us as Archer vacillates between the demure May and the
daring Ellen, Archer's final choice seems inevitable.[5] The relationship
between Archer and Ellen can be defined in many ways, as that of pupil
and teacher, or child and parent, or romantic and realist, but it is never
presented as the union of like with like.[6] Thus, the continuing lure of
Ellen for Archer illuminates another, major opposition in the novel: the
contrast of the male sustained and stifled by society, and the female
rejected by—and thus freed from—that world.

Ellen Olenska seems to have been born different. Although her parents were of "good" New York family, they were wanderers, international travelers, and when they died, their little girl became the charge of her eccentric Aunt Medora. Old New York remembers Ellen as "bold" Ellen Mingott (32), the only girl to wear black satin at her coming-out party. As Book One opens, Ellen has become a major embarrassment to her family, having run away from her husband, a rich Polish nobleman, to the sanctuary of old New York and of her class.

The Countess Olenska claims she wants to belong, but she is always, in some way, alone. "I want to feel cared for and safe," she tells Archer, expressing a wish to be, like the inhabitants of old New York, safe in the nursery world of evasion and pretense (75). Yet despite her desire for safety, Ellen chooses not to live with her grandmother, the socially powerful Mrs. Manson Mingott, under whose roof Ellen would find social rehabilitation. Instead, she selects a small house in an unfashionable part of the city, exulting in "being alone in it" (74). On her return to New York, Ellen is both inside society and dissociated from it. Society, quite rightly, views her as a threat. For she sees things. The child Ellen had been "a fearless and familiar little thing, who asked disconcerting questions" (60), and the grown-up Ellen does the same. "Does no one want to know the truth here?" (70), she asks, for she has seen through the pretenses and evasions of her set. She recognizes the child-world for what it is, describing old New York as "being taken on a holiday when one has been a good little girl" (75), a child's heaven, where no one cries (78). And so she cannot take the children's games seriously; she laughs at New York's rituals and reticences. Told she lives in an unfashionable neighborhood, she merely questions, "Why not make one's own fashion?" (74).

Ellen disturbs others not only because of what she dismisses, but because of what she values. She cares about ideas; she even has books in her drawing room, "a part of the house in which books were usually supposed to be 'out of place' " (104). And she mingles with writers and artists, those people who terrify the rich New Yorkers.

And, worst of all, Ellen takes New York's slogans seriously. When she is cautioned that any happiness "bought by disloyalty and cruelty and indifference" (172) is a despicable happiness, she believes it. And, believing, Ellen acts on her faith. Her greatest social error is to accept, as a standard of behavior, the values her group has long since abandoned.

She accepts society's pretense as reality, thus holding the insiders to their own words. That they are hypocrites is repeatedly made clear by their attempts to buy their own happiness with acts of disloyalty and cruelty and indifference to Ellen herself.

Though the New Yorkers know that Ellen's husband is a brute and that his treatment of Ellen has been perverse, they prefer not to recognize the facts. There is no place for pain nor even discomfort in a child's heaven without tears. When Ellen returns to New York, scarred by the miseries of her marriage, she injects the unpleasant into the safe world. The New Yorkers do not like to look at suffering, so Ellen must be persuaded to conceal her pain. No one wants to know the truth here, as Ellen says, when the truth is unpleasant.

Because the group refuses to see the truth of Ellen's marriage, it will not acknowledge her right to a divorce, or even her reason for wanting one. Because they deny pain, the insiders see only a woman foolishly relinquishing her husband's money. Her indifference to such wealth puzzles them and limits their powers of persuasion. Unable to appeal to greed, they must appeal to Ellen's loyalty in order to betray her. She is convinced that she should abandon the notion of divorcing in order to spare the family.

Ellen is posing a double menace to New York: she threatens because she doesn't value what New York really worships (money), and because she does value the loyalty, generosity, and discipline New Yorkers only pretend to live by. As long as Ellen remains in New York, she continues to be dangerous. Her very presence, even as a married woman, challenges the sanctities of family and class. And it challenges the complacency of Newland Archer as well.

At the same time that Ellen upholds the value of family solidarity, she subverts the stereotypes that support it. The New Yorkers live by the easy categorizations that permit them never to think; one such categorization defines the wife in a broken marriage as the guilty partner. Ellen's decision to leave the count automatically relegates her to this role, but her demeanor and behavior do not fit it. While the insiders are eager to condemn Ellen and gossip incessantly about her friendship with the notorious Julius Beaufort, they cannot be sure that Ellen has become a "bad" woman. Appearances suggest that she may simply enjoy male friendship. She is surrounded by men who admire her: the writer Ned Winsett, the Duke of St. Astrey, the patriarch Mr. van der Luyden, the financier Beaufort, the count's secretary, Monsieur Rivière. The idea that a woman can relate to men on a basis that is neither sexual nor filial is a new one in New York.

And the list of Ellen's friends is troubling for another reason. The mix of aristocrat and servant, of artist and businessman indicates Ellen's blithe disregard of the class lines that mean so much to the ruling families. Ellen calls the duke "dull," mocks the van der Luydens' exclusivity, mixes with the *arriviste* Mrs. Struthers, lives among artists and writers, and visits academics. Ellen is interested in ideas, not social identity, and if the Shoe-Polish Queen, Mrs. Struthers, can offer her good music, Ellen will seek her company. She creates her own fashions, but in doing so, she weakens the barriers that have protected and even created old New York's power. The insiders, like their leader, old Mr. van der Luyden, have achieved influence through exclusivity. But Ellen is blurring the lines of insider and outsider, dismantling a sacred structure.

Whenever Ellen troubles the insiders, they send an emissary from their world to negotiate with her. But Newland Archer cannot restore Ellen to the world of innocence; instead, she lures him farther and farther outside. She reverses his values; she makes him see.[7] With Ellen, Archer learns to look within the Valley of Childish Things and beyond it. He credits her with "opening my eyes to things I'd looked at so long I'd ceased to see them" (76), and once he recognizes the deadliness of the child-world, he begins to dream of a different one. Archer is learning to move beyond his world in dreams, yet he can never do so in reality.

Book One of the novel defines Archer as a prisoner of New York's ideas; Book Two depicts him as a prisoner of his own imaginings. In the first half of the novel, Archer's inability to move past New York stereotypes seals his future. Although he is drawn to Ellen, he needs to find a safe way to categorize her before he can learn to trust her. Ellen's exotic qualities attract him, but Archer wants to "own" Ellen in the classic New York way, and his possessiveness and jealousy cloud his vision. Like his peers, he is obsessed with Ellen's innocence. He wants certainty before he commits to her: he wants assurances that she committed no sexual sin before she left her husband, and that she has been equally unblemished since. Archer wants to limit Ellen by defining her according to his rigid polarities, and he wants to be sure she will be fully his, not Beaufort's, not Monsieur Rivière's.

Because Archer is thinking New York thoughts, he cannot see the woman before him as she is; looking for evidence of her innocence, he overlooks her humanity. His decision to treat her in the New York way, to regard her as a source of potential scandal and thus someone who must be controlled, reflects his deepest allegiance. When Archer convinces Ellen not to seek a divorce, he denies her complexity and rejects the widened vision and richer life she offers. Ellen suggests an exciting life, but she also suggests an ambiguous one. Adults can deal with ambiguities; children cannot. And so, at the end of Book One, Archer retreats to innocence (and May), leaving Ellen alone.

Book Two, parallel in structure, explores the same conflict, more deeply analyzing the dynamics at work in the romantic triangle. By focusing further on the contrast between Archer and Ellen, as well as on that of Archer and May, this section explores Archer's sanctuary: his imagination. In Book One, Archer retreats to New York ways and attitudes to protect himself from his desire for Ellen; in Book Two, he hides within the world of his imagination to protect himself from both Ellen and New York.

Safely, if unhappily, married to May, Archer has achieved some measure of tranquillity until Ellen re-enters his life. Their re-encounter underlines their differences. Ellen, the adult, has learned to accept the consequences of her choice. Agreeing not to divorce, she remains free yet restricted; as a solitary woman, she has achieved great social success in Washington even as she has severed her ties to Archer. She has chosen to remain unconnected to either her husband or to Archer, and she is willing to pay the price in loneliness and in the increasing financial pressure the Mingotts apply. Ellen's family attempts to force her back to her husband by cutting back her allowance, but Ellen resists. Her loyalty to her family, demonstrated in her not seeking a divorce, is rewarded by repeated family betrayal. But Ellen will accept relative poverty and isolation in return for independence.

Archer, however, wants what children want—to escape the consequences of his choice. His characteristic strategy in this book is to run away, to find comfort in poetry, in visions, in cliches and evasions, in anything but a clear recognition of his dilemma.

Even before Ellen returns to his world, Archer has found his study and his books to be a secret cave where, he thinks, he can live a "real" life. When that sanctuary proves inadequate protection against his longing for Ellen, Archer can only suggest another escape. He is startled when Ellen bluntly describes their romantic alternatives, asking him if he wants her to be his "mistress" (289). "I want," he replies, "somehow to get away with you into a world where words like that—categories like that—won't exist. Where we shall be simply two human beings who love each other...." Ellen can only sigh and then laugh. "Oh, my dear—where is that country?" (290).

Ellen must caution Archer to "look, not at visions, but at realities" (289). There is no country for Archer and Ellen, and Archer has already decided against joining Ellen *outside* of country and clan. When she uses the word "mistress," she defines what Archer actually proposes—the New York way. Although Archer is too evasive to speak of it, he wants Ellen to become a prisoner for him. As his mistress, Ellen would be a consumable, a throwaway, defined solely by her dependence on her man. As in Book I, Archer, loving Ellen, wants to limit her. Ellen perceives the trap, saying, "We're near each other only if we stay far from each other. Then we can be *ourselves*" (290-91, emphasis added).

Ironically, in refusing Archer, Ellen both upholds New York family values and maintains the identity so threatening to New York. Her final movement outside is characterized by similar ironies. Although Archer perceives it as New York's casting out of the enemy, the taking of life "without effusion of blood" (335), it is largely Ellen's choice, another decision reflecting her free, adult status. Ellen is leaving because May is pregnant. Having previously agreed to sleep with Archer once, and then to separate, Ellen has subsequently decided that her pleasure cannot be bought by betrayal and cruelty. Ellen demonstrates her moral growth in this final choice. She considers May (and the family that is soon to be) before herself. New York, as always, is blind. While the tribe celebrates the expulsion of the troublemaker as a victory achieved after great unpleasantness, it cannot see the real Ellen. The insiders cannot see her free movement beyond them—past their rigid stereotypes, evasions, and hypocrisies. Ellen chooses to travel out of this heaven, to a grown-up's world.

Her leaving is also her way of holding Archer to his word. It is significant that Ellen leaves because Archer is to be a father, for he must now demonstrate that loyalty to family he once urged on her. Once, in a deeply ironic moment, Archer defended Ellen against the rumors circulated by his male friends. "Women ought to be free—as free as we are," he had declared (42), but by the end of the novel, Ellen is far more free than Archer. For how free can Archer, in his child-world, be? For the rest of his life, he dabbles in politics and philanthropy, but he is by nature a dilettante. His is the nursery-world in which every day is the same. There is, of course, the old escape into fantasy, so much a part of Archer that even in old age, when he is free to see Ellen, he chooses not to. She is "more real" (361) to him in imagination, more comforting, than she would be in physical reality. Her life is "too dense...too stimulating" (358).[8] Archer has always preferred visions.

Ellen is free precisely because she sees not visions, but reality. Choosing to escape a heaven without tears, she has, instead, "had to look at the Gorgon," who "dries one's tears" (288). She has risked sorrow and pain and transcended them. She has lived by the credo of her champion, Monsieur Rivière, and looked life in the face, not run from it. And so Ellen lives an independent life in Paris, free to see, to analyze, to judge. She is solitary, but she is therefore free of both her husband and of New York. And she lives among the ideas she craves.

Ellen Olenska is everything a heroine should be: intelligent, fearless, lively, beautiful, generous, kind. Like so many American heroes, she is a loner, a fighter, and a survivor. But we do not usually think of Ellen when we think of lonely courage. For Ellen fights alone within a group; the Gorgon she faces is not an animal, or an Indian, or a military foe. It is society itself. The loneliness of her struggle is exacerbated by the hero of this novel, who, like other American heroes, prefers vision to reality. By looking life in the face, Ellen moves beyond Archer's reach, beyond the confines of his society and the consolations of his imagination. There is, indeed, no "country" in which she and Archer can both feel at home.

Section Two:
Loss and Renewal

They Stooped to Folly

"What a help, what a support are definite classifications," muses Virginius Littlepage, one of the central characters of Glasgow's *They Stooped to Folly* (294). A major intelligence in the novel, Virginius seems surrounded by characters who can be succinctly and definitively classified. He himself can be typed as a genteel Southern lawyer of great manners and small imagination. And then there are all the women, most of whom can be easily labeled: the perfect wife, the fallen woman, the sexpot, the Calvinist, the clubwoman, the New Woman. Only one character, throughout the novel, never seems to fit a type and never chooses to wear a mask. Milly Burden, simply by being herself, acts as a catalyst for a series of unmaskings. She stands at the center of this cluster of characters like a mirror, challenging the others to look—at her, and at others, and at themselves. Gradually, in this social comedy, the classifications begin to disintegrate, and it becomes clear that they have never been a "help." Instead, the classifications divide the characters, so that they never know each other and are denied the intimacy, the "loving kindness" they crave. The parallel processes of disintegration and recognition begin in the troubles of Milly Burden, who scorns lies and masks.

We see much of the story through the eyes of Virginius and Victoria Littlepage, who might appropriately be called Newland Archer and May Welland grown old. Nice, well-meaning, conventional people, they suffer a series of shocks that begin when Milly Burden, Virginius's secretary, has a love affair with a young writer, Martin Welding. When Martin goes off to World War I, Milly spares him the news of her pregnancy, and the baby subsequently dies. After the war, Milly advises Martin, who is anxious to experience more of the Old World, to return to Europe. He is still ignorant of Milly's pregnancy and the scandal it caused. Back in Europe, Mary Victoria Littlepage, Virginius and Victoria's daughter, decides to "save" Martin from a nervous breakdown and from Milly's influence, by marrying him. The elder Littlepages are horrified, not only at Milly's sexual transgressions and her refusal to hold Martin to his duty to her, but by their saintly daughter's deliberate appropriation of a man committed to another.

As they struggle to understand their daughter, Virginius and Victoria try, sincerely, to understand their daughter's victim, Milly Burden. But Milly is a puzzle. She seems to have created her own values, and, in some way, to have convinced others to judge her by these standards. Virginius senses that Milly's "indifference to what in a Victorian lady he would have called her frailty appeared in some incredible fashion to redeem her character" (7). Initially Milly rejects any call to duty except duty to herself; she speaks often of her right to live her life freely, as long as she plays fair, of her right to pleasure. While such statements perplex Virginius, he admires Milly's "steady courage in facing reality" (284).

Milly's personality is further defined by contrast. She becomes an increasingly sympathetic character when she is compared to that virago of virtue, Mary Victoria. Milly may believe she has a right to her own life, but Mary Victoria, that great appropriator, moral conqueror of the postwar Balkans, "demanded, from the purest motives, the right of moral encroachment upon the lives of others" (39). Mary Victoria might be mistaken for a New Woman in her solitary war work, but she is merely the innocent destroyer in a new guise. She can move freely through battlefields and terrorize men because she is non-human, utterly sexless, humorless, driven only by her mission "to curb the lower nature of man" (12). Caught in her fantasy of rescue, Mary Victoria is a mean and spiteful child. Virginius always thinks of her as a little girl in white, and, like a spoiled child, Mary Victoria takes what she wants—Martin Welding. Unlike Milly Burden, however, Mary Victoria lies about her actions. She couches her acquisition of Martin in terms of "duty" and "rescue."

Milly is thus unlike this "good" woman, and her difference subverts the classification itself. Around her swirl other apparently typical characters: Victoria Littlepage, the perfect wife, born with no lower nature and grateful her husband has none; Louisa Goddard, the energetic, no-nonsense spinster clubwoman; Mrs. Burden, Milly's mother, a religious fanatic. Milly is not like these "good" women, either.

And she is not really like the "bad" ones. She bears no relationship to old Aunt Agatha, seduced years ago and relegated to a life of seclusion and shame; now, in old age, enjoying a renewed adolescence of movie matinees and banana splits. She is no Amy Dalrymple, the town's scarlet woman, divorced for immorality at fifty and a continuing object of desire for every middle-aged man in town.

Because Milly seems untypical, the types themselves begin to fall apart, and then the pain and loneliness behind the masks appear. Mary Victoria's casual disregard for Milly and manipulation of Martin reveal her cruelty. And Milly's rebellion becomes a kind of virtue, so that Mary Victoria's mother perceives Milly as "more human," more "exciting" and "vital" than her own daughter. The perfect wife, programmed for virtue, begins to wonder if perhaps "ruined women" are a social construct that will vanish "as soon as the world ceased to believe in them" (240). She, who had never "for an instant,...forgotten herself and her duty to others" (150), begins to ask why any woman should "be responsible for the moral sense of a man" (146). Her husband Virginius, increasingly disillusioned with his daughter, imagines the "light and darkness....tears and laughter" (256) of having a child like Milly.

Other definite classifications begin to blur. Mrs. Burden is more pitiful than hateful in her righteousness. Amy Dalrymple, the sexual temptress, longs for security and kindness, not passion. Her dalliances are described as the adventures of a woman with no other outlet for her energies. Martin Welding, the writer who claims to want to write about real life, turns out to be a coward. Laura Goddard, ostensibly content with her civic activities and clubs, has pined for Virginius, her best friend's husband, for years. As for Virginius, he lusts for Amy Dalrymple. And his perfect wife longs "for something more satisfying than any love Virginius was able to give" (144).

People are unhappy behind the masks. Virginius considers his marriage merely a "serene monotony" disguised as happiness (20), and fears that he has never lived. He senses that he is a prisoner of innocence, "had life...ever meant to him anything more than escape from experience?" (306). Martin feels suffocated by his inability to live up to his wife's ideals. Victoria, dying, feels hollow inside.

And yet, because categories are so comforting, they are hard to relinquish. And thus they divide people, and the individual is never truly known, never touched. Dying, Victoria tries to leave an important message for her husband, but she cannot write it. Days after his wife's death, Virginius realizes that he never really understood her; trying to embrace his grieving daughter, he asks why, "even now,...he could never touch, the real Mary Victoria?" (314).

Linked to this concern with classification is the novel's other major theme, the nature of "loving kindness." The phrase and its variations are used repeatedly by Milly, Mrs. Dalrymple, and Victoria. It defines an ability to see beyond roles and to deal generously with the person damaged by such categories. Even the characters caught in roles are capable of loving kindness. Thus, Victoria sees the pathos in Milly's judgmental mother, and sympathizes with and even admires Milly herself. Virginius, too, is what Milly describes as an "angel" to her (242), a significant word in a novel filled with angels—of devastation

(Mary Victoria) and purity (Victoria). Amy Dalrymple, too, despite her reputation, is essentially generous and forgiving. Each of these characters sees and acts in unconventional ways,[9] in moments of kindness.

Among a multitude of ironies in the novel, one major irony is the fact that those individuals who can give loving kindness are often blind to it in others. Victoria remains threatened by Mrs. Dalrymple, unable to see her as anything but a rival. Victoria's compassion for Milly does not draw her any closer to her equally kind husband, because they remain prisoners of conventional attitudes toward marriage.

Just as Milly is the central figure in exploring the theme of deception and truth, she is clearly tied to the theme of loving kindness. Her decision to encourage Martin, whom she loves, to return to Europe shows generosity of spirit, but there is also a hard, cold, narcissistic edge to Milly. Frederick McDowell says that Milly initially chooses happiness or pleasure at all cost; then, discovering the futility of her passion, she "attains a more substantial inner freedom and peace" (179). Milly's development in the novel is different from that of the other characters. At each stage of her growth, she is honest. She begins in an open avowal of her selfish hungers; she will please herself in her affair. Her courage emerges in her pregnancy. But her generosity in freeing Martin to return to Europe becomes anger and bitterness when she loses him for good. Her strength is her honesty; soon she confronts the truth that her lover "was always afraid of life" (7) and thus is too timid to be her partner. She has no choice but to accept his betrayal and Mary Victoria's cruelty. For a while, there is no loving kindness within her. She has learned to hate Martin Welding, and she says she wants only freedom and a truth "that you could believe in, not just shams and labels" (293). Having given herself to a sham of love, Milly closes her eyes to the possibility of a real one.

By the end of the novel, however, Milly has grown beyond her deliberate blindness. She has moved past hatred and she is reaching, as she says in ecstasy, "into the world!" (346). Alone, Milly is not running away from the possibility of all human ties, but toward a better, more genuine connection. "The happy ones are those who have found something worth loving" (294), she declares, and her discovery marks her progress. Her honest, open vision will teach her what to value, and her loving kindness, how to value it. All the main characters of *They*

Stooped to Folly are alone. But of them all, Milly Burden emerges fully alive.

Democracy

Another woman character claims to be looking for *something* but is actually looking for someone. When Madeleine Lightfoot Lee, protagonist of Henry Adams's *Democracy*, begins her quest, her search becomes a parable of the dangers of passivity and an exposé of the effects of power. This novel of education explores both the nature of power and its enticements for the powerless. Much of the social criticism is expressed through continuing metaphors of high and low, appropriate to an ironic novel called *Democracy*, set in Washington, D.C., after the Civil War.

Madeleine Lightfoot Lee is the intruder. Harry Henderson III notes that "Adams' heroines are no Jamesian innocents, but hardy intellectuals" (213). and Madeleine is both experienced and intelligent. The 30-year-old widow of a rich stockbroker, she has already become an alien on her home ground, New York. She "had lost her taste for New York society; she had felt no interest in the price of stocks, and very little in the men who dealt in them; she had become serious" (1-2). Bored by a group of people "as monotonous as the brown stone houses they lived in" (2), Madeleine samples a number of diversions. She reads German philosophy in the original, dabbles in philanthropy, tries religion. She is "eating her heart out because she could find no one object worth a sacrifice" (4). New York offers a variety of people, occupations, aims, and ideas, but "all these, after going to a certain height, stopped short" (6). Madeleine is weary of such arrested growth; she wants a land of giants. Her discontent makes others uncomfortable. The average member of New York society becomes defensive under Madeleine's gaze: "If she cannot be contented like other people, what need is there for abusing us just because she feels herself no taller than we are?" (9).

Madeleine cannot stop reaching higher. She is simply too different to be contented like other people; she is brighter, braver. A voracious reader, she is, "perhaps, the only woman in New York who knew something of American history" (9-10), thus another woman with connections to a past. And her personal past has formed her, too. "To lose a husband and a baby...and keep one's courage and reason, one must become very hard or very soft," she explains. "I am now pure steel" (10-

11). Because she is so different, she is not satisfied with what satisfies others. She wants more than money and status, she wants

to get all that American life had to offer, good or bad, and to drink it down to the dregs, fully determined that whatever there was in it she would have, and that whatever could be made out of it she would manufacture. (5)

Henderson says that her purpose "is described in tones almost deliberately echoing Thoreau's in going to Walden Pond" (213), but Thoreau sought self in solitude, and Madeleine is secretly looking for a partner. When she moves to Washington, she believes she wants "to see with her own eyes the action of primary forces," to get to "the heart of the great American mystery of democracy and government" (10). But any woman seeking power in Washington will find a powerful man. Madeleine thinks she can merely look at power without being touched by it. Yet the omniscient narrator warns that "Perhaps...however strongly she might deny it, the passion for exerting power, for its own sake might dazzle and mislead a woman" (12) intruding into this bastion of male force.

"Why will not somebody grow to be a Lee and cast a shadow?" she wails (9). And when she enters Washington, she finds Senator Silas P. Ratcliffe, the Prairie Giant of Peoria. Is he the man of stature or the rat? His relationship to Madeleine is repeatedly defined as a war, the two as combatants. In Washington, Madeleine fights her own civil war, divided by her longing to submit to male power and her need to escape it.

The personal is political in this novel.[10] Madeleine's search for power in the abstract exposes her to the concrete realities of force, for her and for the nation. Silas Ratcliffe is Madeleine's enemy and an enemy of the people. Ratcliffe's manipulation of Madeleine mirrors his unscrupulous tactics in government. Marshalled behind Ratcliffe are all the forces of tradition and the lure of the feminine role. On Madeleine's side are only her own intelligence and two curious allies. There is the typical woman, Madeleine's conventional but loving sister Sybil, and the atypical man, John Carrington, a Southern lawyer, sensitive, responsible, and in love with Madeleine. Because both are remote from the sources of power, they are little help in resisting it.

The war is waged in the face of a group that disapproves of Madeleine, for they can judge her only by their own values. Like the

New Yorkers, the Washingtonians are puzzled by Madeleine. Unsure what the woman wants, they label her an adventuress seeking to marry Ratcliffe. Madeleine herself is unsure what she wants. Ratcliffe amuses her; he gets her into the recesses of government, places she might not otherwise see. When he appears to fall in love with her, she feels safe from any reciprocal emotion. But Carrington senses that Madeleine is drawn to Ratcliffe's "strong will and unscrupulous energy." Ratcliffe "flattered all Mrs. Lee's weaknesses by the confidence and deference with which he treated her" (99); he is tempting her with the role of the helpmate, the dutiful, sacrificing wife.

When Ratcliffe does propose, he is as manipulative as he is in the Cabinet or on the Senate floor. Knowing he cannot reach Madeleine by an appeal to religious feeling or ambition or love, he relies on the fact that "she was a woman to the very last drop of her blood. She could not be induced to love Ratcliffe, but she might be deluded into sacrificing herself for him" (179). He offers her a life of duty—and of vicarious power as First Lady, when he achieves the presidency. Madeleine came to *see* power; now she is tempted to submit to it.

Madeleine is confused. She has seen what Washington is like; she has studied the Senate and "read with unerring instinct one general characteristic of all Senators," an addiction to flattery so strong that only perpetual sycophancy can satisfy it (32). To marry Ratcliffe is to join his circle of fawning dependents. She has witnessed the newly elected President and the First Lady standing in a receiving line, robot-like, the leaders of "democracy" aping the manners of royalty. She has thus seen two versions of the role proposed for her. The third is no better. The most powerful man in Washington (next to Ratcliffe) is his crony Baker, a lobbyist, and Madeleine observes Mrs. Baker. The lobbyist's wife is powerful by association, and also vulgar, crude, corrupt—an image of what Madeleine could become.

And Madeleine has seen the nature of Ratcliffe himself, a man whose greatest talent is "the skill with which he evaded questions of principle" (161). She watches as Ratcliffe steals control from the President and shares the spoils with his cohort, Baker. Madeleine, who came to Washington in search of something tall and towering, has fallen in her quest; she is "deep in the mire of politics and could see...how the great machine floundered about, bespattering with mud even her own pure garments" (195). She does not want to accept what she sees.

Instead, she rationalizes that beneath the "scum" on the surface of politics there must be "a sort of healthy ocean current of honest purpose" (196), and she deceives herself into thinking she can guide Ratcliffe to that purpose. Significantly, the woman who once described her goal as an upward movement is now describing a descent into the underworld, through scum and mud.

Madeleine is self-deceived and troubled because she is still a prisoner of the stereotype. The narrator makes this quite explicit: "Mrs Lee sat still and let things take their course; a dangerous expedient, as thousands of women have learned, for it leaves them at the mercy of the strong will, bent upon mastery" (311). Playing the feminine role, she had questioned "whether any life was worth living for a woman who had neither husband nor children" (334). Seeking a meaningful life, Madeleine Lee, in reality, sought a man to give it meaning. Claiming to want to see a hero, she is trapped by her need to belong to one.

Although both Sybil and Carrington work to free Madeleine from her fascination with force, Madeleine must free herself. She must acknowledge what she sees around her and within. She must admit that there are no heroes in Washington, no tall trees but only a "wilderness of stunted natures" (174). Those who appeared to be heroes were merely masters; "democratic government...was nothing more than government of any kind" (342).

The great force at the center of the nation, Madeleine discovers, is characterized by manipulation, intrigue, and deceit.[11] Power has nothing to do with principle, even if the principle is democracy. Force is the same everywhere, whether it is political, or financial, or sexual dominance. Madeleine must look elsewhere for something to value.

Madeleine's search leads her to herself. She has been looking for a "Lee," but she is a Lee, Mrs. Lightfoot Lee. She keeps her name and her principles by refusing Ratcliffe.[12] It is up to her to become the hero she seeks, by acting, not acquiescing. "She had barely escaped being dragged under the wheels of the machine, and so coming to an untimely end" (341), the end of identity and purpose. Madeleine's story ends with her renewal, as she recognizes that the "true democracy of life" is "her paupers and her prisons, her schools and her hospitals" (342), the sphere, however limited, in which she can act freely and generously and even heroically. New York society was right about one thing: Madeleine's dissatisfaction was with herself; she was unhappy because she was no taller than the others. She came to Washington to escape the arrested growth she saw in New York and in herself. In the center of male power, she nearly lost the chance for any growth. Finally, alone, she can begin to nurture "true democracy": her money can sustain, maybe even elevate, the poor, the sick, the outcast. Madeleine must design a new machinery of liberation, not control. It is *something*, not *someone*, worth sacrificing for.

Chapter Seven:
Designs for Marriage

To take what you would give me, I should have to be either a very large man or a very small one, and I am only in the middle class.

Willa Cather, *O Pioneers!* (112)

Section One:
Revision and Reversal

Main Street

For the intruder, marriage is often a trap. It is a compromise at best, a disfigurement at worst. Repeatedly, the "successful" heroines refuse the tie of marriage because it binds too closely. The independent woman who can achieve some substitute closeness in an extended family of blood relations or friends appears to be the most successful of the lot. Thus Ellen Olenska has her cultural network and Madeleine Lee her sister Sybil and loyal friend Carrington. The good marriage is so rare as to appear non-existent. There, are, however, a few heroines who manage to marry and retain their selves.

The primary requirement for this kind of marriage is self. Female identity must precede the union, not be defined by it. Thus the marriage demands a strong woman. Only a very secure, strong woman can resist the lure of the traditional marriage, with its promise of security through submission. And only a strong woman can defy convention in choosing her mate and in choosing how to live with him. Given the strength of the forces opposing the new marriage, it is not surprising that it remains imperfect and in process, an experiment that is never completed, a reality that never meets the ideal.

Such a marriage is like the heroines that attempt it: ambivalent, puzzling, hard to classify. There is no "republic of the spirit" or "secret cave" in which these women can find perfect happiness alone, and there is no country for their dream of perfect union, either. There are only rough drafts, tentative versions of marriages, some more satisfying than others.

All such versions share one thing: there is to be no father in this marriage. Carol Kennicott of Sinclair Lewis's *Main Street* must learn this lesson after years of discontent. Her marriage must be drastically revised when she grows up and relinquishes her search for an approving father. In some instances, the reaction against the father-husband results in a role reversal: in Lewis's *Ann Vickers*, Ann's lover must be stripped of power and moral authority so she can rise to meet (and marry) him; Willa Cather's Ántonia Shimerda is the great mother of "Cuzack's Boys," but she is also the dominant partner in the Cuzacks' marriage. Such marriages may be described as merely adaptations of a traditional structure of one strong partner and one weak one. But clearly, the men who ally themselves with strong women show a certain strength themselves. The man who plays the socially imposed role in marriage finds support and security in society; the man who rejects the role must have resources elsewhere—within. What appears to be a role reversal may, in fact, be the first step in a movement beyond any conventional role at all.

Such ambiguity makes it difficult to classify the marriage of Alexandra Bergstrom in Willa Cather's *O Pioneers!* Alexandra is strong, but not entirely so. Carl takes from Alexandra but gives to her as well. Their union seems to redefine itself continuously, as their needs and energies balance and re-balance.

There is no perfect equilibrium, no linking of exact equals in Alexandra and Carl's marriage. And when partners appear more evenly matched, as in Cather's *The Song of the Lark*, there is still no perfect balance—and no ideal romance. No intruder finds her identical twin, but some do find men, not boy heroes, of insight, courage, and generosity. In every case, the good marriage is one of the heroine's later steps to fulfillment, not her first. Like the American Adam, the intruder grows in loneliness. But she grows beyond the Huck Finns and Ishmaels and Nick Adamses to risk the final adventure. Designing a new model of intimacy, the intruder drafts a new world. It will be no Eden of wonder and innocence and space. It will be a place where the past and experience are neither evaded nor revered, where adults can come together. Unlike Eden, it will not be static. It will be a perpetually changing territory, subject to revision and redefinition. When the intruder finds her mate, they step together into the new territory of marriage. It is not a final step, but a stepping off—with all the promise and uncertainty that beginnings and new lands provide.

There is such a design, and a perilous beginning, in *Main Street*. Although Mark Schorer speaks for many in calling the novel a period piece (438), the novel remains interesting for several reasons. Sinclair Lewis's portrait of American smugness and insularity is startlingly relevant, and his perceptions of a woman's inner struggle are astute. Unfortunately, the typical reading of the novel focuses on nearly everything but Carol Kennicott's development. Critics who consider Carol are prone to want to hurry past her to another question: Does she speak for Lewis? Others attempt to schematize the novel as a battle between Gopher Prairie and Carol, searching for a winner, and for evidence of Lewis's allegiances.[1] A reconsideration of the novel as a story of one person's growth opens the book to different questions. Carol Kennicott's conflicts then become the center of several kinds of stories: growing up, growing together, and learning what—and how—to fight. Such a reading proposes that Carol's inner struggle must be resolved before she can match herself against Main Street.

Carol is, ostensibly, an intruder heroine. She has the vitality and vision of the type: "Even when she was tired her dark eyes were observant" (8), and she questions and examines "unceasingly" (9). She wants to wake up the farmers, enlighten the burghers, and generally reform the town of Gopher Prairie. Carol means to change things— everything, that is, but herself. Although she follows the recognizable pattern of the intruder by entering an alien world, exposing its vices and challenging its values, Carol is an ineffectual heroine. She is an intelligent, perceptive, and energetic force without focus because she is still a child.

"I want everything," Carol says (15), with the voraciousness of a little girl. She shares other innocents' qualities. She is essentially sexless,[2] enduring, not enjoying, her husband's love-making; dallying in a virtuous and idealized adultery. And, most importantly, she wants a Daddy, an ideal father as lover. Her dream mate is a replica of her father, "the gray reticent judge who was divine love, perfect understanding" (339). It is the fantasy of a person without self, for it promises an easy, ready-made identity and perfect, unconditional approval. Carol wants not just a father, but a special one, a man qualified to esteem her and never, ever, to criticize her. She wants a judge who will never really judge her.

Love, for Carol, is validation by a parent. Whenever she is drawn to a man, she sees him as a rescuer, someone who will save her from an unsatisfactory situation and, on a deeper level, from herself. She marries a doctor—not as good as a judge, perhaps, but still a romantic figure of solace and healing. She marries him when she feels bored with her job and "sees no glory ahead," and partly because "the firmness of his personality enveloped her" (20). When Gopher Prairie threatens her idealized image of herself, she turns to Erik Valborg, young and sensitive and aesthetically inclined, for support, not for sexual release. Erik will be her ally, protector, and judge. He, not Will Kennicott, is to be the embodiment of her cultured, indulgent father. When the artist fails her, she turns to the Philistine father, Perce Bresnahan, millionaire executive. "He made her feel young and soft—as Kennicott had once made her feel" (297). Each man fails her, for no one can supply the boundless approval Carol desires. No one can give her herself.

The key to Carol's character is Lewis's constant and complicated use of the word "play." Carol repeatedly yearns for "someone to play with" (337); as a young bride, she plays house (64), and Will's mother credits her with teaching Will to play (107). Bresnahan tells her she'd be fun to play with (277), and she dreams of playing "incredible imaginative games" (352) with a lover like Erik. "Play" is what children do, and it signals Carol's arrested development, but it has many more positive connotations in the context of the novel. It represents humor, spontaneity, receptiveness to novelty and to experience in general. Ironically, the child-Carol has, in this sense, never learned to play at all.

The most telling use of the word occurs when Carol gives her first party. The citizens of Gopher Prairie dismay her, for it is clear "they had lost the power of play as well as the power of impersonal thought" (77). The linking of the "playful" with the "impersonal" is so close as to make the terms interchangeable. Carol, like her neighbors, cannot "play," if we take the term to mean a movement beyond the personal, beyond the self. If play requires humor, Carol cannot indulge, for she has a keen sense of irony but little sense of fun. She lacks spontaneity, for she is forever conscious of the gaze of others. Carol is self-conscious precisely because she has no self.

Vida Sherwin advises Carol about changing the village, but her exhortation may also refer to a change of character. Carol must "work from the inside," Vida tells her, "with what we have, rather than from the outside, with foreign ideas. The shell ought not to be forced on the spirit.... The bright shell has to grow out of the spirit, and express it" (137).

Gopher Prairie is massed against Carol Kennicott, imposing a rigid shell on the free spirit. But Carol herself repeats the same process, trying on a variety of identities, forcing the potential adult within into the tight, uncomfortable, unsatisfying spaces of others' values. It is a childish way of seeking approval. Playing roles is the only kind of play Carol knows.

The question of the novel thus becomes, who is Carol to be? She seeks answers anywhere but within. "Whenever she was restless she dodged her thoughts by the familiar vagabond fallacy of running away from them, of moving on to a new place" (389). Thus, the move to Gopher Prairie. If a new place cannot satisfy, a new role will. And so Carol resorts to play-acting: impersonating the "Clever Little Bride" (48), becoming as unreasonable as an amateur actress on a first night when she gives her first party (75). She assumes the roles of reformer, progressive, historian, devoted wife, doting mother. But shells are not substance. It is a lesson she learns when she directs other actors. Her amateur theatricals fail because she cannot "carve intaglios in good wholesome jack-pine" (222). External changes constrict and deform; foreign surfaces do not express the spirit.

Carol play-acts because she is afraid of judgment, and yet she craves it so badly. "Always she was acting, for the benefit of everyone she saw—and...of the ambushed lurking eyes she did not see" (100). Changing roles is her way of escaping the most hurtful judgment. When the leering eyes condemn the progressive Carol, she can assume a new disguise and be the loyal wife or the dedicated mother. Her eagerness to please empowers those she most despises. Dependent on others for identity, Carol must interpret every glance, every word, as personal. She becomes the victim of others' cruelty, but also of her own evasions. Her playing is the nervous rebellion of a frightened little girl.

She hints at her dilemma in her advice to Erik Valborg. She tells him to run away, and to "play 'till the Good People capture you" (330). She defines freedom as a moment of disobedience, a temporary eluding of other peoples' control. To Erik, freedom is the expression of spirit by the shell: "I don't just want to play. I want to make something beautiful.... And I don't know enough" (330). Erik is Carol's dream of an artist, and she can only advise him to live her fantasy of incredible imaginative games. She cannot understand that Erik dreams of art as inner discipline, as a manifestation of experience and learning that moves from inside to out. Deeply afraid to look within, Carol has nowhere to look but to others. Thus the whole world impinges on and threatens her as she watches it watch her. She is the harshest judge of her own failings, for she denies her own capacities for growth. Carol directs her energies and vision outward, hoping to change her audience rather than to change herself.

When change comes, it comes through Carol's redirected gaze. In the outcasts of the village Carol finds an image of her own alienation. Learning to understand the outsiders and even to love them, Carol develops a new tolerance for her hidden self. Lewis uses the scenes of Carol and the outsiders in several ways: to detail the callousness and cruelties of the insiders, to explore Carol's weaknesses, and to track her development.

Even Carol's restless yearning appears admirable when it is contrasted with Gopher Prairie's complacency. The vulgarity, ignorance and materialism of the insiders is surpassed only by their drive to protect what is theirs and to deny others a share of the goods. The geniality that welcomes Carol to the insiders' set gives way to fury when Carol creates a "servant problem" by paying her maid more than other hired girls get. It is her first lesson in the viciousness of the town, where civic virtue and respectability are concepts used as weapons against the slightest personal rebellion. Carol learns to be afraid of Gopher Prairie by observing its treatment of Miles and Bea Bjornstam, Fern Mullins, and Erik Valborg, all of whom can be characterized by a greater sensitivity and intelligence than their persecutors. As Carol begins to identify with the deviants, she rightly classes the insiders as "the quiet dead....scornful of the living for their restless walking" (257).

Carol makes no conscious decision to ally herself with the enemies of Boosterism. Her connection to the poor or the unorthodox is often tainted by the same failings and foolishness Carol shows elsewhere. Thus, her initial horror at the drab, dirty, stifling atmosphere of the town is undercut by a contrast with the farm girls' awe. For Bea Sorenson, coming to town to seek her fortune, escaping the squalor and isolation of the farm, Gopher Prairie is lovely. The juxtaposition reveals as much about Carol's impossible longings as it does about the town.

Carol's subsequent encounters with the lower classes are equally ambivalent. Carol learns to know and like her maid Bea and to rate her "a companion altogether superior to the young matrons" of Main Street. But she is still posturing; she and Bea are "two girls playing at housework" (108). The slums bother her, but she doesn't know what to do about them, for she senses that she cannot "play Lady Bountiful" in Swede Hollow (113). She is uncomfortable when the reality of poverty demands more than role; she is afraid to think of millions of workers in rebellion, for they would threaten her pose before the "Beas and Oscarinas whom she loved—and patronized" (267). Carol's dream of revolution is a fantasy of more art, dance, and drama—more prettiness— for the town. Such changes would be as superficial as her changing roles. Carol can see dirt and drabness and dullness, but she doesn't look deeply. it takes years of patronizing her hired girls before Carol realizes that the room she provides for them is a sty (287).

However flawed her encounters with outsiders may be, Carol learns from them. Miles is her greatest teacher, for he treats her as if she were "her own counselor....not a Respectable Married Woman but fully a human being" (117). And more than anything, Carol's involvement in the Bjornstam family pulls her toward an open break with Main Street. Inside the Bjornstam house, Carol finds easy acceptance and camaraderie; there is no reason for Carol to look for approval here, among those without status. Ironically, the pariah Miles and his family embody many of the values Carol respects. Miles is intelligent, perceptive, strong and skillful, and he is careless of public opinion. The Bjornstam family group possesses a sweet, spontaneous joy, courage, and an optimism more genuine than any Boosterism. When sickness takes Miles's family and the town breaks his spirit, Carol loses her friends and learns a new lesson. The experience teaches her not to fear, but to hate. And growing hate, contempt, and anger drive her farther from the town.

Carol must go away from Main Street to leave her childhood behind. For years, she has been the little girl using make-believe as a survival tactic. Playing the rebel one day, she has played the good child the next. And always, there has been Will Kennicott to give her permission or to judge her, and thus to act as scapegoat for her failures.

The spirit within Carol can emerge only when she can stop looking to others—fathers and judges—for permission and reward. The physical separation from Main Street is simply a metaphor for her emotional distancing and decreasing dependence. At many earlier points in her life, Carol had hoped that a new place would bring her a new self, and now her hope is realized. But moving transforms her only because the place no longer matters to Carol. It cannot define her. Only she can do that. Alone.

In Washington, "she caught something of an impersonal attitude" (413), and she learns a new way to play. Her new friends "played, very simply, and they saw no reason why anything which exists cannot also be acknowledged" (411). This is a new, extended definition of "play," implying an activity that takes a person outside of herself to the world of ideas, and to a clear, comprehensive vision. Carol finally learns to play. Becoming a person, she becomes capable of impersonal thought.

Inner change transforms her marriage and her mission. *Main Street's* ending has been widely attacked as discordant and unsatisfying. Schorer says that Carol has learned little and seen less (439); Bradbury, that she is defeated by her town (54), and Spindler is disturbed by a perceived shift from satire to sentimentality in the final pages of the book (174). Carol returns to the husband she scorned and the town that damaged her. The move, however, is no retreat to safety or reduction of self. It is a beginning for Carol and Will Kennicott.

There have been earlier indications that Carol's perception of her husband was distorted by her own neediness. No man could be the perfect model of divine love, the benevolent father she sought. And so Will became the focus of her discontent, representative of all the judges in Gopher Prairie who would not give her her idealized vision of herself. But Will is almost always on Carol's side in her battles with Main Street; his quarrel is not so much with her goals as with her strategies. In his own way, he is an alien, too. One of Carol's poses was as an advocate of progress, "spieling [a German word for "playing"] about how scientists ought to rule the world," Will says. But the doctor *lives* what Carol preaches. As he tells her, "I'm all the science there is here"; "trying my damnedest to heal everybody" (381). He, like Carol, is brighter and kinder than the Boosters or the Thanatopsis Club or the Jolly Seventeen. But Carol cannot see her husband until she stops looking for a father: "It had not occurred to her that there was...a story of Will Kennicott,...that he had bewilderments and concealments as intricate as her own" (422).

In a turning point in their marriage, Carol is tempted to revert to the old patterns and practices, and Will is tempted to use them to his advantage. After a year in Washington, Carol is uncertain about her future. She is attracted to the "new" husband she is beginning to see, but she is not sure whether she should follow that husband back to Gopher Prairie. Retreating to her old and childish habits, she asks Will to decide for her. Lonely, missing his wife and child, Will, too, is tempted by his old role. If he decides for Carol, he gets what he wants, but he also re-assumes responsibility for Carol's life. Both husband and wife resist the enticements of the old ways: Will urges Carol to "do your own deciding" (421), risking the consequences of her choice. She, too, takes a risk—the risk of acting like an adult, one who must take responsibility for her own decisions.

Whether Carol is satisfied by her decisions is questionable. When she returns to Gopher Prairie, she faces conflicts with Will over the raising of their son and over her crusades. But Carol has her own bedroom (at Will's insistence), and a new sense of purpose as well as a new self. She first came to Gopher Prairie a spoiled child; she returns a grown-up. The adult Carol knows she cannot have "everything," and so her projects are limited and practical, not sweeping and superficial. A suffragette in Washington advised her to live by the "most dangerous" of doctrines: "You can keep on looking at one thing after another in your home and church and bank, and ask why it is, and who first laid down the law that it had to be that way" (423). Carol knows that she has always done this, but feels that she has always failed. Still, she returns to do it again.

This is no surrender to the forces of Main Street, nor is it an idealizing of its values. It is, instead, a small victory. Carol has changed herself, and thus she has changed her connection to Gopher Prairie. And she has found a new partner in the old one—the man she never really saw. Nothing is as it was, not Carol, nor her marriage, nor even Main Street. Gopher Prairie can only be as powerful as Carol allows it to be. Perhaps she cannot change it, but in looking at it, *impersonally*, she diminishes its power over her. In a sense, Carol Kennicott winds up, once again, in a new place. And she is a new person. Change has come from within, and we cannot know what its expression will be. "I haven't even started," Carol says (432).

Ann Vickers

Ann Vickers is Main Street rewritten—badly. It is another novel about a woman's growth, depicting the same external and internal struggles. Ann, like Carol, fights society, but this time the battle is not concentrated in one town. Moving from city to city, Ann fights the same foes as Carol, and the two novels taken together make it clear that deliberate ignorance and smug materialism are not limited to middle America. Ann's inner conflict mirrors Carol's battle to define herself in the face of opposing needs and desires. *Ann Vickers*, however, is an unsatisfying novel because it is grounded on simplistic alternatives and rigid polarizations. There is no imagined revision of roles, but instead merely a reversal, or an appropriation, of stereotypes. Change occurs within the context of accepted norms, and the narrowing of choices is matched by a heavy-handed symbolism and imagery.

The novel is interesting, however, because it explores a new facet of an old theme. Once again, the story of an intruder focuses on her quest for identity. But *Ann Vickers* recognizes that there are two ways for a woman to obliterate self: by submitting to the strictures of society, and by fighting them.

The polarities are introduced at once. As an adolescent, Ann is caught between roles. The tomboy dominates boys', games, and yet she knows her assertiveness loses her the very boys she admires. "The boys, the ones I want, they'll never like me! And...I do like them! But I've just got to be satisfied with being a boy myself!" (34). Ann is a prisoner of categories, and she cannot imagine any relationship that is not defined by existing categories. What, then, is she to be? And who is she to love? As an adult, she is rejected by a man who tells her he'd like to marry her, but "you're a little too big for me. I have a career of my own. And if I married you, I'd simply become your valet" (406). Her lover cannot see past the union of one large person and one small one, and neither can Ann. She mourns her early faith in feminism, when she believed that women could be "just like men." Disillusioned, she complains, "We can't. Either we're stronger...or we're weaker" (409).

Ann is not sure what to be—in love or work. Like Carol Kennicott, she assumes a number of identities: feminist, radical, humanist, social worker. Unlike Carol, she commits deeply to each one, and that is her problem. The enormity of the cause envelops the self, obliterating it. The woman becomes the embodiment of the cause. Ann feels she must commit herself "even at the cost of hating myself as a prig—a sentimentalist—a charlatan" (265). It is a self-imposed imprisonment, but a prison nevertheless.

The dual conflict is Ann's teacher. The radical Ann learns solidarity with other women, prostitutes and shoplifters, in jail. The prison symbolism is incessant, almost intrusive. Ann's crime is to *be* a woman, for all women, caught in society's net, must break its rules or die. Later, Ann commits those crimes society most condemns; she becomes pregnant with an illegitimate child and then aborts it. There is terrible pain and guilt and loss. And there is a parallel loss of identity. Having an abortion makes Ann a criminal, but she is not punished by society. Other, poorer women go to jail for what Ann has done. But she is free; in fact, she is the warden of a prison. Her connection to those women in prison must be hidden and is thus doubly painful. As Sally Parry says, Ann "becomes a prisoner of her own actions" (71).

Love, causes, loss, and guilt all threaten the self. All are prisons. Judgment, external and internal, seems inescapable and harsh. And so Ann, like Carol, seeks escape from self in others.

Her first attempt is to do the expected thing, to marry. Her marriage to Russell Spaulding, a fellow social worker, fits a socially defined framework, but not the right one. Russell is a child, feeding upon Ann's energy and purpose, wanting only that she be "Big enough to hold an office which would make them both socially important" (434). Ann dearly wants a child, but she does not want Russell to father it. And so she remains Russell's mother, instead.

Then Ann becomes a child herself, in her affair with a married, older, powerful man. Barney Dolphin is, literally, a judge, the father-lover who may save her from the prison of self, the father of her child. Loving Judge Dolphin, Ann is reduced in many ways. She is dependent and submissive, and she betrays her feminism in her betrayal of Barney Dolphin's wife. It is a corrupting, distasteful union.[3]

Ann constantly refers to the baby she aborted, a girl, as Pride, and perhaps that child represents the confidence and security Ann lost in the abortion. When Ann does give birth, the new baby may be perceived as her own rebirth, the emerging self. This child is a boy. And, in many ways, in her changing relationship with Judge Dolphin, Ann emerges as a male.

Ann's commitment to an ideal is replaced by her commitment to her lover. She becomes manipulative, calculating, and hard in concealing the affair and in tricking Russell into believing the child is his. She assumes those masculine traits that lead to success in a man's world. At the same time, she lives for her Judge, subservient, childlike, satisfied now with "being a boy" in the workplace so that she can be a little girl in secret.

The solution to Ann's problems is another reversal. As Ann assumes male status, Barney Dolphin falls from power. When Dolphin is caught taking bribes, he is discredited and diminished. No longer the master, in love and law, he is sent to prison. Ann, remaining devoted, further compromises herself and her principles to raise money for his release and their future. The crusading social worker becomes a syndicated columnist and a lecturer-for-hire. And then, when Dolphin is freed, Ann cries exultantly, "we're out of prison!" (562).

Perhaps only a man who has suffered his own guilt, shame, and confinement is a suitable mate for Ann. Perhaps Ann feels freed because, with Dolphin released, she can return to her real work and her feminism: "I'll always have jobs," she tells him, "it makes me only the more stubborn a feminist, to be in love!" (539). Ann is no longer restricted to one commitment, forced to choose between love or a cause. And commitment to any one thing, she has learned, can narrow identity.

But this ending, which purports to free the characters, locks them into stereotypes. Conventional structures have not been dismantled but merely reversed. Ann Vickers has gained power in a relationship, and she has become her own judge, but this has happened because her mate has lost his power and his moral authority. Lewis's mouthpiece in this novel is often Malvina Wormser, an enlightened doctor. Discussing marriage, she tells Ann, "In a long life devoted to meddling with other peoples' intimate affairs, I don't know of half a dozen successfully married couples who are both important people" (413). Perhaps Wormser speaks for Lewis here, and perhaps this novel is meant to describe the strength of false polarities. Those who live within a world of such categories may be unlikely to envision any union besides that of strong and weak, big and small. Perhaps even a reversal of vision is a step toward a more positive revision. But, like the conventional bond of strong man and weak woman, the marriage of Ann Vickers and Barney Dolphin seems to reduce them both.

Section Two:
Redefinitions

My Ántonia

Some readings have found the marriages of Willa Cather's heroines troubling. Maxwell Geismar, for example, asks whether

> it is the fate of Cather's dominant and increasingly inaccessible women to be "always surrounded by little men," as in the case of Alexandra Bergson, to be worshipped from afar and to marry for convenience, as in the case of Ántonia Shimerda, and to sacrifice marriage, love, and, finally, friendship in the interests of an artist's career, as in the case of Thea Kronborg? Isn't it something of a catastrophe to avoid all deeper involvement, as her women really seem to be doing here, though it may be in the interests of the most admirable and illustrious career? (172)

Geismar's questions, posed in 1947, assume a number of conventional attitudes: that in any male/female union, one partner must possess the power since power cannot be shared; that therefore a dominant wife necessitates a weak husband; and that women with careers become pseudo-men, less interested in deep human involvements as they focus their energies outside the family. Attitudes change, and so does our reading of Cather. New interpretations of Cather's three novels—*0 Pioneers!*, *My Ántonia*, and *The Song of the Lark*—indicate that Cather imagines a range of possibilities for marriage, proposing new models for love as she creates new, near-mythic heroines who trespass into conventionally male regions.

My Ántonia is another novel of contrasting worlds. The novel, which celebrates the American dream of immigrant struggle and success, is also a novel about class. Ántonia Shimerda is the daughter of Bohemian immigrants; Jim Burden is solidly middle class in heritage, and he maintains that status (or even improves it) in his education and career. Granted, the novel is an account of the immigrant' rise in class; as they become prosperous, the immigrants adopt the conventions of the class above. But not Ántonia. To do so, she would have to become the feminine stereotype, virtually to destroy what makes her vital and interesting. Instead, remaining a strong woman, Ántonia becomes an alien in both the Burdens' world and in the increasingly conformist world of the immigrants. Ironically, she cannot be "my" Ántonia for Jim unless she stops being herself; he can possess her only if she moves, defeated, into the confines of his environment. And then she would not be Ántonia at all.

Jim remains safely within the world he was born to. The impact of Ántonia on his consciousness is to teach him to despise that place. His story is the story of Miles Coverdale or Lawrence Selden, for he is another male drawn to an intruder by her difference. Ántonia represents an alternative to his world, a place he both desires and fears: first, she is the exotic territory of the Bohemians; later, she is the new place she is creating for herself, different from both her past and his. Fascinated by the "foreign" countries Ántonia represents, Jim is too timid to migrate. Like Coverdale or Selden, he prefers the safety of a snug retreat.

The novel is full of movement as the two characters meet, learn about each other's worlds, and establish neutral ground for a developing friendship. At first, the prairie-playground is just such a neutral territory for the young girl and boy; then each separation of Ántonia and Jim is followed by the establishment of a new meeting place: the Harlings' house, the dancing tent. But there is no permanent connection, just a pattern of union, division, reunion, and loss. In the end, there is further movement. Whenever Jim becomes disgusted by his own world and threatened by Ántonia's, he runs away. In the course of the novel, he escapes to a variety of sanctuaries. But the greatest of these is memory.

David Stouck discusses the pastoral mode of *My Ántonia*, focusing on the narrator as hero, and his retreat from an unsatisfactory personal life "to the fuller life of his memories" (45). As Jim tells his life story revolving around Ántonia, "he attempts to shape a happy and secure world out of the past by romanticizing disturbing and unpleasant memories" (46). Thus, as Judith Fryer says, Jim "creates 'his' Ántonia, just as, in the telling of the story, he creates himself. Like the pastoral shepherd, Jim Burden remembers and represents a time and a place in which a great deal of human suffering occurs in an idealized landscape" (*Felicitous Space* 278). Stouck and Fryer both identify the unreliability of Jim's narrative, for he is using the past as solace, transforming it to meet his needs. Ellen Moers says that "the starting point of the tale is Jim Burden's telling of it; for *My Ántonia* is not *mine* at all. To possess her is for the narrator as impossible as the possession of what he calls...'the precious, the incommunicable past.' Memory itself is an act of possession in Willa Cather's work: thwarted possession, ruthless in intent. It kills as it brings to life" (*Literary Women* 238).

In the inevitable distortions of memory, Jim makes one more attempt to hold (and thus change and limit) the woman who changed his life. His story, then, is his narrative, but Ántonia's story is largely the account of that suffering Jim romanticizes. Much of the pain in the pastoral is Ántonia's, but she is not left with the final misery of regret and loss. There are two parallel movements in the novel: Jim Burden's retreat, Ántonia's progress. By the end of the story, Ántonia has rejected the two worlds of the novel's beginning and constructed a third community. Ántonia thrives within a network of deep human ties; on a flourishing land, where there are none of the definitions that damned Jim Burden, she becomes partner in a new marriage, part of a loving family. In the end, she is still moving forward, with a partner, while Jim retreats, alone.

Although Ántonia's first partner is Jim Burden, their periods of closeness are always followed by division. The childhood turf, the prairie, seems a place where two children can meet as friends. Here Ántonia is Tony, and the boy and girl learn from each other without the restrictions of sex and class. Sharon O'Brien calls this period one of "freedom and unselfconscious wholeness when sisters were both equal to and indistinguishable from their brothers" (111).[4] But even in this Eden, there is no bliss for Ántonia. She is never truly a child. Her playtime is a respite from the poverty of the family, the petty meanness of her mother and brother, the despair of her father. Pain is her beginning and her teacher. In memory, Jim Burden evades the pain, but he hints at his fear of it.

The land itself frightens Jim. To him, the Nebraska prairie signals that "the world ended here"(14) and he is terrified of moving too far, of being lost in endless sun and sky. Thus the new place hints at Jim's limitations, the coming reduction of self. But for Ántonia, the land, full of violence and death, is a source of what Fryer calls "regenerative power" (*Felicitous Space* 249). Jim shrinks from it; Ántonia is compelled to embrace it.

An open break between the children occurs when Ántonia must assume adult responsibilities. She must go to work, while Jim, still a child, remains at school. His new perception of Ántonia is grounded in the attitudes of his class. Ántonia is no longer a comrade but an inferior.

Not only is she a peasant, but her brother's cruelty in loading her with "chores a girl ought not to do" makes her unfeminine. Her brother allows her to be hired out, like a man, and worse, Jim thinks, she glories in her strength. Ántonia is now doubly distasteful to Jim, for she is violating the codes of both his world and her own. She has fallen to the level of a farm hand, and, even at this level, she is an alien to her peers: "the farm hands around the country joked in a nasty way" about her doing man's work (84). Jim wants *his* Ántonia back and asks her why she can't be "nice" all the time. Ántonia points out the crucial distinction. "If I live here [the Burden farm] like you, that is difference. Things will be easy for you. But they will be hard for us" (93).

A reconnection begins in town, where both meet, again on the level of children. Jim moves to town with his family, Ántonia as a hired girl, but in reality as a kind of ward of Frances Harling. The Harling house is a safe place apart from both the Burden and Shimerda worlds. Frances Harling becomes a model for Ántonia. "There was a basic harmony between Ántonia and her mistress.... They knew what they liked, and were not always trying to imitate other people.... Deep down in each of them there was a kind of hearty joviality, a relish of life, not over-delicate, but very invigorating" (120). Mrs. Harling becomes Ántonia's ideal mother: bright, generous, compassionate, rich. In her house, Ántonia learns good English, and she is encouraged to tell her wonderful stories. She has her own voice. And in the Harling house, a bridge between the two territories, Jim comes to visit.

There is, however, no permanent middle ground. Ántonia cannot be the Harlings' child forever. She must move out, and she moves into dangerous territory. When she enters the world of Black Hawk, Ántonia becomes its prey.

She leaves the Harlings hungry for the pleasure the other hired girls enjoy. Becoming one of them, she becomes vulnerable to the judgments and actions of Black Hawk society. She demeans herself by accepting Black Hawk's values; reaching for a better life, she falls. By joining the hired girls in the dancing tent, Ántonia becomes, like them, "a menace to the social order. Their beauty shone out too boldly against a conventional background" (133). The middle class town boys are attracted to these immigrant girls, so "unusual and engaging" (131), and Jim sees the dancing tent as "neutral ground" where the groups can meet (134). But it is not really a safe place. Within its shelter, Ántonia becomes available to the males of Black Hawk, who think of her not as a potential wife but as an amusement. Reaching for some joy, Ántonia becomes a cheap copy of a society woman, imitating her costumes, aping her longing for picnics, parties, and dances. To the men of Black Hawk, she becomes a cheap diversion. The sons of American families will play in the dancing tent, but their "respect for respectability" is stronger than any desire for a hired girl (139).

Jim is no rebel. Like the other middle-class males, he enjoys his moments in the tent. More sensitive than his peers, he compares the vitality of the immigrants to the "furtive...repressed" life of the town, where the citizens "in those houses...tried to live like the mice in their own kitchens; to make no noise, to leave no trace, to slip over the surface of things in the dark" (143). Stouck describes Jim's dilemma at this time of his life as part of his encounter with "the complexities of sexuality, for what Jim once admired as her [Ántonia's] impulsiveness is now a sexual freedom" (52). Ántonia's sexual liberation, however, is also her acquiescence in her role as sexual prey. And Jim, the nightly visitor to the dancing tent, joins the others of Black Hawk in the hunt. But a part of him wants more than a dalliance with Ántonia. When he tries to express his passion for her, Ántonia must be the adult and advise him to go away, to make something of himself, away from the town.

Moving apart, the pair continue the behavior that damages them. At college, Jim reconstructs the two environments that torment him: there is the middle-class world of the University of Nebraska, and the exciting one of his affair with Lena Lingard. When Lena's attractions impinge on the academic world, Jim runs away to Harvard. Ántonia, caught more tightly by the role she has accepted, is further degraded. As the submissive, unquestioning bride-to-be, Ántonia invites betrayal. Seduced and abandoned, the mother of an illegitimate child, she has no status in Black Hawk or out of it.

When she and Jim meet again, they are far apart in experience and understanding. The 24-year-old is what she was at 14, her brother's drudge. Burden, seeing her again, can see only his own disappointment. "I could not forgive her for becoming an object of pity" (194). His is the child's perspective, in which all external reality is defined by his ego. He is still the boy-student, about to begin law school. Yet, in a sense, his growth has been arrested since that moment, whenever it was, when his fears conquered his desire. Perhaps it was when he came to the prairie and saw endless space as endless obliteration, or when he first saw Ántonia as a peasant, not a person. At any rate, his course will be as furtive and as predictable as any life in Black Hawk. But Ántonia, who has "a new kind of strength in the gravity of her face" (207), is beginning again.

Because Ántonia's fall occurs within society, it is a fortunate one. Ántonia cannot run from the townspeople and the farmers who judge her. She is compelled to face her accusers, and her strong, defiant nature impels her to resist their judgment. She develops a new power by enduring loneliness and censure and even pity. She survives the massed forces of two worlds and travels past them. Jim, too, moves—but his journey is a retreat. His farewell to the broken Ántonia indicates his conformity and his evasion. "I'd have liked to have you for a sweetheart, or a wife, or my mother or my sister—anything that a woman can be to a man. The idea of you is a part of my mind...." (208).

We must keep in mind that Jim says this when both he and Ántonia are in their 20s, both unmarried. "I'd have liked," he says, "to have you for a wife," the verb indicating that this is impossible. It is impossible because Ántonia is not a suitable wife for a man of Jim's status. To choose her would mean a violation of every class and social structure Jim claims to despise. Far safer to keep Ántonia a part of his mind, to console himself with the *idea* of her. It is impossible to bridge such different worlds.

Or is it? Ántonia's marriage challenges that cliché. While it may not be a merging of disparate classes, it is, in many other ways, a breaking of barriers.

Anton/Ántonia. The names suggest a complement as well as a difference. Anton Cuzak is a city dweller who, at first, hates the country. He is a philosopher. If he is spirit, Ántonia is earth; she is the land alien to him. However dissimilar the two halves of the new whole may be, they are joined by several important qualities.

Both are outsiders, objects of society's disdain. Ántonia has been an object of social scorn since she began doing men's work. Cuzak has, in conventional terms, "submitted" to his wife's wishes in settling on a farm. Such behavior only reinforces society's misperception of the marriage as a reversal of the traditional power structure. But there is more than enough power to share. Ántonia *is* a strong woman, and her strength sustains Anton Cuzak in his early, dispirited days on the farm.

Anton has a corresponding power of his own, the courage to move from his world to Ántonia's, to risk the judgment of the group and to acknowledge his own dependence. In each partner, courage is blended with generosity, so that Anton can accept not only Ántonia's past but her illegitimate child. And Ántonia can give her husband the support he needs without condemning him for needing it.

In this marriage, different spheres meet and merge to create a new place. Such action is possible, it seems, when both partners are strong enough to defy social codes and to survive social disapproval. Ántonia is a strong person, but Anton is no weakling. Together they build a world where the old definitions no longer apply. On the Cuzak farm, the old polarities blend toward androgyny and equality. Even the class lines blur as Anton and Ántonia become prosperous, but not homogenized.

Kazin says of Cather that "she seemed in her own way so complete that she restored confidence to the novel in America. There was no need to apologize for her or to 'place' her; she had made a place for herself, carved out a subtle and interesting world of her own" (190). The process is what Ántonia and her husband undertake in this novel.

As for Jim, he prefers the safe world of memory and regret, and the even safer, but deadlier, world of his class. Fearing the judgment of his peers, he has met their standards, even surpassed them. He has become a respected lawyer for a great railway, and married well. His wife is rich and handsome. But she is dead inside, "unimpressionable and temperamentally incapable of enthusiasm" (1). His marriage is Jim's last move backward—to the place that Ántonia has made him disdain.

Jim can dream of life and even write of it. But he cannot ever live it. He has arrested his development by his choices, and so he can only go back. He can remember his childhood, even attempt to re-create it. He can return, again, to the woman who "had not lost the fire of life" (218) to find what he needs. He comes as he always came, as a child, seeking to reproduce those moments of free and fearless camaraderie. But Jim's attempts to return to Ántonia will always be futile. She has moved beyond Jim, to adulthood and to a new union. Burden is the alien now. In Ántonia's territory, where adults are not afraid of the earth, Jim Burden is merely one of Cuzak's boys.

0 Pioneers!

Cather carved out her own place in American fiction and created heroines who do the same, constructing alternatives to conventional worlds and to conventional relationships. Women who build new places must also create themselves, so that they can summon the energy, defiance, and courage necessary in the new territory. Because such heroines act in ways other women might imagine but never attempt, they become figures of near-fantasy, of wish fulfillment. As models of female rebellion and growth, they are necessarily mythic. In *My Ántonia*, the progress of such a figure is tracked through the eyes of an observer. The male narrator, the social insider, helps to define the heroine by contrast: Jim Burden's hesitations and retreats underscore the rare courage of the woman who moves out of his territory. Nevertheless, our view of Ántonia remains limited to externals. Cather's earlier work, *O Pioneers!*, describes an equally mythic figure, using a different technique. The novel employs a dual process. In the first half, it involves itself in mythmaking, presenting a model of heroism so flawless as to be almost boring. Then the novel begins to dismantle the myth to reveal the human being beneath the model. When we move within Alexandra Bergson, we recognize that the woman who has been both Earth Mother and Provident Father is lonely inside the labels. Her economic independence isolates her, and the second half of the novel describes Alexandra's temptation to relieve her loneliness in a dangerous way. Alexandra is seduced by the conventional dream of conventional love; she is drawn toward female surrender, enticed by the promise of an all-protecting, all-controlling lover.

Thus the second part of *O Pioneers!* exposes the model woman as a human being attracted by traditional feminine rewards. In this section of the book, Alexandra's alienation, temptation, fall, and redemption are explored through two relationships: her changing connection to Carl Linstrum, and the fantasy romance she plays out, vicariously, in Marie Shabata and Emil Bergson's affair. Taken together, these two relationships define the nature of Alexandra's final union, and they define the human being, not the mythic figure.

My Ántonia tells two stories. Ántonia's life is described only as it relates to Jim Burden's experience of her. *O Pioneers!*, in contrast, keeps us close to the heroine so that Alexandra's inner life becomes as important as her impact on others. It is a lengthier, more complex analysis of how a strong woman can imagine and initiate a new kind of marriage.

At first, Alexandra Bergson seems destined for divinity. Even as a child, she seemed to know "exactly where she was going and what she was going to do next" (6). She is a Nebraskan Amazon; in her man's coat, with her flowing gold hair, she is a figure of androgynous force. David Stouck says her name evokes "an image of conquest on an epic scale" (9), and, like Ántonia, it is a feminized version of a man's name. As Sharon O'Brien notes, she is the heroine who "cannot be easily categorized," "who cannot be understood if we apply our polarized categories of gender" (429). She transcends type in another way as well: like many intruder heroines, she is never a child, she "had to grow up too soon" (17). Her father's death forces her to assume a male role as head of the family, the manager of the farm and provider for her mother and younger brothers. Soon she acts like the forceful male entrepreneur, taking risks that others will not and winning by her gambles. She keeps the high land when everyone around her rushes to get river land; she mortgages her property to extend her domain: "Down there [on the river] they have a little certainty, but up with us there is a big chance" (64). Father-businessman, she is also Earth Mother. The vastness and distance of the stars fortifies her, "the great operations of nature" give her "a sense of personal security" (70). She is fully alive out of doors; as Fryer notes, she cannot "be contained or expressed by" her house (*Felicitous Space* 256).

Sixteen years of struggle bring her success. There are heavy, rich harvests, gorgeous gardens, orchards, and fields. In triumph, she appears "sunnier and more vigorous" then she did in youth, but she has "the same calmness...the same clear eyes" of the Amazon/goddess (87). She is a near-perfect blend of the new and old. Disdaining the opinion of her neighbors, she shelters a religious eccentric the others want to put away. When the immigrant families, eager to assimilate, scorn their Scandinavian past, Alexandra cultivates it. She is the bane of her conventional brothers, the novel's Greek chorus of conformity.

Thus, the first half of the novel presents the empowered, nearly omnipotent woman. Harry Hartwick identifies Cather's strength as her ability to "fuse soul and body into a symbol of cosmic importance, to raise the literal into the figurative" (400), and in Alexandra, Cather creates such a symbol. But the symbol seems to have no soul. Stouck calls Alexandra an epic figure, and, as such, a one-dimensional character.[5] And in the first half of the novel, she is indeed so nearly flawless as to be flat. This part of the book reads like the perfect assignment for high school students: an inversion of the pioneer saga, with a heroine instead of a hero, a literary lesson in social studies. Alexandra stands too tall, like a figure in a poster for a Soviet collective.[6]

But this is the figure seen from the outside. In the second half of the novel, we move within, to a deeper understanding of a character who is less a symbol and more a person.[7] The process of demythologizing the heroine is conducted through an exploration of her closest relationships: to Carl Linstrum and to Marie Shabata.

Carl is the childhood friend whose losses counterpoint Alexandra's conquests. Intimidated by the land, Carl leaves for the city. He returns to Alexandra's farm a self-described failure, one of thousands who "have no ties...know nobody...own nothing" (123). Alexandra welcomes him and shelters him the same way she shelters other needy people. Carl's re-entry into her life re-creates the patterns of their adolescence, when they reversed gender roles in their friendship. At that time, Alexandra seemed to be looking toward the future while Carl seemed preoccupied with the past. The adult Alexandra has learned to cherish and nurture the past, and she treats Carl as an important part of her past.

Meeting after years apart, Carl and Alexandra do not know how to connect. The only relationship they can imagine for themselves is that of a mother and child.[8] Alexandra's censorious brothers define it for her, voicing society's disapproval. Carl is after her money, they say; he will try to marry her because he "wants to be taken care of." Alexandra counters, "Well, suppose I want to take care of him?" (167). Her reply reflects her disregard of public opinion, but it also shows her feelings for Carl are essentially maternal.

Carl is more vulnerable to the criticism of others, and he is perceptive enough to know that any connection to Alexandra would further diminish him, in his eyes and hers. "To take what you would give me," he explains, "I should have to be either a very large man or a very small one, and I am only in the middle class" (182). And so he leaves, afraid of others' judgment and of becoming the child Alexandra's generosity would make of him.

When Carl leaves, hoping to become a bigger man and thus worthy of Alexandra, she is lonelier than she has ever been. While she had never considered Carl as a lover, she misses his companionship. In isolation, Alexandra is forced to consider her own confused emotions, the feelings she has often repressed. Alexandra's personal life is "almost a subconscious existence," an "underground river" that rises "only here and there" and then sinks for long intervals (203). Carl's return and subsequent departure cause Alexandra to confront what has been hidden for so long. Never having loved, Alexandra imagines love in conventional terms. In her inner life, Alexandra is still the child, longing for a fantasy romance.

She can watch her fantasy of love played out in her shadow self, Marie Shabata. Her best friend, Marie is like her in many ways, especially in her vitality and courage. But she also represents the dark side of Alexandra, the part of her that longs to be the conventional female in the conventional love story. Alexandra was once her father's favorite child, but her father's death forced her to assume a parental role. Marie Shabata is forever Daddy's Girl. She is the child Alexandra, secretly, would like to be.

Marie was the little girl indulged and petted by men. Sweet, delicate, ultra-feminine, she was indulged by both her father and her uncle, and even by strange men who would give her candy as a reward for her flirtatiousness. She never grows up. She is a creature of impulse,[9] and men repair the damage of her impulses. When she elopes in her teens, her father gives the newlyweds a farm. Her husband Frank is as possessive as any father, and with him, Marie plays the submissive role, soothing his discontents with her adoration.

Marie is everything Alexandra is not. Alexandra has never really been a child; no man has ever indulged her, taken care of her. Alexandra has never been permitted an impulse, for the running of a farm demands the "slow, truthful, steadfast" mind (61). Marie Shabata is, and lives, what Alexandra dreams of.

This is made explicit by an actual dream. After Carl leaves her, Alexandra dreams of "being lifted up bodily and carried lightly by someone very strong. It was a man, certainly, who carried her, but he was like no man she knew; he was much larger and stronger and swifter...." (206). This is a fantasy of dependence, of surrender of her own power to a lover who is even more powerful.[10] It is a dream Alexandra observes as reality when Marie Shabata falls in love with Emil Bergson.

Repeatedly, after the love affair has ended, Alexandra blames herself for her blindness to it. She cannot understand why she did not see the signs of the adultery and did not prevent its consequences. But this affair, as an enactment of Alexandra's own desires, is part of that underground river of Alexandra's personal life. It surfaces, and then is pushed back. Alexandra is not really blind to it. She sees what she desires, but she denies the vision. Subsequently, she suffers a double guilt: the guilt of denial, and the guilt of the vicarious participant.

Marie, the child-wife, finds the strong lover of Alexandra's dream. Ironically, he is Alexandra's brother, Emil. Alexandra herself considers Emil a person apart, the one family member "who was fit to cope with the world" (213), who is superior to the constraints of the plow, free from the demands of the land.

He is of the world in another way. He embraces the world's values. Like Alexandra's neighbors, he finds Alexandra's relationship with Carl "indecorous," "somewhat ridiculous" (179). Emil cannot imagine any love that does not fit accepted patterns. And in his connection to Marie, he assumes the accepted role.

Marie hates the land. To her, it represents an endless cycle of yearning, "the same pulling at the chain" (248) until the spirit is destroyed. Emil, the man of the world, is to carry her away from the farm and rescue her from the land. This land is what defines but also limits Alexandra, for her close relationship with it has left her little time for other relations. Alexandra dreams of a man who will carry her *above* the earth, rescuing her from its demands. The goddess, "armoured in calm," a figure of white and gold serenity (135), longs to be Marie, who seems "to kindle with a fierce little flame if one but breathed on her" (136).

Marie and Emil play at a dangerous, child's game.[11] Emil recognizes the connection for what it is: "I can't play with you like a little boy any more" (156), he tells Marie, but this is the only kind of love he can imagine. It is a play filled with images of death, from Emil's appearance in the garden with a scythe to the killing of the ducks. Emil shoots them because of Marie's whim, and then she cries. The incident is ominous for several reasons. As O'Brien says, it foreshadows the murder of the lovers, and it links lover and husband, drawing "a close relationship between man's violence to nature and to women." Emil, the hunter, kills with a gun, just as Frank Shabata will. "Such violence is possible because the hunter objectifies what he destroys, separating himself from the object he wants to possess and control; but such possession...kills the object of desire" (435).

Marie Shabata is the center of a triangle of possession and violence, and the dream of love is played out to a nightmare climax. And so Alexandra, mourning the loss of her brother and her friend, dreams her dream again. This time, she "knew at last for whom it was she had waited, and where he would carry her" (283). The dream lover is death.

Alexandra is no longer blind to her own emotions. She has learned that she cannot surrender her strength, but she has also admitted her own weaknesses. Human, flawed, she has become a "middle person," and so she can love a man who is neither large nor small.

Carl Linstrum's return initiates a different relationship. Alexandra has discarded her dangerous fantasy of love, and she is ready to accept a new union.[12] It will give Carl the ties he longed for, the feeling of being needed that he lost in the city. Earlier, Alexandra had complained to Carl that "I'd rather have your freedom than my lands" (122), but in this marriage she will have both.

The new relation can be defined by both partners' relation to the land. Even as a child, Carl had believed the land "wanted to be let alone, to preserve its own full strength" (15). He felt he could not, or should not, make his mark on it. Alexandra, as the novel repeatedly notes, *is* the land. Her husband will not try to mark her, to own her; he will leave her free. Alexandra, as O'Brien says, is the conqueror who wins the land by yielding to it (429); she "gives herself up to its power and beauty" (154). She is safe in giving herself to Carl because he is not the possessor that kills. As a person neither great nor small, Carl will not efface her strength nor sap it.

In all her earlier dreams of love, whether they involved Carl Linstrum or Marie Shabata and Emil, Alexandra visualized oppositions: parent/child, protector/protected, dominance/submission, strong/weak. This new marriage of friends is "safe" not because it is a diminished version of love but because a true friendship can be based on a mutual trust and generosity rare in conventional marriages. Friendships are less likely to be founded on those sexual power patterns that result in manipulation, resentment, deceit, and even death.

Before she is ready to love Carl Linstrum, Alexandra must fall from her mythic place. She must become a person not by relinquishing her strength, however, but by accepting it. She must give up her last ties to the traditional world, her secret dream of salvation through another, someone stronger than she. Only then is she ready to marry. A goddess is no match for a man. But a woman should not long for a god.

Alexandra's final comment on her recurring dream, "It will never come true now, in the way I though it might" (308), is not a statement of regret. It expresses her release from the fantasies that kill. In their place, Alexandra has accepted a new tie. Choosing to marry Carl, she once again defies society, for he is poor and thus considered powerless, a "failed" man. Yet by marrying Alexandra, Carl manifests his own growth: he has lost his fear of others' judgments, and he is brave enough to accept the label of the "weak" partner. Carl and Alexandra join in a radical union, two aliens against the group. It may be a flawed marriage, but it is founded on honesty and experience, not illusion and impulse. It is different from what Alexandra dreamed, but much better.

The Song of the Lark

Alexandra Bergson lives a dream of love through Marie Shabata until that shadow self and destructive fantasy are destroyed. In Cather's *The Song of the Lark*, a circle of failed men live through one woman, Thea Kronborg. "In the determined, uncompromising girl," Stouck says, "they see the possibility of their own dreams being fulfilled, and in the lives of these characters Thea in turn catches a reflection of that elusive emotion which drives her relentlessly on with her music" (188).[13] Thea defines the relationship in terms of the "two selves" conflict that dominates the novel: she senses that the men are drawn to something "that had to do with her, but it was not she. Perhaps each of them concealed another person in himself, just as she did. Why was it that they seemed to feel and to hunt for a second person in her and not in each other?" (217). Thea's question draws an important distinction. Many of Thea's admirers are men with two selves, the external, failed identity, and the inner, longing self. They discover the carefully hidden self in Thea and focus their desires for fulfillment on the woman. But Thea, the artist, discovers the second self within herself, not as it is mirrored and magnified in another. And her survival as an artist depends on her capacity to nurture her hidden identity alone, not in relationship to another.

This difference between Thea and her admirers is at the center of the plot. Thea's men support and sustain her, but they also threaten to drain her of the very qualities they admire. Thus she must repeatedly distance herself from the circle and avoid the temptations that have defeated them until she can survive alone. Only when she has found her own second self, developed in isolation, can Thea give her men their best selves. Only then can she answer her own question, "What if one's second self could somehow speak to all their second selves? What if one could bring them out?" (217). And only when Thea has learned to distance herself, so that she can preserve her newly integrated identity, can she begin to re-connect, in a deeper relationship.

The first section of the novel signals the theme of division. The 11-year-old Thea is ill, and her pneumonia becomes a metaphor for her conflict. She is unaware of her pain, "she seemed to be separated from her body.... It was perplexing and unsatisfactory, like dreaming." She wants to wake up and "see what was going on" (9). These are the images of dreaming, division, and vision that characterize many intruders. For Thea, like the other intruders, is torn. The adolescent girl loves what she has always known, the familiar people, houses, and trees of Moonstone, Colorado, yet hungers for the "unknown world beyond Denver. She felt as if she were being pulled in two" (139). She needs to explore the unknown, not only outside herself, but within. She must relinquish the familiar and cut her allegiance to familiar values.

Thea has already shown parts of her concealed self. A minister's daughter, she is an outsider drawn to other outsiders, outcasts, railroad men, the inhabitants of the Spanish section of town.[14] Her mother notes that she has never had any real childhood; like Alexandra Bergson and Ántonia Shimerda, she assumes adult responsibilities in her teens. Her first music teacher, Wunsch, credits her imagination and stubborn will as her most distinctive qualities. The townspeople, however, resent her seriousness and discipline. Thea the young music teacher is criticized because she expects too much of her pupils, boys and girls of her own age. Already, those parts of Thea that make her distinctly herself are misread: her high standards for her pupils are considered arrogance; her affection for Spanish Town is suspect. Her seriousness and discipline earn her the label "hard," which will follow her throughout her life.

Thea is afraid to reveal much of her hidden self. Cather notes that the minister's family is more keenly afraid of "the tongue, that terror of little towns" than any other household (126), and Thea thinks she can placate public opinion. She perceives conformity as a way of protecting her second self, believing that "by doing all that was required of her...she kept that part of herself from being caught up in the meshes of common things" (216). Aware that there is a part of her that is different, Thea tries to save it through concealment and submission.

Her fear of her judges is intensified by the lessons in sorrow and longing she learns by observing the town. At the prayer meetings of her father's church, she hears the secret pain of the very community she fears. And the town's callousness toward a miserable tramp, dying of typhoid, enrages as well as frightens her. The men she is closest to are all in some way broken. Dr. Archie feels that he has destroyed his potential by making the wrong marriage. Spanish Johnny, Thea's first image of the artist, is self-destructive in his wandering and drinking. Professor Wunsch is driven out of Moonstone for his alcoholism, his genius betrayed by his own weakness. And Ray Kennedy, Thea's first lover, is haunted by his unworthiness, dreaming only of "striking it rich" to win Thea, working to learn more to be Thea's intellectual equal.

These are good but damaged men, all somehow haunted by a second self. They can give her no model of integration of the two identities, and the women she knows best are no help, either. They are long suffering and resigned, like her mother and Spanish Johnny's wife, or self-centered and coldly conventional, like Mrs. Archie. How is Thea to learn to nourish her hidden self when she sees only models of compromise, evasion, and defeat?

The pattern of her conflict is a repeated sequence of temptation, resistance, and growth. Thea's first temptation is the lure of marriage. Ray Kennedy has loved Thea faithfully and silently since she was 12, but this good and generous man nevertheless poses a trap. With Ray, Thea feels the serenity of surrender; he rests her soul because "he never set lively fancies going in her head;.... with Ray she was safe; by him she would never be discovered!" (109). Thea knows that Ray wants only to care for her; he would be a loving father. But she knows that because he cannot see the hidden Thea, he would help her to repress it forever, to "rest" in her conventional role. Ray's unqualified love is a great offering, especially to a girl scorned by society and exploited at home. She is "saved" from this first temptation by the death of the father/lover, which liberates her in two important senses.

"For Thea, so much had begun with a hole in the earth" (216). Ray's death teaches Thea her own power. When she is called to his deathbed, she is initiated into her own capacity "to bestow intense happiness by simply being near anyone" (147). She never forgets that moment. When Ray dies, so, too, does the proposed image of Thea as child bride. The new self, the woman who brings joy merely by her presence, begins to emerge. And then Ray's legacy to Thea frees her from Moonstone and allows her to see a world beyond.

Harsanyi, Thea's new teacher, sees a woman who is changing, one who charges to confront difficulties, who "ran to meet" pain. This is no longer the child who is divided from her own suffering and thus lives in a dream. Harsanyi becomes another man moved by her second self, believing her "uncommon, in a common, common, world" (212). Sensing her division, he warns her that "the strongest need of your nature is to...emerge *as* yourself" (208).

As Thea begins to find that emergent identity in art, she learns to identify the group, the common world, as the enemy of the self and of art. In the famous symphony scene, Thea is transformed by the music. And then, outside the hall, she is harassed by crowds, propositioned by men: "they were there to take something from her. Very well; they should never have it" (201). There is no longer room for compromise with the familiar world.

The artist Thea, the hard, hidden core of the woman, is first seen at the Mexican Ball. Significantly, the emergence is paralleled by a merging. For Thea, it is the first time she has sung for "a really musical people," and self calls to selves, so that Thea "felt as if all these...people debouched into her" (232). Finding her voice, she becomes linked to her audience. The union is accompanied by a severing of other connections; on this same visit home, Thea breaks with her family and with those who judged her in the town: "Their ambitions and sacred proprieties were meaningless to her" (240). She is more alone and yet committed in a new way.

When she leaves, Dr. Archie warns her that her fulfillment requires her to scorn what is easy and cheap, and he thus anticipates the next two temptations. Dispirited by a financial struggle, Thea is caught in the conflict of money vs. art. Her newest teacher, Madison Bowers, elicits Thea's worst self. Cold, greedy, cynical, Bowers knows what art is but prefers to teach the tricks of the art trade, to cheapen others' talent and to sell his own. Under his tutelage, Thea's dedication to her own art develops into a contempt for the "stupid faces" of everyone who cannot meet her standards. Bowers trains his pupils to please an audience but not to challenge or move them, and Thea's ideals are nearly buried under his opportunism.

Rescue brings further temptation. Fred Ottenburg, the "beer prince," heir to a fortune and patron of the arts, introduces Thea to new worlds and new possibilities. He offers her two escapes—from her money problems, by bringing her to wealthy supporters, and from overwork and discouragement, by offering her refuge on his Arizona ranch. But Fred is the "easy" avenue to destruction, for he is another of Thea's father/protectors, seeking to use her self as a substitute for his own.

Fred, like Ray Kennedy, baits the conventional trap. He is generous, admiring, and kind, and he promises the same safety Thea sensed with her earlier suitor. Fred is the same kind of man, a failed man. His marriage is his mark of compromise; Fred has already chosen to join the "common world" by marrying a child-woman, extravagant, spoiled, ignorant, discontented. Like Dr. Archie, Fred feels that his life has been ruined by his marriage, and he sees a second chance in the uncommon Thea. He is a rescuer who asks too much of Thea, for he wants to control her. Because he is a powerful, rich, father figure, Fred tempts the powerless woman. He is the prince of a fairy tale, but his rescue is a domination. He is particularly dangerous because he deceives. He attempts to manipulate Thea into committing her emotions by concealing his marriage. He is willing to trick her into a supposed "quiet marriage" that would be no marriage at all. His maneuvering shows how badly he misreads Thea even as he attempts to control her. Thea would defy convention as Fred's lover, but she refuses to be a victim of his deception. Fred loses Thea because he forces them both into unacceptable roles: he, the vile seducer seeking mastery; she, the blind child trusting her master.

Dr. Archie, Thea's "old" father, helps her to escape this new paternal relationship. She becomes "Dr. Archie's Venture," as Part Five of the book is called. She is his business venture, as he finances her training in Europe, but also his adventure, since her foray into new places enacts Dr. Archie's dreams. Moving to Europe, even under the father's auspices, helps Thea to move further away from all her fathers and from her family as well. Even Thea's dying mother does not bring her back.

She does not return until years later, and then she comes in triumph. She returns to her circle of men, and, as they witness her success, they share it.[15] Dr. Archie feels an "exhilaration," as "Something old died in one, and out of it something new was born" (413). Regeneration comes from the new Thea, the woman who has made herself, through isolation and sacrifice and discipline. The transformation is not without its dark side; as Fred realizes, Thea is only "wholly present" when she is singing (442); offstage, the prima donna can be cold, distant, arrogant.[16] Thea acknowledges that she has no personal life, but her distance has assured her survival. She tells the story of a love affair in Europe, and she describes its most dramatic moment in terms that show her fear of destroying herself. She and her lover were caught in a storm on a glacier-like lake: "If we hadn't both been strong and kept our heads, we'd have gone down" (456). Thea knows the danger of an all-consuming love, of passion that drowns. If she is to become herself, to become the voice that can transport others beyond the personal, she must beware of her own personal desires.

Finally, Thea is strong enough to love without fear of obliteration. When she marries Fred Ottenburg, both he and she are stronger than they were as lovers in the Canyon, and they are more evenly matched.[17] Thea is no longer the recipient of Fred's charity; she is rich and famous. Fred has dissociated himself from his conventional attitudes and ties. The death of his wife breaks his last link to the common world, and Fred's enormous financial success reveals that he can build an empire as well as inherit one. Most important, Fred's continuing devotion to Thea shows his growth. To be near her, he has moved to her world, not trapped her in his. His money cannot buy the new Thea; in her kingdom, he is a courtier-prince.

The love affair in Arizona was tainted. The partners were not free of the values of others; they were not yet themselves. Only when Fred learns to love without possessing and Thea learns not to fear such love, can they marry. In the Canyon, the lovers showed the potential for such love: there, they played like two boys, there Fred was Thea's ideal, someone who is never tired, who can "catch an idea and run with it" (306). But the Canyon was another of those fairy tale countries, a physical symbol of changes that must come from within. When Fred and Thea have become themselves outside the Canyon, when they have endured a lonely confrontation with the world, with its cheap ideals and stupid faces, they are ready to unite.

Ellen Moers says that the opera singer is a perfect heroine for feminists. She is "strong, willful, and grand; an international traveler; a solitary, but with a subservient entourage in attendance. Men adore her, but there is no other kind of heroine, not even the saint, who can so plausibly be made a chaste as well as a mature and desirable woman" (*Literary Women* 189).[18] Thea is indeed all of the above, but we must keep in mind that she relinquishes her chastity to explore a new territory in marriage. Her final step completes the journey so many intruder heroines undertake. In novel after novel, the conflicts of the intruder tell us that, to be fully human, a woman must allow her hidden self to emerge and to grow. To do so, she must fight the society that suppresses, weakens, or kills that self. She must sever all traditional attachments that deface or destroy her. When she has emotionally separated herself from the culture that stifles her, the woman can cultivate her hidden self. Then, and only then, a new and radical love is possible.

This is Thea's pattern. Hester Prynne, Lily Bart, Madeleine Lee, Edna Pontellier—all these women follow the same pattern, but they do not complete it. In a sense, all intruders are artists, for they must re-design themselves. Their only chance to live adult lives, open-eyed, comes from their choice of the artist's "uncommon" life. For the common fate of women is innocence.

American literature depicts artists like Priscilla, or Verena Tarrant. They have voices, but their voices are not their own. They are instruments of their culture, the medium of their masters' values. The greatest of these artists is Carrie Meeber. And she is not like Thea Kronborg.

Granted, there are similarities. Carrie and Thea share celebrity, acclaim, and economic success. They also share the isolation of the famous at the same time that they are magnets, drawing a circle of admirers. But there is a crucial difference. Carrie's story, as well as each of her performances, ends in longing. Thea brings fulfillment. The heroines play different parts, one enacting the drama of innocence; the other, of vision.

Carrie is what others make her. She is passivity and drift and hunger. She feeds on what others give her. Her success comes from a series of negatives: she conquers by not seeing, by not choosing. Thea is what she made herself. She is energy and activity; she charges to confront difficulties. Like Carrie, she is given things, but she gives back far more. And her success is a product of her vision. As Fred tells her,

Thea's audiences know that "you've sometime or other faced things that made you different" (463). And her difference is her power.

Carrie is a mirror. Because Carrie sees only as others see, she can give them merely their own limited vision, their own seedy imaginings of beauty and joy. She returns her audience to their worst selves, to the emptiness they can never fill. Thea, like Carrie, begins in longing. But she finds her satisfactions within. Her money, fame, and adoration are merely accessories. There is a person beneath.

On stage, Carrie imitates the central activity of her times. She becomes the thing to be displayed and devoured. The process fails to satisfy, and so it must be repeated over and over, each time further dehumanizing the buyer and his purchase. On stage, Carrie performs the deal, imitating what is already a sham happiness, a pseudo-fulfillment.

Carrie imitates; Thea transforms. The disciplined Thea has transformed herself. By discovering and nurturing the person within, Thea becomes the true artist. She is not what Madison Bowers taught her to be, the performer who pleases but never challenges or moves the audience. She is the strong woman who faces the crowd, assumes its secret burdens, accepts its hidden failures. And she transforms the people of the crowd by merging with them, sharing her personal triumph. She becomes the voice of the weak, a voice transmuted by her own powerful song. She contains others' longing and gives it back—as fulfillment. She can do this only because she has fought to be uncommon in a common world.

The epilogue of *The Song of the Lark* assumes a new point of view. It is that of old Aunt Tille, the only significant woman in Thea's inner circle of admirers. Tillie is the failed woman, the potential artist: "As she often says, she just missed going on the stage herself" (485). She is the social eccentric broken by the world, brave enough to risk ridicule in her amateur theatricals and recitals, dreaming of fame, but relegated to the spinster's role of housekeeper and nanny. She, like the men in Thea's circle, lives in Thea's triumphs. Her frustrated hopes, her courage, her eccentricities are somehow vindicated in her niece's victories, for, after all, she was almost an artist herself.

Tille is sustained, like Dr. Archie and Professor Wunsch and Harsanyi, by a woman who has lived their second life. Unable to reconcile their uncommon longings with their ordinary lives, they find solace and hope in a new bond. In their love for Thea, they connect to a woman who is living a dream.

How many men and women never know of a Thea? How many readers of American literature never see an intruder? Those who do not see her are deprived of an image of solace and hope, an image at once powerful, positive—and threatening.

Epilogue:
Transformation in a New Age of Innocence

A Mother and Two Daughters

Intruders do not disappear from American literature in mid-twentieth century; neither do child brides. To track the continued appearance of innocents like Phillip Roth's Brenda Patimkin (*Goodbye, Columbus*), John Cheever's Nellie Nailles and Marietta Hammer (*Bullet Park*), or of intruders like Anne Tyler's Muriel Pritchett (*The Accidental Tourist*) would require another lengthy study. Such a study would doubtless reveal new variations of the American patterns of evasion and confrontation, and new versions of the child bride and intruder heroine. Evidence of the persistence of old patterns in new times is clear and abundant in one book of the 1980s: Gail Godwin's *A Mother and Two Daughters*. This popular novel is a clear demonstration of the enduring power of American myth and of the ongoing struggle to challenge that myth.

A Mother and Two Daughters incorporates both kinds of American literary heroine; it replays and revises the heroines' dilemmas at the same time that it reverberates with allusions to earlier heroines in parallel plots. Sly references to *The Scarlet Letter* are not merely amusing,[1] for this is another novel about resistance and renewal. Equally significant are the constant links to Hawthorne's *The Blithedale Romance*, Chopin's *The Awakening*, and Wharton's *The Age of Innocence*. The parallels to earlier fiction are presented in two heroines. Modern dress may disguise the twinning, but Hawthorne's little performer, Priscilla of The *Blithedale Romance*, is surely sister to Lydia Mansfield, talk-show hostess, just as the rebellious Hester Prynne of *The Scarlet Letter* is kin to Cate Galitsky, the free-lancer who loves a platform. The paired heroines may be characterized along the same lines as the innocent May Welland and the unsettling Ellen Olenska of *The Age of Innocence*, and Cate and Lydia experience a number of

277

"awakenings" in their struggles to see, to understand, and perhaps even to resist.

The allusions enrich a novel already characterized by subtlety, complexity, and wit, but they do something else, too. They suggest that readers of contemporary literature must keep looking at the same things they look at in novels written 50 or 100 years earlier.

A Mother and Two Daughters explores the same themes covered in the classics of heroinism: escaping the power of the father, learning to see, challenging evasion, growing in solitude, and dealing with the past. It its exploration, it relies on many of the same motifs of the lover-as-father, the fairy tale country of romance, the sleeping beauty, and the awakening adult. As the title indicates, the book tracks the progress of three heroines, Nell Strickland, the mother, suddenly widowed after a happy marriage; Lydia Mansfield, her younger daughter, separated from her husband; and Cate Galitsky, her elder daughter, a scholar-gypsy with a Ph.D., twice divorced. All three move in a pattern of separation from and loss of the father, to individual growth and concurrent division from each other, to reconciliation and renewal. The parallel movements are both humorous and painful, triple variations on the novel's theme that "Everybody has her own starting point" (145) on this difficult but critical journey.

The family dynamics of the Stricklands determine both the nature of the women's conflicts and their individual responses. Leonard Strickland, the father, is Leo, the king of the house on a high hill in Mountain City, North Carolina, and he rules by evasion. A respected lawyer, he is most remembered for a case in which he extolled the need to trust in one's foundations. Ironically, however, he was representing a company whose building was sinking into the ground.

Such irony permeates the characterization of the entire family. Leonard was not always a spokesman for tradition nor a follower of convention. Like Newland Archer of *The Age of Innocence*, he once had his dreams of rebellion and a young woman who encouraged them. Leonard had longed to fight in the Spanish Civil War, but he was persuaded to choose the sensible course, to stay home and practice law. The choice lost him his first love; later, Leonard "rescued" Nell from loneliness and angry cynicism by marrying her. He was a good husband and a loving father, but he was also, like Archer, a man who retreated from the family. At home, Leonard had his study with his beloved essays

by Montaigne and Emerson, and even when he was within the family
group, he was frequently absent in spirit. On Saturday afternoons, for
example, while the conflicts of the little girls swirled around him,
Leonard sat serenely in his corner of the living room, his headphones on,
listening to opera.

A gentle, measured soul, Leonard Strickland deplored shrill
women. And so the women in his family learned to accommodate. Years
later, Cate remembers her mother's routine transformation. Alone with
her daughters, Nell could be anything from "wry humorist" to "ferocious
disciplinarian," but as soon as Leonard came home, Nell became the
subdued helpmate. The change

had confused her and Lydia, as little girls, when their mother suddenly became
smaller and smoother when Daddy came home. Cate's way of steadying herself
against the sudden chemical change in the family mixture had been to assume
the more ferocious properties of the vanished mother, while Lydia...had
retreated into the quiet, neat shell of herself. Which...made Lydia resemble a
small copy of the mother. (223)

Thus the sisters become "good" girl and "bad," modern versions of
May Welland and Ellen Olenska in *The Age of Innocence*, both formed
by the repressed environment common to this novel as well as to
Wharton's. Even the "good" Lydia realizes that "people like us" relegate
disturbing topics "to the outer fringes by simply not mentioning them.
As long as they are not mentioned, they do not exist in our world. And
how can they be a threat if they don't exist?" (296). North Carolina and
old New York are both hieroglyphic worlds.

Lydia's insight demonstrates a major difference between *The Age
of Innocence* and *A Mother and Two Daughters*, for Godwin's novel
does not focus on the impact of one heroine on a male protagonist.
Instead, it charts the movement of three heroines away from the evasive,
small world and analyzes their relationships to men and to each other. It
is as if May Welland and her mother were seen from the inside, and also
through the eyes of women who knew them best. While there is a
Newland Archer figure in Leonard Strickland, as the novel begins,
Leonard dies. Thus Leonard becomes the past and represents the
traditions each woman must conform to or confront. And the plot of the
novel describes the women's choices.[2]

Tracking female choices and changes, *A Mother and Two Daughters*, like its predecessor, relies on an intruder as instigator. Cate Galitsky, the bad daughter, is a disrupter figure, bringing discord and dismay to every family gathering. Her classmates at the Mountain City high school called her Joan of Arc, and she is indeed a kind of self-created martyr. In the early 1970s she lost her teaching job at an exclusive private school when she lined her charges up, blocking rush hour traffic in New York City, to protest the invasion of Cambodia. Cate is a zealot, with all a zealot's flaws: she is rigid in her attitudes, sarcastic, hypercritical, prone to what Lydia calls "steamroller judgments" (371). Her mother thinks Cate tends to focus her "faultfinding propensity" "out in the world when she might do better to focus a little closer to home" (164). Cate loves a platform, and from it, she cannot always recognize when she becomes a parody of her own best self.

And there *is* an admirable self. Cate's entrance into any gathering brings excitement, energy, and intelligence. Her tales of even the most mundane events are always thrilling, because she seems to see so many interesting things. Cate is another heroine-as-seer, another woman wanting to see more. By age 10, Cate sensed a "conspiracy at home, at school, and even in books, to withhold from her the very information she needed to make sense of the world" (40). As a grown-up, one of her missions is "smoking people out of their hideouts of sweet words" (82), penetrating the hieroglyphic barrier. The habit makes her threatening, infuriating, and, of course, exciting to be with.

Years after her Cambodian protest, Cate receives a letter from one of the girls she recruited. The young woman calls Cate "the only real-life heroine she'd ever known," and says that, when she needs to "summon courage," she thinks of Cate (388). And Cate, for all her silliness, is a model of courage. As her ex-husband once told her, "you always keep your chin up even when you're crying" (81); she maintains her defiance through pain and loss.

Cate's "starting point" in the novel is loss and fear. When she returns to Mountain City for her father's funeral, she is suffering from a loss of confidence and certainty. She has been through two failed marriages; she is teaching at a college that is about to shut down. She is beginning to question her values, and her return to the family brings no solace. The bad (but interesting) daughter Cate is eternally jealous of the good Lydia, envying what she thinks of as Lydia's complacent, superficial but secure existence. Cate returns home as the failed child— untenured, unwed, unhappy. And her father's final message to her, the will he leaves behind, further erodes her identity.

Leonard, loving and admiring his daughter's rebelliousness yet fearing it, too, has damned Cate in his will. He has chosen not to give her her inheritance outright, but to apportion it, in small amounts, in a kind of allowance. Thus Cate cannot generously and nobly give the money away to the latest of her causes; she will be protected from her own impulses. And thus Cate, by her father's action, is discredited and reduced. Leonard is still king, exercising his power, and Cate is his child-princess, toying with dangerous ideas.

Losing a father and a father's approval, Cate needs some validation beyond that of her increasingly shaky ideals. Her fear makes her vulnerable to the attractions of a new father, the father-lover. Roger Jernigan appears to be a near-perfect model of both roles.

Presenting the character of Cate's new lover, Godwin reverses our expectations and then, in further explaining Jernigan's appeal, reverses them again. Jernigan is the Pesticide King, "Mr. Poison in the Sky" (103), millionaire founder of a chemical empire. Endlessly in trouble with the EPA, Jernigan is endlessly powerful. Like Cate's real father, he seems to control Cate's world. He owns the apartment she lives in, subsidizes the college she works for, and, on their first date, takes Cate to dinner at a restaurant he owns, ominously called The Power Plant. He appears so powerful he is not Dracula, but Dracula's *father.*

The fairy tale motif is central to understanding Cate's relationship to Jernigan. Jernigan's son, Jody, plays Dracula in a student production, and Dracula seems to be everywhere in this book. Cate and her nephew watch a television documentary about Dracula, and Cate admits that she's fascinated by vampires but doesn't like sadism. The program concludes by attributing the longevity of the Dracula myth to the fact that people fear death, but fear some things even more than death. When her nephew asks Cate what she fears more than death, her offhand response is, "The loss of my will to resist" (69), and she recognizes the deep, personal truth of the casual remark. Her answer, however, is undercut in the scene's context: Cate is greedily eating peanut brittle as she expounds on resisting the status quo, and as she tries to "declaim and chew at the same time" (70), she breaks her tooth.

Should she fear her own bite or Jernigan's? Cate acknowledges that the lure of Dracula might be tied into the "eternal pull between Eros and Thanatos" (69), "the wish to be transformed" (70). If Dracula is a thread in the novel, so is Eros. Another woman in the book speculates that the search for Eros is "a striving for what one lacks" (148), and the yearning for completion may lead to obliteration. Cate has recently lost her father, and she is losing the certainties of self and ideals that sustained her will. Roger Jernigan seems to offer her an easy transformation, but is he Eros or Thanatos?

Jernigan is no villain of melodrama. He is an ardent lover, a generous and devoted father to his sons. He keeps Cate warm through a long Iowa winter; like a father, he supports and protects her. He is no evader but talks frankly about his ethical problems balancing business and environmental demands. Cate loves his "sheer personal energy" (214), and his paternal qualities do not seem to limit her. He loves to talk to Cate; the "more independently and assertively she expressed herself," the more he likes it. She makes him see there are "more worlds than his" (214).

Jernigan appears in Cate's life just when she most needs rescue, and he is steadfast, loyal, and open. When Cate becomes pregnant with his child, he takes her to his mountain castle and proposes marriage. He promises to love and care for Cate, to share his power and never to limit hers. She will be free to teach, to travel, to think her own thoughts. She is touched, honored—and tempted by the offer. But she must refuse him.

Jernigan offers the dream-come-true, and Cate, in spite of her loneliness and fear, accepts that "outside of a storybook, it [the marriage] would be doomed to failure.... I would feel as if I had retired from the struggle without having finished facing it" (260).

> He had offered her everything he had. What more did she want?.... She couldn't think of what more she did want, she could only know what she did not want. But how could you tell a man like Roger Jernigan that, though you knew your life was not perfect, your hopes for the future lay in keeping a space ready for what you did want, even though you didn't know what it would be until it came. (259-60)

When Newland Archer declares his love to Ellen Olenska, he dreams of some place where they can live protected from the realities of their circumstances. Refusing him, Ellen asks, "Where is that country?" Cate, too, recognizes that what her lover proposes is only a dream, and she rejects it in favor of some distant, perhaps unattainable, perhaps even illusory goal.

While what Cate waits for may never come and may not be real, what Jernigan offers, protection and independence, is definitely not real. The storybook motif makes this clear. Roger offers Cate a place in his castle, called Rollingstone. But Rollingstone was named after its first owner's real estate project, a swindle. Rollingstone was a land fraud, a selling of acreage in a city that did not exist. Its owner got rich, but those who believed in the swindle lost a great deal. Rollingstone has its double in Jernigan's ubiquitous billboards, which depict a beautiful farm area, tranquil and unspoiled. The only words on the billboards are "Sunny Enterprises," but everyone knows that this is the name of Jernigan's pesticide company, a tacit admission of poison in the air or vermin on the ground. Every sunny day, every castle, takes a trade-off, and Cate is afraid of the bargain. At Rollingstone, she would be safe; there would be nothing to resist, just secure surrender. But Cate fears losing the will to resist.

She suffers further losses: the loss of her father-lover, the sadness and guilt of her abortion, a loneliness even greater than before. As she fights against a restricting role and against her lonely desire to accept it, her sister Lydia copes with other losses. Lydia loses the roles that defined her.

A swimming metaphor, reminiscent of *The Awakening,* contrasts the way the sisters handle conflict. As a child, Lydia watched her sister confront each wave, then rise, battered and virtuous, from its blows. Lydia was afraid; Cate's invitation to join the battle upset her. She was too scared to imitate her sister and yet hated herself for her cowardice. As an adult, Lydia thinks she has finally found her own gradual and systematic way of coping with the waves, independent of Cate's standards.

Lydia's system is initially based on roles. She married the right man and became the perfect wife and mother. She was her husband's "kitten" (64), as well as a Cordon-Bleu cook. She seemed to love being the suburban matron: one of her favorite activities was to get dressed up to drive to the city and shop; another was to walk graciously and charmingly past her husband's subordinates on her way to his private office at the bank. But this perfect figure slept a great deal, rewarding herself for successful completion of her duties with naps, "a kind of umbilical cord connecting her to her childhood" (126).

Then Lydia wakes up, leaves her husband, goes back to college, and takes a lover: Stanley Edelman, younger than she, sexy, ethnic. She is learning to think, to be spontaneous, assertive, and sensual. But the neat categories of her system are falling apart.

When her older son Leo gets into trouble at school, a child psychologist hints that Lydia may not be the best of mothers. Did she ignore Leo because, like her, he was the "good" child in the family? When her lover Stanley meets her ex-husband, Lydia is appalled. She is, in fact, a little ashamed of Stanley. He is only a podiatrist, and she was married to a prominent investment banker. She wanted Stanley safely relegated to the category of secret lover. Like so many child brides, Lydia defines herself by others' assessments. She worries that her connection to Stanley demeans her. Stanley brings Lydia a tenderness and vulnerability she saw only in her sons, never in her husband, but these very qualities confuse her. Even as she is learning to think and to feel, Lydia, like her sister, is losing the foundations she trusted. She is learning to be braver, but she is, as she did in childhood, measuring herself against Cate, who seems so much bolder.

Nell, too, is lost and afraid. She dreams of climbing into her husband's lap, seeking comfort "as if she were a little girl" (170). Years of marriage taught her to mask her essential difference from the other wives of Mountain City, and now, widowed, she begins to regain her independence. She retreats into the luxuries of solitude. But she is pulled from the safety of isolation by her needy daughters and their troubles.

Months after Leonard's death, the women come together again to experience a bitter division. What was to have been a quiet vacation for Lydia and Nell becomes a family drama when Cate intrudes. She is the disruptive element again, provoking a confrontation between the sisters. The quarrel, significantly, ends when their father's favorite place, the cottage, burns down. It is their last family haven, destroyed as each sister wounds the other in her most secret, vulnerable, place.

The daughters come to each other for solace; pain makes them cruel. Lydia accuses Cate of failure, of developing nothing from all her advantages except "an endless capacity to criticize." Cate attacks Lydia's "safe, circumscribed, orderly little kingdom, your pretend world" (486).

Each, ironically, describes what she most fears in herself. Anger breaks the last tie between the women.

Growth comes in subsequent isolation. As a first step, Cate must accept her own shortcomings. Directing her criticism within, she realizes she was "contemptible" in making Lydia and all her goals seem worthless (493). The recognition seems the final step toward Cate's defeat. Cate has lost her lover, her job, her child, her family. Her own body seems to betray her when she develops a disfiguring palsy. She seems broken, thinking, "What *may* I do" in the face of "the progressive diminishment of all that was hers"? (508). Yet surrender brings a kind of peace, for even as she stops resisting, Cate finds transformation—from the tense readiness she lived by to "a different kind of readiness: a bemused, restful way of offering of herself" (509). This is no "easy transformation" through submission to another's will, but a self-created beginning, a reconstruction on a new foundation.

Lydia, too, finds herself by herself. She feeds her hunger for both approval and power by building a new image around old strengths. As the star of a television show for housewives, Lydia becomes a role model for all those women like the old Lydia of the naps and the fears. By pretending that there is no one out there, watching her, and by focusing on the moment, the nervous Lydia is able to project a winning media personality. She thus achieves the approval of a whole world of viewers, the public she has always longed to please. Significantly, in her first television appearance, Lydia talks about her father and her family and city history, as she expertly prepares a soufflé. She uses her old roles to create a new one.

Nell, alone, confronts her own needs and restructures her world. Moving away from the friends of her marriage, learning to be comfortable with herself, she moves on—to reconnection and renewal. She is the first of the three women to travel so far.

Nell's past forms her future. An old school friend who is dying asks Nell to nurse her through her last illness. Nell has come to love her solitude, her pleasant, self-contained existence. To reconnect is no easy matter, yet Nell realizes that "you can be self-contained in the coffin" (551) and takes care of her friend Merle. One involvement leads to another; eventually Nell marries again. When Merle dies, her husband, Marcus, and Nell fall in love. The marriage is different from Nell's first. While Marcus is an Anglican priest, he is not a father. When Cate asks if she should call him "Father," or "Reverend," he suggests "Marcus." He is no king of a mountain or even of a church; he has lost his congregation to a lesbian minister. Like Roger Jernigan, Marcus is hard to type: he deplores the idea of women priests and yet loves Cate for her feistiness. Like Leonard, he likes to retreat to his books, but he reads them in bed with Nell. He brings her devotion and companionship and sexual rapture. Marrying him, Nell chooses another "starting point," another renewal of her life.

Four years after the sisters burned their father's cottage, they come together again, and the transformed heroines reconnect. Nell has a new husband, Lydia is a figure of power and influence, but Cate is the most changed. She has found a certain peace—and a measure of security. Four years earlier, her godmother had deplored Cate's situation, warning, "Nobody can live on the edge of possibility forever, especially not women...a middle-aged woman with no base attracts more pity and censure than her male counterpart" (16). In the novel's epilogue, Cate has acquired her base, her own mountain kingdom. It is the legacy of her spiritual father, cousin Osgood, an Appalachian craftsman, an eccentric, disfigured loner. From this base, the flamboyant Cate may still attract censure, for she is still unwed and unorthodox. She has given up a secure job at a New York foundation to free-lance, selling her courses in the humanities around the country, still grabbing the platform wherever she can.

But she is not to be pitied. Cate has redefined herself and reconnected to others. Osgood has given her a heritage, and she is forming new attachments and re-establishing old ones.

Present at the family celebration on Cate's mountain are new friends and new family members, but two older ties pull hardest. The meeting of the sisters is difficult; Cate and Lydia are estranged more by shame and guilt than by anger. Slowly, tentatively, they signal forgiveness: Lydia, by disparaging her work, Cate, by advising, "Don't underestimate what you do," the sisters cautiously trying out each others' viewpoints, trying on each others' selves (587).

If Eros is, indeed, a search for what one lacks, the sisters have found at least part of what was lacking, and found it in themselves. Lydia has become braver and more assertive, less the child-woman, more like Cate. Cate has found an order and a system to her life, a base. Selling her courses, she has become the pragmatist, anticipating the market, living on others' approval. She has become a little like Lydia.

These have not been simple transformations, nor are they complete ones. Lydia will always be afraid, will "never quite believe in her security" (557). Cate admits she is a "die-hard idealist and will always expect more than I can get" (567). But the sisters have changed; they can see through each others' eyes now. Such widened vision creates a widened world, with room for new relationships. When the self is stronger, others can help to supply what one lacks. There is no Dracula on Cate's hill, no one promising easy transformation but threatening death.

There is, however, Roger Jernigan. Cate called him back; Cate pursued him. But he, too, is different. He has given up Sunny Enterprises, and, like Cate, is an itinerant consultant now. The lovers meet as two free-lancers, still loving, but with a re-distribution of power and a re-definition of roles. Jernigan is no longer the omnipotent father, but he is still a source of energy and security for Cate. She came back to him, not in desperation, but out of concern for his welfare. Free of her own neediness, Cate offers Jernigan visions of worlds he has never seen.

Lydia is about to commit herself as well. Her long-postponed acceptance of Stanley's proposal is, at least in part, based on Lydia's endless fear. She doesn't want to grow old alone, to be the only Strickland woman without a man. But Stanley is also much loved, for he brings Lydia that part of herself she hides—softness, tenderness, sweetness. And Lydia's decision to accept Stanley, now that she is famous and he is still a Jewish-Italian podiatrist, indicates a change in her values.

What we must note, however, is that Lydia chooses to marry Stanley because of Cate: in the beginning, in the end, Cate is the catalyst. The good sister cannot escape the challenge of the bad one. In what she calls "Cate's kingdom," Lydia feels a "sudden yearning, profound and unfulfillable" (590), and this emptiness prompts her to turn to Stanley for what is missing. Lydia has achieved exactly what she wanted: to be greatly admired and powerful. But she is not Cate. Millions of people observe Lydia with approval; very few come to Cate's seminars. Lydia has taken and held the public eye, and she has learned to see far enough to know that something is still missing, something that Cate can see or enjoy or learn.

And so, in spite of Lydia's growth and courage and strength, there is still the reproach of the bad sister. At the end of it all, there is still the disrupter Cate, the lone woman challenging others, resisting their certainties. Godwin's sisters, who fight, envy, criticize, emulate, and love each other, represent the two strains of American heroine, re-enacting the battles of their predecessors. *A Mother and Two Daughters*, one novel of the 1980s, stands as an explicit model of continuity in character, conflict, and theme. For more than a century, American novels about good little girls and disruptive women have told of the dangers of resistance and the difficulties of transformation in a world that prefers sightless, subservient, and static women. For more than a century, these novels have chronicled the perils of the struggle to see and grow. Stories of American heroines have never depicted the battle as easy, but they have described it as a necessary engagement of women's force. The will to resist—to look closely and critically for what is lacking in oneself and in one's world—is the beginning of transformation of self and others. Lured into innocence, lulled by myth, each generation of women, like Hester Prynne or Cate Galitsky, must find its own starting point.

Notes

Introduction

[1] Judith Fryer explains the disappearance by relating it to the dream of the new Eden: "If Eve was the cause of the original Adam's downfall, the role of the New World Eve must be minimized. This time she must be kept in her place so that in the American version of the myth there will be no fall." *The Faces of Eve: Women in the Nineteenth Century American Novel* (New York: Oxford UP, 1976).

[2] Annette Kolodny's *The Lay of the Land: Metaphor as Experience and History in American Life and Letters* (Chapel Hill: U of North Carolina P, 1975) is an excellent study of the symbolism of the land as woman.

[3] This is R.W.B. Lewis's term in *The American Adam* (1955; Chicago: U Chicago P, 1968).

[4] Lillian Robinson calls such a focus on inner struggles a characteristic approach of "bourgeois literature," a literature that evades any discussion of social remedies, or of sex, class and culture. *Sex, Class, and Culture* (1978; New York: Methuen, 1986)

[5] My category of child bride is thus different from Leslie Fiedler's Fair Girl. He defines the Fair Girl as opposite to the Dark Lady and sees no fusion until the twentieth century, when Fitzgerald introduced the prototype of the "fair goddess as bitch" in Daisy Buchanan (*Love and Death in the American Novel*, New York: Criterion, 1960, 300). I perceive the bitch/destroyer not as the shadow self of the innocent, but as its essence. As the figures reappears in a series of novels, its dangerous qualities become more obvious, but they have been there from the beginning. And my definition of the intruder is far more positive than that of the Dark Lady.

[6] Tony Tanner (*The Reign of Wonder*, London: Cambridge UP, 1965) analyzes the conflict of the naive eye thrust into society, as Henry James explores it. In this analysis, he discusses several qualities of the intruder heroines.

[7] Discussing the work of Jewett, Freeman, and Gilman, Julia Bader notes that, in fiction by these women, "to see and to describe clearly is to become (or to create) a self." "The Dissolving Vision," 189. I would extend her point to encompass all intruder heroines.

289

Part One

Chapter One

[1]Leo B. Levy notes how the silk purses also define her inaccessibility. *"The Blithedale Romance*: Hawthorne's 'Voyage Through Chaos,' *"The Blithedale Romance*, Nathaniel Hawthorne, Eds. Seymour Gross and Rosalie Murphy, 322. Rpt. from *Studies in Romanticism* 8 (1968).

[2]Barbara F. and Allan B. Lefcowitz link Priscilla to Dreiser's *Sister Carrie* and note Hawthorne's ambivalent treatment of the "supposedly immaculate white heroine." "Some Rents in the Veil: New Light on Priscilla and Zenobia," *The Blithedale Romance*, Nathaniel Hawthorne, Eds., Seymour Gross and Rosalie Murphy, 346. Rpt. from *Nineteenth Century Fiction* 21 (1966).

[3]Two excellent studies of heroines explore other dichotomies. Sandra M. Gilbert and Susan Gubar, in *The Madwoman in the Attic: The Woman Writer and the Nineteenth Century Literary Imagination* (New Haven: Yale UP, 1979) consider the Victorian "angel in the house," obviously a sister to the early American child brides, and they analyze her double, the monster. However, their study of British literature reveals critical differences: the British angels and monsters are extremes, opposed to one another, representing male images of the spiritual otherness of women (the angel) or the otherness of the flesh (the monster), 28. The images are repeatedly presented in two opposing characters; the angel is *in* the house, the monster outside it; i.e., Amelia Sedley and Becky Sharpe, 29. The American innocents contain both images within one character.

Nina Auerbach's equally important study, *Woman and the Demon: The Life of a Victorian Myth* (Cambridge, MA: Harvard UP, 1982) places two images within one kind of heroine, but Auerbach's images of angel/demon, victim/queen stress the positive force of the heroine, her transfiguration from "humanity to beatitude" (40), her more-than-human power. The child brides of American literature are devouring angels, not super-human but dehumanized.

[4]Nina Baym calls Priscilla at Blithedale "the perpetual reminder of ideals the community has presumably tried to reject," "the woman in history, distorted by her social role and misrepresented by the ideals derived from her." *The Shape of Hawthorne's Career*, 198, 196, respectively. Baym contrasts Zenobia's vitality and Priscilla's distorted self, but she emphasizes Zenobia's lack of sisterhood as the cause of her downfall.

[5]Note that when Coverdale sees Priscilla back in the city, she is so beautiful and transformed, she seems to have just emerged from a chrysalis, the city being her true milieu.

[6]Paul John Eakin, comparing Zenobia to Margaret Fuller, notes that one danger of Fuller's quest for self-culture was the danger of hero-worship. *The New England Girl* (Athens: U Georgia P, 1976): 52.

[7]Rudolph Von Abele notes the irony of the innocent, simple child drowned in stocks and bonds. "Holgrave's Curious Conversion," *The House of the Seven Gables*, Nathaniel Hawthorne, Ed. Seymour Gross, 403. Rpt. from *The Death of the Artist: A Study of Hawthorne's Disintegration* (The Hague: 1955).

[8]Eakin notes that Hilda's only resource in dealing with the experience of evil is repression. *The New England Girl*, 78.

[9]Arlin Turner says they carry consciousness of their own guilt home with them. *Nathaniel Hawthorne* (New York: Oxford UP, 1980): 340.

[10]She gives Selah Tarrant a check so that Verena will live with her for one year.

[11]Fetterley remarks on the brutality and sadism in Ransom's language for thinking about Verena. *The Resisting Reader*, 145.

[12]Fetterley notes this jealousy: "His obsessive desire to interpose himself between her and the realization of her career [her public speaking] is certainly motivated by jealousy" (*The Resisting Reader*, 120). She also notes that Ransom proposes to Verena only after his first article is accepted for publication, 121.

[13]Judith Fryer analyzes Isabel's fear of passion and her resulting choice of Osmond, with whom Isabel thought she could remain in control. *Faces of Eve*, 137-38.

[14]An early review of the novel hinted at this interpretation of Isabel. Margaret Oliphant, writing in *Blackwood's* in 1882, said she was "quite unable to understand how Isabel falls into Osmond's toils" unless it was because "so elaborate and self-conscious a personality recoils instinctively, even though full of abstract admiration for truth, from the downright and veracious." Rpt. in *The Portrait of a Lady*, Ed. Robert Bamberg, 659.

[15]She also says Isabel is afraid of substantial men.

[16]Dorothy Van Ghent notes how structurally important Pansy is to the second half of the novel. "On *The Portrait of a Lady*," 699.

[17]Michael Spindler makes this point about the Marches' retreat from understanding. *American Literature and Social Change: William Dean Howells to Arthur Miller* (Bloomington: Indiana UP, 1983): 81.

[18]Ellen Moers discusses Marian as Niel's teacher. *Literary Women* (New York: Doubleday, 1976): 238-39.

[19]David Stouck notes that Marian's disintegration is the story of society's decline. *Willa Cather's Imagination*, 59. Carolyn Heilbrun says that the novel shows women as defaced property, like the land, but she identifies Niel's attitudes as Cather's. *Reinventing Womanhood*, 81.

[20]Pizer notes his lack of direction and need to derive strength from the act of possession. *The Novels of Theodore Dreiser*, 120, 111, respectively.

[21]Philip Fisher calls this a world of "might-be" and "has-been," a world that excludes the possibility of full present being. "Acting, Reading, Fortune's Wheel: *Sister Carrie* and The Life History of Objects," *American Realism: New Essays*, Ed. Eric Sundquist (Baltimore: Johns Hopkins UP, 1982): 264.

[22]Pizer says Carrie rises "not because she is honest or plucky but because she has the native shrewdness to allow others to ferry her in the direction she wishes to take." *The Novels of Theodore Dreiser*, 89.

[23]Eric Sundquist, in "The Country of the Blue," says, "Carrie's easy transformation from consumer to consumed is a concise illustration of the character of success in the age of Capitalism: the 'possession of self' becomes indistinguishable from the 'self of possessions' and the hero of desire, rather than diverging from society, tantalizes that society by containing and expressing it in an erotic materialism of the self." *American Realism: New Essays*, 21.

[24]Grebstein says Carrie does manage to get inside the worlds she desires, and she is disappointed. "Dreiser's Victorian Vamp," 556.

[25]Fisher ("Acting, Reading, Fortune's Wheel," 267) talks of a romantic deadness in Carrie, and Pizer (*The Novels of Theodore Dreiser*) notes that Hurstwood is "a man without a center" (78) and that all three central characters live by "a code of selfish amoralism" (42).

[26]Ironically, Moers calls Dreiser "a master of the use of senseless speech to establish character" ("The Finesse of Dreiser," *Sister Carrie*, Theodore Dreiser, ed. Donald Pizer, 563. Rpt. from *American Scholar* 33, Winter 1963-64), while Richard Poirer calls Dreiser's vision one "in which character—as a derivative of language and the power of language—is regarded as relatively negligible." *A World Elsewhere*, 240.

[27]Fisher discusses the importance of roles in the novel, exploring a hierarchy of work that moves from selling objects to more directly selling the self. "Acting, Reading, Fortune's Wheel," 263-68.

[28]Fisher notes this. "Acting, Reading, Fortune's Wheel," 268.

[29]An important essay on this theme is William J. Freedman's "A Look at Dreiser as Artist: The Motif of Circularity in *Sister Carrie*." *Modern Fiction Studies* 8 (Winter 1962-63): 384-92.

[30]Blanche Gelfant (*The American City Novel*, 78) says, "The attempt to satisfy innate aesthetic and spiritual desires with materialistic ends—fashion, wealth, and power—is the basic irony, as well as the tragedy, in Dreiser's novels."

Chapter Two

[1]Margaret McDowell's article, "Viewing the Custom of Her Country: Edith Wharton's Feminism," *Contemporary Literature* 15 (1974): 521-38, is a groundbreaking study. In it, she notes that destructive women in Wharton's

fiction gain power because they can manipulate the hypocrisy and pretense which characterized American relations between the sexes in the late nineteenth and early twentieth century, 528.

[2]Wolff's study of the novel in *A Feast of Words* (229-58) is an exploration of this point.

[3]Elizabeth Ammons says Undine is associated with mirrors throughout the novel because not she, but the marital custom of the country she reflects is the major target of Wharton's satire. "The Business of Marriage," 328.

[4]Wolff says, "the black comedy of domestic life has become a distillation of all the infamy that contaminates the public world, and the ladies, with their mutilated selves and monstrously realized dreams, are as fully appropriate to a representation of a spirit of the age as the story of any of its generals might have been." *A Feast of Words*, 251.

[5]McDowell says that Undine identifies with the values of whatever group captures her attention, assimilates those values, mirrors them, and illuminates their weaknesses. *Edith Wharton* (Boston: Twayne, 1976) 79.

[6]Wolff calls Ralph a narcissist. *A Feast of Words*, 237.

[7]McDowell says that Ralph eventually "recognizes in himself, in at least latent form, those qualities that he most hates in Undine." *Edith Wharton*, 81.

[8]This is a phrase Wharton uses to describe the appeal of the Nouveau Luxe (273), but the hotel is Undine's real home, and thus a mirror of her charms.

[9]This blurring of polarities is very like the blurring of subject and object in *Sister Carrie*.

[10]Elizabeth Ammons makes this point about Pauline. "Edith Wharton's Heroines: Studies in Aspiration and Compliance," diss., U of Illinois at Urbana-Champaign, 1974: 164-65.

[11]*Ellen Glasgow and the Ironic Art of Fiction*, 186. McDowell also compares her to May Welland of *The Age of Innocence*, another young girl who knows nothing and expects everything, 190.

[12]Of this moment, in which the innocent Stanley is revealed as the killer of a child, Frederick McDowell says, "Though she [Stanley] ruins all who come into her sphere, human beings are yet so imperceptive of reality that they flock to console her." *Ellen Glasgow and the Ironic Art of Fiction*, 220.

[13]This may be the second child Stanley has "killed." Earlier, there is a reference to her having brought on the miscarriage of her baby.

[14]Frederick McDowell (*Ellen Glasgow and the Ironic Art of Fiction*, 216) says the novel chronicles "the maladjustments of modern man to the world around him, maladjustments engendered by his sense of outrage at the disproportion between his expectations from life and the oppressive reality he confronts."

Chapter Three

[1]Maxwell Geismar notes that American audiences have a distaste for tales of incest even though it is a basic theme in American literature. *The Last of the Provincials* (Boston: Houghton Mifflin, 1947): 350.

[2]Even though Priscilla's money "buys" Hollingsworth, she cannot make the deal until he chooses her over her more willful sister.

[3]She is mainly referring to the American stereotypes of dark lady and fair girl.

[4]For more, but certainly not all, on the negative qualities of the Ververs, see Jean Kimball, who compares the Ververs to the Osmonds of *The Portrait of a Lady*; "Henry James's Last Portrait of a Lady: Charlotte Stant in *"The Golden Bowl*," *American Literature* 28 (Jan. 1957): 449-68; Joseph Firebaugh, "The Ververs," *Essays in Criticism* 4 (Oct. 1954): 404-10; Ferner Nuhn, *The Wind Blew From the East* (New York: n.p., 1942): 133-38; Judith Fryer, *Faces of Eve*, 115-19.

[5]Michael Millgate says that "the much-criticized insubstantiality of the social setting" of the novel "may in part represent a deliberate comment on the unreality, the impossibly sheltered and rarefied lives of the characters." *American Social Fiction*, 14.

[6]Leslie Fiedler calls Maggie "more Christ than woman, more angel of death than Christ." *Love and Death in the American Novel*, 293.

[7]F.O. Mattheissen says that, in the Pym analogy, James has not caught "the horror of its unrelieved light." *American Renaissance*, 303. This is exactly what I think he has caught. Arthur Mizener thinks that perhaps Maggie is more like Chillingworth (the cold heart of *The Scarlet Letter*) than James meant her to be. *The Sense of Life in the Modern Novel* (Boston: Houghton Mifflin, 1964): 115. Warner Berthoff says that the Ververs hide their true natures behind the curtain of blankness. *The Ferment of Realism*, 120.

[8]Tony Tanner says that the level of metaphor in the book, where almost everything takes place, is also "the level of consciously fabricated lies both of utterance and repression." *Adultery in the Novel*, 86.

[9]According to Eakin, Squire Gaylord is there to "vindicate his daughter's innocence" and to prove "the existence of a moral design in the universe which Bartley's crime would deny." *The New England Girl*, 115.

[10]For more discussion of the theme of lost spiritual values, see Paul John Eakin, *The New England Girl*, 110-16, and Mary Suzanne Schriber, *Gender and the Writer's Imagination*, 100.

[11]Henry Nash Smith says that Howells set out to show how the breakdown of a marriage resulted from the undisciplined characters of husband and wife, their lack of childhood religious training. *Democracy and the Novel* (New York: Oxford UP, 1978): 94.

[12]Eakin notes Marcia and Bartley's self-deception. *The New England Girl*, 107, 109.

[13]Dietrichson notes that Bartley's moral decay is measured by his relationship to money. He says that the couple's inability to live within their means caused Bartley to "act in a manner to show up his basic moral depravity" by selling out. *The Image of Money in the American Novel of the Gilded Age*, 315.

[14]Frederick Hoffman says that Howells links Bartley's "untidy morality" to "dishonest business practices." *The Modern Novel in America* (1951; Chicago: Henry Regnery, 1963): 25.

[15]Eakin says she is trying to conceal the defeat of her womanhood from herself and others. *The New England Girl*, 114.

[16]See, for example, Henry Nash Smith, *Democracy and the Novel*, 95.

[17]He also notes the irony of Marcia's assessment of Halleck as a model of goodness and of Halleck's sentimental elevation of Marcia. *The New England Girl*, 111.

[18]John F. Callahan says that Dick Diver "unconsciously uses Victorian genteel values and forms to mask his failure actively to seek risks and satisfactions beyond the family." *The Illusions of a Nation* (Urbana: U Illinois P, 1972): 104.

[19]This is Maxwell Geismar's phrase. *The Last of the Provincials*, 291.

[20]Callahan notes that Fitzgerald's heroes often define women as symbols rather than persons, thus denying themselves the complexity of human contact and annihilating their own personalities. *The Illusions of a Nation*, 215.

[21]Edwin Fussell calls them the "objectified images of Fitzgerald's 'brave new world'." "Fitzgerald's Brave New World," *F. Scott Fitzgerald: A Collection of Critical Essays*, ed. Arthur Mizener (Englewood Cliffs, NJ: Prentice-Hall, 1963): 54. Rpt. from *ELH* 19 (Dec. 1952).

[22]Callahan ties this theme to three Fitzgerald heroes: Gatsby, Diver, and Stahr (of *The Last Tycoon*), all of whom seek approval from those in power and secretly cherish the values of the dominant group. *The Illusions of a Nation*, 212-15.

[23]Brian Way says this scene shows Dick at his most manipulative and insincere. *F. Scott Fitzgerald and the Art of Social Fiction* (New York: St. Martin's, 1980): 144.

[24]Way notes the air of falsity in Dick's social gifts (134), and also notes that Fitzgerald relates this to certain equivocal aspects of Dick's personality (15). *F. Scott Fitzgerald and the Art of Social Fiction*.

[25]Also undermining patriarchy, they say, were industrialism, the disappearance of God, the decline of the British empire.

[26]Michael Spindler's book, *American Literature and Social Change*, studies this change in detail.

[27]Cynthia Griffin Wolff links *The Reef* and *The Age of Innocence* as triangle romances. *A Feast of Words*, 220. Blake Nevius (*Edith Wharton: A Study of Her Fiction*, 189) rightly links Wharton's criticism of evasion and irresponsibility in *The Age of Innocence* to her later novels. For more on the triangles of innocence, see Wershoven, *The Female Intruder in the Novels of Edith Wharton* (East Brunswick, NJ: Associated UP, 1982) 75-123.

[28]Margaret McDowell says that the van der Luydens represent "the deadness of the conventions that attempt to preserve intact the values whose efficacy has long ago disappeared." *Edith Wharton*, 102.

[29]There are also parallels to the Prince and the white curtain of *The Golden Bowl*.

[30]This point is made by Jacobson ("Perception, Communication, and Growth," 76), Louis O. Coxe ("What Edith Wharton Saw in Innocence, *New Republic* 27 June 1955: 16), Gary Lindberg (*Edith Wharton and the Novel of Manners*, 107), Cynthia Griffin Wolff (*A Feast of Words*, 322) and Margaret McDowell (*Edith Wharton*, 98).

[31]Jacobson says the pattern of Archer's marriage, his giving up "any real sense of responsibility for the sexual, intellectual, and emotional growth of his wife" reflects "how deeply Archer is entrenched within his own culture." "Perception, Communication, and Growth," 78.

[32]Blake Nevius makes the connection to "The Beast in the Jungle." *Edith Wharton: A Study of Her Fiction*, 187.

[33]There is a direct parallel to Fitzgerald's concluding in *This Side of Paradise* that "The problem of evil had solidified for Amory into the problem of sex.... Inescapably linked with evil was beauty.... Beauty of great art, beauty of all joy, most of all the beauty of women." (1920; New York: Scribners, 1948): 280. Maxwell Geismar identifies "a strong sexual coloring...to the fits of revulsion" Amory feels in this novel, particularly on the occasion of his first kiss. *The Last of the Provincials*, 297.

[34]Geismar also relates the romances of Fitzgerald's couples to the incest theme of Poe, specifically the incest of brother and sister in "The Fall of the House of Usher" (335). And Elizabeth Hardwick (*Seduction and Betrayal: Women and Literature*. 1970; New York: Random House, 1974, 87-88) makes a relevant comment on Scott and Zelda Fitzgerald: they were not "especially appealing" as persons. "Their story has a sort of corruption clinging to it, the quality of a decadent fairy tale.... They seem, most of all, like incestuous brother and sister—brilliant, perverse, selfish—their handsome, self-loving faces melting into a mask." She notes the twinning, as "In this couple defects were multiplied, as if by a dangerous doubling; weakness fed upon itself without a counterstrength and they were trapped...."

³⁵Joan M. Allen makes much of the Chevalier O'Keefe story. She says that its moral is that women hurt men by "their debilitating love," by "keeping them from their ideals," and "actually destroy men through the allure of beauty and base sensuality." Allen identifies this moral as "the major theme of both Fitzgerald's life and work." *Candles and Carnival Lights: The Catholic Sensibility of F. Scott Fitzgerald* (New York: NY UP, 1978): 89.

³⁶Geismar notes that the emphasis on youth and pleasure depicted in Fitzgerald's novels is an inheritance from the Gilded Age, a reflection of society's belief that "maturity is the infinite extension of adolescence." *The Last of the Provincials*, 305. It is interesting, then, that the representative of the Gilded Age, Adam Patch, provides Anthony with the means to remain a child.

³⁷He is therefore even more passive than Carrie, who envisions herself as an actress and then becomes one.

³⁸Donald Pizer discusses Clyde's tendency to denigrate any girl who surrenders to his desires since he considers such desires evil. Pizer notes Hortense's role as sexual entrepreneur, and Clyde's reluctance to marry Roberta because she has given sex away. However, Pizer believes that Clyde's attitude to Sondra is asexual and idealized, since Clyde cannot reconcile the dirtiness of sex with the ideal Sondra. *The Novels of Theodore Dreiser*, 236-41.

Part Two

Chapter Four

¹Nina Baym says that in "The Custom-House," Hawthorne creates an image of Hester as "an unambiguous heroine" even before the reader meets Hester. "The Romantic *Malgré Lui*," *The Scarlet Letter* by Nathaniel Hawthorne, Eds. Sculley Bradley, Ricmond Croom Beatty, E. Hudson Long, Seymour Gross (New York: Norton, 1978), 283. Rpt. from *ESQ: A Journal of the American Renaissance* 19 (1973).

²Margaret Higonnet notes that many writers have "projected culturally repressed values onto 'outside' female characters in order to criticize the established order. Such writers may represent a woman simultaneously as part of the social code, her position determined by set roles, and as a disrupter of norms who unmasks their teleology and their limits." "Introduction," *The Representation of Women in Fiction*, eds. with intros. Carolyn Heilbrun and Margaret Higonnet, Selected Papers from the English Institute, New Series 7 (Baltimore: Johns Hopkins UP, 1983): xviii.

³Ernest Sandeen says, "Her apparent humility and patience conceal her inner subversion of the penance imposed on her at the same time that they express her devotion to her lover." "*The Scarlet Letter* as a Love Story," *The*

Scarlet Letter, Nathaniel Hawthorne, Eds. Sculley Bradley et al. Rpt. from *PMLA* 77 (1962).

⁴Baym calls Dimmesdale a dependent personality who doesn't so much want power as he wants approval. *The Shape of Hawthorne's Career*, 127.

⁵Note Richard Poirer's explanation that the hero of American classics "creates a world elsewhere—bearing little relation to the real world, emanating only from the self." *A World Elsewhere*, 7.

⁶Ernest Sandeen says that "Hester gives the impression of strength because of her complete self-knowledge," but Dimmesdale "is presented, up to the last few chapters in the book, as a person the reader can know better than Arthur can know himself." "*The Scarlet Letter* as a Love Story," 376.

⁷Compare this scene to Pearl's view of herself in a reflecting pool. Initially entranced by her image, the practical Pearl soon decides that "either she or the image was unreal" and "turned elsewhere for better pastime" (128).

⁸Seymour Gross makes this point. "'Solitude, and Love, and Anguish': The Tragic Design of *The Scarlet Letter*." *The Scarlet Letter*, by Nathaniel Hawthorne, Eds. Sculley Bradley et al., 362. Rpt. from *CLA Journal* 3 (March 1968).

⁹For comments on the insider/outsider motif, see Judith Fryer (*Faces of Eve*, 82); Nina Baym (*The Shape of Hawthorne's Career*, 12-18); and Seymour Gross (" 'Solitude, and Love, and Anguish'," 360, 365).

¹⁰R.W.B. Lewis (*The American Adam*, 112) says that Hester "incarnates those rights of personality that society is inclined to trample upon. The action of the novel springs from the enormous but improbable suggestion that the society's estimate of the moral structure of the universe may be tested and found inaccurate."

Chapter Five

¹Annis Pratt identifies this as a typical conflict of women's fiction, saying "even the most conservative women's authors create narratives manifesting an acute tension between what any normal human being might desire and what a woman must become." *Archetypal Patterns in Women's Fiction*, 5-6.

²Gary Lindberg argues that Lily's social fall is accompanied by a moral decline. *Edith Wharton and the Novel of Manners*, 60-61. Louis Auchincloss, however, perceives Lily as morally superior to her class. "Afterword." *The House of Mirth*, New York: New American Library, 1964: 344-47. Elsewhere I argue at greater length that Lily's moral development occurs largely *because* she falls from social grace. *The Female Intruder in the Novels of Edith Wharton*, 43-59. David Stouck discusses the "images of people in motion, of a life as a procession," that inform "almost every scene" of *Lucy Gayheart* and says that movement "for Lucy is the essence of her vitality." *Willa Cather's Imagination*, 218.

[3]Elizabeth Ermath says that the conflict "between individuals and the prevailing consensus is...the preoccupation of representational fiction." She notes the "high proportion of important female casualties" of the conflict, saying, "Their common fate poses a fundamental challenge to the norm of consensus confirmed formally by the novels that destroy them." Although she is discussing British and European novels, I think her point is equally applicable to American ones. "Fictional Consensus and Female Casualties." *The Representation of Women in Fiction*, 10.

[4]Judith Fryer (*Felicitous Space*, 44-45) says that Wharton's novels repeatedly discuss the idea that "when one discards the old patterns, without being able to generate a new mode of being, one's environment fails to cohere in a meaningful way," and relates this theme to *The Awakening*. Elaine Showalter notes that both these novels "deal with the futile struggle for consciousness." *A Literature of Their Own: British Women Novelists from Brontë to Lessing*, Princeton: Princeton UP, 1977: 131.

[5]Spacks notes Edna is nonetheless dependent in a traditionally feminine way.

[6]Donald Ringe discusses how Chopin compares and contrasts Edna's state through the use of a number of contrasting characters. "Romantic Imagery in Kate Chopin's *The Awakening*," *American Literature* 43 (Jan. 1972): 580-88.

[7]Mademoiselle Reisz also never goes near the water.

[8]Judith Fryer (*Faces of Eve*, 257) discusses the bird imagery at length.

[9]George Arms characterizes Edna as essentially a drifter, a romantic fatalist. "Contrasting Forces in the Novel," *The Awakening*, by Kate Chopin, Ed. Margaret Culley, New York: Norton, 1976: 175-80. Rpt. from "Kate Chopin's *The Awakening* in the Perspective of Her Literary Career," *Essays on American Literature in Honor of G. B. Hubbell*, ed. Clarence Ghodes, Durham: Duke UP, 1967.

[10]Jules Charnetsky also says that the novel never answers the question of how to be free within one's self but still connected to others. "Edna and the 'Woman Question'," *The Awakening*, by Kate Chopin, Ed. Margaret Culley, 200. Rpt. from "Our Decentralized Literature," *Jahrbuch fur Amerikastudien* (1972).

[11]Spacks says that Edna's ambiguous view of the swim "mingles fantasy and realism in exactly the same way as her view of herself as a woman," and that both overestimate her strength. *The Female Imagination*, 74.

[12]Per Seyersted says "it is less important for her [Edna] to live than to have a self, to be able to exert a conscious choice which can bring out her own essence." "Introduction," *The Complete Works of Kate Chopin*, I, 28.

[13]Judith Montgomery says that Lily learns to appreciate and extend human kindness as she falls. "The American Galatea," *College English* 32 (May 1971):

897. Margaret McDowell says that as Lily moves toward tragedy she moves toward understanding of herself and others and reveals her superiority to those who reject her. "Viewing the Custom of Her Country," 527.

[14]Joan Lidoff says that Lily, "like many other heroines, acts out a cultural dilemma: when society provides no female adult role of active responsibility and initiative, women are confined to passive and childlike states and cannot mature." "Another Sleeping Beauty: Narcissism in *The House of Mirth*." *American Realism: New Essays*, Ed. Eric Sundquist, 254. Lidoff, however, argues that Lily cannot grow because she is frozen in narcissism.

[15]Margaret McDowell says that by the end of the book, Selden has become "enmeshed in the social values which restrict his ability to love." "Viewing the Custom of Her Country," 527. George Spangler compares Selden to Robert LeBrun, identifying their conventionality and their lack of masculine force. However, he feels that the introduction of such men into the plots leads to a kind of feminine self-pity aimed at sentimental readers. "Kate Chopin's *The Awakening*: A Partial Dissent," *Novel* 3 (Spring 1978): 249-55.

[16]Richard Poirer says that Selden lacks a sense of human solidarity, that he knows others "not by loving but only by judging them." *A World Elsewhere*, 232.

[17]Lidoff notes these mood swings. "Another Sleeping Beauty," 242.

[18]Diana Trilling says that, in the world of the novel, "Money rules where God, love, charity, or even force of character or distinction of personality might once have ruled." "*The House of Mirth* Revisited," *Edith Wharton: A Collection of Critical Essays*, Ed. Irving Howe, Englewood Cliffs, NJ: Prentice-Hall, 1962: 111. Judith Montgomery ("The American Galatea," 897) says "marriage has become a public market in this novel."

[19]Geismar (*The Last of the Provincials*, 211) notes that "the lyrical opening of the central romance in *Lucy Gayheart* is soon qualified by the unpleasant revelations of love: by Lucy's 'discovery' that passion, dark and terrifying, can drown like black water." He identifies Cather's technique of undercutting the romance-novel tone, but I do not think it is passion that kills Lucy.

[20]In the very first scene of the novel, Lucy is skating on the ice.

[21]She cites *0 Pioneers !*, for example.

[22]Stouck notes that the woman's vitality and "human sympathy...transform the tired song into a living, moving experience" and that Lucy goes back, not to "Art," but to "Life" enriched by the arts. *Willa Cather's Imagination*, 224.

[23]This is true even if, in the case of Rose Sellars of Wharton's *The Children*, what she gets is confirmation of her belief that Martin Boyne is a fool and reinforcement of her prejudices.

[24]Spacks feels that the novel glorifies this kind of female heroism based on endurance and denial. *The Female Imagination*, 106. But Glasgow's portrait of Ada Fincastle is ambiguous enough to allow a more ironic reading.

[25]Frederick McDowell (*Ellen Glasgow and the Ironic Art of Fiction*) notes difficulties in Glasgow's characterization of both men. He believes that Fincastle symbolizes Glasgow's own life of intellectual isolation but that he is not persuasively shown as a great teacher (206, 209). McDowell also notes an absence of irony in the attitudes of the other characters toward Ralph and feels that such irony is needed to underscore Ralph's narcissistic self-pity (213). However, if we read the novel as a study in wasted sacrifice, in the female suppression of self in the service of weak men, there is little inconsistency.

[26]Judith Fryer says that whatever Howells intended, his question, " 'Can a woman have both professional satisfaction and marriage?'—can only be answered in the negative in this novel." *Faces of Eve*, 234.

[27]Schriber also notes that Grace shows the same Puritan temperament as Olive Chancellor, 91.

[28]Schriber says that Howells attempts to create sympathy for Grace by giving her such "womanly" qualities as a broken heart, a desire to treat children, a distancing from feminism. *Gender and the Writer's Imagination*, 93.

[29]Eakin says Mulbridge is like Gilbert Osmond, adopting the heroine's rhetoric as a screen for bending her spirit. *The New England Girl*, 101.

Chapter Six

[1]*Democracy* was published in 1908, but the novel's manuscript was submitted to Henry Holt in 1879.

[2]Judith Fryer (*Felicitous Space*, 139) says that Ellen suggests disorder, threatening to "pollute the little sphere of order and purity with a sexual and cultural richness that would destroy it."

[3]James A. Robinson says that Ellen represents the life of impulse; May, the life of repression, in a "classic Freudian confrontation between id and superego." "Psychological Determinism in *The Age of Innocence*," *Markham Review* 5 (Fall 1975): 3.

[4]Louis Auchincloss calls Archer "burstingly complacent," "the roundest possible peg in the roundest possible hole." *Edith Wharton: A Woman in Her Time*, New York: Viking, 1971: 129. Geoffrey Walton describes Ellen as a revolutionary force. Edith *Wharton: A Critical Interpretation*, Rutherford, NJ: Fairleigh Dickinson UP, 1970: 134. Jacobson ("Perception, Communication, and Growth," 69) says that the novel is about an "Outsider, Ellen Olenska, who cannot be accepted into the Tribe—New York society—and an Insider, Newland Archer, who cannot break out."

[5]Wolff says that Wharton's earlier outlines of the novel had Archer marry Ellen, but the two are not happy together. *A Feast of Words*, 327.

[6]Gary Lindberg sees Ellen as the agent of rescue for Archer, liberating him from the taboos and sanctions of his tribe. *Edith Wharton and the Novel of Manners*, 82.

[7]Wolff says, "Ellen is the catalyst that forces Newland's self-confrontation." *A Feast of Words*, 316.

[8]According to Wolff, Archer's "yearning for Ellen is indescribably intense, yet for the most part it belongs to another world." *A Feast of Words*, 327.

[9]Frederick McDowell says that Virginius and Victoria are harsh in judging when conventional prejudices rule them, but more charitable when they obey the dictates of the heart. *Ellen Glasgow and the Ironic Art of Fiction*, 172.

[10]Henderson says that Madeleine's social role as a young attractive widow becomes entangled with her philosophical quest, and "sexual politics are inextricably confused with national politics." *Versions of the Past*, 215-16.

[11]Fiedler notes that in refusing her lover, Madeleine rejects the corrupt modern state he represents. *Love and Death in the American Novel*, 338.

[12]The irony is, of course, that she got the name by marrying.

Chapter Seven

[1]For discussions of Carol as Lewis's mouthpiece, see, for example, Michael Spindler (*American Literature and Social Change*, 178), and Michael Millgate (*American Social Fiction*, 100). As to how closely Lewis allies himself in the battle, see Schorer, who thinks Lewis spares Carol much needed satirical comment ("Afterword," 437), Malcolm Bradbury, who thinks Lewis "sees round" Carol (*The Modern American Novel*, 59), Alfred Kazin, who notes Lewis's satire of American life but believes Lewis is "fundamentally uncritical of American life" (*On Native Grounds*, 176), and Sally E. Parry, who feels Lewis sympathizes with Carol's difficulties in adjusting to Main Street but condemns her air of superiority ("The Changing Fictional Faces of Sinclair Lewis' Wives," *Studies in American Fiction* 17, Spring 1989: 67).

[2]Geismar notes that Carol's first revulsion against the immigrant farmers is linked with her sexual revulsion against Will (*The Last of the Provincials*, 85).

[3]Sally E. Parry, "The Changing Fictional Faces of Sinclair Lewis' Wives," 71-72, and Harry Hartwick, The *Foreground of American Fiction*, 1934; New York: Gordon P, 1967: 275, discuss this corruption.

[4]O'Brien says the "fall" occurs when "the adolescent must notice the fallen world of sex roles and repress the part of the self then assigned to the other gender."

⁵Stouck also says that Alexandra does not change throughout the novel. *Willa Cather's Imagination*, 23, 26-27.

⁶Geismar calls her "almost too stoical, remote, and unfaltering" (*The Last of the Provincials*, 163) and says that sometimes Cather's pioneer portraits become like a "tableau of Grant Wood's" (170).

⁷Sharon O'Brien makes this point about the divided structure, but she says we best understand Alexandra when "we learn of her need for human attachment when she despairs of life after her brother's death" (*Willa Cather: The Emerging Voice*, 429). I believe Alexandra is defined more extensively in two love relationships, her own and Emil's.

⁸Stouck says, "The emotional quest to be reunited with the strong parental figures of the past describes something of Carl's relationship to Alexandra" (*Willa Cather's Imagination*, 29). But Stouck does not discuss the later changes in this relationship.

⁹Berthoff notes that Cather deplores self-indulgence "of sense or desire" (*The Ferment of Realism*, 257).

¹⁰Judith Fryer makes this point and connects it to Zenobia's dream, in *The Blithedale Romance*, of a godlike man (*Felicitous Space*, 262). Annis Pratt (*Archetypal Patterns in Women's Fiction*, 22, 24) connects the dream lover to a corn god, embodying "the natural cycles of fertility and drought," and says the figure does not dwarf Alexandra. O'Brien rightly notes that the "male figure's meaning and function change over time," but "the dream always involves the woman's yielding." She says the dream expresses feelings Alexandra "enacts only with the land, but never, in reality, with another person" (*Willa Cather: The Emerging Voice*, 438).

¹¹Stouck calls it a child's romance (*Willa Cather's Imagination*, 20). O'Brien (*Willa Cather: The Emerging Voice*, 44) calls it narcissistic.

¹²Stouck (*Willa Cather's Imagination*, 3) sees this as merely a marriage of companions. So does Fryer (*Felicitous Space*, 262). O'Brien (*Willa Cather: The Emerging Voice*, 445) discusses it as neither a traditional marriage nor a token one.

¹³He compares the circle of men, with Thea at its center, to the characters of *Winesburg, Ohio* who tell their stories to George Willard (187).

¹⁴Stouck says that "her complicity with these failures also suggests a source for her artist's drive in alienation from her peers" (*Willa Cather's Imagination*, 189).

¹⁵Stouck makes this point (*Willa Cather's Imagination*, 198).

¹⁶Among those who note Thea's negative qualities are Stouck (*Willa Cather's Imagination*, 9, 197) and Geismar (*The Last of the Provincials*, 178).

¹⁷Stouck says their love affair never involved the submission of one to the other (*Willa Cather's Imagination*, 196) but I see the early economic imbalance and Fred's early links to convention as significant.

[19]Moers also says Cather uses Thea as "a heroic stand-in for the woman of letters" (*Literary Women*, 190).

Epilogue

[1]Allusions to *The Scarlet Letter* are particularly evident: Nell's book club discusses it (and the mini-series on public television), an unwed mother lists Arthur Dimmesdale as her baby's father on the birth certificate.

[2]Carolyn Heilbrun says, "Godwin's later novels are extraordinary in their development of female heroes who are not only aware of the need for an independent destiny, but struggling toward it." *Reinventing Womanhood*, 90-91.

Works Cited

Adams, Henry. *Democracy*. 1908. New York: Henry Holt, 1933.

Ammons, Elizabeth. "The Business of Marriage in Edith Wharton's *The Custom of the Country*" *Criticism* 16 (1974).

_____. "Edith Wharton's Heroines: Studies in Aspiration and Compliance." Diss., U of Illinois at Urbana-Champaign, 1974.

Auchincloss, Louis. "Afterword." *The House of Mirth*. New York: New American Library, 1964.

_____. *Edith Wharton: A Woman in Her Time*. New York: Viking, 1971.

Auerbach, Nina. *Communities of Women: An Idea in Fiction*. Cambridge, MA: Harvard UP, 1978.

_____. *Woman and the Demon: The Life of a Victorian Myth*. Cambridge, MA: Harvard UP, 1982.

Bader, Julia. "The Dissolving Vision: Realism in Jewett, Freeman and Gilman." *American Realism: New Essays*. Ed. Eric Sundquist. Baltimore: Johns Hopkins UP, 1982.

Baym, Nina. "Melodramas of Beset Manhood: How Theories of American Fiction Exclude Women Authors." *American Quarterly* 33 (Summer 1981).

_____. *The Shape of Hawthorne's Career*. Ithaca: Cornell UP, 1976.

_____. *Women's Fiction: A Guide to Novels by and about Women in America, 1820-1870*. Ithaca: Cornell UP, 1978.

Bell, Daniel. *The Cultural Contradictions of Capitalism*. New York: Basic Books, 1976.

Bennett, George N. Introduction. *A Modern Instance*. By William Dean Howells. Bloomington: Indiana UP, 1977.

Berthoff, Warner. *The Ferment of Realism: American Literature, 1884-1919*. New York: Free, 1965.

Bewley, Marius. *The Eccentric Design: Form in the Classic American Novel*. 1957. New York: Columbia UP, 1963.

Bradbury, Malcolm. *The Modern American Novel*. Oxford: Oxford UP, 1983.

Brownstein, Rachel. *Becoming a Heroine: Reading About Women in Novels*. New York: Viking, 1982.

Callahan, John F. *The Illusions of a Nation*. Urbana: U Illinois P, 1972.

Cargill, Oscar. *The Novels of Henry James*. New York: Macmillan, 1961.

305

Carpenter, Frederic. "Scarlet A Minus." *The Scarlet Letter*. By Nathaniel Hawthorne. Eds. Sculley Bradley, et al. Rpt. from *College English* 5 (Jan. 1944).

Cather, Willa. *A Lost Lady*. New York: Knopf, 1923.

_____. *Lucy Gayheart*. 1935. New York. Knopf, 1976.

_____. *My Ántonia*. 1918. Boston: Houghton Mifflin, 1949.

_____. *O Pioneers!* 1913. Boston: Houghton Mifflin, Sentry Ed., n.d.

_____. *The Song of the Lark*. 1915. Boston: Houghton Mifflin, 1923.

Chase, Richard. The *American Novel and Its Tradition* . New York: Doubleday, 1957.

Cheever, John. *Bullet Park*. 1969. New York: Bantam, 1970.

Chopin, Kate. *The Awakening*. 1899. New York: Norton, 1976.

_____. "Confidences." *Atlantic Monthly*. Jan. 1899. Rpt. *The Complete Works of Kate Chopin*. Ed. Per Seyersted. 2 vols. Baton Rouge: Louisiana State UP, 1969.

Crews, Frederick. *The Sins of the Fathers: Hawthorne's Psychological Themes*. New York: Oxford UP, 1966.

Dietrichson, Jan. *The Image of Money in the American Novel of the Gilded Age*. Oslo: Univeritetsforlaget. New York: Humanities P, 1969.

Dreiser, Theodore. *An American Tragedy*. 1925. New York: New American Library, 1964.

_____. *Jennie Gerhardt*. 1911. Cleveland: World Publishing, n.d.

_____. *Sister Carrie*. 1900. New York: Norton, 1970.

Eakin, John Paul. *The New England Girl*. Athens: U Georgia P, 1976.

Erlich, Gloria. *Family Themes and Hawthorne's Fiction*. New Jersey: Rutgers UP, 1984.

Feidelson, Charles. "The People of Boston." *The Scarlet Letter*. By Nathaniel Hawthorne. Eds. Sculley Bradley et al. Rpt. from "The Scarlet Letter." *Hawthorne's Centenary Essays*. Ed. Roy Harvey Pearce. Columbus: Ohio State UP, 1964.

Fetterley, Judith. *The Resisting Reader: A Feminist Approach to American Fiction*. 1978. Bloomington: Indiana UP, 1981.

Fiedler, Leslie. *Love and Death in the American Novel*. New York: Criterion, 1960.

Fisher, Philip. "Acting, Reading, Fortune's Wheel: *Sister Carrie* and The Life History of Objects." *American Realism: New Essays*. Ed. Eric Sundquist. Baltimore: Johns Hopkins UP, 1982.

Fitzgerald, F. Scott. *The Beautiful and Damned*. 1922. New York: Scribners, n.d.

_____. *The Great Gatsby*. 1925. New York: Scribners, n.d.

_____. *Tender Is the Night*. 1933. New York: Scribners, 1960.

Friedenberg, Edgar. *Coming of Age in America*. New York: Randon House, 1965.

Friedman, William J. "A Look at Dreiser as Artist: The Motif of Circularity in *Sister Carrie*." *Modern Fiction Studies* 8 (Winter 1962-63).

Fryer, Judith. *Faces of Eve: Women in the Nineteenth Century American Novel*. New York: Oxford UP, 1976.

_____. *Felicitous Space: The Imaginative Structures of Edith Wharton and Willa Cather*. Chapel Hill: U North Carolina P, 1986.

_____. Gass, William. "The High Brutality of Good Intentions." *The Portrait of a Lady*. By Henry James. Ed. Robert Bamberg. Rpt. from *Accent* 18 (Winter 1958).

Geismar, Maxwell. *The Last of the Provincials*. Boston: Houghton Mifflin, 1947.

Gelfant, Blanche. *The American City Novel*. 1954. Norman: U Oklahoma P, 1970.

Gilbert, Sandra M., and Susan Gubar. *The Madwoman in the Attic: The Woman Writer and the Nineteenth Century Literary Imagination*. New Haven: Yale UP, 1979.

_____. *The War of the Words*. Vol. 1 of *No Man's Land*. New Haven: Yale UP, 1988.

Gilligan, Carol. *In a Different Voice*. Cambridge, MA: Harvard UP, 1982.

Glasgow, Ellen. *In This Our Life*. New York: Harcourt, Brace, 1941.

_____. *The Sheltered Life*. New York: Doubleday, Doran, 1932.

_____. *They Stooped to Folly*. New York: Literary Guid, 1929.

_____. *Vein of Iron*. New York: Harcourt, Brace and World, 1935.

Godwin, Gail. *A Mother and Two Daughters*. 1982. New York: Viking, 1983.

Grebstein, Sheldon. "Dreiser's Victorian Vamp." *Sister Carrie*. By Theodore Dreiser. Ed. Donald Pizer. New York: Norton, 1970. Rpt. from *Midcontinent American Studies Journal* 4 (Spring 1963).

Griffith, Clark. "Substance and Shadow: Language and Meaning in *The House of the Seven Gables*." *The House of the Seven Gables*. By Nathaniel Hawthorne. Ed. Seymour Gross. New York: Norton, 1967. Rpt. from *Modern Philology* 51 (Feb. 1954).

Gross, Seymour. " 'Solitude, and Love, and Anguish': The Tragic Design of *The Scarlet Letter*." *The Scarlet Letter*, by Nathaniel Hawthorne. Eds. Sculley Bradley, et al. Rpt. from *CLA Journal* 3 (Mar. 1968).

Hardwick, Elizabeth. *Seduction and Betrayal: Women and Literature*. 1970. New York: Random House, 1974.

Hartwick, Harry. *The Foreground of-American Fiction*. 1934. New York: Gordon 1967.

Hawthorne, Nathaniel. *The Blithedale Romance*. 1852. New York: Norton, 1978.

_____. "Hawthorne's Notebooks and Journals." *The Scarlet Letter*. By Nathaniel Hawthorne. Eds. Sculley Bradley, et al.

_____. *The House of the Seven Gables*. 1851. New York: Norton, 1964.

_____. *The Marble Faun*. 1859. New York: New American Library, 1961.

_____. *The Scarlet Letter*. 1850. New York: Norton, 1978.

Heilbrun, Carolyn. *Reinventing Womanhood*. New York: Norton, 1979.

_____. *Toward a Recognition of Androgyny*. New York: Knopf, 1973.

Henderson, Harry. *Versions of the Past*. New York: Oxford UP, 1974.

Hoffman, Daniel. *Form and Fable in American Fiction*. New York: Oxford UP, 1961.

Howells, William Dean. *Dr. Breen's Practice*. 1881. Westport, CT: Greenwood, 1969.

_____. *A Hazard of New Fortunes*. 1889. Bloomington: Indiana UP, 1976.

_____. *A Modern Instance*. 1882. Bloomington: Indiana UP, 1977.

Jacobson, Irving. "Perception, Communication, and Growth as Correlative Themes in Edith Wharton's *The Age of Innocence*" *Agora* 2 (1973).

James, Henry. "The Art of Fiction." *Partial Portraits*. London: Macmillan, 1911.

_____. *The Golden Bowl*. 2 vols. 1909. New York: Scribners, 1937.

_____. *The Bostonians*. 1886. New York: Dial, 1945.

_____. *The Portrait of a Lady*. 1908. New York: Norton, 1975.

_____. "Preface" to the New York edition of *The American*. 1907. New York: Norton, 1978.

Janeway, Elizabeth. *Man's World, Woman's Place: A Study in Social Mythology*. New York: Delta, 1971.

Kaul, A.N. "Community and Society." *The Blithedale Romance*. By Nathaniel Hawthorne. Eds. Seymour Gross and Rosalie Murphy. New York: Norton, 1978. Rpt. from *The American Vision: Actual and Ideal Society in Nineteenth-Century Fiction*. New Haven: Yale UP, 1963,

Kazin, Alfred. *On Native Grounds*. 1942. New York: Doubleday, 1956.

Kolodny, Annette. *The Lay of the Land: Metaphor as Experience and History in American Life and Letters*. Chapel Hill: U of North Carolina P, 1975.

Laing, R.D. *The Divided Self*. 1960. London: Tavistock, 1969.

Lasch, Christopher. *The Minimal Self*. New York: Norton, 1984.

Lawrence, D.H. *Studies in Classic American Literature*. 1923. New York: Viking, 1964.

Lebowitz, Naomi. *The Imagination of Loving*. Detroit: Wayne State UP, 1965.

Lefcowitz, Barbara F. and Allan B. "Some Rents in the Veil: New Light on Priscilla and Zenobia." *The Blithedale Romance*. By Nathaniel Hawthorne. Eds. Seymour Gross and Rosalie Murphy. Rpt. from *Nineteenth Century Fiction* 21 (1966).

Levy, Leo B. "The Blithedale Romance: Hawthorne's " 'Voyage Through Chaos'." *The Blithedale Romance*. Nathaniel Hawthorne. Eds. Seymour Gross and Rosalie Murphy. Rpt. from *Studies in Romanticism* 8 (1968).

Lewis, R.W.B. The *American Adam: Innocence, Tragedy, and Tradition in the Nineteenth Century*. 1955. Chicago: U Chicago P, 1968.

Lewis, Sinclair. *Ann Vickers*. Garden City, New York: Doubleday, Doran, 1933.

_____. *Main Street*. 1920. New York: New American Library, 1961.

Lidoff, Joan. "Another Sleeping Beauty: Narcissism in *The House of Mirth*." *American Realism: New Essays*. Ed. Eric Sundquist. Johns Hopkins UP, 1982.

Lindberg, Gary. *Edith Wharton and the Novel of Manners*. Charlottesville: U Virginia P, 1975.

Lynn, Kenneth. "*Sister Carrie*: An Introduction." *Sister Carrie*. By Theodore Dreiser. Ed. Donald Pizer. Rpt. from *Sister Carrie*. New York: Rinehart, 1957.

Matthiessen, F.O. *American Renaissance*. 1941. New York: Oxford UP, 1962.

_____. "A Picture of Conditions." *Sister Carrie*. By Theodore Dreiser. Ed. Donald Pizer. Rpt. from *Theodore Dreiser*. New York: Sloane, 1951.

McDowell, Frederick. *Ellen Glasgow and the Ironic Art of Fiction*. 1960. Madison: U Wisconsin P, 1963.

McDowell, Margaret. "Viewing the Custom of Her Country: Edith Wharton's Feminism." *Contemporary Literature* 15 (1974).

Millgate, Michael. *American Social Fiction: James to Cozzens*. New York: Barnes & Noble, 1964.

Millet, Kate. *Sexual Politics*. New York: Doubleday, 1970

Moers, Ellen. "The Finesse of Dreiser." *Sister Carrie*. Theodore Dreiser. Ed. Donald Pizer. Rpt. from *American Scholar* 33 (Winter 1963-64).

_____. *Literary Women*. New York: Doubleday, 1976.

Nevius, Blake. *Edith Wharton: A Study of Her Fiction*. 1953. Berkeley: U California P, 1961.

O'Brien, Sharon. *Willa Cather: The Emerging Voice*. New York: Oxford UP, 1987.

Parry, Sally E. "The Changing Fictional Faces of Sinclair Lewis' Wives." *Studies in American Fiction* 17 (Spring 1989).

Pizer, Donald. *The Novels of Theodore Dreiser*. Minneapolis: U Minnesota P, 1976.

Poirer, Richard. *A World Elsewhere: The Place of Style in American Literature*. New York: Oxford UP, 1966.

Pollard, Percival. "The Unlikely Awakening of a Married Woman." *The Awakening*. By Kate Chopin. Ed. Margaret Culley. Rpt. from *Their Day in Court*. New York: Neale, 1909.

Porte, Joel. "The Dark Blossom of Romance." *The Scarlet Letter.* By Nathaniel Hawthorne. Eds. Sculley Bradley, et al. Rpt. from *Romance in America.* Middletown, CT: Wesleyan UP, 1969.

Pratt, Annis. *Archetypal Patterns in Women's Fiction.* With Barbara White, Andrea Lowenstein, Mary Wyner. Bloomington: Indiana UP, 1981.

Reeves, Nancy. *Womankind.* Chicago: Aldene-Atherton, 1971.

Richardson, Robert. *Myth and Literature in the American Renaissance.* Bloomington: Indiana UP, 1978.

Robinson, Lillian. *Sex, Class, and Culture.* 1978. New York: Methuen, 1986.

Schorer, Mark. "Afterward." *Main Street.* By Sinclair Lewis. 1920. New York: New American Library, 1961.

Schriber, Mary Suzanne. *Gender and the Writer's Imagination: From Cooper to Wharton.* Lexington: UP of Kentucky, 1987.

Spacks, Patricia Meyer. *The Female Imagination.* New York: Knopf, 1975.

Spindler, Michael. *American Literature and Social Change: William Dean Howells to Arthur Miller.* Bloomington: Indiana UP, 1983.

Stouck, David. *Willa Cather's Imagination.* Lincoln: U Nebraska P, 1975.

Sundquist, Eric. *Home as Found.* Baltimore: Johns Hopkins UP, 1979.

_____. "The Country of the Blue." *American Realism: New Essays.* Ed. Eric Sundquist. Baltimore: Johns Hopkins UP, 1982.

Tanner, Tony. *Adultery in the Novel: Contract and Transgression.* Baltimore: Johns Hopkins UP, 1979.

_____. *The Reign of Wonder.* London: Cambridge UP, 1965.

Tintner, Adelaide. "The Spoils of Henry James." *PMLA* 61 (Mar. 1946).

Tocqueville, Alexis de. *Democracy in America.* Trans. George Lawrence. Ed. J.P. Mayer. Garden City, New York: Doubleday, 1969.

Turner, Arlin. *Nathaniel Hawthorne.* New York: Oxford UP, 1980.

Van Ghent, Dorothy. "On *The Portrait of a Lady.*" *The Portrait of a Lady.* By Henry James. Ed. Robert Bamberg. New York: Norton, 1975. Rpt. from *The English Novel: Form and Function.* New York: Holt, Rinehart and Winston, 1953.

Veblen, Thornstein. *The Theory of the Leisure Class: An Economic Study of Institutions.* 1899. New York: Modern Library, 1934.

Von Abele, Rudolph. "Holgrave's Curious Conversion." *The House of the Seven Gables.* By Nathaniel Hawthorne. Ed. Seymour Gross. Rpt. from *The Death of the Artist: A Study of Hawthorne's Disintegration.* The Hague: Martinus Nijhoff,1955.

Wagner, Geoffrey. *Five for Freedom.* Rutherford, NJ: Fairleigh Dickinson UP, 1973.

Way, Brian. *F. Scott Fitzgerald and the Art of Social Fiction.* New York: St. Martin's, 1980.

Wharton, Edith. The *Age of Innocence*. 1920. New York: Scribner's, 1970.

_____. *A Backward Glance*. 1934. New York: Appleton-Century, 1936.

_____. *The Custom of the Country* . 1913. New York: Scribner's, 1941.

_____. *French Ways and Their Meaning*. New York: Appleton, 1919.

_____. *The House of Mirth*. 1905. New York: Scribner's, 1933.

_____. *Twilight Sleep*. New York: Appleton, 1927.

_____. "The Valley of Childish Things, and Other Emblems." *The Century Magazine* 52 (July 1896). Rpt. *The Collected Short Stories of Edith Wharton*. Ed. and intro. R.W.B. Lewis. 2 vols. New York: Scribners, 1968.

Wolff, Cynthia Griffin. *A Feast of Words: The Triumph of Edith Wharton*. New York: Oxford UP, 1977.

_____. "Thanatos and Eros." *The Awakening* by Kate Chopin. Ed. Margaret Culley. Rpt. from "Thanatos and Eros: Kate Chopin's *The Awakening*." *American Quarterly* 25 (Oct. 1973).

www.ingramcontent.com/pod-product-compliance
Lightning Source LLC
Chambersburg PA
CBHW062159270326
41930CB00009B/1585